＊

The Social Worker and Psychotropic Medication

D1564055

The Social Worker and Psychotropic Medication

Toward Effective Collaboration with Clients, Families, and Providers

Fourth Edition

KIA J. BENTLEY
JOSEPH WALSH
Virginia Commonwealth University

BROOKS/COLE
CENGAGE Learning

Australia • Brazil • Japan • Korea • Mexico • Singapore • Spain • United Kingdom • United States

BROOKS/COLE
CENGAGE Learning·

The Social Worker and Psychotropic Medication: Toward Effective Collaboration with Clients, Families, and Providers,
Fourth Edition
Kia J. Bentley, Joseph Walsh

Executive Editor: Mark Kerr D

Senior Acquisitions Editor: Seth Dobrin

Editorial Assistant: Coco Bator

Media Editor: Elizabeth Momb

Senior Brand Manager: Elisabeth Rhoden

Market Development Manager: Kara Parsons (Kindstrom)

Senior MarComm Manager: Linda Yip

Manufacturing Planner: Judy Inouye

Rights Acquisitions Specialist: Thomas McDonough

Design, Production Services, and Composition: PreMediaGlobal

Cover Image: Vector Glass Glossy Sphere. Abstract Background/ © andkuch

For product information and technology assistance, contact us at **Cengage Learning Customer & Sales Support, 1-800-354-9706**.
For permission to use material from this text or product, submit all requests online at **www.cengage.com/permissions**
Further permissions questions can be e-mailed to **permissionrequest@cengage.com**.

Library of Congress Control Number: 2012953689

ISBN-13: 978-1-285-41900-8

ISBN-10: 1-285-41900-6

Brooks/Cole
20 Davis Drive
Belmont, CA 94002-3098
USA

Cengage Learning is a leading provider of customized learning solutions with office locations around the globe, including Singapore, the United Kingdom, Australia, Mexico, Brazil, and Japan. Locate your local office at **www.cengage.com/global**.

Cengage Learning products are represented in Canada by Nelson Education, Ltd.

To learn more about Brooks/Cole, visit **www.cengage.com/brookscole**

Purchase any of our products at your local college store or at our preferred online store **www.cengagebrain.com**.

Printed in the United States of America
1 2 3 4 5 6 7 17 16 15 14 13

Contents

List of Tables   xv
Preface to the Fourth Edition   xvii
About the Authors   xxi

PART I THE CONTEXT OF SOCIAL WORK ROLES IN MEDICATION MANAGEMENT   1

1   **The Larger Context of Psychopharmacology and Social Work**   3

A Critical, Balanced Social Work Perspective   4
  A Social Work Perspective   4
  A Critical Perspective   5
  A Balanced Perspective   10

Neuroscience, Biology, Mind–Body Connections, "Causality," and the Scientific Context of Psychopharmacology   12
  "Big Pharma," Public Scrutiny, and the Social Context of Psychiatric Medication   14

Changing and Expanding Roles and the Disciplinary Context   19

Summary   22

Topics for Discussion and Learning Activities   23

**2   Overview of Social Work Roles in Medication
Management Across Settings   24**

Practice Settings, Roles, and Activities   25
  Mental Health   25
Case Examples   26
  Child Welfare   27
Case Examples   28
  Aging, Health, and Hospitals   30
Case Examples   31
  Corrections and Jails   32
Case Examples   33
The Partnership Model of Social Work Practice   33
  Appreciate Participants' Strengths and Limits   34
  Embrace a Client-Centered Practice   35
  Reconceptualize the Client–Clinician Relationship   36
  Conceptualize the Role of the Social Worker as a Resource   37
  Appreciate the Family Members' Perspective   38
Social Work Role Categories   38
  Physician's Assistant   38
  Consultant   39
  Counselor   40
  Monitor   40
  Advocate   41
  Educator   42
  Researcher   43
Social Worker Roles and Professional Values   44
Current Medication-Related Activities of Social Workers   44
Summary   48
Topics for Discussion and Learning Activities   49

**PART II A PRIMER ON
PSYCHOPHARMACOLOGY   51**

3   Basic Psychopharmacology   53
The Central Nervous System   54
  The Brain and Nervous System   54
Properties of Nerve Cells   59

Neuron Structure 59
Neuron Function 61
Neurotransmitters 63
Acetylcholine 64
Norepinephrine and Epinephrine 65
Dopamine 65
Serotonin 66
Gamma-Aminobutyric Acid (GABA) 66
Glutamate (Glutamic Acid) 66
How a Drug Moves Through the Body 67
Absorption 68
Distribution 68
Metabolism 69
Excretion 69
The Effects of a Drug on the Body 70
The Placebo Effect 72
Five Classes of Psychotropic Medication 73
Antipsychotic Medications 73
Antidepressant Medications 74
Mood-Stabilizing Drugs 76
Antianxiety Medications 77
Psychostimulants 78
A Word About Pharmacogenomics 79
Adverse Effects of Psychotropic Medication 80
Adverse Physical Effects: Definitions 81
Adverse Physical Effects: Factors in Their Production 82
Adverse Psychological Effects 83
Adverse Social Effects 83
Summary 84
Topics for Discussion and Learning Activities 84

4   The Five Classes of Medication   **86**
Medications That Treat Symptoms of Psychosis 87
The Symptoms of Psychosis 87
Specific Medications 88
Origins 88
Current Medications 89

The "First Generation" Antipsychotic Drugs   92
The Second-Generation Antipsychotics   94
Case Examples   97
Antidepressant Medications   99
  Symptoms of Depression   100
Specific Medications   100
  Origins   100
  Current Medications   101
  The MAO Inhibitors   102
  Cyclic Antidepressants   104
  The Serotonin Reuptake Inhibitors and Other New Drugs   107
Case Examples   109
Mood–Stabilizing Medications   110
  Symptoms of Mania   111
Specific Medications   112
  Origins   112
  Current Medications   112
  Lithium   113
  Anticonvulsant Medications   117
Case Examples   121
Anti–Anxiety Medications   124
  Symptoms of Anxiety   124
Specific Medications   125
  Origins   125
Current Medications   125
  Benzodiazepines   125
  Buspirone   128
  Other Anti-Anxiety Medications   130
Case Examples   131
Psychostimulants   133
  Attention Deficit Hyperactivity Disorder   133
  Ethical Issues in the Drug Treatment of Children   134
Specific Medications   135
  Origins   135
  Current Medications   136
  Other Drugs Used to Treat ADHD   139
Case Examples   140

Summary   143

Topics for Discussion and Learning Activities   143

5   Intervention Concerns with Special Populations   145

Gender Differences   146
 General Considerations   146
 Neurotransmitters   147
 Absorption   147
 Distribution   147
 Metabolism   148
 Classes of Medication   148

Pregnancy   149
 Classes of Medication   150

Sexual Adverse Effects of Medications   151

Older Adults   152
 General Considerations   152
 Classes of Medication   154

Children and Adolescents   156
 General Considerations   156
 Classes of Medication   157

Ethnopharmacotherapy   160
 African Americans   162
 People of Hispanic Cultures   162
 Asian Americans   163

People with a Dual Diagnosis of Mental Illness and Substance Abuse   164
 Mental Illness and Alcohol Abuse   167

Summary   167

Topics for Discussion and Learning Activities   168

PART III KNOWLEDGE AND SKILLS FOR EMBRACING PSYCHOSOCIAL ROLES   169

6   Referrals, Decision-Making, and the Meaning of Psychiatric Medication   171
 Parallel and Integrated Care Across Settings   172
 Excellence in Making Referrals for Psychiatric Medication   175

The Meaning of Psychiatric Medication   180
*Shared Decision-Making and Collaboration with Clients and
Families*   191
Summary   193
Topics for Discussion and Learning Activities   194

7   **Medication Education for Clients and Families**   **195**
The Effectiveness of Medication Education   197
Issues in Implementing and Evaluating Medication
Education   199
Developing Clear and Appropriate Objectives   199
*Understanding the Specific Needs and Abilities of the
Learners*   199
Creating an Atmosphere Conducive to Learning   200
Knowledge of the Material   200
*Skills for Selecting and Using Appropriate Teaching
Methods*   201
*The Ability to Assess One's Performance and the Learner's
Acquisition of Educational Outcomes*   202
Special Considerations for Children and Older Adults   203
A Word about Recruitment Challenges   203
Examples of Medication Education Programs   204
Content of Medication Education Programs   204
The Patient and Family Education Program   206
Multifamily Group Intervention for Schizophrenia   207
The Family Survival Workshop for Schizophrenia   208
Family-to-Family   208
Group Psychoeducation for Bipolar Disorder   209
Family Focused Treatment   210
Education for Adolescent Clients   211
The Multi-Family Psychoeducation Group for Depression   211
Content Recommendations for All Education Programs   212
Summary   213
Topics for Discussion and Learning Activities   213

8   **Medication Monitoring and Management**   **215**
Client Self-Monitoring of Medication   217
Using Existing Measures to Guide Monitoring   223

Concrete Steps for Coping with Adverse Effects   225

Problem Solving in Medication Management   228

Negotiating Medication Issues with Health Care
Providers   232

Advocacy in Medication Management   236

Summary   238

Topics for Discussion and Learning Activities   239

9   Medication Adherence   241

Models for Understanding Adherence   243

   The Self-Efficacy Model   243

   Characteristics of the Client   244

   Aspects of Treatment   246

   Aspects of the Social Environment   247

   Aspects of the Symptoms   248

Legal and Ethical Issues in Adherence and Refusal   250

Interventions to Assist in Medication Adherence   253

   Motivational Interviewing   253

   Dynamic Adherence   256

   The Harm-Reduction Model   257

   Compliance Therapy   258

   Cognitive and Behavioral Interventions   258

Summary   259

Topics for Discussion and Learning Activities   260

PART IV FUTURE DIRECTIONS   261

**10   Future Directions in Psychopharmacology:
Implications for Social Workers   263**

The Drug Development Process   263

New Pharmaceutical Treatments   266

Herbal and Vitamin Treatments   268

Expanding Prescription-Writing Privileges   272

Keeping Up with Drug Developments and Client
Experiences   275

Summary and Final Words   278

Topics for Discussion and Learning Activities   279

Glossary   281

References   297

Name Index   329

Subject Index   337

List of Tables

2.1	Frequency, Competence, and Appropriateness of Social Work Roles and Activities with Psychiatric Medication	46
4.1	Antipsychotic Medications	90
4.2	Adverse Effects of Antipsychotic Medications	91
4.3	Types of Side Effects of Antipsychotic Medications	91
4.4	Adjunctive and Side-Effect Medications Used with Antipsychotic Medications	94
4.5	Drug Interactions with Antipsychotic Medications	97
4.6	Monoamine Oxidase Inhibitors	102
4.7	Side Effects of MAO Inhibitors	103
4.8	Foods and Drugs to be Avoided When Taking MAO Inhibitors	103
4.9	Drug Interactions with SSRI Antidepressants and MAO Inhibitors	104
4.10	Cyclic Antidepressants	105
4.11	Drug Interactions with Cyclic Antidepressants	106
4.12	SSRI Antidepressants	107
4.13	Atypical Antidepressants	108
4.14	Side Effects of Serotonin-Reuptake Inhibitors and Related Drugs	109
4.15	Drug Interactions with SSRI Drugs	109
4.16	Mood-Stabilizing Medications	113
4.17	Side Effects of Lithium Carbonate	115
4.18	Signs of Lithium Toxicity	116
4.19	Drug Interactions with Mood-Stabilizing Medications	117
4.20	Side Effects of Other Mood-Stabilizing Medications	119
4.21	Benzodiazepine Medications	126
4.22	Adverse Effects of Anti-Anxiety Medications	127
4.23	Benzodiazepine Withdrawal Symptoms	128
4.24	Drug Interactions with Benzodiazepines	129
4.25	Other Anti-Anxiety Medications	129
4.26	Medications for ADHD	136

4.27 Side Effects of Psychostimulant Medications   137
8.1   Symptom Checklist   219
8.2   Dimensions of Partnership in Medication Management   239
9.1   Possible Risks and Protective Factors for Medication Non-Adherence   249
10.1 Websites with Information on Psychiatric Medications   277

Preface to the Fourth Edition

I t turns out we have a bit more to say about the interface of social work and psychopharmacology. And thankfully our loyal publisher has granted our request to update our text once again and to continue the process of rethinking our perspective and considering even more deeply the messages we are conveying about what social work is and is not, especially the role we should play in an arena still fraught with ambiguity, skepticism, changing beliefs, new discoveries, and powerful personal experiences. As in previous editions, we lean on empirical research across the methodological spectrum to guide our literature reviews and suggested practices; this edition integrates even more results of our own published research and scholarship into the content. This new fourth edition is undergirded by two clear motivations: to provide more content on critical perspectives about psychiatric medication use and to draw more attention to the relevance of content about psychiatric medication across practice settings. More specifically, our fourth edition offers these changes:

1) a brand-new Chapter 1 presents in more detail the sociopolitical context of social work and psychopharmacology and defines more explicitly what it means to maintain a critical yet balanced perspective on psychiatric medications and their use.

2) an expanded second chapter presents an array of social work roles in psychopharmacology, and this time it emphasizes how these roles are enacted, not just in mental health settings and psychiatric facilities, but also in hospitals, health care settings for older adults, in jails and other forensic facilities, and in school and child welfare settings, to name a few.

3) the main section on classes and types of medication has been completely updated to reflect new discoveries of medications and new uses of medications across diagnostic categories.

4) the material on culture and special populations has been significantly updated and expanded to reflect new research.

5) a brand-new chapter has been added to fully present new content on a relatively new concept in the health care arena, shared decision-making, which is a systematic approach to working with clients that is congruent with our partnership model of care.

6) content on the meaning and impact of taking psychiatric medication on clients' sense of self and identity is greatly expanded, using qualitative research conducted by the senior author as well as updated literature reviews.

7) the material on prescriber referrals has been greatly expanded both in terms of its scholarly discussion and the inclusion of "how to" ideas and considerations.

8) all content on medication education, adherence, and medication monitoring have been updated, including the addition of exemplar programs and content on motivational interviewing.

9) future directions content now includes an updated discussion of prescription-writing privileges as well as content on how social workers can keep up with relevant developments in practice through exploitation of Internet resources.

10) learning objectives and questions for further consideration and classroom activities have been revised to reflect social work roles across settings.

We started back in the mid-1990s with the hope that *The Social Worker & Psychotropic Medication* would be a practical and useful resource for social work students and practitioners as they fulfill their daily roles in medication management in social work and human service settings. We hoped the book would contribute to the conceptualization and clarification of the social worker's role in psychopharmacology. We are referring here not only to the expansion of the social worker's roles in this area but also to a shift toward more client-centered "partnership" models of practice. Ideally, we wanted the book to begin to fill the acknowledged gap between current real-world practice and current curriculum materials.

We still have three specific goals for our readers. We hope that when they have finished the book: (1) they will be **aware** of the relevant facts and fictions about psychotropic medications, as well as have a good sense of the historical, sociopolitical, economic, and ethical context of their administration; (2) they will be **articulate** with clients, families, and other providers regarding the basics of psychopharmacology and the language of the field; and (3) they will be **active and assertive** with regard to helping their clients' with medication-related concerns using a range of approaches, techniques, and strategies in collaboration with clients, families, and other providers. In essence, we hope that our book will help social workers be more responsive to, and compassionate about, the comprehensive and complex needs of their clients.

The book is still divided into four parts. Part One, "The Context of Social Work Roles in Medication Management," as noted above, is completely reworked and provides the context and philosophical foundation for the rest of the text. We discuss how social work's unique lens relates to practice roles as they are—or in some cases, should be—practiced today. Part Two, "A Primer on Psychopharmacology," provides social workers with relevant information about psychopharmacokinetics, pharmacodynamics, and the theory and science of medication. We provide up-to-date content on drugs and their use across five major classes of psychiatric medications. Part Three, the heart of the book in terms of practice content, is called "Knowledge and Skills for Embracing Psychosocial Roles." It includes extensive content on decision-making, referrals, managing the meaning of medication, psychoeducation, adherence, medication monitoring and advocacy. All are presented both conceptually and in terms of the interventive knowledge needed to address the issues with clients and families, and indeed, prescribers. Part Four, "Future Directions," looks ahead to developments in psychopharmacology, including new drugs on the horizon, new uses for herbal treatments and vitamins, prescription privileges, and some ideas for keeping up with developments in the field. The book closes with an easy-to-read glossary, which provides social work students and working professionals with demystifying definitions (and pronunciations) of the terms commonly used in this ever-expanding field.

A note about language: We have chosen to predominantly use the term client throughout the book, even though some recipients of social work or human services prefer to be called consumers, patients, psychiatric survivors, customers, or other descriptive terms. Since our book's main focus is the social worker's interaction with service recipients, we believe that client is the most appropriate, non-stigmatizing term. Also, we frequently use the generic term "prescriber" to refer to psychiatrists, non-psychiatrist M.D.s, nurse practitioners, physician's assistants, and other professionals who prescribe because it is the most broadly descriptive of today's medication providers.

We believe that the two most salient features of the book are that it is profession-specific to social work and is a practice-focused treatment of the topic. Despite the fact that social workers are the number one mental health professional providers in the country and the fact that treatment with psychotropic medication is at least part of the treatment of choice for most mental, emotional, and behavioral disorders, challenges, and struggles, no book before ours had ever addressed the role of social workers in medication management. This book has been used primarily as a major text for social work courses in psychopharmacology or a required supplemental text in clinical practice, human behavior, or mental health courses at either the B.S.W. or the M.S.W. levels. We are pleased with the course adoptions over the past 16 years since the publication of our first edition, and we hope this edition will be a well-received response to changing practices. We certainly welcome and invite comments and criticism.

ACKNOWLEDGMENTS
FOR THE 4TH EDITION

Throughout the decade or so of publishing these editions, we have expressed gratitude to those who in some way shaped and stimulated our thinking about, and interest in, psychopharmacology and social work. These have included long lists of names of mental health consumers and families, academic colleagues near and far, doctoral students, local practitioners, and past manuscript reviewers. For this edition, I would first like to simply acknowledge a few folks who have been and are so important to my life and career. First and foremost, I remember with deep affection, really undefinable gratitude, our former editor-turned-friend, Lisa Gebo, whom we lost several years ago to breast cancer at way too young an age. She showed unwavering confidence in our product and demonstrated a relentless commitment to quality in every aspect of the publishing process. I love her and miss her and will still think of her every time I pick up a copy of this book that she really brought to life. I am grateful to three very special VCU colleagues. Sarah Kye Price and I are collaborators and friends and try to find ways on a daily basis to help each other to make a difference in our respective worlds and make sure we take time to celebrate professional achievements along the way. Patti Aldredge and I go back 34 years to the days of MSW student process recordings and role plays. She finally landed at VCU in 2012, quite remarkably, and is a breath of fresh air in my everydayness. Patti has never done anything but affirm and validate all that I am professionally and personally, and my appreciation for all that grows exponentially as I age. Finally, I have to acknowledge my buddy and coauthor, Joe Walsh. I am still so very grateful for our continued mutual affection and for the interesting collaboration that remains exceedingly comfortable and cozy. Thanks, too, to Seth Dobrin and Suzanna Kincaid of Cengage for saying "yes" to this new edition and shepherding the process so seamlessly. We would also like to thank the reviewers whose important and extensive feedback informed this new edition: Carol Drolen, University of Alabama; R. Anna Hayward, Stony Brook University; Anthony Schefstad, Rollins College; David Townsend, Ivey Tech Community College; Lara Vanderhoof, Tabor College; Vikki Vandiver, Portland State University; and Joy Willmott, Case Western Reserve University. Thank you, thank you, thank you.

Kia J. Bentley
August 28, 2012

I would like to thank my former students Sara Van Tongeren and Rachel Wojciechowski for contributing several case illustrations to this new edition. Thanks, too, to Kia, for keeping me on task and contributing to my slow development as a wine connoisseur.

Joe Walsh
August 28, 2012

About the Authors

Dr. Bentley is a tenured professor at Virginia Commonwealth University where she has taught since 1989. She served as VCU's Ph.D. Program Director from 1999 to 2012 and as their Associate Dean for Strategic Initiatives from 2007 to 2009. Dr. Bentley has all three degrees in social work: a BSW from Auburn University (1978), an MSSW from the University of Tennessee (1979), and a Ph.D. from Florida State (1987), where she received a "Distinguished Alumni Award" in 1997. In addition to being lead author of this book, Dr. Bentley is the editor of both *Social work practice in mental health: Contemporary roles, tasks & techniques* (2002; Brooks/Cole) and *Psychiatric medication issues for social workers, counselors and psychologists* (2003, Haworth) and has published approximately 50 other works on social work topics in mental health. She is now involved with a project that looks at decision-making about psychopharmacology among pregnant women. She serves as a consulting editor for the *Journal of Social Work Education* and *Best Practices in Mental Health* and regularly reviews for several publishers and other journals. She was the chair and chair-elect of the Group for the Advancement of Social Work Education in Social Work from 2011 to 2013. In terms of community service, Dr. Bentley is a member of the Council of Advocates for Gateway Homes, a residential facility near Richmond, Virginia; the former chair of Central State Hospital's Human Rights Committee, a state psychiatric facility in Petersburg, VA; the former chair of the statewide Virginia Mental Health Planning Council; and served six years on the Board of Virginia's chapter of the advocacy organization, the National Alliance on Mental Illness. In the classroom, she can be found teaching a Ph.D. course in practice theory and intervention research. In the MSW program, she teaches courses on mental and emotional disorders, psychopharmacology and social work, community mental health, and mental health policy and services. She has been active with the Council on Social Work Education for many years, serving on their Commission on the Role & Status of Women for 6 years and their Commission on

Accreditation for 3 years. She is currently an active CSWE site visit chair and accreditation consultant, as well as a consultant to doctoral programs in social work.

Joseph Walsh, Ph.D., L.C.S.W., is a tenured Professor of Social Work at Virginia Commonwealth University, having joined the faculty in 1993 after a long career in community mental health practice and specializing in services to persons with serious mental illness and their families. He is a graduate of Ohio State University's MSW and Ph.D. programs. He currently teaches courses in direct practice, community mental health, and mental and emotional disorders and continues to provide direct services to clients at a university-affiliated counseling center. Joe was the 1998 recipient of the prestigious National Mental Health Association's George Goodman Brunei and Ruth P. Brudney Social Work Award, given annually to recognize significant contributions to the care and treatment of persons with mental illness. He is the author of several other books, including *Endings in clinical practice: Effective closure in diverse settings* (2007) and *The recovery philosophy and direct social work practice* (2013), both published by Lyceum, and *Theories of direct social work practice*, published by Brooks/Cole. Dr. Walsh was recently appointed to the Virginia Board of Social Work.

PART I

The Context of Social Work Roles in Medication Management

Chapter 1

The Larger Context of Psychopharmacology and Social Work

Chapter 2

Overview of Social Work Roles in Medication Management
Across Settings

1

✳

The Larger Context of Psychopharmacology and Social Work

Learning Objectives

Upon completion of this chapter, the reader will be able to:

1. Articulate dimensions of both a critical perspective and a social work perspective on psychopharmacology.
2. Define a "balanced perspective on medication."
3. Understand the tensions between embracing advances in neuroscience and biological psychiatry and continuing to hold fast to an "ecological" model of human behavior.
4. Understand the controversies and criticisms associated with "Big Pharma" and the role of pharmaceutical companies in defining care.
5. Appreciate the challenges and opportunities for social work in effectively fulfilling medication-related roles in the real world of multidisciplinary practice across many human service settings.

This introductory chapter attempts to paint a picture of the larger context in which social workers function with respect to psychiatric medication. To define the perspective, we will bring the discussion of social work roles into this arena. We will detail what it means to hold a critical, balanced social work perspective on issues related to psychiatric medication, and then we will place our roles in context to "nature nurture" debates and current thinking about neuroscience, public scrutiny of medications, the power of pharmaceutical companies, and the place of our profession in the array of helping professions.

A CRITICAL, BALANCED SOCIAL WORK PERSPECTIVE

A contemporary social worker brings to her or his job multiple lens and perspectives, and this is certainly true when cultivating effective collaboration with clients who take psychotropic medication, their families, and professional helpers. Here we talk briefly about what it means to embrace a social work perspective when working around medication-related dilemmas, and what it means to cultivate a critical and balanced perspective in the face of complex issues related to both clients' rights and professional roles.

A Social Work Perspective

What exactly is a social work perspective, and what does it look like when it comes to a discussion of psychopharmacology? To us, a contemporary social work perspective means that we look at phenomena through a specific disciplinary lens. A social work lens includes, at a minimum, a person-in-environment perspective, a social justice perspective, and a strengths and empowerment perspective. It will be helpful to provide a brief reminder of these key dimensions that have relevance for assuming the roles we put forth in this book.

Person-in-Environment Perspective.   Social workers are taught to view people within the context of larger systems, like families, communities, neighborhoods, and societies, as well as to see them in cultural and historical context. They are taught that problems that people face are complex biopsychosocial phenomena, likely caused or related to multiple factors and often, if not always, related to the interaction of the individual with things outside themselves, the "environment" or ecological context. Typically, social workers reject unicausality for the kinds of problems they address, and this frees them up from blaming the individual for their woes or offering up simplistic, unsatisfying, and potentially naïve answers to questions that they grapple with on a daily basis.

Social Justice Perspective.   The social work perspective is undoubtedly also a *social justice perspective*. Building on the ecological person-in-environment perspective, social workers are taught and socialized to be critically aware of the impact of social, political, and cultural institutions and structures on the life of individuals, families, communities, and organizations. They have a special sensitivity to the inequities in the social distribution of rights, privileges, goods, and services and are taught to recognize the role of ignorance, bias, discrimination, and privilege in creating or maintaining inequities, especially in the human service arena. Thus, social workers are taught to see and question how those with power, authority, and influence often work to maintain those privileges, even when it systematically, incidentally, or even unknowingly oppresses and marginalizes other voices and limits the human experience of others. All social workers yearn to remedy these inequities and to create innovative and effective responses to human need through professional practice or teaching and scholarship. One might argue that the heart of social work is to improve the equitable access of people, especially those who are particularly vulnerable or oppressed, to needed resources and opportunities. That basic function of social work will be no different when it comes to enacting our roles across settings with respect to psychiatric medication.

Strengths and Empowerment Perspective.   A social work lens is one of *strengths and empowerment* and has historically included a strong values orientation. We will speak much about the role of the social worker, indeed, that is the focus of the book. There can be no question, however, that contemporary social workers first strive to see clients' capacities, talents, assets, positive traits and qualities, skills, and social supports and to use knowledge of these strengths to help clients achieve the positive psychosocial changes they seek. The mirror of this intention is the rejection of the lens of pathology. Even in a profession centered in understanding problem-saturated situations and then applying problem-solving strategies to address them, social work strives to see people as humans, intrinsically worthy of respect and dignity and compassion. Social workers strive to not define people as labels and instead to see any struggles, problems, symptoms, or challenges as only a piece of their humanity and lived experience. Social workers center most of their work in self-determination, the notion that clients choose their paths. It is their right and responsibility. Social workers, then, are facilitators of client choices and strive to reject manipulation or coercion in any form. Related to strengths and self-determination is the notion of empowerment, which suggests that clients be seen as competent, capable, and resourceful, they develop a consciousness about the situation, and they participate actively in making life changes. These ideas undergird the partnership model of practice presented more fully in Chapter 2.

A Critical Perspective

What do we mean by a critical perspective? A critical or analytical perspective demands attention to power when it comes to language and the presentation of knowledge and "facts." With respect to psychiatric medication in particular, it means social workers should intentionally apply critical thinking skills to their professional development related to psychiatric medication and be aware of arguments made by so-called antipsychiatrists.

Awareness of Antipsychiatry.   Antipsychiatry is a categorical term given to those who provide often searing social critiques of mainstream psychiatry and challenge the assumptions put forth by mainstream psychiatry, especially as they relate to currently biologically focused psychiatry and the use of psychotropic medications. In a well-written scientific and historical analysis, Valenstein (1998), for example, strongly advocates increased attention to the adverse effects of psychiatric drugs and also makes a persuasive case that a more critical perspective is needed to fully grasp the social and psychological implications of the use of medications in mental health treatment. He exposes what he believes to be erroneous assumptions made about the causes of mental illnesses and the exaggerated claims regarding the effectiveness of drug treatments. These arguments echo the work of Tomi Gomory, Stuart Kirk, and David Cohen in our own field of social work. They have charged the field with being intellectually dependent on psychiatry or, said more passionately, with overidentification with the "reigning paternalistic drug-centered biomedical ideology in mental health" (Gomory et al., 2011, p. 135). In Cohen's (1988) seminal review of the history of social work and drug treatments, he urged social workers to avoid repeating the failures of the past, when social workers either ignored or rationalized the negative effects of shock treatments on their clients. His more recent work builds on this foundation by criticizing the methodologies and conceptualizations underlying current drug research that he believes "raise serious doubts about the widespread use" of many psychiatric medications today (2002). Based on these arguments and others, he, along with coauthor Peter Breggin, offers a concrete approach for consumers of medication to actually stop taking their psychiatric medications (see Breggin & Cohen, 2007).

For decades, others in this field (Davidson & Jamison, 1983; McCollum, Margolin, & Lieb, 1978) suggested that social workers pay more attention to not only the negative physical effects of these medications but also their negative psychological and social effects. These latter effects include the overuse of medications, their use for social control, and their potential to reinforce a negative sense of self. Gerhart and Brooks (1983) also urged social workers to be aware of the "seriously substandard" administration of antipsychotics in hospitals and community mental health centers (p. 454). More recently, Gomory and colleagues (2011) write a compelling argument that the "medicalization of distress and misbehavior," including the problematic practice of confusing a label of disorder as the cause of the disorder, has threatened our integrity as a profession and literally distracted us from both understanding and addressing psychosocial distress and maladjustment. The authors present a history of social work's problematic "alliance" with psychiatry, including our being overly enamored with the medical model, institutionalization, forced care, the DSM, and psychotropic medications. The association of social work with psychiatry, according to these authors, may be motivated by a desire for prestige and legitimacy. While tempting to dismiss the entire argument due to overstatement, we would rather argue that such critics of psychiatry and social work are needed and many of their concerns warranted. And it is precisely this critical lens that is needed by contemporary social workers across settings if those working in the field are to both honor and embrace what social workers are really called to do. Where social workers fall into the same harmful traps of oversimplifying mental illnesses as "brain diseases," underestimating the influence of pharmaceutical companies on the structure of medical care, buy into the expansiveness of the DSM, or, closer to home, refuse to examine how subtle coercion or professional arrogance can creep into our professional repertoire, then they should be admonished. These authors argue that it is time for social workers and others to "rededicate themselves to the supportive, educative and problem-solving methods unique to their disciplines" (p. 135). Toward this end, we wholeheartedly agree. This text has always rejected the notion of social workers as "handmaidens" and instead stressed the application of core social work values and functions to the issues and concerns of people with respect to psychiatric medications. This edition indeed stresses those roles across settings beyond inpatient and outpatient mental health settings and includes child welfare and school settings, health and aging service settings, and corrections and juvenile justice settings, for example.

The Application of Critical Thinking.   Talking about a social work perspective and the recent criticisms of social work and its relationship to psychiatry provides a comfortable and seamless basis for more explicitly noting the importance of embracing that critical perspective, that is, vigilantly applying critical thinking to our knowledge and value base. Ennis's well-used definition of critical thinking is that it is "reasonable and reflective thinking focused on deciding what to believe or do" (Ennis, 1989, p. 4). Beyer (1990) likewise says that critical thinking involves such things as trying to distinguish the relevant from the irrelevant, identifying and evaluating unstated assumptions, identifying points of view and biases, and determining the credibility of sources and support. It is an examination of the quality of thought and argument with the hope of improving thinking, which is the basis for action. The work of Richard Paul and Linda Elder may be helpful in trying to ascertain what is really meant by a critical perspective. Here are several characteristics they list of a "well-cultivated critical thinker" (2009, p. 2) and we add how that quality is particularly relevant in thinking about social work and psychopharmacology. The critical thinking person:

- *Raises vital questions and problems.* The interaction of a social work perspective and a critical perspective supports social workers raising questions about, for example at the global level, the increasing frequency of antipsychotic medication use for children, the lack of research on the long-term effects of psychiatric medication, the role of direct advertising in the increase in psychotropic drug use, or the profit margins of pharmaceutical companies. It is also quite appropriate, if not expected, that social workers raise closer-to-home practice questions on a daily basis. Example: "Does this referral to a prescriber suggest to my client that she and I have failed? Am I suggesting it because I think we have?"

- *Gathers, assesses, and interprets relevant information.* It is certainly appropriate for social workers to ask clients about their current and past experiences with medication, both therapeutic effects and negative side effects, as well as the impact on sense of self and quality of life. Social workers also gather and assess information about varying aspects of psychiatric medication relevant to any practice situation from reputable sources, including websites, journals and books, and directly from collaborators such as prescribers. Example: "How might all the information I have on risks of non-adherence to medication be relevant in this case with my young male client, José, with substance use issues and all that I know about him?"

- *Comes to well-reasoned conclusions and solutions, testing them against relevant criteria and standards.* A social worker's skepticism about the use of antipsychotic medication with older adults in long-term care may actually support its use in one of her client's when she sees the dangerous self-injurious and combative behaviors the client engages in without medication and hears from her client's adult children of their fears and inability to cope without this medical intervention. Examples: "How can I help this family look at the relative costs and benefits of allowing treatment with antipsychotic medication for the family matriarch? Can I keep my own biases in check? How can I not go too far and actually subtly coerce the family into one position or another? How can I convey unconditional positive regard and have them experience me as a caring resource no matter what they choose to do in their loved one's situation?"

- *Thinks open-mindedly within alternative systems of thought, recognizing, assessing, as need be, their assumptions, implications, and practical consequences.* A social worker collaborates with his client to plan and implement any number of strategies to help her withdraw from her long-term use of benzodiazepines, including examining the possible positive and negative impacts on her mood and affect, her relationships, her sense of self, her work performance and together try to anticipate the issues, both physical (insomnia and irritability) and psychological (doubt, fear), that may arise. Example: "Shall we make some backup plans of 'what to do just in case' some of your concerns about discontinuation of your Ativan are realized?"

- *Communicates effectively with others in figuring out solutions to complex problems.* The social worker can be a leader—or a team player—in offering her expertise and "lens" to difficult situations. For example, the school social worker may involve the school psychologist, the special education teacher, the child's pediatrician, and both the child's mothers to gain multiple perspectives and problem-solve about the student's seeming lethargy, persistent inattention, poor grades, and more recently, his practice of selling his ADHD medication to peers at school. Example: "When we come together this Thursday on the conference call, let's start with sharing our experiences and perspectives about Matt's struggles and our hopes for how we might effectively address his concerns."

In our own field of social work, Gibbs (1991) argues that another part of critical thinking is the identification of fallacies in other's ways of thinking. He describes ten fallacies to watch out for. Here they are, along with problematic examples related to social work and psychopharmacology:

- *Appealing to personal experience: When someone asserts something is true because they have had some personal experience with it.* "I have been using Celexa for years, and it's just great for depression. And I went to a nurse practitioner to get it, not a psychiatrist, cause they are so much better, not always in a rush and looking at their watches." Actually, the person should stay close to their own experience and say that Celexa has worked well for them, not overgeneralize and imply that it is great for all people with depression. The same is true for the overstatement about nurse practitioners. Instead, she should own her own experience and speak with "I" messages.

- *Making ad hominum arguments: When someone attacks the person making the argument, rather than the argument itself.* "I don't buy his story that social workers are nothing but handmaidens to the medical profession. He is clueless about social work and is just trying to get his name in the paper so he can get grants." Obviously, all people are entitled to voice opinions and share experiences and perspectives, even if they are critical of social work. Attacking the messenger, or distorting the message, is disrespectful and off-base in this case.

- *Making ad verecundiam arguments: When someone asserts something as true simply because some authority or well-known person says it is.* "According to Dr. Torrey, my brother John should not be the one to decide about his diet or his medication since people with mental illness are literally brain-disordered and thus not in any position to make their own decisions." E. Fuller Torrey has indeed made some arguments about brain diseases and their implications for decision-making among people with severe mental illnesses. However, there are many in social work and beyond who do not see his views as "truth," and do not embrace his perspectives or its implications.

- *Making ad populum arguments: When someone asserts something as true because the notion is popular or because large numbers of people hold it to be true.* "Everyone is using Straterra now so I think that's the way to go for sure." Actually, this is an overstatement as well since "everyone" is certainly not using Straterra. Drug choice is a complex individual matter and should not be one based solely on popularity of types or brands.

- *Accepting uncritical documentation: When we believe something is true simply because it is documented somewhere without looking at the nature and quality of the documentation.* "No way pregnant women can ever take an antidepressant. The newspaper ad [soliciting clients for a class action suit] showed a graph of recent increases in the numbers of birth defects." Actually, many pregnant and postpartum women take medication for depression and anxiety and other mental and emotional difficulties, because they have weighed the pros and cons with prescribers and others and have come to the conclusion that it is in their own, their child's, and/or their families best interest. Appropriate skepticism, but admittedly not a dismissal of claims outright, might accompany solicitations for class action suits. Further review of information or data is called for.

- *Accepting testimonials: Believing something must work or not work after hearing the personal testimony of others who have received the service or used the product.* "Everybody on the NAMI panel was raving about the Family to Family program, so it must really help." The program may very well help a specific family. Hearing other people enthusiastic about a program might indeed provide motivation to seek it out, but it certainly does not warrant overstatement of potential results for a specific family.

- *Acquiescing to the manner of the speaker: Believing something to be true, often unknowingly, because of the attractiveness or persuasiveness of the speaker or the manner in which the assertion is presented.* "Maybe if you take your bipolar medication, you can be famous. I heard Glenn Close's sister speak at a conference in Canada, and after she started taking medication for her bipolar, she started writing novels. Bipolar people are just more creative." In this day of celebrity, marketers are aware of how the public is swayed to trust a message offered by someone we invite into our homes through television and other print and electronic media. Again, social workers need to be wary of overgeneralization and subtle seduction in arguments for what might be the wrong reasons and to help their clients do the same.

- *Appealing to either newness or tradition: When someone asserts something is true simply because it's been held to be true for a long time or, conversely, just because it's different and new.* "They have my husband on two antipsychotic medications and an antidepressant and a beta blocker! Now that's crazy." Polypharmacy, a term that used to have a negative connotation, is the practice of using multiple medications with the same person. Actually, it is now not uncommon for some clients to have very sophisticated and complex regimens involving two, four, or even six or more medications. While polypharmacy is more common, questions about the underlying rationale for such a plan are, of course, still very fair.

- *Oversimplification and half-truths: Reducing a complicated message to a simple statement or suppressing relevant information in order to convince others of something.* "The newer antipsychotic medications don't have as many side effects as the older ones so you get your doctor to prescribe one of those right away." Actually, a good bit of recent attention and clinical research has exposed the early overstatements about the newer antidepressant and antipsychotic medications when they were just out. We have examined our own content in this book to insure that we did not fall into the same trap.

A Balanced Perspective

Finally, we argue that in addition to a social work perspective and a critical perspective, social workers should maintain a balanced perspective with respect to psychiatric medications. This means they must appreciate the relationship between the rights of individual clients, their families, and society, as well as the interplay among the costs and risks of using psychotropic medication versus the benefits and, finally, between the social worker's role in medication management and the legitimacy and uniqueness of other helping professions.

Rights of Individual, Family, and Society.   How do we hold in balance the rights and perspectives of individuals, families, neighborhoods, and even society at large? One could argue that the entire court system is an attempt to establish an impartial mechanism to decide the distribution of rights between individuals and society. Determining the appropriate balance between various interests becomes more difficult when the individual has a mental illness or an emotional disorder. Although clients' rights issues gained attention in the 1970s with landmark court battles and passage of a client bill of rights, the struggle for balance is still seen in debates about such issues as involuntary commitment and the right to decline treatment. Today's constriction of clients' rights seems to be related to many mental health providers' continued presumption that clients are incompetent and to "bureaucratic paternalism" rooted in stigma that too often characterizes the mental health system (Bentley, 1991; Winslade, 1981). That is, mental illness and involuntary hospitalization are often seen as synonymous with incompetence. Such attitudes can lead mental health professionals to make inappropriate decisions on behalf of clients and undermine their basic right to self-determination (Keast, 2011).

At the same time, while the enhanced involvement of families in recent years has been welcomed by all who embrace a partnership model, it has raised some important questions related to the appropriate role of families in clinical decision-making. What does client confidentiality really mean in light of the caregiving family's "need to know"? What voice should family members have when it comes to clinical treatment decisions? As families have pointed out, their lives can be dramatically impacted by the choices clients make. Indeed, an entire body of literature exists about the family's burden of such caregiving. This literature speaks to the frustration, anger, grief, and pain that many families experience as they try to cope with mental illness in a loved one. Trained to understand the systemic effects of individual choices, social workers must recognize the family's rights to pursue their ideas of what is their own and their loved one's "best interest."

However, the rights of clients, families, and society can and do clash, especially regarding psychiatric medication management. Social workers can be caught between their desire to collaborate with families and their ethical and legal obligation to honor the decisions and confidence of their clients. Zipple et al. (1990) offer several helpful strategies for resolving such conflicts, such as sharing nonconfidential information with families, providing them with written information when appropriate, referring them to educational groups in the community, using release-of-information procedures, and, when necessary, using mediators. While it is true that in social work the client's rights hold the preeminent position, effective collaboration is achieved by trying to balance the rights of all who have a stake in the process. Establishing a partnership model of practice is an important factor. While social workers' obligation to hold the client's well-being in highest regard is clear, their obligations to themselves, their agency, and society are also recognized (National Association of Social Workers [NASW], 2008).

Appreciating Both Costs and Benefits of Medications.   Responding specifically to Cohen's (1988) original essay, Johnson (1989, p. 659) critiqued what she believed to be his overstatement of the risks of psychotropic medications, calling for a fuller evaluation of both the risks and benefits of drug treatment and the "wrenching dilemmas" that practitioners and clients face in this area. We also have some disagreement with Cohen's positions. For example, we do not believe that social workers should avoid encouraging consideration of psychotropic drugs in some cases merely because they have adverse effects or because they bring up issues of authority and coercion.

We argue that research on the clinical efficacy of psychotropic medication as a therapeutic intervention has largely affirmed their role as an important aspect of treatment for many people. We also know that for many people their "lived experiences" with medication is quite positive, if not transformative, and for many others, not positive at all (e.g., Bentley 2010; Karp, 2006). We argue that social workers should stand for balance and common sense. That is, while acknowledging the significant contribution that psychotropic drugs can make toward reducing symptoms and improving the quality of life for many people, social workers should not ignore the disturbing adverse effects of medications or the sociopolitical aspects of their use, as discussed with respect to the critical perspective social workers apply. British social work scholar Nick Gould ties his own balanced perspective into larger frameworks of the conceptualization of mental illness. He seems to reject both "social constructivism," which suggests that mental illness does not exist and is created by language and context, as well as "biological determinism" which suggests problems are all physiological. His pragmatic approach is integrated with what he calls critical realism: mental disorders do indeed have some external reality but exist within social contexts, thus social workers "have the responsibility to be both critical and proactive about its inequitable and discriminatory consequences" (p. 10). He articulates our own intent for this book in his own book's position statement found in *Mental health social work in context*:

> This book steers a middle course that acknowledges the problematic and contested nature of medical psychiatry and advocates for psychological and social interventions where they have demonstrated to be beneficial, but at the same time acknowledges that there are forms of pharmacological and other medical interventions that offer some respite for some people from mental distress. It also recognizes that an important source of "evidence" in relation to best practice is the perspective offered by people who use services themselves, the "experts by experience." All this may be imperfect and untidy but offers the best options we have at present. (Gould, 2010, p. 2)

As Davidson and Jamison (1983) stated three decades ago, psychotropic drugs are a "mixed blessing" (p. 140) and should be cautiously accepted as an ethical, humane alternative to deterioration. When medications are used as prescribed, many clients and their families are helped, hospital stays may be shortened, and significant improvements in the quality of life can be achieved.

NEUROSCIENCE, BIOLOGY, MIND-BODY CONNECTIONS, "CAUSALITY," AND THE SCIENTIFIC CONTEXT OF PSYCHOPHARMACOLOGY

The scientific context of social work roles in medication management is obviously crucial to understand, especially as it may relate to the political context of our practice domain. What is the current thinking about the connection between mental, emotional, and behavioral "disorders"; symptoms, struggles, and challenges; and scientific evidence around "cause," "correlation," or "cure." While we hinted at these questions in sections above, several new and old texts reflect a growing trend to try to articulate the connection between social work in general and biology and neuroscience in particular. Ginsberg, Nackerud, and Larrison (2004) may have been among the first out of the gate. Their text *Human Biology for Social Workers*, published in part in response to increasing accreditation requirements around biology content, was the first comprehensive social work text to explicitly address such varying topics as human anatomy and physiology, genetics, intelligence, disease, mental illness, substance use and abuse, human sexuality, and aging. A year later came Applegate and Shapiro's *Neurobiology for Clinical Social Work* (2005). This text emphasizes the practice implications of new knowledge around attachment and neurobiology, and how it specifically affect regulation and the impact of experience on brain development. Most recently, our colleague Rosemary Farmer (2009) has published *Neuroscience and Social Work Practice,* which more comprehensively presents the content on "missing links" to practice, namely the neuroscientific links not only to attachment but to understanding and addressing trauma and addiction and the impact of psychotherapy and psychotropic medications. With respect to psychotropic medication, for example, she notes how knowledge of genetic variations in enzyme function can help explain differential metabolism (and thus differential drug effects) among various ethnic groups.

Importantly, the Ginsberg text discusses the tension between biological and "ecological" determinism and, to no one's surprise, calls for a rejection of either and an integration of both. Chapter 3 opens with the incredible understatement that "the ramifications of the nature versus nurture debate are widespread" (p. 42). Indeed, conceptualizations about the biological causes are entangled with professional domain and societal sanction to provide the "cure," if you will. If you have a physical problem, you go to the physician. If you are in a spiritual crisis, you seek help from a minister, priest, or rabbi. Tensions develop when there is competition over professional domain that occurs when there is ambiguity about "cause"; thus, disciplines, on some level, compete for causation claims so they can then compete for the dollars and social status that are associated with owning the "cure." This had led to the medicalization of many woes that some would see as psychological or social issues. In the physical illness realm, impotence is a glaring case in point. Advertisers for "erectile dysfunction" have been successful in portraying (very attractive, sexy, and happy) patients as "victims" of a physical malady that can and should be treated by physicians using products they manufacture. There is no mention of any social, emotional, or psychological aspects to the condition.

Such has been true with mental illnesses as well. Many mental illnesses are consistently portrayed in advertising as genetic or biological disorders that demand "medical treatment" by a physician. Lacasse and Leo's analysis of selected consumer advertisements for the SSRI type of antidepressant (See Chapter 3) makes a compelling case on the tendency of advertisers to go beyond the existing data in drawing conclusions for why some psychiatric medications "work" that does not always connect with evidence (Lacasse & Leo, 2005). Ads noting that depression and anxiety, for example, are "caused by chemical imbalances" are common, yet according to numerous other scholars (France, Lysaker, & Robinson, 2007; Leo & Lacasse, 2008), this is insufficiently supported, and even some researchers making those claims can not substantiate them. So called "backward reasoning" does not work. As France and colleagues put it, "[R]esponse to antidepressants is not by itself proof that an imbalance of brain chemical causes depression. Psychotherapy can alleviate depression; therefore (using the above logic), a deficiency in psychotherapy causes depression" (p. 412). Entire textbooks have been written in attempts to expose "errors of logic" and the "pseudoscience" in biological psychiatry (e.g., Ross & Pam, 1995) that social workers need to be aware of.

What that leaves us with is a complex biopsychosocial understanding of mental, emotional, and behavioral disorders, struggles, and challenges with likely multiple etiologies, all of which belie simplistic answers or formulas. Are there any models that adequately address or propose this kind of truly integrative "both and" conceptualization of mental health issues? We think so. One model that attempts to explain the interplay between biological and environmental influences is the *stress-diathesis* (or stress vulnerability) model of mental illness (Mazure, 1995). This model asserts that although the cause of mental illnesses and disorders may be associated with genetic factors and abnormalities in brain chemistry and structure, the course or progression of disorders is partly related to environmental factors. Vulnerability and stressors are moderated in their impact by the presence of protective factors such as skills in coping and competence, medication, and social support (Liberman, 1988). This model bears resemblance to a more general *risk and resilience* framework for practice (Fraser, Richman, & Galinsky, 1999) in which the social worker's interventions are intended to build or amplify a client's particular set of protective factors to offset any risks to impaired social functioning. If social workers can help build up protective factors, they can decrease the impairments and handicaps experienced by clients and their families. Although the model was originally developed to explain the course of schizophrenia, social workers will find it useful because it clarifies how they can contribute to improved psychosocial functioning in clients and their families, particularly through medication management. This model suggests that although social workers most likely will not influence genes, chromosomes, or the size of frontal lobes, they surely can help build protective factors and, through psychosocial interventions, can help clients maximize the benefits of their psychotropic medication. While psychosocial interventions do have effects on neurotransmission, the nature of this impact is not yet known, even though knowledge is beginning to develop in this area (e.g., Beitman et al., 2003).

"Big Pharma," Public Scrutiny, and the Social Context of Psychiatric Medication

As we have noted, many authors (e.g., Brown, 1985; Cohen & McCubbin, 1990) caution that the renewed interest in psychiatric drugs is most likely related to the medical profession's desire to remain dominant in the field and for drug companies to reap healthy profits. Clearly, such factors as the economic and sociopolitical aspects of prescription practices, drug research budgets, managed care, and insurance reimbursements must be faced head on. There can be little doubt that the increased public scrutiny is connected with the dis-ease, at best, and outrage, at worst, about the sheer size and magnitude of "Big Pharma," the pejorative term meant to refer to the whole pharmaceutical industry. This includes companies like Pfizer (maker of Zoloft and Xanax), Eli Lilly (maker of Cymbalta and Prozac), GlaxoSmithKline (maker of Paxil and Wellbutrin), Roche (maker of Valium and Klonopin), Astra Zeneca (maker of Seroquel), and Novartis (maker of Clozaril and Ritalin), to name a few. Indeed, in the past several decades, numerous books have caught headline news including Petersen's (2008) *Our Daily Meds: How the Pharmaceutical Companies Transformed Themselves Into Slick Marketing Machines and Hooked the Nation on Prescription Drugs*, Law's (2006) *Big Pharma: How the World's Biggest Drug Companies Control Illness*, Blech's (2006) *Inventing Disease and Pushing Pills*, Angell's (2004) *The Truth About Drug Companies,* Goozner's (2004) *The $800 Million Pill*, Greider's (2003) *The Big Fix* and others (e.g., Caplan, 1995; Valenstein, 1998; Walker, 1996). All describe the massive size and power of these companies to shape what we think of as malady and to control their treatment. They harshly criticize not only psychiatry in general, but the use of psychotropic medications in particular and especially the pharmaceutical industry. Petersen is one of the few to acknowledge that "medicines can and do save lives" (2008, p. 11) and notes the unmistakable contributions of antibiotics, vaccines, and protease inhibitors, for example. However, she says the "tragedy lies not with the medicines but with the marketing and the unprecedented power these companies have over the practice of medicine" (p. 11). She argues that it is not surprising that 65% of Americans take some kind of prescription medication when there is one drug company marketer per six physicians. As we have seen with the antipsychiatrists, some attack the overreliance on chemical imbalances in general to explain commonplace human problems and urge their readers to see medications not as miracles but as chemical lobotomies. Others attack the irrational or seemingly arbitrary cost formulas derived by the drug industry and point to high profits and overzealous marketing efforts (Relman & Angell, 2002). Of late is the increasing sensitivity of medical journals for publishing research where the researcher has a vested interest in the product tested, including being recipients of speaker fees and other "freebies" by drug companies (e.g., Reist & VandeCreek, 2004). New policies about disclosers of advisory board memberships, the sources of one's research funding, consultation relationships and fees are now commonplace in medical journals. Social work researcher Jeff Lacasse's most recent work has focused on exposing the practice of ghostwriting and other conflicts of interest in academic medical centers. Ghostwriting, a mostly prohibited practice, is when a pharmaceutical company secretly approaches medical researchers to "author" a paper that in fact has already been crafted by the company to show specific results. Misrepresentation and ethical conflicts of interest are obvious and the potential for real human harm is well established (Lacasse & Leo, 2010). In fact, Lacasse's research showed that when clinicians were exposed to two vignettes of a fictional antidepressant clinical outcome study, perceived credibility was lower when close financial connections to the company and ghostwriting were disclosed (Lacasse & Leo, 2011).

The cautions about "Big Pharma's" influence, however, extend beyond the antipsychiatrists and have really gone mainstream. In an editorial published in one of the most respected psychiatric journals, Steven Sharfstein (2008) writes that when the profit motives of drug companies and the quality of care motives of psychiatry align, there is a "win win." However, he too expresses concern about overmedicalization of distress, overmedication, direct marketing, and the nature of drug advertisements. Echoing an earlier question from preeminent psychiatrists David Healy and Michael Thase (2003) who ask "Is academic psychiatry for sale?", Sharfstein (2005), president of the American Psychiatric Society, calls for the development of "a new professional ethic" including more transparency about financial support from the industry and the "reining in" of enticements and gifts. Psychiatrist Steven Dubovsky and his medical student daughter, Amelia Dubovsky, collaborated to write a "survival guide" for psychiatrists as an aid to help them manage their day-to-day practices in the face of intense, pervasive, and powerful marketing of medications, usually provided under the guise of "education" about medications (Dubovsky & Dubovsky, 2007). One of their tools is for practitioners to fully understand the complex context of medication discovery and development and to bring a critical perspective to clinical trials of research and the subsequent sale of drugs.

The unmistakable increase in public scrutiny around psychotropic medications can be seen in the cry for more attention to the negative impact of these medications. Keshavan and Kennedy (1992) devote an entire edited volume to dysfunction related to the use of psychotropic medications. Topics include overdosing, problematic interactions, drug-induced neuropsychiatric symptoms (dystonias, parkinsonism, TD, NMS, akathesia), abuse of and dependence on benzodiazepines and anticholinergics, and drug-induced systemic syndromes such as cardiovascular problems, sexual dysfunction, and immunological problems. However, the controversies surrounding the use of psychotropic medication have moved beyond scholarly journals, medical books, and college classrooms and toward newspapers and the popular press. Perhaps the best-known example of this is Prozac, the best-selling antidepressant. Tens of millions of people have received prescriptions for Prozac since its introduction in 1986. Some tout its wonders to treat depression, help reduce anxiety in people who struggle with panic, decrease the intrusive thoughts and rituals in people diagnosed with obsessive-compulsive symptoms, and treat bulimia. Others are amazed by its ability to improve concentration and productivity, even in asymptomatic persons. In his best-selling book, *Listening to Prozac*, Kramer (1993) enthusiastically endorses the medication, claiming that it has more power to change people's behavior than long-term psychological treatments.

On the other hand, Barondes (1994) writes that he is disturbed by such support for Prozac and wonders if it is really just an expensive placebo, a question echoed first by Ann Blake Tracy's title *Prozac: Panacea or Pandora* (1994). Since then there has been an explosion of popular books published that criticize Prozac, including *Let Them Eat Prozac* by David Healy (2004). They all question just how long-lasting the changes are, how long someone has to take it, and at what cost. Hundreds of suits have been filed against Eli Lilly, the makers of Prozac, for its connection to acts of violence in some users. Most are dismissed. Mason and Pollack (1998) note a decade ago that to date there has never been a successful suit against the company and that such suits are decreasing in frequency. To our knowledge this is still true today.

This public debate about the "truth about drugs" grows particularly active regarding the medication of children (Bentley & Collins, 2013). It rages in the popular press with such popular books as *And They Call It Help: The Psychiatric Policing of America's Children* by Louise Armstrong (1993). It hits close to home in agency and facility philosophies and policies, as well as among family members. New clinicians usually take little time to determine on which side of the falsely dichotomous "medication fence" a certain child mental health facility falls: behavior management or medication. One concern arises that, by medicating, clinicians may avoid proper focus on the "true" genesis of children's disorders (such as physical, sexual, or emotional abuse). Widespread concern exists about overmedicating children, especially those diagnosed with attention deficit disorders, learning disabilities, and mood disorders. In fact, public controversy surrounding worries about the impact and overuse of Ritalin is but one of many concerns voiced in the media. One case involved a drug company (Pfizer) who admitted to fraud and illegal marketing of Neurotin (to treat disorders for which there was no FDA approval) and was forced to pay a multimillion dollar fine (Schmit, 2004). In addition, there has been considerable controversy around pediatric drug testing and whether the FDA exceeded its authority by actually mandating the testing of psychiatric medications on children, a development that had been widely applauded in clinical circles. Much attention today, however, relates to uncertainties about the increased risk of suicide by users of some SSRI's. The FDA has recently asked manufacturers to strengthen the language on warning labels but some are going even further and questioning the effectiveness of these medications with children at all.

However, others worry more about an under-medicated society. What about all the adults and children who suffer from treatable illnesses and conditions but receive insufficient treatment and services or no treatment at all? What about those who receive inadequate dosages or an inadequate trial? What about people who receive some type of psychotherapy alone when a combination of medication and psychotherapy or psychosocial intervention would be best? For instance, Dr. Osheroff, a physician, sued Chestnut Lodge for failing to provide him with adequate treatment (medication) for his severe depression, instead providing long-term intensive insight-oriented psychotherapy on an inpatient basis. Over the course of many months, he deteriorated to such a poor physical and mental state that his family, worried about his survival, had him discharged and arranged for alternative treatment that included medication. In a relatively short time, he was back working in his medical practice and resuming his life. Although the case was settled out of court and thus set no legal precedent, it spurred an important debate about the future of psychodynamic approaches for disorders and illnesses known to respond to medication (see Klerman, 1990; Stone, 1990).

As in the cases of SSRI's, Ritalin, and Dr. Osheroff, increased public attention on psychotropic medication and warnings about overreliance or under-reliance have numerous legal and ethical implications. In fact, improper medication management is the most common legal claim against psychiatrists (Wettstein, 1992). Most complaints relate to negligence and lack of informed consent, such as failing to take an adequate history, prescribing an improper dose, prescribing a drug without proper indicators, failing to recognize or treat adverse effects and interactions, and failing to discuss the benefits, risks, and alternatives. Thus far, the courts have been unwilling to hold manufacturers liable for failing to warn consumers about the risks and adverse effects of prescription medication because of a "learned intermediary" rule. This says that since physicians decide which medication will be prescribed and how much, injury is best avoided by a direct warning from the physician (Walsh, 1993). Walsh, however, describes the case of a woman who sued Upjohn, claiming that Halcion (triazolam) was responsible for her severe anxiety, sleeplessness, decreased appetite, and suicidal ideation. In this case, the court looked not only at the warnings the physician had given his patient but also at the warning given by the pharmaceutical representative to the physician. The case record reports that a reasonable warning is one that not only conveys a fair indication of the nature of the dangers involved but also warns with a degree of intensity demanded by the nature of the risk. A warning may be found to be unreasonable in that it was unduly delayed, reluctant in tone, or lacking in a sense of urgency (Walsh, 1993, p. 68).

Because the costs of medication affect availability and use, they have clear social and ethical dimensions. For example, tremendous controversy centers on the availability of the second-generation antipsychotics to clients served by public programs and settings, such as community mental health centers or state psychiatric hospitals. Even though research strongly supports the efficacy of these drugs with persons diagnosed with treatment-resistant schizophrenia, the drugs themselves and the required blood-monitoring system for some make the cost prohibitive for many community mental health centers and state hospitals. Although these drugs have been on the market for several years, those who might really benefit from it have very limited access to it (Reid et al., 1993). The great tragedy may be that even though the cost of the medications themselves is greater, the overall costs of care may not be dramatically increased because of lowered hospitalization costs of people on the newer medications (Nightengale et al., 1998). The National Alliance for the Mentally Ill (NAMI) has fought long and hard on moral grounds alone for making the new atypical antipsychotics and SSRIs more widely available. At one time NAMI actually began legal action against Sandoz, the maker of Clozaril (clozapine), claiming unreasonable price fixing, because the drug had been available in Europe for thousands of dollars less per year than in the United States.

Clearly, some of these issues have implications for the types of advocacy in which social workers become involved. Developing clearer ethical guidelines around psychopharmacology issues may also help clarify the advocacy role. For example, what should the relationship be between social workers' organizations and drug companies? Should drug companies be allowed or even encouraged to set up booths at social workers' national conferences, as they do at conferences sponsored by the American Psychiatric Association? Why or why not? Because the pharmaceutical industry invests up to 40% of its revenue on promotional activities, such as advertising, direct mail, and sales representatives, we have noted concerns that have arisen about the relationships between this industry and practicing physicians (Caudill, Lurie, & Rich, 1992), as it has for the relationship between the industry and researchers. Neill (1989) notes that "a complex ideological and financial relationship exists between the drug industry and the prescribing psychiatrist, the vendor and the consumer, which has yet to be explored" (p. 333). For example, after reviewing hundreds of drug advertisements in medical journals, Neill notes that even as drug companies exploit and manipulate physicians, drug advertisements minister to the psychological needs of physicians for prestige, identity, potency, and self-satisfaction. Unfortunately, as we have noted, drug advertisements can also reinforce medical concepts of illness that tend to locate pathology in individuals, de-emphasizing the social context and competing psychosocial interventions (Lacasse, 2005). Additional remedies, such as psychosocial rehabilitation, improvements in housing, education, and jobs, are sometimes considered "totally beyond the pale" (Kleinman & Cohen, 1991, p. 868). Social workers are thus challenged to maintain their psychosocial emphasis and perspective even as they take on roles traditionally ascribed to the medical sphere. It should be pointed out that although drug companies do not currently court social workers, if their role in medication management continues to expand, such subtle influences on autonomy may need to be confronted and a mandate to disclose our own connections to these companies may emerge.

Health care professionals are still a long way from understanding how new modes of financing health and mental health services, including managed care, will affect psychopharmacology practice. Should they worry that it may lead to even greater reliance on medications because of their sheer efficiency? Will people be "treated only from the neck up" (Flynn, 1994, p. 16)? Or should they be hopeful that the rhetoric of managed care, which supports empirically validated treatments such as combined psychotherapeutic or rehabilitative approaches, will finally be realized? Similarly, what will changes in Medicare and Medicaid coverage do to psychopharmacology practices? Regrettably, we may already have a hint to some of those answers. Scheid (2003), for example, after reviewing data on organizational structures, service offerings, and provider experiences in managed care, concludes that the primary effect of managed care has been on cost containment and *not* on accountability, outcome assessment, or quality of care. She notes a decreased commitment to those needing long-term mental health services.

CHANGING AND EXPANDING ROLES
AND THE DISCIPLINARY CONTEXT

To appreciate the sociopolitical context of social work roles in psychopharmacology, social workers need to see with open eyes issues of professional sanction and professional "turf." Heller and Gitterman (2011) summarize some of the developments that have influenced social work's place in the disciplinary landscape in the delivery of mental health and other human services today. Noting our status of primary mental health care providers to people with serious mental illnesses, they point to the development of licensure protections for clinical practice, and third-party payments that accompany those developments, and shifting roles for psychiatrists to those that emphasize prescription writing and medication management as opposed to talk therapy. Social workers, however, still need to define what is unique about their own professional perspective, what is shared with related disciplines, and what falls outside their purview. This is a great historical challenge in and of itself. It is even more interesting in an area—psychopharmacology—so closely identified with other professions. Importantly, we will also need to better understand the unique contributions that professionals in fields such as nursing, psychology, and psychiatry, and even nonprofessionals such as folk healers bring to client care.

Although social workers see themselves as highly trained and knowledgeable clinicians, they constantly face having to explain and demonstrate who they are, often making a case for their indispensability, especially when in settings not dominated by social workers (Dane and Simon, 1991; Mailick & Jordan, 1977). Because often what they do is influenced by other professions who do not fully understand them, social workers have noted a discrepancy between what they can do, want to do, or were trained to do, and what they actually do (Harrison, Drolen, & Atherton, 1989). For example, Pray (1991) notes that the gatekeeping function of physicians and psychiatrists often subtly defines what is deemed an appropriate role for social workers.

Dane and Simon (1991) relate this continued misunderstanding of social work in part to the devaluing of women's work, because women constitute a large majority of social workers. They also note the divergent missions and training of other helping professions, as well as the poorly defined and stressful roles that exist in many settings. In an analysis of the sources of strain between social workers and physicians, Mizrahi and Abramson (1985) provide insight into the social worker's long-standing struggle to be understood. Specifically, they note that physician training stresses hard science knowledge, puts little emphasis on the clinical relationship, and offers little opportunity for them to process their feelings. They also state that physicians are socialized to be the autonomous decision-makers and authority figures. In stark contrast to social work training, which emphasizes values, relationships, and "process," the training and socialization of physicians leads to differing perspectives in a number of important areas, such as the role and rights of clients and families and the role and function of social work. Similarly, Mailick and Jordan (1977) note how differences among professional knowledge, values, and methods of communication influence collaboration. Weil (1982) suggests that social workers consider the barriers to collaborative relationships and openly address differences in socialization and status. Avoiding stereotypes is also crucial to prevent negative attitudes toward other professions. Greater interdisciplinary collaboration begins with mutual respect and mandates the bold confrontation of misperceptions and ignorance (Gibelman, 1993).

The benefits of interdisciplinary collaboration are well articulated. For example, Sands (1989) notes that such collaboration "helps us arrive at a comprehensive understanding of the client [and] solve complex problems" (p. 1). Similarly, in their classic article, Toseland et al., (1986) note how teamwork improves services to the client as well as work satisfaction for professionals. A comprehensive review (Rice, 2000) confirms the positive impact of collaboration in health care on client outcome and continuity of care, quality of care, and reduced hospital stays, as well as job satisfaction of workers and the promotion of professional identity.

Abramson and Mizrahi's innovative work on collaboration between medical social workers and physicians adds an interesting dimension to our understanding of differing styles of collaboration among people and among different disciplines (Abramson & Mizrahi, 2003; Mizrahi & Abramson, 2000). Using the interviews of 50 pairs of social worker–MD collaborators, they generated a typology of "transformational," "transitional" (in-between), versus "traditional" collaborators. Traditional collaboration is most associated with dissatisfaction among both physicians and social workers. This kind of collaboration is characterized by limited or unclear or subservient roles by social workers and minimal communication between collaborators. They recommend we strive for more transformational styles. For social workers, this refers to the tendency to educate and involve physicians in psychosocial issues, regularly share information and responsibilities, contribute actively to the team, and assume nonhierarchical relationships. For physicians, it means integrating psychosocial aspects of care into their own role, initiating contact with and involving social workers, and engaging in joint decision-making with social workers.

In mental health and health settings in particular, social workers have tended to play key roles on interdisciplinary teams. In the Toseland et al. (1986) survey of 71 team members from seven disciplines, social workers were reported as having a high degree of influence, second only to psychiatrists. Further, it showed that social workers tended to play a wide range of roles, including some that overlapped with other professions. Interestingly, there were strong differences of opinion among the team members in two areas: (1) whether or not team members ought to have equal power and (2) whether there ought to be a clear differentiation of roles among the professions. Claims of a unique perspective and expectations about roles may be interrelated. For example, social workers often refer to their unique "holistic perspective" as their profession's strength (Dane & Simon, 1991). However, nurses have also cited a "holistic perspective" as a key distinguishing aspect of their profession. One survey of physicians found that they perceived hospital social workers as having a limited understanding of clients' psychosocial problems and as performing only as discharge planners who arrange for concrete services (Pray, 1991). A large-scale survey of social workers, physicians, and nurses in a medical setting (Cowles & Lefcowitz, 1992) found disagreements among the three regarding professional roles. Unfortunately, other professionals did not think social workers had the ability to assess emotional problems. Overall, however, differences in the way roles were perceived related less to what social workers did in everyday practice than to what roles they performed that are their *exclusive* domain.

Clearly, more training in interprofessional collaboration is needed if we are to truly embrace our unique perspectives and roles, as well as more fully appreciate our colleagues contributions to care and treatment of those in need in sibling disciplines. Henkin and Dee (1998) stress the teaching of specific collaborative skills, such as empathy, adaptability, group process skills, assertiveness, and emotional expressivity and sensitivity. Because of the connection between interdisciplinary collaboration and role issues, King and Ross (2003) recommend that cross-disciplinary training directly address role ambiguity and professional identity. Mailick and Ashley (1981) summarize this view:

> Of utmost importance in working with a collaborative group is the capacity to listen, to be respectful, to understand the implications of other professional opinions, to be willing to recognize and accept areas in which the expertise of colleagues is unique, and to defer to special knowledge when appropriate. (p. 135)

A few examples of innovative interdisciplinary education models or projects can be found in the literature (e.g., Burns et al., 2000; Cameron & Mauksch, 2002; Talen, Fraser, & Cauley, 2002). These involve such components as simple as sharing coursework to periodic shadowing of other discipline's work, conjoint client visits, and interactive sessions with video and role-play. Regrettably, as Rice (2000) notes, even innovative efforts to enhance interdisciplinary practice are too often tied to time-limited funding streams that dry up. The barriers to sustainability of specific educational initiatives, including lack of accreditation mandates, lack of faculty expertise and experience, turf issues, and entrenched institutional structures, are significant.

Several reviews report the results of research into factors that seem to be associated with successful collaboration. Dozens of factors across a number of different dimensions—environmental context, personal characteristics of collaborators, process and structure, communication, purpose, and resources—are identified, a number of which we have highlighted above (Bronstein, 2003; Mattessich, 1992). Clearly, a favorable political climate, shared vision, open and frequent communication, trust, adaptability, and respect, and a successful history of collaboration are all helpful. Also identified as key are clear roles, the presence of concrete, attainable goals, and a leader with strong interpersonal skills.

SUMMARY

This chapter describes the intriguing context in which contemporary social workers enact their roles in psychopharmacology across settings. That context includes the disciplinary lens of social work and a mindfulness about social justice dimensions of all we do, as well as a plea for a balanced perspective on psychiatric mediation use. However, we also stress more emphatically in this edition a critical perspective on psychiatry and medication in general, as well as an appreciation of the scientific and sociopolitical dimensions of psychopharmacology, including neuroscience and tension between biological and ecological determinism, as well as the influence of drug companies on the structure of health and human service delivery. Social work is presented here and throughout the book as being especially well suited to respond to the client's medication-related dilemmas across settings, given our commitment to the whole person in biopsychosocial context, our appreciation of social justice, and a critical yet balanced view of psychiatric medication use, and especially to collaboration and client-centered care.

TOPICS FOR DISCUSSION
AND LEARNING ACTIVITIES

1. What are the benefits and costs of embracing a "balanced perspective" on medication? A critical perspective? For you? For clients and families?

2. How would you explain your own "biopsychosocial perspective" on mental illness, emotional distress, or behavioral disorders to a client? Her or his family? A family tells you that low levels of serotonin "caused" their family member's depression? Do you say anything?

3. A pharmaceutical company is hosting a breakfast at your agency. Do you attend? Under what circumstances? Have you ever, or would you, accept a logoed coffee cup or pen as a token gift from a drug company?

4. Social work has continued to be a female-dominated profession. Do you believe that plays a role in our continuing struggle for legitimacy in some professional arenas?

5. What aspects of social work or social work education and training do you think equips social workers to be particularly well suited to respond to client's psychiatric, medication-related dilemmas?

2

✳

Overview of Social Work Roles in Medication Management Across Settings

Learning Objectives

Upon completion of this chapter, the reader will be able to:

1. Understand the range of roles for social workers in four practice settings.
2. Define the five essential components of the partnership model of social work practice.
3. Identify and define seven roles for social workers when working with clients who use psychotropic medications.
4. Define three interventions that can be used within each role.

All social workers engaged in direct practice across various settings work, at least occasionally, often frequently, with persons who use psychiatric medications as part of their intervention plans. Social workers have only recently, however, begun to elaborate a range of specific professional roles with regard to medication issues. Historically, some would say they have functioned too often as physician's assistants, merely supporting consumer compliance with medications according to the physician's recommendations. However, the range of service delivery modalities for many client populations has expanded to a point where clients and families often ask social workers to help them make difficult decisions and address a variety of dilemmas related to their use of psychotropic medication. Social workers thus must possess a sound knowledge of medications and understand their consequences for clients' lives, but not merely to complement the physician's role. Instead, the social worker brings her or his unique perspective to medication issues based on its appreciation of client self-determination, its view of the person-in-environment as the basis for assessment and intervention, and its perspective that medication is only one part of comprehensive psychosocial intervention. Social work also promotes a partnership model of practice, which bases relationships with clients and families on an appreciation of their strengths and viewpoints and an assumption that the helping relationship should be nonhierarchical.

In all practice settings, the assessment of a client's mental, emotional, and behavioral status and the monitoring of their medications (when indicated) should comprise a significant part of the person-in-environment perpective, as discussed in Chapter 1. Traditionally, social workers have not emphasized knowledge of medications as a key component of their professional training or continuing education, but a continued ignorance of this topic will only result in disservice to clients. Although medications seem to affect functioning at a bio-chemical level, they equally affect the psychological and social concerns of clients and their significant others. In this chapter, we outline the range of roles that social workers should be prepared to assume in working with clients who use or consider using psychotropic medications in the practice areas of mental health, child welfare, aging (including health and hospitals), and corrections. We also describe our "partnership model" of practice as the foundation for all role functions. To begin we provide brief overviews of social work practice in four major practice areas noted above, as well as some case examples of how social workers typically interface with adults and children taking psychiatric medication.

PRACTICE SETTINGS, ROLES, AND ACTIVITIES

Mental Health

Mental, emotional, and behavioral disorders are unfortunately widespread throughout the U.S. population. While the prevalence of such major disorders as schizophrenia and bipolar disorder are 1% and 3%, respectively, others are more common. Kessler et al. (2005) found in a national survey that other life-time prevalence estimates are as follows: Anxiety disorders (28.8%), mood disorders (20%), impulse-control disorders (24.8%), substance use disorders (14.6 %), and any disorder (46.4%).

Social workers are the nation's largest providers of mental health services, with 122,000 professionals so employed (Bureau of Labor Statistics, 2011). Sixty percent of mental health professionals are clinically trained social workers, compared to 10% of psychiatrists, 23% of psychologists, and 5% of psychiatric nurses (National Association of Social Workers [NASW], 2008). Social workers provide services in a variety of settings including community mental health centers, private agencies, state and county hospitals, psychiatric units in general hospitals, veteran's affairs facilities, psychiatric rehabilitation agencies, and private practice settings.

Social workers occupy many roles in mental health, including case manager, therapist, advocate, and administrator. As *case managers* in public mental health agencies, social workers work with people who have serious mental illnesses, such as schizophrenia, bipolar disorder, depression, anxiety, and personality disorders. In that capacity, social workers spend time individually or as a member of an interdisciplinary team to determine consumers' strengths, goals, and needs, and to help them find formal and informal services aimed at recovery from mental illness (and sometimes substance abuse). Social workers provide counseling, help consumers locate appropriate housing and vocational services, and advocate for consumer needs with landlords, law enforcement officers, and others. They also work as advocates in the policy arena, developing and promoting legislation that will help people receive equitable treatment. *Clinical social workers* provide individual and family counseling in mental health, private practice, drug treatment centers, and in school-based programs. In all settings social workers need to recognize the biological, psychological, and social aspects of mental health, although these factors may be targeted differently during intervention.

Many clients in mental health settings use psychotropic medication from the antipsychotic, antidepressant, mood-stabilizing, antianxiety, and psychostimulant drug categories to help them achieve stability. One challenge, though, is that psychiatry's emphasis on biological intervention, supported by the availability of effective drugs, has compartmentalized the medical and social approaches to the treatment of mental illness. A sharper distinction has evolved between psychiatry, on the one hand, and social work and related disciplines on the other. This distinction has provided a rationale for social workers to assume more active roles in helping clients who use psychotropic medication to also utilize psychosocial interventions in their community adjustment. Social work's emphasis on holistic intervention has received a boost with the emergence of the consumer-generated Recovery Movement, which refers to a consumer's journey toward holistic wellness (Walsh, 2013).

CASE EXAMPLES

John is a 34-year-old single Caucasian male, living with his sister and brother-in-law. He experiences dysthymia and demonstrates dependent personality traits. Although he is intelligent, cares about others, and has a notable self-deprecating wit, John shows extreme anxiety in all social situations and has a poor self-image. For several months, the social worker has intervened to help John reach his goal of self-sufficiency as he sought better social skills, employment, and junior college enrollment. Making significant strides, John applies for jobs, attends interviews, and visits a regional college campus. However, with each initiative, he becomes almost incapacitated with a fear of failure. The social worker decides to refer him to an agency physician, who will evaluate medication that can help John deal with his depressed mood through this difficult time.

John impresses the physician as someone working hard to overcome his problems. The physician decides to prescribe a small dose of an antidepressant medication that may help John sleep better at night, stabilize his mood, and reduce his anxiety. The medication seems effective, and John's dose is gradually raised into an average therapeutic range. During their weekly sessions, the social worker helps John monitor the effects of his medication. Several months later, John begins working. He seems committed to making the experience a success, but the stress of his job responsibilities and his need to interact regularly with coworkers overwhelm him. One evening, John abruptly quits. In a panic, fearing that he has blown a rare opportunity to work, he takes a serious overdose of his medications. He survives but is hospitalized for one night for observation.

Learning of the overdose, the physician becomes angry and tells the social worker that he will no longer prescribe medications for John. He states that doing so would constitute irresponsible practice because the client is a suicidal risk. However, the social worker continues to see John, who seems truly remorseful about his action. He recovers from the crisis and states that he wants to continue focusing on the same goals. Further, because the medication has helped him move forward, John hopes that he can resume taking an antidepressant drug. The social worker has been placed in a difficult bind. She tends to agree with John, but the physician will not meet with him again. The social worker will violate agency policy and put her reputation as a team player in jeopardy if she arranges to transfer John's psychiatric care to another agency physician.

Child Welfare

The child welfare system includes all programs and policies that are intended to improve the well-being of children (Segal, Gerdes, & Steiner, 2013). Social workers are prominently represented in child protection, foster care, adoption, school social work, and juvenile justice services. The social service needs of children are great. In the United States, more than 13 million children (18%) live in poverty (DeNavas-Walt, Proctor, & Smith, 2008), 8 million (11%) do not have health insurance, and even more do not receive regular medical care. In 2010, 900,000 children were confirmed to have been victims of abuse or neglect, and 400,000 children, most under age 11, were in foster care (Administration for Children and Families, 2010). About 20% of children and adolescents have experienced mental and behavioral disorders, and 12% have serious emotional disturbances. Since the 1990s, there has been a substantial increase in the numbers of children diagnosed with oppositional defiant, attention deficit/hyperactivity, autism spectrum, and bipolar disorders. Only about one-third of children who need mental health services receive them (Hochman, 2006).

Child protective services (CPS) include designated state, county, and local departments responsible for investigating allegations of abuse or neglect, protecting children at risk for abuse or neglect, and placing children who have been maltreated into alternative settings. Social workers serve as investigators, intake workers, caseworkers, and supervisors. Family preservation services are activities designed to help families alleviate crises that might lead to out-of-home placements. Social workers provide in-home support and counseling so that families can be helped to stay together. The roles of school social workers vary among states and school districts. In some districts, they are solely responsible for assessing and meeting the needs of students through special education services. In other districts, they provide group and individual counseling for regular education students and sometimes their families. In many schools, the social worker is part of an interdisciplinary team, including teachers, school administrators, psychologists, nurses, parents, and perhaps a speech or hearing therapist. They participate in making ongoing assessments and plans regarding students' social, emotional, and physical needs.

In working with children and their families, social workers embrace the major roles of case management and direct practice. Case management with children involves assessing a child's problems and needs and determining what steps are necessary for alleviating them. Case managers often must advocate for a child to obtain services in a service system that includes many barriers to comprehensive care. Case management is also involved when a social worker works with a foster family to provide counseling services for a child placed in their home and works in a hospital to help a family find aftercare health services. Direct practice with children and their families involves face-to-face contact with children and family members to form a therapeutic relationship and work through family problem issues. Because young children do not have verbal skills or insight, interventions often include forms of play therapy.

Children rarely bring themselves to the attention of a social worker; someone else has decided that they need help. As such, self-determination can be difficult to facilitate with children. By virtue of their age, they cannot be empowered in the same way adults can. This complicates the process of medicating children, which is often done when mental or behavioral problems emerge. There are special risks in this process related to informed consent, possible long-term adverse physical effects, and communicating to children that problems in living can be addressed with interventions besides drugs (Walkup et al., 2008). It often falls to the social worker to advocate for ethical practices in this area.

CASE EXAMPLES

Students referred to the Metropolitan Behavioral Health Authority's Youth Day Treatment Program (YDT) must be identified by their parents or a public schoolteacher as having a behavioral or emotional problem that prevents them from succeeding in a school setting. The goal of the program (comprised of three social workers who maintain contact with a consulting psychiatrist and schoolteachers) is to enable targeted students to display more age-appropriate behaviors at home and in school. These goals are attained through interventions that are provided entirely in the school and classroom.

Monique was a 7-year-old African American female, the fourth of ten children, who presented to YDT aggressive behavior demonstrated by a lack of respect for adults and authority figures, negative interactions with peers, and difficulty staying focused at school. These concerns were brought forth by the kindergarten teacher, but her mother indicated that Monique's behavior had become unmanageable at home. Recently, Monique had begun to describe auditory and visual hallucinations. Her mother stated that her daughter's problem was "aggressive, rageful, and defiant behavior" as well as "attention to voices and objects that are unseen." Monique believed she had been referred to YDT services because she does not have friends. The child was diagnosed by a psychiatrist as having attention-deficit/hyperactivity disorder and a psychotic disorder not otherwise specified. The psychiatrist prescribed Tenex, .5 mg twice daily for hypertension, Clonidine .1mg at bedtime to reduce the ADHD symptoms and manage her anxiety, and Ritalin 5mg three times a day to further treat the client's ADHD. The YDT social workers had no role in the medication process except to monitor Monique's adherence and her mental status.

Monique was highly dependent on her mother who had been diagnosed with bipolar disorder and received medications herself. Each of her nine living siblings were fathered by different men who did not live in the home. Her biological father had a criminal history marked by multiple incarcerations. Additionally, the client's younger sister died suddenly one-and-a-half years ago (there was a CPS investigation after the death but no direct evidence of abuse was found) and the client had not adjusted well to this transition. She often talked to her deceased baby sister out loud.

The YDT staff were asked to develop a set of behavioral interventions for Monique while the psychiatrist monitored the medications (which the social workers did not think she was taking as prescribed). Monique's goals were to reduce disrespect toward adults and authority, demonstrate positive peer interaction, acquire skills to increase her ability to focus, participate in weekly individual and group therapy with a social worker to explore current stressors, learn to identify her feelings, and be able to recognize the differences between hallucinated states and reality. The interventions consisted of:

- YDT staff monitoring the client's behavior in the classroom daily, coordinating observations with other school staff.
- Weekly individual and group therapy by a YDT staff member to resolve Monique's inattention, distractability, and disrespectful behaviors, and to provide social skills training.
- A referral to family intensive in-home counseling to monitor and improve family interactions in the home.
- YDT staff utilization of a daily point system to reward Monique's positive behaviors.
- Weekly telephone consultations with the psychiatrist to discuss mental status observations.

By the end of the school year Monique continued to display rigid and odd cognitions not grounded in reality. Her impulsive behaviors decreased, however, and she began to increase her peer interactions. She was able to concentrate more effectively in school and earned B's in her last grading quarter. Overall, the client was showing progress in her behaviors, but was still showing evidence of psychosis. Monique would be followed by the psychiatrist over the summer and family preservation services would continue, but the social workers in the YDT program, which corresponded to the academic year, would no longer participate.

Aging, Health, and Hospitals

One out of every eight Americans, or 12.4% of the population, are older adults, persons aged 65 years and older (Segal, Gerdes, & Steiner, 2013). The oldest-old (aged 85 and older) are the fastest-growing segment of the population. In 2006 there were 5.3 million Americans over the age of 85; in 2050 there could be as many as 21 million. While most older adults live healthy, satisfying lives, they are at risk of living in poverty, suffering from depression, being victims of abuse, or experiencing health problems associated with aging. The goal of social work with older adults is to promote and advance older clients' social, emotional, and physical well-being. About 5% of professional social workers are primarily employed in the practice area of aging.

Knowledge areas relevant to work with older adults include the biological and psychological aspects of aging, cognitive processes and emotional development, sociological aspects of aging, and legal and economic aspects of aging (Zarit & Zarit, 2007). Social workers also need to be aware of the actions of commonly used medications used to treat the physical and mental health of older adults. The vast majority of older adults (81%) use at least one prescription medication, and more than half use five or more medications, including over-the-counter drugs and dietary supplements (Qato, et al., 2008).

The roles of social workers in older adult and health care include case manager, group facilitator, therapist, and advocate. Social workers in health care settings, such as skilled nursing facilities, hospitals, home health care agencies, and hospice care facilities provide a variety of services for older adults. Psychosocial assessments are a crucial part of social work practice in health care settings. Social workers in hospitals and hospices provide family support services, discharge planning, and death and dying counseling. They decide the type and scope of supportive care needed and link the client to community resources and family supports. Social workers who serve older adult clients must be prepared to work as part of a multidisciplinary team that can include psychiatrists, physicians, nurses, physical therapists, occupational therapists, and nutritionists, all of whom attempt to coordinate their areas of expertise in holistic services for older adults.

Critical issues in older adult services include elder abuse and neglect, managing dementia, caregiving for aging parents, grandparents caring for grandchildren, mental health, and depression. Depression is the primary emotional disorder among people who are older, affecting as many as 2 million older adults each year (National Institute of Health, 2003). About 25% of people over age 65 with a chronic medical illness suffer from depressive symptoms and 15% suffer from major depressive disorders (Sheikh et al., 2004). Other mental health problems commonly associated with older adulthood include anxiety, paranoia, and substance abuse. Special challenges for social workers who intervene with older adults include an awareness of their greater sensitivity to the adverse effects of medication.

CASE EXAMPLES

Roger Trimble is an 88-year-old Caucasian widower and father of 11 children. After his wife died 21 years ago, Mr. Trimble retired and moved into his daughter's urban home. Mr. Trimble stayed active by attending church, attending his grandchildren's sports activities, visiting with family members, and engaging in volunteer activities. Mr. Trimble also walked two miles every day to stay healthy. Beginning 10 years ago, however, Mr. Trimble's family noticed that he frequently misplaced his keys, hats, wallet, and other items. In addition, his volunteer supervisors reported that Mr. Trimble was found wandering the parking lot, confused about where he was.

Six years ago Mr. Trimble suffered an atrial fibrillation, a heart rhythm disturbance that caused him to experience a series of minor strokes. He was admitted to the hospital for several days. Upon returning home, Mr. Trimble's family noticed a marked decline in his functioning. Mr. Trimble could not remember card games he had played his whole life. He called family members by the wrong name. He occasionally forgot how to get to church and back. Mr. Trimble soon retired from all volunteer activities because his family members took his car away from him. He also began to worry about intruders at night. He would get up to check the doors, the hallways, and the kitchen. He hid his personal items and could not find them. As the years passed, Mr. Trimble's mental functioning continued to deteriorate, and he became more stubborn and agitated.

At this time his physician diagnosed him with both Alzheimer's disease (with an onset before his strokes) and vascular dementia (following his stroke-related decline). The physician referred him to an older adult home services program, which included a social worker, nurse, and nurse's aid. The medical team has been prescribing Neuron tin, Ativan, and Zyprexa to stabilize Mr. Trimble's mood and to control hallucinations, Depakote to decrease his tremors, Vasotec for his blood pressure, and folic acid and Razadyne for his dementia. The team's psychosocial goals for the client were to develop and follow a consistent daily routine, increase his level of physical functioning, reduce his feelings of anxiety, stabilize his blood sugar through diet, maintain his support systems, and help the family become more knowledgeable of available community services.

These goals required coordination between Mr. Trimble, the medical professionals, the in-home care team, and Mr. Trimble's family. The social worker and nurse helped the family develop and follow a routine of consistent care for Mr. Trimble so that he was not left alone so often. The nurse's aid worked with Mr. Trimble to move around during the day, thus helping him to sleep better at night and increase the quality of his physical functioning. Referrals to senior center activities were helpful toward this end as well. Having a consistent routine with the same people and the medications helped Mr. Trimble maintain his current level of cognitive functioning.

Mr. Trimble continued living with his daughter and her husband who provided his basic care. Three of his other children visited him weekly, and the others visited him twice monthly and called him each week. Mr. Trimble maintained close relationships with his children and grandchildren, attended Mass, and saw his friends on Sundays. Mr. Trimble occasionally speaks with his former coworkers and volunteers. The family reports that Mr. Trimble functions best at home during the day and when there are a lot of people around. He suffers most at night after a long day of visitors. Mr. Trimble is more alert when he eats regular meals that are low in sugar. He denies suicidal thoughts, although he says that he is lonely and sleeps when he is alone. His cognitive decline continues, although more slowly than before, and he seems physically comfortable.

Corrections and Jails

In 2008 the United States had 2.3 million criminals behind bars or 1 in every 100 adults (Liptak, 2008). The primary goals of the criminal justice system are to maintain public safety and punish lawbreakers by confining or controlling them (Miller, 1995). Despite its lack of emphasis on rehabilitation, the criminal justice system represents a major practice arena for social workers. Social workers may specialize in juvenile corrections, the rehabilitation of adults, the case management and counseling of people on probation and parole, police social work, and victim assistance services. Social work's person-in-environment theory requires practitioners to consider both individual and sociological factors that affect human behavior. Social work values require that offenders should be given access to effective therapies, including medication, and perhaps be removed from prisons to be given treatments in other environments.

The functions of social workers in the juvenile and family court system include making psychosocial assessments, conducting court investigations, giving courtroom testimony, supervising probation, and fulfilling court-assigned social services. In juvenile corrections, social workers conduct comprehensive assessments following adjudications so that the corrections system can implement effective interventions based on offenders' strengths. In adult correctional facilities, social workers write comprehensive psychosocial histories, prepare reports for parole boards, administer treatment programs to sex offenders and substance abusers, conduct individual and group therapy to teach life skills, and advocating for prisoners' rights.

Community corrections refers to punishments that occur outside of secure facilities in halfway houses, work/release programs, community service programs, or diversion programs. Social workers have many opportunities to provide counseling and arrange for rehabilitative services in those settings. Finally, in victim assistance programs, social workers are advocates and counselors, helping victims receive the services to which they are entitled and facilitating victim/offender mediation.

One of the unintended outcomes of psychiatric deinstitutionalization is that some persons housed in jails may be detained there in lieu of psychiatric hospitalization. Additionally, some criminals have mental illnesses that may contribute to their antisocial behaviors. Correctional facilities are legally required to provide services to people with disabilities, and these may include mental health screenings, evaluations, and treatment for the estimated 30% of offenders with mental disabilities (Pollack, 2005). Most community service boards designate a staff member with the responsibilities of being a liaison to jails, and most prisons employ full-time social workers on staff. While comprehensive mental health services are rare, one literature review has demonstrated that prison inmates are more likely to be medication-adherent when such systematic programs are in place (Shelton et al., 2010). A recent meta-analysis of 26 empirical studies found that interventions with offenders with mental illness effectively reduced symptoms of distress, including institutional adjustment and behavioral functioning, and produced significant reductions in psychiatric and criminal recidivism (Morgan et al., 2012).

CASE EXAMPLES

Rachel is a social worker at the Anderson Correctional Facility, an all-female prison that houses up to 800 women in a northeastern state. Women are incarcerated in one of the prison's five residential buildings for a variety of crimes, many of which are drug-related but span the range of felonies and include murder. Almost 80% of the incarcerated women take some type of psychotropic medication, and most were using these at the time of their admission. In her role on the health care team, which includes a social worker, physician, nurse, and several case managers, Rachel provides biopsychosocial assessments of all new prisoners, a process that includes determining what psychotropic medications they might be using. It is then her responsibility to verify the accuracy of the prescriptions by consulting with relevant pharmacies in the prisoner's former place of residence. Rachel then refers the inmates to the psychiatrist (who provides part-time work at this and other correctional facilities in the region) who further evaluates their mental health status and either continues with, or alters, the medication regimen.

Rachel also provides individual therapy for women who are assessed as having mental health problems, and she meets with the health care team monthly for case reviews. Women who appear to develop mental health problems after their admission to the prison are referred to Rachel for mental health assessments by the security staff or other corrections officers who interact with the prisoners on a regular basis. All prisoners who use medication receive their prescriptions from a nurse as part of the daily "medline," where they stand in line to receive their drugs. When prisoners are being prepared for release, Rachel participates in their mental health discharge planning, although most other discharge arrangements are carried out by designated case managers.

We believe that in all service settings the social worker's activities should be based on a partnership model of practice, a topic to which we now turn.

THE PARTNERSHIP MODEL OF
SOCIAL WORK PRACTICE

We believe that the key component for achieving this success is effective collaboration—with clients, their families, and also other health care providers, such as psychiatrists, nurses, and physicians. A key theme that undergirds effective collaboration across fields of practice is the partnership model of practice. In a partnership model of practice the social worker appreciates both the strengths and the limits of clients and their families, embraces a client-centered perspective, reconceptualizes the helping relationship, redefines the social work role as a resource to clients, and appreciates the perspective of family members.

Working toward partnership implies working toward a nonthreatening alliance of participants and a mutual sharing of expertise. With respect to medication, partnership calls for good communication on both an informational and relational level (Schneider et al., 2004). Indeed, the ideas of decreasing distance and affirming the humanity of clients presented here have been validated by qualitative research into the experiences of clients with regard to their relationships with clinicians. Ware, Tugenberg, & Dickey (2004) analyzed interviews with 51 people with schizophrenia and identified eight client "priorities" in relationships with helpers. First, they appreciated the small, "beyond the call of duty" things that some practitioners do, such as telling a joke or the brief sharing of personal information. They also appreciated when practitioners noted similarities in their own life with theirs and when they "felt known" and affirmed by clinicians who conveyed an empathetic understanding of the client's life situation. Participants emphasized the importance of talking freely to accessible clinicians, being consulted, and having one's requests honored and included in decisions. Again, these respondents wanted to be treated like intelligent, competent adults. Readers will notice that this approach echoes the principles often discussed in relationship to empowerment practice (Lee, 2003).

Appreciate Participants' Strengths and Limits

The "strengths perspective" for social work is a strategy that suggests a reorientation of practice toward the individual client's unique strengths and aspirations and away from pathology, symptoms, or weaknesses (Saleebey, 2011). In its fullness, the perspective goes beyond a minor shift in a practice emphasis or a simple reframing of client problems into more positive terms. Work with clients should "reek of 'can do'" in every phase of helping because all clients can learn, grow, and change.

Although Weick and colleagues (1989) acknowledged long ago that most social workers are intuitively comfortable with the strengths perspective, they also pointed to the difficulty that many experience in adopting this perspective as their primary orientation. One such difficulty arises from the widespread reliance on what some would call a pathology-based classification scheme, such as the *Diagnostic and Statistical Manual of Mental Disorders* (DSM-IV-TR), for decisions about treatment and reimbursement. In this book we openly struggle with how to reorient social work practice toward clients' strengths while still responding when the stated need of clients is to directly reduce their problems or so-called deficits.

Appreciating clients' limits is as complex as appreciating their strengths. The key is to avoid automatically defining a client's mental, emotional, or behavioral symptoms as given limitations; in other words, avoid presuming incompetence or poor judgment. According to Deegan (2000), automatically viewing people with psychiatric problems as irrational or unreasonable is fueled by "mentalism" (akin to sexism and racism). Deegan saw this attitude as a "spirit breaking central attitudinal barrier" that leads to a cycle of disempowerment and despair among clients. By "limits" we mean any existing barriers to progress, such as a lack of skills or inadequate resources. Social workers need to help clients realistically define their own situational limits and personal challenges, both of which may or may not be related to symptomatology, just as they would help identify their clients' unique strengths and assets. Ignoring or underplaying the sometimes severe limits that clients have in social functioning can result in exaggerated and harmful expectations on the social worker's part. Similarly, ignoring or underplaying strengths can contribute to the demoralization that clients often feel in the mental health system.

Embrace a Client-Centered Practice

The client's perspective should be the centerpiece of practice. Although some see this as a given in social work, others will recognize it as a call to shift their focus away from the practitioner's or the agency's preconceived notions of where clients should be headed and truly "begin where the client is." It means that the agency agenda is not the centerpiece of practice and therefore should not be dictating the nature and direction of the helping process; it also means that the funding source of a program is not the centerpiece and therefore should not be defining the goals of helping. Instead, social workers should assist in defining the client's goals in a way that truly emerges from the client's current life situation and desired outcomes, even if the result is some sort of reframing of the purpose of the helping endeavor. Knowing what the client really wants to work toward is the most important piece of information the social worker can have. It defines the direction and pace of practice. A partnership model, however, does not mean that social workers are passive participants or quasi-servants or that the agency context is totally irrelevant.

Self-determination is clearly a relevant issue here. It has been described as perhaps "the most confounding concept in the intellectual underpinnings of social work" because of its "illusive" and "clouded" nature in real-world practice (Rothman, 1989, p. 598). Self-determination is considered by many human service practitioners as a moral imperative and a practice tool that fosters change and growth even though it has limits related to a client's economic circumstances, resources, mandates and pressures, and mental acuity and skill (Ryan & Deci, 2008). The controversy then arises as to what extent a client's symptoms affects the actualization of his or her self-determination.

As far back as 1963, Soyer argued that the self-determined aspirations of clients should be the focus of practice, even if those aspirations appear unrealistic. Soyer offered two reasons to justify this strong stance: (1) the client just might be right, and (2) perhaps only by living life can clients "try, test, and temper" their goals (p. 77). Recently, consumers who are active in the recovery movement emphasize that making the client the director of the helping process is central to maintaining the value of self-determination in social work (Piat et al., 2009). It also enhances the control clients have over their own lives.

Rapp (2007) pointed out that the stated wants of clients do not differ from their needs (and do not seem different from most people's). The tendencies of social workers to avoid risks or their desires to save clients from failure, as Soyer (1963) stated, too often "dampen rather than fire" their aspirations and desires. Yeung, et al. (2010) support helping processes based on clients' needs as clients perceive them, but they acknowledge that negotiation and compromise, as well as interdisciplinary cooperation, may help temper certain unrealistic wishes. However, social workers sometimes tend to let clients self-determine only when they happen to agree with their clients' decisions or direction. Too often they define their own professional perspective as more valid, particularly when disagreements arise related to issues of medication adherence (Deegan & Drake, 2006). In later chapters we will see how concerns about self-determination and clients' strengths and limitations affect medication management.

Reconceptualize the Client–Clinician Relationship

For decades, researchers have called for a reconceptualization of the client–clinician relationship in the human service professions, including social work (Anderson, 2008; Pare & Larner, 2004). They think that clinicians should try to reduce the social distance between them and their clients and families, demystify the relationship and process, and reconsider power issues. Saleebey (1992) summarized the needed reconceptualization as a give-and-take that begins with the demystification of the professional as expert, an operating sense of humility on the part of the helper, the establishment of an egalitarian transaction, the desire to engage clients on their own terms, and a willingness to disclose and share.

With this reconceptualization social workers seek to redistribute power among themselves, clients, and families and to see them as equals in the helping arena. Although the social worker–client relationship clearly has some built-in power differentials arising from education and societal sanctions, Burti and Mosher (2003) suggested that by acknowledging such differentials through open and direct discussion, social workers can minimize them. However, like the models of feminist therapy in the 1970s, the partnership model of social work practice calls for clinicians to go beyond a mere acknowledgment of power issues to the actual redistribution of power. What does this mean in terms of the client's role or the family member's role? The answer is active participants in the helping processes based on their own individualized expertise and experience. So long as providers, clients, and families are each seen as experts with rich experiences, unique perspectives, and specialized knowledge, achieving this ideal is realistic.

The social worker can teach the client or family member basic strategies that have been shown over time to be useful in helping people reach their goals, whether this is problem solving, skills training, psychoeducation, cognitive–behavioral techniques, or other psychosocial and environmental interventions. But the client and family also share their own experiences, provide extensive input, generate and weigh options, and make decisions along the way. The social worker may serve to facilitate most of the "structure," whereas clients and families may provide most of the "content" of helping. Both the clinician and client should constantly share information, negotiate, and offer feedback. These activities are no different when addressing issues related to medication management.

The ideal, then, is to bring together the strengths and ideas of the client, perhaps the client's family and the provider, to produce the most productive overall partnership. The client shares her or his experiences and knowledge as an equal participant, offering a perspective that serves as important "data" to be incorporated into every step of the helping process. The role of the client is to make choices and to validate and legitimize the actions of the providers on her or his behalf. The social worker helps clients learn through experience and may ask questions that point to previously unrecognized issues; she or he also continuously highlights the choices available to clients. The social worker adjusts techniques or conditions in the treatment system to ensure that it is client-driven.

Just as clients must be offered greater power in their relationship, social workers must come to terms with the loss of power (Greene, 2009). Although social workers may find themselves in the unfamiliar territory of defining roles and boundaries for practice, they will also be freed from the pressure to be something other than their genuine selves (such as the all-knowing, dispassionate expert). Because clients may not be familiar with such ideas about the helping relationship, social workers must model mutuality and partnership, especially in the engagement process. This calls for a dynamic working relationship between the social worker and clients and families that is characterized by mutuality, authenticity, and a sense of being "in process." Partners should constantly seek greater empathy and understanding of each other and work for clearer communication.

Conceptualize the Role of the Social Worker as a Resource

The demystification of the helping process and the redistribution of power have many implications for the role of the social worker. What is the role of the social worker in such a reconceptualization? In the partnership model, the essence of the social worker role is to be a resource for clients and families. Obviously, social workers are a resource on a number of levels (emotional, strategic, concrete/practical, informational) and in a number of capacities (educator, advocate, researcher, monitor, counselor, consultant). But the bottom line is that social workers are a source of whatever information, support, or "supplies" are called for to achieve relief or recovery or to reach clients' specific "wants" and goals. The "supplies" we stress in this book are the assessment, planning, and intervention skills and techniques drawn from a problem-solving approach to social work.

As a resource, the clinician focuses on assessing and clarifying issues to be addressed, teaching new skills, and emphasizing the use of environmental supports and resources (Browne, 2006). Describing the role of a case manager in mental health, Vourlekis and Ell (2007) state that she or he should be one who provides the conditions, knowledge, and linkages needed to address the concerns of the client. Less emphasis is put on the techniques of insight-oriented psychotherapy. Even so, purposeful conversation and reflective discussion are still major aspects of the helping process, not only as the means to establish relationships, define goals, and explore potential strategies of intervention but also as the means to ventilate, sort out feelings, and receive support and validation.

Interestingly, in terms of being a resource, not only can social workers share what they know, but they may go even further by sharing what they do not know. That is, when gaps in their own knowledge base become apparent, social workers may share with clients their search for answers in the literature, lectures, or workshops. In this way their clients can see the clinical thought process right before their eyes, further demystifying the helping process.

Appreciate the Family Members' Perspective

Another significant dimension of the partnership model of practice is the clinician's appreciation of the opinions, thoughts, and beliefs of the client's family members. Specifically, we suggest that the social worker view these as valid and valuable. Just as the client's perspective must be validated, so must that of the family, especially because the family often provides expert observations of family interactions and the client's behavior (Anuradha, 2004). But on an even more basic level, we know that listening to the stories of family members—and we would add clients—even repeatedly, will deepen relationships among all participants. Thus, the partnership model involves the client's family in the helping process to the extent possible, given the client's desires.

In a survey of 453 clinicians serving people with mental illness in community mental health centers, Kim and Salyers (2008) found that the most significant variable related to the extent of social workers' collaboration was their attitude toward family involvement in treatment and care. Further, a more recent study of 904 adult caregivers of youth with mental health concerns found that treatment gains were greater when family members perceived a desire to help from their providers (Davis et al., 2011). Clearly, the partnership model of practice produces beneficial outcomes for clients.

With this brief introduction to fields of practice where social workers will likely encounter clients who use, or might consider using, psychotropic medications, we now review the related professional roles that social workers may occupy when working with these clients.

SOCIAL WORK ROLE CATEGORIES

Physician's Assistant

In the role of physician's assistant, the social worker accepts the physician's decisions about psychotropic drugs and, as such, is limited to helping clients take their medications according to those recommendations. The worker is not expected to offer advice about any decisions involving the prescription and use of medication or any compliance strategy, although he or she does play a role in the assessment process. Psychiatric social workers were thought to function mainly as physicians' assistants through the 1970s.

For many years, the role of a physician's assistant was the most common because of factors that included the relatively limited legal scope of the practice of social work, traditions of authority among the core helping professions, the focus of professional social work education on other areas, and social workers' negative attitudes about the relative appropriateness of medication as a primary means of intervention (Gerhart, 1990). Psychiatrists and physicians are still the primary providers of biological interventions for all types of emotional problems and mental disorders, but over the past four decades, the new emphasis on community-based care has prompted social workers to broaden their psychosocial framework to include interventions using psychotropic medication. Although social workers are still limited to the role of physician's assistant in some settings, they have moved away from this role in many other settings.

Consultant

In the past 30 years much of the professional literature concerning psychotropic medication discusses the roles that social workers play or ought to play regarding their clients' use of medications, thus augmenting the original physician's assistant role. As far back as the 1970s, McCollum, Margolin, and Lieb (1978) wrote that the social worker needs to be skilled in three areas. First, the worker must be able to assess clients for possible referral to physicians. This involves evaluating the client's current levels of functioning, the intensity of the observed suffering, and the client's capacity to manage that suffering. Second, the worker must prepare clients to actively participate in the process of assessment by the physician. To prepare the clients for referral, the worker's responsibilities include articulating the reasons for the referral, reviewing the client's attitude toward psychiatrists, discussing the client's expectations about medications, and monitoring the client's subjective experiences of effects after medications have been prescribed. Third, the worker must monitor clients (we will discuss this in a separate section below). Finally, we add another necessary worker skill: assessing the client's ability to pay for medication, the cost of which may be quite high.

Diamond and Scheifler (2007) emphasize the need for social workers to conceptualize her or his relationship with the physician as well as clients. Both social workers and physicians need to see themselves as consultants and collaborators with each other. They need to work together to specify the range of social workers' roles in medication management, interpret how important it is for clients to take their medication as instructed, devise procedures to evaluate each medication's effectiveness, and record relevant data in a client's file when monitoring their response. Physicians can provide in-service training to other professionals on such issues as drug categories, adverse effects, and interviewing techniques. Social workers, in turn, can teach physicians about various aspects of psychosocial intervention. Of course, disagreements may arise among the physician, social worker, and client over many issues, and they must be openly dealt with to move toward constructive resolution.

Another part of the consultant role is validation, or working to empower clients to make decisions about the use of medication (Tobias, 1990). The validator confirms, legitimates, or verifies the feelings and values of the client as well-grounded. Validation promotes active client participation in treatment planning and intervention. As a validator, the social worker seeks to uncover the client's perceptions and experiences, supporting as legitimate those components that can be channeled into action on the client's part. With regard to the use of medication, the validator can assist the client to become a stronger consultant in interactions with all helping professionals.

Counselor

The term "counselor" is often used interchangeably with that of "therapist," but distinctions can be made between the two concepts. Counseling is generally concerned with helping people cope with "normal" problems and opportunities (Ivey & Ivey, 1999). A counselor is more of a teacher and coach, while a therapist is more of a detective and analyst (Corsini & Wedding, 2004). Counseling is thus a process of providing clients with information and practical help, as well as delineating alternatives, teaching problem solving, and helping to articulate goals (Barker, 1998). The counselor always demonstrates empathy for the client, defined as the ability "to perceive accurately and sensitively inner feelings of the client and to communicate understanding of these feelings in language attuned to the client's experiencing of the moment" (Hepworth et al., 2012, p. 88). Research has consistently demonstrated that effective intervention depends on the client's sense of trust in the worker as a caring individual who understands his or her perspectives (Hewitt & Coffey, 2005; Spaulding & Nolting, 2006).

In the role of counselor, then, the social worker helps the client problem-solve and make decisions about practical matters related to medication use. This role overlaps at times with that of educator and advocate and may of course extend beyond medication management issues. The process of problem solving helps the client become a better problem solver by increasing both the number of effective response alternatives for resolving a problem and the probability that the most effective response will be selected from the alternatives (Hepworth et al., 2010).

Monitor

To monitor medication, the social worker must observe and help the client observe their positive and negative effects and the appearance or persistence of symptoms. The social worker may also help to check the client's use of medications as prescribed. He or she needs to help evaluate the client's responses to any discomfort, the relative importance of the physiological adverse effects (i.e., dry mouth versus impotence), and any impairments in social functioning. Finally, the worker conveys information from the monitoring process back to the client, perhaps to the family, and to the physician. Through these activities, the social worker both helps the client monitor medication and serves as a resource to the physician.

There are three types of adverse effects for social workers to monitor: physical, psychological, and social. Through self-study and collaboration with medical personnel, the social worker can become educated about adverse physical effects. Adverse psychological effects involve any changes in the client's self-image and identity that emerge as a result of using medications. For example, clients may come to view themselves as "sick" people or may become overly dependent on medication as a solution to perceived emotional problems. They may also avoid potentially healthy challenges in the social environment. The adverse effects may make them appear even more disturbed to others, so that clients see themselves as marginal.

Adverse social effects include any potentially negative consequences that go beyond the individual client to include the effect of medication use on one's standing with certain social institutions, such as employers who may lack confidence that the consumer is able to manage his or her required responsibilities. Further, medications initially used for symptom relief so that psychosocial treatments could be initiated can become the complete treatment. To this listing of adverse social effects, we add that if the client is dependent on the family, families have been given the difficult responsibility of monitoring both the client's response to medications and his or her development of additional self-care skills. This topic of extra-physical side effects merits close attention by social workers because the health professions have largely neglected it.

Advocate

Gerhart and Brooks (1983) asserted 30 years ago what is still true today: social workers do not objectively weigh the benefits and risks of medication with regard to both physical and psychological adverse effects. They proposed a third role, that of the client advocate, based on their perception that medical expertise is not always the rule and that medication can have serious negative effects that might outweigh its benefits. They defined advocacy as the "representation of mentally ill individuals and groups by social work practitioners in an effort to present the client's expressed desires to those in the mental health system who have the power" to assess how medications are administered (p. 456).

The social work advocate ideally has a peer relationship with the physician and participates in all phases of decision-making regarding the choices made for medication. This role is crucial because of the emphasis on community care, which makes the responsible monitoring of a client's medication needs and outcomes difficult for any single person to maintain. To function as an advocate, the worker must have a good working knowledge of mental illness, psychotropic medications, and laws and regulations about such issues as forced medications and the rights of consumers. Social workers can competently carry out the advocacy role when they represent the client's position from a sound base of knowledge and professional values, although this can be difficult at times.

Higgins (1995) went beyond the types of advocacy we have just outlined. She suggested that social workers should function as political advocates for clients who cannot access medications they want to use. This situation developed quite dramatically with the introduction of clozapine in 1991. The medication had demonstrated benefits for some people with schizophrenia who had not responded to more traditional antipsychotic medications. However, the cost of the medication coupled with the need to monitor blood counts weekly created an expensive treatment regimen. Because some clients and families who could not afford the drug filed suits to gain access to it, adjustments were made in public insurance policies, helping to broaden the drug's availability. Because issues related to the cost of medication are serious and because restrictions on the availability of medication may arise, Higgins argued that social workers need to serve as advocates before not only physicians but also agencies, funding sources, and government regulators. Further, when funding caps limit a client's access to medication, social workers may need to become involved in decision-making about which eligible clients should have access to medications such as clozapine. The relevance of Higgins's perspective is a reminder that medication issues should be considered in their broadest contexts. Bachur (1986) also stressed this point, arguing that considerations of drug use and misuse need to be studied not merely in the context of the individual and family but also more broadly, including informal helpers, such as friends and neighbors, local community agencies, and government policy makers.

Hughes and Cohen (2010) agree that, of all professional helpers, social workers have the primary responsibility to serve clients as advocates. Concerned about the negative effects of medication, Cohen is skeptical of psychiatry's willingness to address this issue adequately and further states that adherence to the medical model of treatment tends to result in some abuses in somatic intervention. He proposes that social workers as advocates undertake a greater amount of activity with clients in several areas, including knowledge of the prior history of drug reactions; identification of negative physical, psychological, and social effects; and provision of oral and written drug information.

Social workers need to be aware that empowerment and advocacy efforts with clients and families may lead them to decide to refuse medication or to negotiate extensively with physicians about the types and dosages of medication the client should take. These situations often give rise to value dilemmas for social workers. One may hold that social workers need to support the right of refusal of medication or any other treatment for legal, empirical, and ethical reasons in light of the profession's mandate to respect each client's dignity, worth, and right to self-determination. Thus, social workers may find themselves in an ethical bind when clients or physicians choose strategies the social workers do not believe will work.

Educator

The role of educator is crucial to the social work profession's maintenance of collaboration with clients and families. The uses and actions of medication are complicated and confusing for many professionals as well as the general public, so there is a need for social workers to address the topic by directly providing educational materials and other information. With the widespread development of client and family psychoeducational and medication education programs, this area has seen progress (Walsh, 2010). By emphasizing psychosocial themes of adjustment, the educator role complements the kinds of information generally provided to clients by physicians and nurses.

So that they can provide basic information about relevant medication issues during individual client interventions, social workers should strive to keep up with all ongoing developments in the field. Bentley and Reeves (1992) outlined six educational units for social work students. These units can also apply to practicing professionals as areas of continuing education to be shared with clients and families. The topics include public and professional attitudes toward psychotropic medication, changing social work roles in psychopharmacology, medication content in psychoeducation, ongoing medication–management techniques, ethical and legal issues in client refusal of medications, and current research and resources.

Further, Bentley and colleagues (1990) specified as educational four of their nine roles for social workers in helping clients adhere to appropriate medication schedules. These roles include educating clients and families about the purposes, actions, and effects of medication; teaching clients and families how to monitor positive and negative effects; teaching skills in problem solving regarding medication; and offering practical suggestions to help clients take medication appropriately. By emphasizing psychosocial themes of adjustment, the educator role complements the kinds of information generally provided to clients by physicians and nurses.

Researcher

A theme in discussions of all role categories is the need for social workers to develop their own literature about issues of psychotropic medication to advance the profession's holistic perspectives. Social workers should produce more literature on the potentially negative effects of medications, the impact of medicines on self-control and one's sense of personal responsibility for problem resolution, and the engagement of the hard-to-reach client in a comprehensive treatment program that includes medication (Davidson & Jamison, 1983). These represent aspects of medication usage that other professions have not adequately addressed but that are consistent with social work's psychosocial theoretical framework. Cohen (2002) calls for social workers to write more case studies and conduct research on the broad range of medication effects, both positive and negative.

There is broad professional acceptance of the positive effects of the combined interventions of medication, counseling, and psychosocial rehabilitation for clients (Warren, 2011). However, because researchers often cannot separate medication side effects from clients' outcomes, the optimal effects of various types of social work intervention have not yet been fully tested. Social workers are now in a position to conduct research to ascertain the main effects of drugs and psychosocial interventions as well as the interactions of these two types of treatment on clients' outcomes. Through these means they can evaluate the effectiveness of medication in ways that may support more treatment strategies involving low dosages of medication.

SOCIAL WORKER ROLES AND
PROFESSIONAL VALUES

The National Association of Social Workers' (2008) Code of Ethics provides guidelines for the professional conduct of all social workers. We believe that our roles for medication management and themes for practice are consistent with the code's six value principles of service, social justice, dignity and worth of the person, the importance of human relationships, integrity, and competence. Our themes are particularly prominent in four of the six ethical principles. We will refer to these themes and related ethical principles throughout the book, but will introduce them here.

As the code asserts, in challenging social injustice, social workers "strive to ensure access to needed information, services, and resources (p. 5)." This principle relates to our responsibility to educate clients about available medication resources and to serve as advocates when necessary so that clients receive appropriate resources, even when issues of cost and access seem prohibitive. In respecting the dignity and worth of clients, social workers "seek to resolve conflicts between clients' interests and the broader society's interests in a socially responsible manner (p. 6)." One way this is accomplished is through our participation with interdisciplinary teams, where we can integrate our medication roles and psychosocial interventions with the activities of physicians, nurses, psychologists, and others, sometimes with an advocacy stance but always in a spirit of collaboration, with a shared goal of constructing the client's best possible service milieu.

In recognizing the central importance of human relationships, social workers "engage people as partners in the helping process (p. 6)." Our notion of the partnership model of practice (described below) is a primary theme of this book. We believe that collaboration with clients and families as well as with professionals underscores the principle of self-determination. This posture is a hallmark of our profession and a necessary stance with regard to the delicate, complex topic of psychotropic medications. Finally, as social workers practice within their areas of competence, they must "strive to increase their professional knowledge and skills (p. 6)." Because so many clients use medications and rely on social workers for some guidance with that process, we believe that at a minimum social workers should be knowledgeable about the types, actions, purposes, and effects of the medications their clients use. They also have a responsibility to keep abreast of changes in the field of pharmacology, including new types of medication.

CURRENT MEDICATION-RELATED ACTIVITIES
OF SOCIAL WORKERS

In order to gain current information about roles and activities being performed by social workers with clients related to psychotropic medication, we designed and implemented a national study on the topic (Bentley, Walsh, & Farmer,

2005B). Findings from this survey (N=994) are referenced in various chapters of this book; here we focus on the data related to practice roles and activities. We asked a random sample of members of the National Association of Social Workers (who self-identified as "clinical" and with "mental health" as their primary field of practice) a series of questions on this and several other topics. The questions of interest here concerned the kinds of activities they carry out related to psychiatric medication, how frequently they perform those activities, how appropriate they think those activities are, and how competent they feel in carrying them out.

The most frequently performed tasks, as summarized in Table 2.1, in a typical month are talking with clients about their feelings about taking medication (the counselor and monitor roles), making referrals to physicians (consultant), and discussing with clients how medications may work in combination with psychosocial interventions (educator and consultant). These were the only three activities that a majority of respondents said they did often. About half the respondents often helped clients weigh the pros and cons of taking medication (counselor and consultant), and discussed medication issues directly with physicians (consultant and advocate).

The social workers' perceptions of competence and appropriateness are positively associated with the frequency of activities performed. Almost all respondents said it was appropriate for social workers to talk to clients about their feelings about taking medication, ranking it as both the most appropriate social work activity and the one they feel most competent carrying out. The second most appropriate activity, also cited by almost all respondents, is making a referral to a physician for a medication evaluation. This also ranked second in terms of perceived competence. There are a few items where differences in perceived appropriateness, competence, and frequency were notable. While three-quarters of respondents said it was appropriate for social workers to assist clients with decision-making around medication (helping clients weigh the pros and cons), barely half do so often. Similarly, where a large majority of respondents reported that preparing a client for an interview with a physician is appropriate, less than half do so often.

Our study findings suggest that some familiar activities are frequently carried out by social workers (in addition to those related to the physician's assistant role), such as talking about feelings and problems related to medication, discussing treatment effects, and making referrals to prescribers. These are seen as appropriate activities and social workers perceive adequate competence in carrying them out. Some activities are not performed as frequently as might be expected. For example, while a large majority of respondents say it is appropriate for social workers to assist clients with decision-making around medication, only about half do so often, and only about two-thirds feel competent to do so. As we noted in the article that contains the main results of this study, other roles that seem to be underperformed, given their historical centrality to social work practice, include talking to clients' families about medication and communicating with treatment team members. Interestingly, these activities seem to require assertive behavior on the part of the social worker. Similarly, whereas most respondents report that preparing

Table 2.1 Frequency, Competence, and Appropriateness of Social Work Roles and Activities with Psychiatric Medication

Activity	Very Frequently/ Often	Quite Competent	Quite Appropriate
Discussing with a client his or her feelings about taking medication	80.0%	90.9%	95.9%
Making a referral to a physician for a medication assessment with a client	71.9%	89.2%	95.1%
Discussing with a client the desired combined effects of medication and psychosocial interventions	70.1%	79.4%	88.0%
Discussing a problem about medication with a client	61.2%	48.2%	72.7%
Monitoring a client's compliance with a medication	60.8%	73.1%	80.4%
Helping a client consider the "pros" and "cons" of taking medication	51.6%	68.1%	75.8%
Checking for the possibility of adverse side effects	51.4%	38.5%	67.2%
Discussing a client's medication problem with a physician	48.2%	63.6%	86.6%
Consulting with the physician about the effectiveness of a client's medication	46.0%	66.2%	83.0%
Communicating a client's lack of medication compliance with the physician	44.6%	82.7%	82.6%
Encouraging a client to take medication	44.2%	79.9%	76.7%
Documenting the effects of medication in a client's chart	39.6%	57.1%	62.3%
Preparing a client for an interview with a prescribing physician	37.7%	82.1%	84.6%
Monitoring a client for prevention of medication abuse	36.5%	47.3%	66.4%
Providing information to a client about the ways that medication works in the body	31.7%	26.4%	43.8%
Assessing the severity of any adverse side effects	30.1%	22.7%	43.9%
Communicating with members of the client's treatment team	28.5%	62.2%	68.7%
Talking with a client's family about medication issues	27.1%	55.6%	60.8%
Prompting a client to remember to take his or her medication	24.7%	75.2%	64.0%
Presenting data or other information to a client about a medication's effectiveness	22.2%	35.2%	44.4%

Table 2.1 *Continued*

Activity	Very Frequently/ Often	Quite Competent	Quite Appropriate
Assessing a client's ability to pay for medication	21.2%	59.0%	64.5%
Helping a family contact a physician about a client's medication	19.9%	75.9%	70.5%
Helping client locate financial and other resources for medication	19.0%	51.8%	71.4%
Suggesting to a physician that he or she adjust your client's medication dosage	15.4%	32.8%	45.7%
Ensuring that a client's medication blood levels are checked when indicated	13.6%	27.5%	33.2%
Suggesting to a physician that he or she change the type of medication	11.3%	29.8%	45.1%
Facilitating a medication education group with clients	3.5%	22.8%	37.3%
Transporting a client to a prescribing physician's office	2.9%	51.8%	15.0%
Facilitating a medication education group with families	2.2%	23.7%	37.5%
Delivering medications to your client	1.8%	43.1%	11.9%
Filling your client's medication pillbox	0.8%	35.9%	8.5%

SOURCE: Adapted from Bentley, Walsh, & Farmer 2005

a client for an interview with a physician is appropriate, fewer than half do so often. Given that making a referral is the second most frequent task, this finding is a surprise. Finally, activities related to the role of researcher were rarely performed by this group of practicing social workers.

A number of implications emerge from these results. First, social workers need to recognize opportunities to apply their problem-solving skills to issues involving psychiatric medication. Perhaps social workers exaggerate the extent of pharmacological knowledge needed to help clients in these ways. Some knowledge of drug activity is desirable but client concerns are often centered in their subjective experiences rather than complicated pharmacological facts. Second, social workers may need to become more assertive in taking action around medication-related problems, including their interactions with physicians and family members. A third implication is that social workers should increase their activities related to client preparation and referral. There is a need for greater emphasis in practice on the emotional impact of a referral for medication and teaching clients skills in negotiating with physicians, as we will discuss in Chapter 6.

As a final note we consider the views of our respondents about the appropriate stance of social workers regarding medication. The social work respondents in the study did not identify personal reservations about medication as a barrier, and they identified their positive attitudes and beliefs about medication as a key to successful practice. We note the consensus that seems to be emerging in the literature that a critical perspective about medications is appropriate for social workers. Practitioners should understand the beneficial therapeutic effects for clients who use medication but also their adverse effects and the negative influences of economic and political forces in prescription writing (Bentley & Walsh, 1998; Cohen, 2002). We conclude that achieving greater role breadth with psychiatric medications and increasing social workers' sense of competence may be best achieved by increasing their knowledge about medications, increasing their range of specific intervention skills, and increasing the extent of their interactions with prescribing physicians.

SUMMARY

The purposes of this chapter have been to describe four relevant contexts for social work practice with clients who use psychotropic medications, present our partnership model of social work practice, outline the range of roles that social workers may assume in their work with clients who take psychotropic medication, and describe current medication-related roles of social workers. Those roles include the physician's assistant, the consultant, the counselor, the advocate, the monitor, the educator, and the researcher. Which of the roles are utilized and how they are implemented will depend on particular client circumstances as well as the intervention philosophy at the worker's agency. As a means of preparing for such interventions, the social worker should reflect on and be able to articulate responses to the following questions:

- Why is medication being prescribed for my client?
- Why is this particular medication being prescribed?
- What are the specific desired effects of this medication?
- What is the full range of its possible positive and negative effects?
- Is there a long-range plan regarding my client's use of medication? That is, how will it be determined whether it is effective or ineffective or when the medication will be adjusted or discontinued?
- What is the client's attitude about taking the medications?
- What is the client's belief system about how medications work?
- Do I have a clear role or set of roles in the process of my client's use of the medication? Am I assuming these roles or have they been articulated by others involved in the client's care?

- How could my client's use of this medication affect, positively or negatively, other interventions I am providing?
- Do I have the opportunity to speak regularly with the physician and other health care providers about the medication?
- Can the client or family afford this medication?

Barkley et al. (1991) have articulated additional questions for the social worker to consider that are particularly relevant to the interests of both the client and family:

- If the client is a child, is the medication designed to benefit the child or the child's caregivers?
- Have the desired outcomes of the medication been clearly communicated to all persons concerned?
- How will the effects of the medication be monitored? How frequently? By whom?
- Will the physician be available to the client, family, and other caregivers?
- Have the risks and benefits of the medication, as well as those of alternate interventions, been assessed and discussed with all relevant parties?
- Within the family, should someone assume some responsibility for the client's adherence to the recommended dose and schedule?

It falls on social workers to make sure the voices of their clients are heard by all who interact with them. There may be occasions, of course, when social workers' competing values cause them to take different courses of action with clients, for example, in strongly encouraging medication use as a means for clients to meet basic survival needs and preserving life. Although we will amplify these issues in the next chapter, we emphasize here that the seven social work roles are ultimately defined as much by how they are implemented as by their substance.

TOPICS FOR DISCUSSION AND
LEARNING ACTIVITIES

1. Share your experiences in working with clients who use medication. What role or roles did you fill in the process, and what was your comfort level with those roles?

2. Generate examples of real or hypothetical clients with whom the various social work roles would be appropriate and inappropriate. Explain why.

3. Describe the range of social work roles that are enacted at your place of employment or field agency. Compare the different roles available at different settings. Are these differences due to agency philosophy, staff preferences, types of clients, types of medications, or other variables?

4. Do you see any value to clients in an expansion of your roles at the agency? If so, how might you try to expand your range of roles?

5. Pretending you are an agency director, write a memo to the social work staff explaining your views about social workers' roles in psychopharmacology.

6. Identify any real or possible ethical dilemmas in the case illustrations included in this chapter. How might you address and try to resolve them?

PART II

A Primer on Psychopharmacology

Chapter 3

Basic Psychopharmacology

Chapter 4

The Five Classes of Medication

Chapter 5

Intervention Concerns with Special Populations

3

Basic Psychopharmacology

Learning Objectives

Upon completion of this chapter, the reader will be able to:

1. Identify parts of the brain that are significant in the processing of psychotropic medications.
2. Describe the structure and functions of nerve cells.
3. Describe the functions of neurotransmitters.
4. Describe six neurotransmitters believed to be significant as targets of psychotropic drugs.
5. Summarize four critical aspects of pharmacokinetics.
6. Summarize six critical aspects of pharmacodynamics.

Social workers often have limited interest in the details of psychopharmacology—indeed, it can make for esoteric reading. Still, a basic knowledge of the chemical processes associated with medications is essential for social workers whose clients use such drugs. Only with this knowledge can the social worker comprehend the nature and significance of changes in the client's physical and mental status, understand the prescriber's rationales for dosage and administration, and offer explanations to clients and families. When a client describes or demonstrates the effects of medications, positive or negative, these can be fully understood only with an awareness of basic pharmacology. This knowledge applies to the social worker/client relationship in four areas:

1. Understanding theories regarding the effectiveness of medications in symptom reduction.
2. Monitoring adverse effects, including the medication's physical, psychological, and social consequences.
3. Educating clients and families about the course of physical and psychological adjustment to medications.
4. Communicating with prescribers, pharmacists, nurses, and others about the present and potential effects of medicine.

The social worker's understanding of medication cannot be considered complete if he or she is aware only of its effects on thinking and mood. To promote a safe and effective drug regimen and to inform clients fully, social workers must also know the presumed causes of the biological and psychological changes leading to symptom relief.

In this chapter we introduce you to the central nervous system and the basic principles of psychopharmacology, defined as *the study of drugs that affect a person's thinking, emotions, and behaviors.* We describe the structure of the brain and nervous system, the properties of neurons and receptors, the processes by which the human body handles psychotropic drugs, and the effects of drugs on body chemistry. We also introduce some general information about the assumed actions of antipsychotic, antidepressant, mood-stabilizing, antianxiety, and psychostimulant medications (although we discuss these more fully in Chapter 4). We conclude with a careful review of the adverse effects that these medications can produce in consumers. So that you can grasp the rationale for medication treatment in a logical, holistic way, we have ordered chapter topics from the most general (nervous system) to the most specific (types of drugs).

The primary sources we used to research this material include Ingersoll & Rak (2006), Janicak, Marder, & Pavuluri (2011), Julien (2011), Sadock and Sadock (2009), Saija and Mortimer (2011), Schatzberg and Nemeroff (2009), and Stahl (2008).

THE CENTRAL NERVOUS SYSTEM

The social work profession's person-in-environment perspective promotes a focus on transactions within and among *systems* at all levels (micro through macro). To maintain this perspective, the social worker must acquire and assess broad sources of information about social systems. Although no social system can begin to approximate the nervous system's elegance and mystery, a systems perspective will help you appreciate the complexity of the central nervous system's structure and processes. It is a massive and astoundingly intricate information-processing unit consisting of *100 billion* nerve cells and even more connectors between these cells. Because psychotropic medications act on the nervous system, an awareness of its geography is an appropriate starting point for understanding how the drugs work. We emphasize, however, that much remains to be discovered about the specific biological processes within the nervous system. Its complexity should remind the social worker that, despite great gains made each year in knowledge about the human body, scientists are still working to grasp the nature of routine system processes and the effects of drugs on them.

The Brain and Nervous System

The brain consists of nerve cells, glial cells, and blood vessels. Although nerve cells, also called *neurons,* carry out all the brain's functions, they make up only a fraction of its weight. *Glial cells,* which surround the neurons and outnumber them by a 10 to 1 ratio, have the sole functions of providing a supporting environment as the neurons' source of nourishment and a system for carrying away waste products. The brain is richly supplied with an intricate system of tiny blood vessels. Although the brain makes up only 2% of a body's weight, it receives 15% of its blood supply.

All human behaviors, including thoughts and emotions, are the result of, or are reflected in, neural activity, with changes in such behavior prompted by changes in brain chemistry (or vice versa). Chemical processes in the brain are influenced by a range of factors originating both inside and outside the body. For instance, the simple act of greeting a client in the agency's waiting room sets off a complex chain, or *pathway*, of cellular activities by which the social worker's nervous system interprets verbal and nonverbal messages from the client and initiates responses. A pathway is a series of interconnecting neurons working together for some coordinated purpose. Conversations with friends, practice interventions, or psychotropic medications are all prompts for chemical activities within and among neurons, activities that cause emotional or behavioral changes.

A neurobiological perspective does *not* assume a purely materialist view of human functioning. Human behavior is always caused by transactions among biological, psychological, social, and even spiritual systems. In fact, biological science remains unclear about many basic processes in brain functioning. Why do people react with strong emotion to a beautiful sunset, a work of art, or a piece of music? What determines their methods of solving interpersonal problems? How do they come to develop their personal values or decide on ultimate life goals? Although the nervous system is highly interactive with the environment, the means by which thoughts, feelings, and behaviors are mediated by the various sources of stimuli are unclear. Whatever your assumptions about identity, free will, spirituality, or nature versus nurture as the source of personality, we wish to emphasize that all human experiences are accompanied by nervous system activities and responses.

The basic functions of the brain are to receive information from the outside world, use this information to decide on responsive courses of action, and implement these decisions with commands to various muscles and glands. The brain can be divided into sections to differentiate its many activities, but its processes are highly interconnected. The brain is generally conceived of as having three sections: hindbrain, midbrain, and forebrain (see Figure 3.1).

The *hindbrain* consists of the brain stem, cerebellum, and pons. Located at the base of the brain, the *brain stem* links the brain to the spinal cord. It is the oldest area of the brain, appearing before the evolution of mammals. The brain stem is primarily occupied with the maintenance of involuntary life-support functions. It consists of several subsections. At its base the *medulla oblongata* regulates vital functions, including arousal, heartbeat, respiration, blood flow, muscle tone, and movement of the stomach and intestines. The *pons,* located just under the midbrain, links various areas of the brain to each other and to the central nervous system. At the center of the brain stem and traveling its full length is a core of neural tissue known as the *reticular formation*. Nerve fibers from this system extend down the spinal cord and control the position and tension of muscles. The

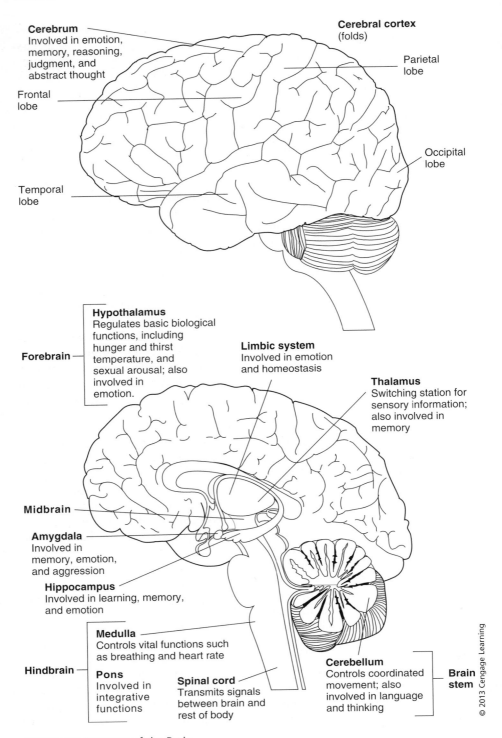

Cerebrum
Involved in emotion, memory, reasoning, judgment, and abstract thought

Cerebral cortex
(folds)

Parietal lobe

Frontal lobe

Occipital lobe

Temporal lobe

Forebrain

Hypothalamus
Regulates basic biological functions, including hunger and thirst temperature, and sexual arousal; also involved in emotion.

Limbic system
Involved in emotion and homeostasis

Thalamus
Switching station for sensory information; also involved in memory

Midbrain

Amygdala
Involved in memory, emotion, and aggression

Hippocampus
Involved in learning, memory, and emotion

Medulla
Controls vital functions such as breathing and heart rate

Hindbrain

Pons
Involved in integrative functions

Spinal cord
Transmits signals between brain and rest of body

Cerebellum
Controls coordinated movement; also involved in language and thinking

Brain stem

© 2013 Cengage Learning

FIGURE 3.1 Structure of the Brain

cerebellum, located behind the brain stem, receives information from the muscles and joints, the organs of balance, the skin, and the eyes and ears. The cerebellum controls bodily functions operating below the level of consciousness, including posture, balance, and movement through space. Memory for certain kinds of simple learned responses may be stored there as well. Although the hindbrain does not include any targeted sites of action for psychotropic medications, some drugs do affect activities there, producing adverse effects.

The *midbrain* is located just above the brain stem. Although quite small, it represents a second level of brain evolution, more advanced than the hindbrain. The midbrain monitors and integrates various sensory functions and serves as a center of visual and auditory stimulation. It encompasses an area called the sub-thalamus that, combined with the basal ganglia, constitutes the extrapyramidal motor system (described later). All information that passes between the brain and spinal cord travels through the midbrain. On the upper surface of the mid-brain, collections of cells relay specific information from sense organs to higher levels of the brain.

The *forebrain* is the largest section of the brain and consists of many specialized areas. The *limbic system,* a group of cell structures in the center of the brain, is the center of activities that create emotions. Many psychotropic medications are tar-geted at neurons in this system. The limbic system also maintains the body's *homeostasis,* a concept from systems theory that should be familiar to social work-ers. It refers here to the constancy and stability of the body's physiological func-tioning. The limbic system permits people to adjust their internal states to maintain a constant climate despite external conditions, such as extreme heat and cold. It regulates such functions as body temperature, blood pressure, heart rate, and blood sugar levels.

The *hypothalamus,* a major component of the limbic system, is a relay station for internal regulatory systems; it monitors information coming from the auto-nomic nervous system (described later) and influences the body's behavior through those pathways. The hypothalamus produces neurohormones (chemicals manufactured in the brain) as one means of maintaining the body's homeostasis. Specialized neurons release neurohormones into surrounding capillaries, where the blood transports them into the pituitary gland. From this "master gland," or regulatory site, the neurohormones are eventually carried to target cells to regu-late such things as temperature, balance, and appetite. Neurohormones also influ-ence motivation, sexual arousal, eating and drinking, sleeping, waking, certain chemical balances, and emotions important to survival.

The limbic system includes other activity centers. The *thalamus,* a mass of gray matter located near the center of the forebrain, relays sensory information from the body to the brain. Because all sensory fibers extending into the cortex must first pass through it, the thalamus is a major integrating center. It helps initiate consciousness and makes preliminary interpretations of external infor-mation. The *hippocampus,* an important center of learning, converts information from short-term to long-term memory. The *basal ganglia,* located on both sides of the limbic system, connect the cerebral cortex to other parts of the brain and help regulate skeletal muscle movements. Like the cerebellum, these nerve fibers are concerned with movement and control, particularly the initiation of movements. When the basal ganglia are unintentionally affected by certain psychotropic medications, adverse effects result. This is the site at which dopamine is depleted in Parkinson's disease and one of the sites at which stimulant drugs act.

The *cerebrum* is the largest portion of the human brain and facilitates its highest intellectual functions. The center of emotion, memory, reasoning, abstract thought, and judgment, the cerebrum integrates highly diverse brain activities. It allows us to organize, remember, communicate, understand, appreciate, and create. The cerebrum is divided into two halves, each of which controls the opposite side of the body. On the surface of each hemisphere is an intricately folded layer of nerve cells known as the *cerebral cortex*. Characterized visually by its many folds, the cortex is an evolutionary product that enables humans to accommodate a much larger surface area than their skull size would otherwise allow.

The cortex is composed of four sets of lobes, each with distinct functions. The largest are the *frontal lobes*, which govern personality, emotion, reasoning, learning, and speech. The primary function of these lobes is motor (muscle) control, including fine motor control (coordinated small muscle movements, such as in the fingers), gross motor control (large muscles, such as those in the thigh), control of eye movements, motor aspects of speech, and motor learning and planning. The frontal lobes are also involved in decision-making and purposeful behavior. The *temporal lobes* affect gross motor skills and the integration of sensory input. Their functions include hearing, perception, and memory storage. The *parietal lobes*, centers of long-term memory and information processing, receive sensory information from the body. Finally, the *occipital lobes* are entirely devoted to processing visual input.

The spinal cord, which runs from the brain stem to the base of the spine, is a part of the central nervous system, but it is also associated with two other systems. First, the *autonomic nervous system* (*autonomic* means, somewhat misleadingly, "autonomous" or "independent") consists of neuron pathways that extend from the medulla oblongata and spinal cord into the body's organs. These neurons regulate the unconscious and involuntary activities of the internal organs and blood vessels. The autonomic system includes two subsystems. The *sympathetic system* functions during the expenditure of energy, and the *parasympathetic system* is more prominent in the body's buildup of energy reserves. For example, the sympathetic system acts to speed up one's heart rate during exercise, and the parasympathetic system slows it down during rest. Because the autonomic nervous system's site of integration is the hypothalamus, this system is affected by some psychotropic medications.

Second, the *peripheral nervous system* consists of neurons that branch into the muscles from the spinal cord. It carries messages to and from the central nervous system to control voluntary muscle activity. Within this system the *pyramidal nerve pathways* manage fine motor activities, and the *extrapyramidal pathways* govern integrated gross motor activities. The entire peripheral nervous system is composed of networks of these pathways, the cells of which are affected by some psychotropic medications to produce adverse effects. The center of integration of the peripheral system is the cerebellum; however, the cerebrum also includes pyramidal and extrapyramidal nerve tracts that connect the cortex to the spinal cord and muscles of the body.

The three sections of the brain represent different levels of the functioning of the nervous system. Much of the rear and base of the brain is specialized and committed to involuntary bodily functions, such as the interpretation of incoming sensations, the control of movement, and the regulation of automatic life support functions. The forebrain, particularly the frontal and temporal lobes, is less specific. Freed from the need to maintain basic bodily functions, its components interact in complex ways to produce thinking and the higher emotions. Psychotropic medications act not only on nerve pathways involved in thinking and feeling but also on other areas of the brain. To the extent that the drugs can reach their desired sites of action without negatively affecting other brain functions, they can serve as successful intervention agents with clients.

PROPERTIES OF NERVE CELLS

As elements in all systems do, neurons exist in the context of a local environment. The structure of that environment is maintained by the glial cells; neighboring organisms include adjacent neurons and cells, such as muscle or gland cells. Each neuron receives input from the environment and then responds toward some externally directed activity. Our discussion here is limited to activities within and among nerve cells that affect human thought and emotion.

Neuron Structure

The cell body, or central area of the neuron, is its metabolic center (see Figure 3.2). Made up of *lipid* (fatty) material, the cell membrane separates the contents of the cell from the fluid enveloping it. Molecules or *ions* (groups of atoms with electrical charges) pass through this membrane to enter or leave the cell, but not at random. Special "channels" must be opened for such movement to occur, and opening these channels is governed by chemical activities within the cell. Each cell includes one single long limb extension called an *axon*, through which the cell body sends signals to neighboring cells (see Figure 3.2 and Figure 3.3). The cell also features numerous short extensions, called *dendrites*, which receive signals sent by other neurons. In the complex maze of the central nervous system, axon terminals are always found close to the dendrites of other cells. However, axons and dendrites do not actually touch each other. The minute amount of space separating them is known as the *synaptic cleft*. Each cell may have access to 1,000 to 10,000 *synapses* (points of union). The synapse includes the *presynaptic terminal*, the cleft, and the *postsynaptic membrane*. A presynaptic terminal is the ending of the axon of the nerve cell; it contains neurotransmitters that extend to the synapse. A postsynaptic membrane is a membrane of the cell body, or dendrite, on which neurotransmitter receptor sites are located.

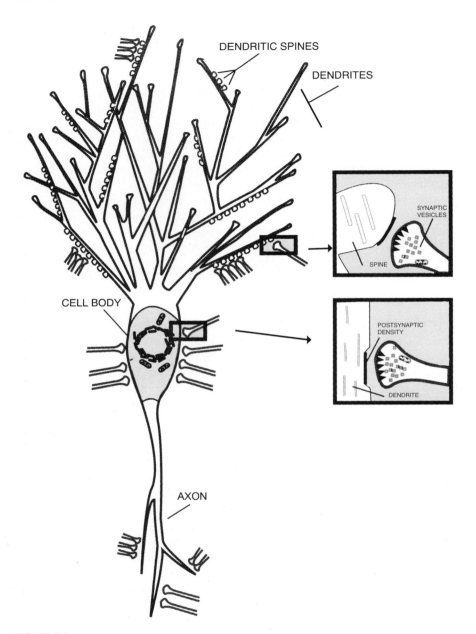

FIGURE 3.2

Organization of the neuron to *receive* synaptic information. Presynaptic input from other neurons can be received postsynaptically at many sites, but especially on *dendrites,* often at specialized structures called *dendritic spines.* Other postsynaptic neuronal sites for receiving presynaptic input from other neurons include the *cell body* and the *axon terminal.*

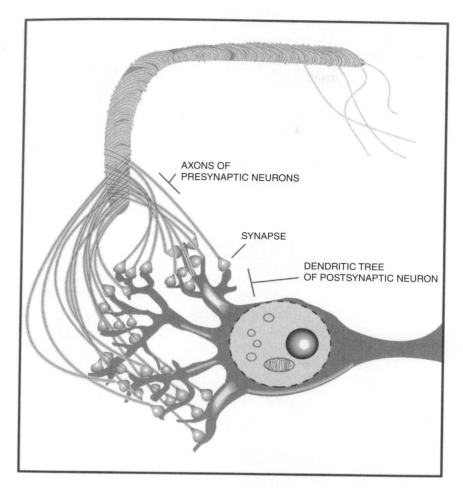

AXONS OF
PRESYNAPTIC NEURONS

SYNAPSE

DENDRITIC TREE
OF POSTSYNAPTIC NEURON

FIGURE 3.3

The *anatomically addressed nervous system* is the concept that the brain is a series of hard-wired connections between neurons, not unlike millions of telephone wires within thousands and thousands of cables. Shown in the figure is a cable of axons from many different neurons, all arriving to form synaptic connections with the dendritic tree of the postsynaptic neuron.

Neuron Function

The transmission of signals through the nervous system involves all the structures of a neuron. The process begins when a cell generates a nerve impulse, a momentary change in the electrical conductivity of the neural membrane. (At rest, neurons maintain a negative electrical charge; an impulse gives the neuron a temporary positive charge.) These impulses are generated at various speeds, sometimes as much as 200 per second. The transmission of an impulse to a receiving cell is facilitated by a chemical neurotransmitter that is released by the axon into the synapse. The neurotransmitter attaches to special receiving areas, or *receptors*, in the dendrite of the neighboring cell. In turn, the receiving cell, having been acted upon, incorporates this impulse as environmental information and determines through its own chemical makeup how to respond. In general, information is passed from cell to cell along a pathway (some of which can be many yards long). The process of signal transmission is no less complex when a social worker lifts a coffee cup than when she or he attends to a client during a lengthy assessment interview. The latter activity simply requires the use of more neuron pathways.

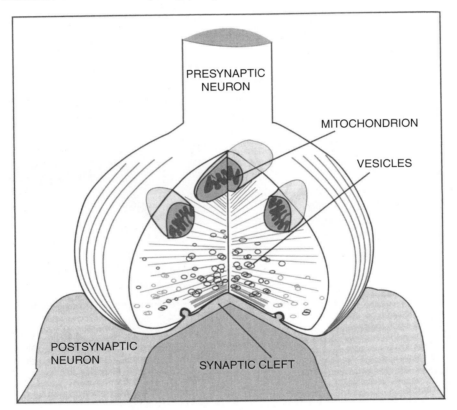

FIGURE 3.4

The synapse is enlarged conceptually here to show its specialized structures that enable chemical neurotransmission to occur. Specifically, a *presynaptic neuron* sends its *axon terminal* to form a synapse with a *postsynaptic neuron*. Energy for this process is provided by mitochondria in the presynaptic neuron. The chemical neurotransmitter is stored in small vesicles ready for release on firing of the presynaptic neuron. The *synaptic cleft* is the connection between the presynaptic neuron and the postsynaptic neuron. Receptors are present on both sides of this cleft and are key elements of chemical neurotransmission.

We offer now a more detailed description of neurotransmission processes so you can understand their implications for psychotropic drug action (see Figure 3.4). The axon terminals include small areas known as *synaptic vesicles*, which contain the molecules of a neurotransmitter produced in the cell body. Activities in the vesicles of the sending cell are called presynaptic because they precede activities in the synapse. The receiving area of the synapse, on the dendrite of the nearby cell body, is called the postsynaptic membrane. Compared to the rest of the cell membrane, both pre- and postsynaptic membranes appear relatively thick and dark because they contain the proteins that are the building blocks of some neurotransmitters. These molecules are like tiny lily pads, floating in the synaptic fluid but attached to the "shore" of the cell membrane. The receptors on presynaptic neurons that regulate the release of neurotransmitters are called *autoreceptors*. Although each neuron releases only one type of neurotransmitter (or sometimes several) at its presynaptic axon terminal, it has receptors to match many different transmitters—thousands, in fact. Receptors are highly specific, however, ignoring all transmitters except the one that matches its "keyhole."

The release of a neurotransmitter into the synaptic cleft occurs when a rupture in the presynaptic axon membrane is followed by a temporary fusion of synaptic vesicles. The process by which a neurotransmitter crosses the synaptic cleft and attaches to a receptor in the postsynaptic membrane is called *binding*, which activates chemical changes in the postsynaptic membrane. These changes can either encourage (excite) or discourage (inhibit) the production of nerve impulses, depending on the chemical composition of the receiving cell. The neurotransmitter does not itself pass through the receiving cell; rather, it penetrates the membrane, and the impulses it generates travel through the cell. After transmission is complete, the neurotransmitter either is discarded as waste by the glial cells or reenters the presynaptic terminal for storage and use at another time (this process is called *reuptake*).

If we conceptualize a neuron as an engine, the receptors are the buttons on the control panel and the neurotransmitters are the fingers pushing the buttons (Pert, 1999). At any given time, a nerve cell may receive a barrage of both excitatory and inhibiting impulses from many sources. Single cells continuously act on or respond to their environment. For instance, in reading this chapter, you have focused on the content before you, but perhaps you have also been listening to music, thinking about certain clients, shifting your posture every few minutes, or smelling the aroma of food cooking in the kitchen. These simple, effortless activities require the exchange of signals among millions of nerve cells along pathways, with each cell doing its part to sustain millions of pathways throughout the nervous system.

NEUROTRANSMITTERS

Drugs are thought to work by modifying natural events in the synapses along pathways in certain areas of the brain. Medication affects these events and subsequently brain function in any of the following ways:

1. Altering presynaptic activity to prompt neurotransmitter release.
2. Altering postsynaptic activity to affect receptor binding.

3. Interfering with normal reuptake processes.
4. Altering the manufacture of receptors.

An *agonist* is a substance (including a medicine) that binds to a receptor and stimulates the same type of cellular activity as a neurotransmitter, thereby increasing its effect. An *antagonist* binds to a receptor but fails to stimulate its activity, thereby decreasing the effect of a neurotransmitter.

The science of neurotransmitters has flourished only since the 1970s. Although more than 40 chemical neurotransmitters have been discovered, and it is suspected that hundreds more exist, our knowledge of them is limited. The intended benefits of psychotropic drugs are at present generally attributed to only seven neurotransmitters: acetylcholine, norepinephrine, epinephrine, dopamine, serotonin, gamma-aminobutyric acid (GABA), and glutamate. All of these except GABA and glutamate are classified as **amines**, or organic substances that are the building blocks of amino acids. GABA and glutamate are complete amino acids.

All primary transmitters except glutamate are present in groups of neurons primarily located in the brain stem but also associated with more diffuse pathways through the central nervous system. Transmitters extend in pathways from the brain stem to other regions of the brain. Interestingly, together, acetylcholine, norepinephrine, dopamine, serotonin, and GABA account for transmissions at less than half the brain's synapses. GABA, the most prevalent of these substances, is found in 25% to 40% of the brain's synapses. Dopamine is used by only 15% of the nerve terminals in those areas where it is most highly concentrated. Acetylcholine is found in 5% to 10% of neuron terminals in the brain. Only 5% of neurons process norepinephrine where it is concentrated, and serotonin is found in less than 1% of central nervous system terminals. However, all these substances are crucial in regions of the nervous system associated with emotional behavior.

The study of neurotransmitters and the effects of drugs on them is a major field of neuroscience. Current knowledge about transmitter processes has been derived primarily from observations of activities within the peripheral nervous system. Establishing that similar mechanisms exist in the central nervous system is a far more difficult and somewhat speculative challenge. In fact, the specific actions of psychotropic drugs on neurotransmitter activity are in some cases still uncertain.

In the following sections we give fuller descriptions of the major transmitters known or believed to be major agents in psychotropic drug treatment.

Acetylcholine

The first major neurotransmitter to be identified almost 90 years ago, acetylcholine is most highly concentrated in the brain stem but is also present elsewhere. It is an excitatory substance released by all neurons that control the activities of the skeletal and smooth (involuntary) muscles, including the heartbeat. It is also released by those autonomic nerve cells in the parasympathetic system that control some glandular functions. Acetylcholine is critical to the transmission of messages between the brain and the spinal cord. It affects arousal, attention, memory, motivation, and movement. Acetylcholine is affected by many types of medications, including the antihistamines, anti-parkinsonian drugs, and medications for dementia. In fact, acetylcholine has been linked to overall cognitive function, and drugs that fight dementia work by enhancing the actions of this neurotransmitter.

Norepinephrine and Epinephrine

Norepinephrine, an excitatory transmitter, is located in the sympathetic nerves of the peripheral and central nervous systems and is secreted by the adrenal glands in response to stress or arousal. Not widely distributed throughout the nervous system, it functions in two major *tracts*, or bundles of nerves that have the same origin, termination, and function. First, norepinephrine influences affective behavior by connecting the brain stem with axons in the hypothalamus and limbic system. The second tract, which extends from the brain stem to the cerebral cortex and hippocampus (the part of the temporal lobe essential in memory regulation), influences alertness. Norepinephrine tracts also extend toward the spinal cord, where they regulate anxiety and tension.

Epinephrine, also known as adrenaline, is also released by the adrenal glands and plays an important role in the body's "fight or flight" response. The transfer of signals between neurons and body cells is governed by epinephrine, which is released during situations of stress or excitement. Epinephrine also increases cardiac output by increasing the rate and the strength of cardiac contraction.

Both epinephrine and norepinephrine belong to the chemical class of the **catecholamines**, which are derived from an amino acid called tyrosine. The major difference between the two neurotranmitters is that epinephrine has a methyl group attached to its nitrogen, while norepinephrine has a hydrogen atom in place of a methyl group. Epinephrine is produced exclusively by the adrenal medulla, whereas norepinephrine is produced by sympathetic postganglionic fibers. Thus, the effects of norepinephrine are largely mediated by the sympathetic nervous system, and the effects of epinephrine are brought about exclusively by the adrenal medulla. Epinephrine is responsible for the control of all body tissues, while norepinephrine controls those parts of the brain that are responsible for the mind–body relationship and responding actions.

Both of these neurotransmitters regulate attention, mental focus, arousal, and cognition. Elevated norepinephrine levels are associated with anxiety, stress, high blood pressure, and hyperactivity. Low norepinephrine levels can cause low energy levels, lack of concentration, and motivation. Release of epinephrine and norepinephrine increases heart and respiration rates and inhibits insulin excretion leading to increased glucose and fatty acids levels in blood. An imbalance of the two substances can cause symptoms of anxiety, depression, premenstrual syndrome, eating disorders, insomnia, and fatigue.

Dopamine

Dopamine is an inhibitory substance that regulates motor behavior and plays a role in pleasure centers of the brain. It is present in four nerve tracts with different functions. One tract extends from the brain stem to portions of the limbic system, which influences emotional behavior, and a closely related tract extends to the cerebral cortex, which affects cognition. Dopamine abnormalities in the limbic system are implicated in schizophrenia. A third dopamine pathway extends from the brain stem to the basal ganglia area of the forebrain, where motor activity is regulated. A lack of sufficient dopamine here causes physical tension, rigidity, and movement difficulties (i.e., the parkinsonian adverse effects of antipsychotic drugs). In its fourth tract, dopamine helps regulate the endocrine system, directing the hypothalamus to manufacture hormones that are eventually released into the bloodstream. There is growing research on the subtypes of dopamine, as we will discuss later.

Serotonin

The tracts of the inhibitory neurotransmitter **serotonin** originate in the midbrain and extend into all brain regions, particularly the hypothalamus. Serotonin is also present in blood cells and the lining of the digestive tract. This substance affects regions in the brain that facilitate sensory processes, muscular activity, and thinking. Serotonin works in large part to calm the nervous system. Strategically positioned in the midbrain, serotonin coordinates complex sensory and motor patterns during a variety of behavioral states. Like dopamine, it has recently been found to include several subtypes and is also a factor in regulating states of consciousness, mood, depression, and anxiety. Serotonin affects basic bodily functions, such as appetite, sleep, and sexual behavior. Some hypothesize that this neurotransmitter contributes to affective disorders, states of high aggression, and schizophrenia.

Gamma-Aminobutyric Acid (GABA)

GABA, an amino acid, is present throughout the central nervous system. Most neurons possess GABA receptors. There are two types of receptors, A and B, but only one of them (type A) has a role in anxiety and its modulation. This transmitter inhibits virtually all neurons; that is, it inhibits the firing of impulses from cells on which it acts and thus plays a major role in controlling neuron excitability. In a sense, it regulates the brain's electrical activity. Almost every cerebral function is likely to be influenced by drugs that act on GABA. These functions include the regulation of motor activity, cardiovascular reflexes, pituitary function, and anxiety. Certain antianxiety medications enhance GABA's effectiveness. Alcohol and sedatives, such as barbiturates, also act on GABA.

Glutamate (Glutamic Acid)

Glutamate has more recently become a topic of major interest in psychopharmacology. It is a primary "excitatory" neurotransmitter in the brain, meaning that it stimulates nerve cell activity. Glutamate is also a chemical that is used in the production of GABA. It is obtained from food and from metabolic processes (including glial cell activity). Glutamate is stored in and released from nerve terminals, and its receptors (four types) are found on the surfaces of virtually all neurons.

Glutamate activity has a major influence on cognitive functions by means of the cortex and hippocampus and on motor functions in the pyramidal and extrapyramidal systems, and it also affects many cerebellar and sensory functions.

Researchers hypothesize that glutamate may influence the development of a variety of mental disorders, including schizophrenia, and other disorders (such as Alzheimer's disease) through a process of *excitotoxicity*. This refers to a normal, temporary process of overstimulating neurons for the purpose of restructuring them. In the nervous system, for reasons that are not known, glutamate can at times overexcite neurons to the point of permanently damaging or destroying them. Medications that diminish this out-of-control process may reduce the symptoms of the resulting disorders. It has also been hypothesized that an alteration (reduction) of GABA function in the prefrontal cortex, initiated by glutamate activity, may produce the symptoms of schizophrenia.

HOW A DRUG MOVES THROUGH THE BODY

The way in which the human body responds to the presence of a drug is called *pharmacokinetics*. Knowledge of pharmacokinetics can help social workers understand why some clients respond differently than others to the same medication and why, when a client stops taking medication, its effects can continue for a while. The four bodily processes important to understanding pharmacokinetics are absorption, distribution, metabolism, and excretion (see Figure 3.5).

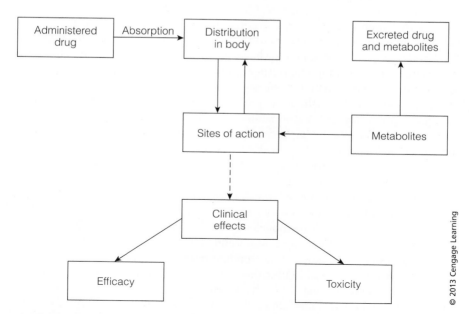

FIGURE 3.5 Psychotropic Drug Pharmacokinetics.

© 2013 Cengage Learning

Absorption

Absorption is the process by which a drug enters the bloodstream, most commonly by the passive diffusion of the drug into the bowel wall. Factors relevant to efficient absorption include the chemical makeup of the drug and the other materials used in its production and the activity of liver enzymes, which break down the drug. With oral medication, this efficiency depends on the drug's strength of concentration, its ability to dissolve into fatty tissue (of which intestinal cell membranes are composed), and the spontaneous movement of a consumer's intestines. Taking a drug on an empty stomach favors rapid absorption because the presence of other substances promotes competition for digestive enzymes and slows the absorption process.

Although most psychotropic drugs are prescribed orally, in tablets or capsules, some are administered intramuscularly. Medications injected into muscles enter the bloodstream more quickly than oral medications because they bypass the digestive process. Intravenous administration of drugs is the quickest, most direct route for absorption; however, it is rarely prescribed because it is impractical and includes the highest risk of adverse effects. As of now, other routes of drug administration, such as the lungs and rectum, are not used to administer psychotropic drugs. The psychostimulant drug pemoline, however, can be administered through the skin with a 7-day patch.

Distribution

Distribution is the process by which a drug, having entered the bloodstream, travels to its desired site of action. Once in the bloodstream, the drug can take one of two routes. It can either dissolve in the blood plasma (the fluid part of the blood) for transport to the site of action, or it can become attached, or bind, to plasma proteins. Binding is problematic because it prohibits the drug from advancing to its site in the brain. After binding, the drug breaks down or is metabolized, diminishing its intended effects. Although protein binding rates vary among drugs and even individuals, most psychotropic drugs are fairly high in protein binding capacity (up to 95% in some cases). Only the unbound portion of the drug can cross into the brain. Because average rates are already so high, small variations in the binding of a drug make a significant difference in its effectiveness.

The blood–brain barrier refers to characteristics of capillaries (blood vessels) in the brain through which a drug must pass to enter neuron sites. Because these capillaries are tightly compressed, this barrier is relatively difficult for a substance to cross. Medications and other substances must be lipid soluble to pass through brain capillaries because the cell membranes of these vessels are lipid, or fatty. In other areas of the body, capillaries are not so tightly bound, and water-soluble substances can leak through them into the surrounding tissue. In general, efficient absorption into the fatty intestinal wall implies that a drug will enter the brain efficiently.

A drug can enter the brain directly, through the circulatory system, or indirectly, through the cerebrospinal fluid after diffusing there from the bloodstream. Access of a drug to the brain depends in part on the blood flow at the intended site—a higher volume of blood increases the likelihood of entry. Access also depends on the drug's relative affinity for the receptors in that area of the brain. Distribution into the brain is facilitated by the large mass of blood vessels that feed it. Nevertheless, the amount of the drug that passes through the blood–brain barrier is usually small compared to the amount that remains in other areas of the body. Prescribers take these facts into account when selecting drugs and dosages.

Metabolism

Metabolism is the process, generally carried out by enzymes in the liver, by which the body breaks down the chemical structure of a drug into derivatives that can be eliminated from the body. The drug's molecules are altered from lipid-soluble substances into water-soluble salts. High water solubility prevents the drug from continuing to recirculate throughout the body. Instead, it can be efficiently absorbed into the body's water and excreted. First-pass metabolism refers to the extensive initial breakdown of the drug in the liver. This process significantly reduces the amount of drug that is available to proceed toward its site of action. *Bioavailability* refers to the amount of a drug that leaves the liver without being metabolized.

The body's cytochrome P450 enzyme system is responsible for drug metabolism. These enzymes are located primarily in cells in the liver and intestines. At least six P450 enzymes are known to exist, and, significantly, certain percentages of the members of different ethnic groups lack one or several of them. This results in a differential quality of metabolism and drug effects (both positive and negative) for members of these groups. This issue will be explored in more detail in Chapter 5.

It is important to note that the products of metabolism, known as *metabolites*, may themselves be pharmacologically active and may promote the primary drug's ongoing effect as they circulate through the bloodstream and nervous system. That is, even though the metabolites represent a chemical breakdown of the drug, they may maintain a set of therapeutic effects on thought or mood similar to that of the original drug. The metabolites of most medications are well known, and prescribers take their effects into account when making decisions about prescriptions. However, metabolism can be affected in a number of ways by physical disease processes in the body and by interactions among drugs. Also, the efficiency of metabolism, as well as kidney function, declines with age.

Excretion

Excretion is the process by which drugs are eliminated from the body, primarily by the kidneys. *Elimination* refers to all processes, including metabolism and excretion, that lower the concentration of a drug in the body. The speed of this process is proportional to the concentration of the drug in the body. That is, elimination proceeds more slowly as less medication remains in the consumer's system. The *blood level* refers to the measure of a drug's presence in the plasma at a given time; *steady state* refers to the point at which a consistent level of a medication is present in the bloodstream; and the *peak level* of a drug refers to the time after ingestion at which the drug reaches its highest concentration in the blood-stream. This peak varies with the type of drug and the amount ingested. Because elimination continues the entire time a drug is in the bloodstream, relative drug-elimination rates determine whether blood levels are increasing or decreasing. That is, the amount ingested and in circulation should correspond to the amount eliminated. *Clearance* is the amount of a drug excreted over a given amount of time. Excretion is carried out through the urine or bile, although sweat, feces, saliva, tears, and even milk in lactating women can also serve this function.

An important concept for understanding the frequency with which a client must take a prescribed medication is that of *half-life*, the time required for a drug to fall to 50% of its peak level. Half-life is determined by metabolism and excretion after absorption and distribution are complete. To clarify a frequent point of confusion, a drug is not completely eliminated, as might be assumed, after two half-lives have passed. In fact, each successive half-life requires the same amount of time as the previous one but accounts for the elimination of only 50% of the remaining medication. For example, the antidepressant trazodone has a half-life of 5 hours; thus 50% of the peak level of a single dose of trazodone is eliminated in 5 hours. However, only 75% is cleared in 10 hours, or two half-lives (50% of the remaining 50% equals 25%); 87.5% is eliminated in 15 hours, or three half-lives (50% of 25%, or 12.5%); 93.75% in 20 hours, or four half-lives; and approximately 97% in 25 hours, or five half-lives. Knowledge of a drug's half-life is essential to determine the dosage that must be taken to maintain a therapeutic level in circulation. If a client takes a drug too frequently, his or her blood level will eventually rise to a point of *toxicity*, or poison. Similarly, taking a drug less frequently than is therapeutically advisable would limit or perhaps even eliminate its effectiveness.

In determining a psychotropic drug treatment, prescribers try to ensure that a steady concentration of medication in the consumer's bloodstream will be delivered to the site of action to produce the desired effect. When a drug's half-life is known, the prescriber can tell the consumer the frequency of dosage that will achieve a steady state; that is, the prescriber provides a schedule so that the amount entering the system will offset the amount leaving it. Logically, medications with longer half-lives should be taken less often than those with shorter half-lives. Of course, taking any medication more frequently than indicated by its half-life would be dangerous, leading to a buildup of the substance in the system and to toxic effects. Many antipsychotic medications and antidepressants can be taken once per day. Mood-stabilizing medications, on the other hand, are generally taken several times per day because of their shorter half-life. Most oral medications are taken at least once per day, but injectable medications can be consumed as seldom as once per month because they are stored and released slowly by muscle tissue.

THE EFFECTS OF A DRUG ON THE BODY

Pharmacodynamics is the study of the effects of a drug on the body. Social workers can use their knowledge of pharmacodynamics to respond to the client's and family's need to learn about medications, including understanding differential

drug response and the reasons for all the drug's effects, both positive and negative. Pharmacodynamics offers several helpful concepts to the social worker,
including therapeutic index, potency, dose response, lag time, tolerance, and
adverse effects. Because drugs interact with body tissues, individual consumer
characteristics account for differences in what the drug can do. In general, drug
action is influenced by a consumer's age (efficiency of metabolism), weight (rate
of absorption), sex (hormonal differences), and any organ problems or diseases
that interfere with the body's efficiency.

The *therapeutic index* of a drug is the ratio of the lowest average concentration
needed to produce a desired effect and the lowest average concentration that
produces toxic effects. In toxicity the amount of an active drug in the body
exceeds the amount required for efficacy, putting the consumer at risk for serious
adverse effects. A high therapeutic index implies that a drug is relatively safe, as
opposed to a drug with a low therapeutic index. That is, a person will not likely
overdose if he or she accidentally takes more than is prescribed.

The *potency* of a drug is its relative strength, in grams, milligrams, or micro-
grams, required to achieve a desired effect. The median effective dose (sometimes signified as ED50) is the dose that produces a therapeutic effect in 50% of
clients. However, a drug's effectiveness cannot be measured merely by its
potency. Two different antipsychotic drugs, for example, may be administered
in very different dosages. One milligram of haloperidol is the equivalent of
10-mg of thiothixene, a similar drug. Although haloperidol is the more potent
of the two, the effectiveness of both may be the same, and they may be equally
safe when given in comparable therapeutic amounts. However, differences in
potency do relate to certain types of adverse effects (see Chapter 4).

The *dose response* is the measure of a drug's therapeutic effect as a function of
increasing the dose. Many drugs demonstrate an enhanced therapeutic effect
when given in greater amounts, but only up to a point. These drugs may
become ineffective or harmful once that peak dosage level is passed. When plot-
ted on a graph, dose responses of different medications can be compared with
each other. Again, this information does not necessarily help the prescriber determine which medication is preferable, because two medicines may have different
therapeutic and adverse effect profiles.

Lag time is the time a medication takes to affect the targeted behavior. Lag
time in part depends on the delay caused by the natural distribution of the
drug, but in some cases it reflects an adaptive response in the central nervous
system. That is, the drug may reach the site of action, but the natural activity
of neurons may change in an attempt to reject the drug, temporarily thwarting
the desired nerve cell activity. Some antianxiety medications demonstrate an
almost immediate therapeutic effect after consumption, whereas antidepressants
may take 2 to 6 weeks to produce a desired effect.

Factors involved in lag time are not well understood, but the time intervals
are predictable. One theory holds that the presynaptic nerve fires more rapidly
than usual in the presence of a psychotropic drug. Eventually, though, the presynaptic neuron can no longer sustain the increased charge. When the neuron
fatigues, the efficacy of the drug can be observed. This phenomenon has clinical

implications; that is, it will do the prescriber no good to increase dosage to obtain a quicker response. To affect the symptoms of the mental illness, one often has to wait.

Tolerance refers to the body's reduced responsiveness to a drug because the sensitivity of receptors changes over time. It affects both the desired clinical effects and the adverse effects. Although tolerance can be observed most obviously with benzodiazepines and can occasionally occur with other medications, tolerance does not affect the therapeutic effects of most psychotropic drugs. Some adverse effects of medications may diminish over time, and in this sense tolerance is positive for consumers.

Adverse or side effects refer to any effects of a drug that are unintentional and unrelated to its desired therapeutic effect. Although these effects are generally considered negative, the client may perceive some as either neutral or positive, such as the weight loss or increased energy that occurs with some of the newer antidepressant medications. Side effects generally occur because a drug acts on multiple sites in the nervous system, even though only one site is targeted for the positive effect. Negative side effects can have serious short- and long-term consequences for the consumer or can be relatively harmless but uncomfortable or inconvenient, such as sedation. Significant side effects themselves may be treated by the prescriber, sometimes with other medications.

The Placebo Effect

Before describing the various psychotropic medications and their effects, we need to consider the interesting issue of the *placebo* effect, which is often observed in medication research. A placebo is a substance that has no pharmacological effect but is given to a client who supposes it to be a medicine. Placebos are used to control for the psychological effects of administering a medication for a particular set of symptoms. In medication evaluation research, the effects of a particular drug are often compared to the effects of a placebo, such as a sugar pill that resembles the actual medication. Surprisingly, consumers often respond to the placebo with considerable symptomatic relief that may be enduring (e.g., Brody & Miller, 2011; Posternak & Zimmerman, 2007). What this implies is that the physical substance of the medication may not be as much the source of impact as the client's attitude toward the provider and the expectation of help. Placebos symbolize the prescriber's healing power and the expectation of the service provider and client that the client will improve.

To establish a drug's pharmacological benefit, its rate or degree of success must be over and above any observed placebo effects. Herein lies a common problem in research reports, because this distinction is not always articulated. For example, if a new antidepressant drug has an effectiveness rate (however defined) of 60% but the placebo effect for a comparison group is found to be 30%, then the drug is said to have only a 30% effectiveness rate beyond the placebo. Some researchers, however, will report a 60% effectiveness rate and ignore the placebo effect.

Clearly, the mere act of taking a drug with presumed benefits can have an effect on the body of the consumer, for reasons that are not well understood.

FIVE CLASSES OF PSYCHOTROPIC MEDICATION

In this discussion we are mainly concerned with psychotropic medications that belong to one of five categories: antipsychotic, antidepressant, mood-stabilizing, antianxiety, and psychostimulant drugs. Drugs in a particular category have been primarily used in the past to treat the same psychiatric symptoms and, with important exceptions, tend to take similar actions. Although this is still largely true, we want to emphasize that drugs from each category are increasingly being found to have effectiveness with other types of disorders. For example, many of the newer antidepressants are also effective in treating anxiety. Because drugs initially developed for one condition or illness are sometimes used to treat other conditions, we must accept that the distinctions between classes of medications are no longer clear.

In the following sections we detail how each type of drug acts on the body and how the body handles each. Each of the drug categories will be discussed in much more detail in Chapter 4.

Antipsychotic Medications

It is widely accepted that people with schizophrenia, the most common psychotic disorder, have a relatively high concentration of the neurotransmitter dopamine or, in pathways extending into the cortex and limbic system, a high sensitivity at its receptor sites. Much evidence exists that stimulating dopamine activity induces psychotic symptoms (Baumesiter & Francis, 2002). Almost all antipsychotic medications are thought to act at least in part by blocking postsynaptic dopamine receptors, binding to these receptors on all four of its pathways. Because of this mode of action, these medications are often termed dopamine antagonists. The medications differ primarily in their potential adverse effects, their potency (as indicated by the number of milligrams in equivalent doses), and their possible effects on other neurotransmitters. We want to emphasize, however, that the "dopamine hypothesis" is far from a certainty, as recent studies have shown fewer correlations between amounts of dopamine and symptoms presentation (Kendler & Schaffner, 2011). It may be that dopamine has an indirect influence on symptom manifestation.

It was once believed that there was only one type of dopamine receptor in the brain, but scientists have since identified five subtypes. These are grouped into two classes, one that produces therapeutic effects and one that produces adverse effects when exposed to psychotropic drugs. The therapeutic actions of antipsychotic medications are believed to result from their blocking one of these types of receptors. The reduction of dopamine activity in people with schizophrenia is accompanied by a reduction in many of the positive symptoms, which feature an excess or bizarre distortion of normal functions (such as delusions and hallucinations). However, for reasons that are not clear, antipsychotic medications are not as effective in reducing delusional thinking or negative symptoms, which feature a loss or reduction of normal functions (withdrawal, poverty of speech and thought, lack of motivation). The negative symptoms may be related to the activity of other neurotransmitters and may be reduced by some of the newer medications.

The antipsychotic medications act on all dopamine sites in the brain, but only one of these is the site of symptom-producing nerve cell activity. Other pathways extend from the midbrain to the basal ganglia and occupy areas of the brain that govern motor activity through the peripheral nervous system. A reduction in dopamine in these other areas causes adverse effects. Clients may experience muscle spasms, tremors, or stiffness, because normal amounts of the transmitter are needed in these areas to facilitate muscle activity. The reduced dopamine in them gives rise to symptoms of parkinsonism and tardive dyskinesia.

The "second generation" of antipsychotic medication, those that have been available in the U.S. market since 1988, seem to act differently than the older drugs. These have become known as serotonin–dopamine antagonists, because they may block the activity of both neurotransmitters. Clozapine, for example, is known to interact with *nine* neurotransmitter receptors (three subtypes of dopamine and three subtypes of serotonin receptors among them). It does not carry the risk of adverse effects for the muscular system. Although the actions of clozapine and the other newer medications are not completely understood, they may selectively act on only those dopamine receptors that produce psychotic symptoms. Their sites of action were once hypothesized as limited to the limbic forebrain and the frontal cortex, but recent evidence suggests otherwise. In blocking receptors for serotonin, the new medications have demonstrated that this neurotransmitter affects psychotic symptoms in some people.

For example, one new medication, aripiprazole, works differently from the other dopamine antagonists. It has the ability to *stimulate* the D2 receptor (a receiving area in the cell membrane) and as such is known as a partial D2 agonist. Further, the drug is believed to stimulate D2 when dopamine levels are low and, conversely, to inhibit D2 levels when the neurotransmitter is high. These processes remain hypothetical, but, if valid, they may help to reverse some of the negative symptoms of schizophrenia, which are believed to be associated with low dopamine levels in the brain.

After oral administration, the peak effects of most antipsychotic medications are achieved within 2 to 4 hours. There is a significant "first-pass" effect in the liver, in which much of the chemical substance is metabolized before it enters the circulatory system. However, the metabolites also act as dopamine antagonists and thus have a therapeutic effect. The drugs are highly protein bound: Fully 85% to 90% remains in the bloodstream. The drugs have a high therapeutic index, making it difficult to overdose accidentally to the point of toxicity. The drugs range in half-life from 10 to 40 hours. Because any point in this range is considered lengthy, antipsychotic drugs can be taken once per day to maintain a steady state.

Antidepressant Medications

There is also uncertainty about how antidepressant medications specifically work. Until the early 1980s it was believed that certain depressions resulted from a deficiency of norepinephrine or serotonin in the limbic area of the brain.

The antidepressants developed in the 1950s and 1960s (and still used today) were thought to work by increasing the prevalence of norepinephrine and serotonin in the nervous system. However, newer antidepressants are known to act differently. Further, it is suspected that antidepressants have additional effects on presynaptic and postsynaptic receptors and perhaps on other neurotransmitter systems. All the antidepressant drugs have antianxiety effects as well, and some have become primary treatments for certain anxiety disorders. The cellular–molecular theory of antidepressant action posits more generally that the drugs increase certain cell nutrients in areas where cells have experienced breakdown due to stress.

Three types of antidepressants, each with different actions, are the monoamine oxidase (MAO) inhibitors, the "cyclics," and those drugs that are serotonin specific. Despite uncertainties about their actions, some general characteristics of the drugs can be described. They must all be taken for several weeks before the client experiences beneficial effects, because their actions are initially resisted by cells at the sites of action. Many of the so-called cyclic antidepressants (see Chapter 4) have a low therapeutic index; that is, the amounts required for therapeutic effect and overdose do not differ greatly. This is a particular problem because these drugs are often prescribed for clients with self-destructive tendencies. Overdose can often be achieved with a 10-day supply of a cyclic drug.

The MAO inhibitors were among the first antidepressants. Although still effective for some clients, they are not frequently prescribed because of rather extensive dietary restrictions that are needed to prevent serious side effects. These drugs act by inhibiting certain enzymes in cells that metabolize norepinephrine and serotonin, so that levels of those transmitters in the central nervous system increase. The MAO inhibitors are effective in some clients who do not respond to other antidepressant medications. It has been found that two types of MAO are present in the nervous system, and only one of these is the desired target of antidepressant action. At present, new MAO inhibitors are in development that are more selective and are also reversible. That is, the drugs will have a therapeutic effect but will be eliminated from the client's system if any recognized toxic substances (certain cheeses, wines, and meats, as described in Chapter 4) enter it. Thus, new MAO inhibitors may become more commonly used in the future.

So named because of their chemical structure, the cyclic drugs (many of which have been called tricyclics and heterocyclics) were the most commonly prescribed antidepressants through the 1980s. They are believed to work by blocking the reuptake of norepinephrine and serotonin and, to a lesser extent, dopamine. The metabolites of cyclic drugs are also active antidepressants. The drugs are highly effective, accounting for their long popularity. As a result of actions in other areas of the autonomic and central nervous systems, many cyclic drugs produce discomforting adverse effects. Fortunately, tolerance does develop to some of the adverse effects but not to the therapeutic effect. These medications are lipid soluble and have a high rate of binding to plasma proteins. With a half-life of approximately 24 hours, they can be taken once per day.

The newer antidepressants, most of which are characterized by their actions on serotonin, add to the uncertainty about how antidepressant drugs act on relevant neurotransmitters. The selective serotonin reuptake inhibitor (SSRI) drugs block serotonin but in general do not interfere with the normal actions of norepinephrine. The dual serotonin and norepinephrine reuptake inhibitors (SNRIs) do not interfere with other chemicals that are affected by the cyclic antidepressants to cause adverse effects. Many advances in antidepressant medication have occurred based on the serotonin hypothesis of depression, but recently, as with dopamine, it has been found that biological correlates of depression are much wider-ranging (Gardner & Boles, 2011).

Bupropion is another type of drug, a norepinephrine and dopamine reuptake blocker, and it has a metabolite that is an even more effective reuptake blocker of these substances in key areas of the brain. Another emerging group of drugs, including trazodone and nefazodone, targets a subset of serotonin receptors as well as its reuptake. The actions of these new drugs may include stimulating certain other neurotransmitter building blocks in the cell body in ways that are not yet understood. More potent than the cyclics, these drugs also have long half-lives. One of their major attractions is that they have fewer adverse effects than the other types of antidepressants. They also offer less potential for overdose.

Mood-Stabilizing Drugs

Since its introduction in the United States as an antimanic drug in 1969, lithium carbonate has been the primary drug treatment for the symptoms of bipolar disorder. The lightest of the solid elements, lithium circulates through the body as a small ion that has a positive electrical charge. It is not clear how lithium achieves its therapeutic effect, but numerous theories have been considered. One hypothesis is based on lithium's high rate of passage through cell membrane ion channels, impeding the activity of the naturally occurring impulses that contribute to mania and consequently stabilizing electrolyte imbalances in the cell membrane. Another hypothesis differentiates the antidepressant and antimanic effects of the drug. The antidepressant effect of lithium may result from its reducing the sensitivity of postsynaptic receptors for serotonin, thus increasing the amount of that transmitter in the nervous system. Its antimanic effect may relate to reduced sensitivity in dopamine receptors and an inhibition of cellular enzymes that produce dopamine. Although highly effective, lithium does not take effect for several weeks after initiation. It is sometimes given, at least temporarily, with an antipsychotic drug to stabilize a manic individual.

Lithium circulates freely throughout the body completely unbound to plasma proteins, unlike antipsychotic and antidepressant drugs. Distributed in the extracellular fluid, it enters body tissues at varying rates. Peak blood levels are reached in 2 hours (4 hours for time-release forms), and there is complete absorption within 8 hours of administration. The half-life of lithium is 24 hours on maintenance doses, defined as the minimum dosage required to maintain a steady therapeutic effect. The drug must be taken two or three times daily, except in its time-release form. Lithium is not metabolized in the liver into derivative compounds. The kidneys excrete 95% of the drug. At steady states, which occur in 5 to 8 days, an equilibrium is reached in that plasma lithium reflects lithium levels in the entire body; thus the drug can be efficiently monitored by measuring levels in the blood. Lithium is excreted by the kidneys in the first few hours after peak levels. Because lithium has a relatively low therapeutic index, adverse reactions (such as muscle tremor and kidney damage) can occur at blood levels only slightly higher than a client's therapeutic level.

Certain antiseizure medications also act as effective mood stabilizers. Like lithium, their mechanisms of action are not clear. One theory holds that they control a "kindling" process in limbic system neuron tracts, a process that contributes to manic states. It is speculated that in mania a repetitive application of low-grade electrical or chemical stimuli is set in motion, eventually producing a manic episode. The drug carbamazepine, a potent blocker of norepinephrine reuptake, inhibits such repetitive firing of sodium impulses. Carbamazepine may also inhibit those enzymes in the central nervous system that break down GABA. The GABA neurotransmitter may have antimanic properties, and thus its increased prevalence in the nervous system may enhance mood stability. Valproic acid, another atypical antimanic medication that has been approved by the FDA for treating bipolar disorder, also has presynaptic and postsynaptic GABA receptor effects. By blocking the convulsive effects of GABA antagonists, valproic acid increases levels of GABA. Other anticonvulsants used to treat bipolar disorder include oxcarbazepine (FDA approved this use in 2002), lamotrigine, topiramate, and gabapentin. Although effective, all these new medications may not be prescribed unless lithium is first ruled out; lithium has been used as a mood stabilizer for a much longer time and has been more extensively tested. The anticonvulsant drugs may, however, be more effective in controlling certain types of mania.

Antianxiety Medications

Several types of anti-anxiety medication are currently available. For many years the most frequently prescribed were the benzodiazepines. The name comes from their chemical structure, in which a benzene ring is fused to a diazepine ring. Speculated to have evolved as fear regulators, natural benzodiazepine chemicals may exist in the brain, potentiated by the GABA neurotransmitter. The benzodiazepine medications are believed to achieve their therapeutic effect by causing the GABA neurotransmitter to bind more completely with its receptor site. GABA receptors in various regions of the brain regulate the anti-anxiety (or anxiolytic) and the sedative and anticonvulsant effects of the benzodiazepines. They act on the central nervous system by binding to specific sites near GABA receptors and produce a blockage of stimulation in areas of the brain associated with emotion. As a general rule, the benzodiazepines reduce anxiety in lower doses and are sedating in higher doses.

Benzodiazepines are usually taken orally. Quickly absorbed in the gastrointestinal tract, they act rapidly—in many cases, within 30 minutes. Having a high therapeutic index, the benzodiazepines do not present a risk for overdose. The numerous brands of these medications vary a great deal in their particular characteristics, but peak levels are generally reached in 1 to 3 hours, and most benzodiazepines form active metabolites. The drugs bind to plasma proteins, with the quality of distribution corresponding to their lipid solubility. Their half-lives vary widely (2 to 60 hours).

An important characteristic of the benzodiazepines is that with continuous use they are physically addictive at some dosages. Long-term use (perhaps no more than 2 weeks) can cause production of the body's natural benzodiazepine compounds to shut down. Thus, if the drug is abruptly withdrawn, no natural production of those substances will occur for some time. Clients must be taken off these medications gradually to prevent the effects of physical withdrawal, which can persist for several months. For these reasons the benzodiazepines are generally designed for comparatively short-term use.

Another widely used anti-anxiety medication is buspirone, a partial agonist of serotonin receptors. Although its impact on anxiety is not yet well understood, serotonin is believed to be anxiolytic in the hippocampus and limbic areas. To be effective, buspirone must be taken regularly, like antidepressant and mood-stabilizing drugs but unlike the benzodiazepines. Buspirone also requires several weeks to take effect. It is quickly absorbed but has a short half-life. It is not potentially addictive. This medication does have limitations, however. Some recent studies have shown it to be generally less effective than the benzodiazepines, and specifically, it is not effective in treating a panic disorder.

An interesting development in psychopharmacology over the past 20 years is the increased use of SSRI medications, most of which were initially developed as antidepressants, for treating symptoms of anxiety. The utility of these drugs supports the hypothesis that serotonin plays a role in the experience of anxiety. Several SSRI medications have been approved by the FDA as anti-anxiety medications: sertraline for posttraumatic stress disorder and panic disorder; paroxetine for generalized anxiety, obsessive-compulsive, panic, and social anxiety disorders; and venlafaxine (a different type of antidepressant drug) for generalized anxiety disorders.

Several other smaller classes of medications are also used to control anxiety. These include the beta-blockers, so named because they compete with norepinephrine at certain receptor sites in the brain and the peripheral nervous system, sites that regulate cardiac and muscular functions. These medications effectively treat anticipatory anxiety; that is, they lower anxiety by reducing its symptoms of rapid heartbeat, muscle tension, and dry mouth. Because the client does not experience these physiological indicators, his or her subjective experience of anxiety is diminished. Finally, the antihistamines are occasionally used as anti-anxiety agents. These drugs block histamine receptors associated with anxiety and agitation. Rapidly absorbed, antihistamines maintain a therapeutic effect for at least 24 hours. These drugs tend to sedate the consumer, however, and work effectively as anti-anxiety agents for only a few months. Although not addictive, they do not treat anxiety as effectively as benzodiazepines.

Psychostimulants

Stimulants have been used in the treatment of attention-deficit/hyperactivity disorder (ADHD) since 1936, with the finding that amphetamine drugs were effective in controlling hyperactivity. Most are currently classified as Schedule II drugs by the Drug Enforcement Agency because of their abuse potential. Schedule II is the most restrictive classification for medications, prohibiting their prescription by phone and the writing of refills without a visit to the prescriber. The psychostimulants are FDA approved for the treatment of ADHD, narcolepsy, and obesity.

As with many drugs, the precise mechanism of action of psychostimulants in treating ADHD is not known. The drugs release dopamine, norepinephrine, and serotonin from presynaptic terminals in the frontal portion of the brain, where attention and impulsivity are regulated. They also inhibit norepinephrine and dopamine reuptake. Between 70% and 90% of children respond positively to the major psychostimulant drugs currently available, which include dextroamphetamine, methylphenidate, and pemoline. Moderate doses appear to improve attention, concentration, and cognitive functioning in adults as well. ADHD in adults remains a somewhat controversial and less thoroughly studied condition, but many adults with the disorder are regularly prescribed methylphenidate.

Three primary medications from this class are prescribed. Methylphenidate, the most widely used and studied psychostimulant, was introduced in 1958 as a treatment for children with hyperactivity. It has a half-life of only 2 to 3 hours, which is advantageous because it does not impair sleep, but the short half-life means that the drug must be taken 2 to 4 times per day. Methylphenidate requires only 30 to 60 minutes to take effect, and it is associated with symptom aggravation 10 to 20 hours after a dose. A time-release form of the drug is available. Pemoline has a longer half-life (2 to 12 hours) and needs to be taken only once daily. Its lesser stimulant effect may also lessen its abuse potential. On the negative side, it may require several weeks to demonstrate a therapeutic effect. Dextroamphetamine remains an alternative medication. It is fast-acting and needs to be taken only twice per day, with a 6- to 7-hour half-life. However, it has a high potential for abuse and illicit use as a street drug,.

Atomoxetine was approved by the FDA for the treatment of ADHD in 2002. It is the first such drug *not* classified as a stimulant. It is a selective norepinephrine reuptake inhibitor and as such works somewhat differently from the other medications in this class. Still, atomoxetine *does* produce effects similar to the stimulants, including some of the same side effects. It can be taken by children age 6 and older and is the first ADHD medication formally approved for the treatment of adults. With a half-life of 5 hours the medication is generally taken twice a day.

Children with ADHD can remain symptomatic through adolescence and early adulthood, but studies about drug effectiveness beyond puberty is not extensive. Some evidence indicates that treatment in childhood leads to better outcomes in adulthood.

A WORD ABOUT PHARMACOGENOMICS

Individuals with similar symptoms respond differently to the same medications because of their unique chemistry, and this has long been recognized as a challenge in psychopharmacology. Being able to better identify in advance how consumers will respond to a drug has the potential to help practitioners avoid lengthy ineffective medication trials, limit client's exposure to adverse effects, and increase their adherence. Toward this end, pharmacogenomics has evolved as a branch of pharmacology that considers the influence of genetic variation in drug response (Malhotra et al., 2007). It aims to develop a more rational means to optimize drug therapy with respect to each consumer's genotype. This approach promises the advent of "personalized medicine" in which medications are optimized with respect to each person's unique genetic makeup.

The premise of pharmacogenomic research is that there are genetic factors that partially affect individual variability to drug response. Evidence for this premise is still developing, but it is supported by observations that members of the same family (including twins) often have similar responses to medications. To date this has most often been observed with antidepressant medications and to a lesser extent with antipsychotic medications. The task for researchers in this field is to identify specific genes that influence drug response, a process that has been facilitated by routine participant DNA collection in many medication trials, as well as the growing availability of databases on variations within the human genome.

There are some limitations and ethical issues emerging in this field of study, however. For example, if a medication has a general rate of effectiveness of 70% and genetic considerations only raise this probability to 80%, it may not be worth the expense of testing. (Some researchers believe that genetic testing should only be done when the potential increase in effectiveness is 40% to 60 %). Further, researchers need to consider the risk–benefit ratio of acquiring genetic knowledge about people and related issues of confidentiality.

ADVERSE EFFECTS OF PSYCHOTROPIC MEDICATION

As monitors, client educators, and possibly the first line of intervention if clients develop concerns, social workers have firsthand involvement with the side effects of medication. As defined earlier, side effects are the physical, psychological, or social effects of a medication that are unintentional and unrelated to its desired therapeutic effect. We use the term *adverse effects* to refer to bothersome and potentially harmful side effects. Clients may experience some side effects as pleasant, such as the mildly sedative effect of some anti-anxiety drugs, but even these may present health and safety concerns. Because all medications act on areas of the nervous system, adverse effects are most readily recognized in their physical form. However, such effects may also be psychological (they affect the consumer's sense of self) and social (they affect how the client is viewed by others). Still, the adverse physical effects are frequently of most immediate concern to the prescriber and social worker because of their potentially negative effect on physical well-being. All three types of adverse effects, however, are important to monitor, as we will discuss later in the text.

Adverse Physical Effects: Definitions

The major adverse physical effects are the following:

Anticholinergic effects (ACEs): Dry mouth, blurred vision, constipation, and urinary hesitancy. These effects result from the suppressive action of some antipsychotic and antidepressant medications on the pyramidal nerve pathways (those parts of the peripheral nervous system that govern fine motor activities). Specifically, the drugs block cholinergic receptors, which is the source of the name of these effects.

Extrapyramidal symptoms (EPSs): Akathisia, the dystonias, parkinsonian symptoms, and tardive dyskinesia. These effects are related to the actions of drugs on extrapyramidal nerve pathways by means of basal ganglia pathways. They occur most commonly with the antipsychotic medications. *Akathisia* is an internal state of restlessness, or the perceived need to be in constant motion, accompanied by muscle discomfort. *Dystonia* refers to the uncoordinated and involuntary twisting movements produced by sustained muscle spasms. *Parkinsonian effects* include the reduction in range of one's facial and arm movements, muscle rigidity and tremor, shuffling gait, drooling, and difficulty either starting or stopping movements. In *tardive dyskinesia*, the word *tardive* is defined as "appearing late" (because these effects occur often, but not always, in some consumers who have taken a medication for many years), and *dyskinesia* refers to a distortion of voluntary movements. In contrast to dystonia, this condition refers to involuntary rhythmic movements in facial muscles, including spasms of the eyelids, repeated puckering of the mouth, licking or smacking movements, and lip tremors. The tongue may curl or push on the cheek. This disorder can also affect the body's extremities and trunk region.

Neuroleptic malignant syndrome: Hyperthermia (high fever), muscle rigidity, fluctuating levels of consciousness, and instability in the autonomic nervous system. A rare (0.1% of consumers) but potentially fatal (15% to 25% of those afflicted) toxic complication of antipsychotic drug treatment, this syndrome generally occurs within 2 weeks after treatment has started.

Orthostatic hypotension: A sudden drop in blood pressure that occurs when rising from a lying or sitting position to a standing one, accompanied by dizziness, lightheadedness, weakness, and an unsteady gait. Although transient, this effect may cause the client to fall and thus is of particular concern with physically frail people, including older adults.

Sedation: Drowsiness.

Sexual dysfunction: Changes in sexual desire and capacity, including problems with erection, ejaculation, and impotence in men and orgasmic dysfunction in women. These symptoms relate to a disruption in the normal functioning of the autonomic nervous system. Adverse effects related to sexual functioning are quite common, particularly with the antidepressant class, and are a major reason for non-adherence. Consumers often do not share these "embarrassing" experiences with professionals, however.

Tachycardia: An increase in heart rate resulting from adverse effects of antidepressant medications acting on the autonomic nervous system. Tachycardia is a serious concern for consumers with heart problems.

Weight gain: Weight gain is not a technical term, but we mention it here because it is a common side effect of many psychotropic medications and is related to changes in the body's rate of metabolism.

Other adverse effects of the psychotropic medications are discussed in Chapter 4.

Adverse Physical Effects: Factors in Their Production

So far in this chapter we have outlined the adverse physical effects of psychotropic medications. However, factors besides the chemical makeup of a drug also determine possible side effects. One factor, for example, is dosage. In general, the higher the dosage, the greater the likelihood of adverse reactions. The following five characteristics of clients also influence the occurrence of adverse effects:

Age: A person's rate of metabolism slows down during later life. For this reason, elderly consumers are particularly susceptible to such adverse effects as sedation, weight gain, and parkinsonian symptoms. Orthostatic hypotension (lowered blood pressure), although not more common among older adults, is potentially more serious because the clients are relatively frail and prone to injury if they fall. However, young people are more at risk for dystonias (muscle spasms), indicating that there is not a simple correlation between age and all adverse effects.

Sex: Women are at higher risk than men for tardive dyskinesia, parkinsonian symptoms, and akathisia. Women with bipolar disorder are also at higher risk for experiencing a manic reaction to antidepressant medication than are men. On the other hand, men are at higher risk for dystonia than women. These differences are apparently due to hormonal characteristics, but there is a need for more research to understand more fully how sex influences the effects of medication (see Chapter 5).

Diagnosis: People with organic brain damage and affective disorders demonstrate a greater propensity for tardive dyskinesia and neuroleptic malignant syndrome than people with other diagnoses. Those with medical illnesses have an increased risk of neuroleptic malignant syndrome with antipsychotic medication and delirium with the antidepressants. Furthermore, people with depression seem to be at a higher risk for orthostatic hypotension than other diagnostic groups, for reasons not yet clear.

Personality: There is some indication that consumers who are action-oriented and have a high need to control their environment may react paradoxically to sedating medications, becoming agitated and confused rather than calmed.

Ethnicity: As discussed in Chapter 5, race and ethnicity are not frequently differentiated in research on drug effectiveness, but they may be relevant factors in a consumer's response because of differences in enzymes for drug metabolism. Asian clients improve on lower doses of antipsychotic medications than people of European ancestry do, but they also experience extrapyramidal symptoms at lower doses than comparison groups. Asian clients may also metabolize antianxiety medications at a slower rate and experience toxicity more often. Asian and Hispanic clients also respond more quickly to, and have more adverse effects from, cyclic antidepressant medications than other groups. African Americans seem to respond more rapidly than European Americans to cyclic antidepressant medications.

Adverse Psychological Effects

Psychological side effects occur when the act of taking medication negatively affects the client's self-concept. No less important than adverse physical effects, psychological effects probably account for an equal number of cases in which clients discontinue medications (Barnett, 2012; Kranke et al., 2012). We note the psychological effects briefly here and discuss them in detail in Chapter 4.

The ongoing use of any type of medication raises several concerns for clients regarding dependency. For instance, consumers must perceive at some level that, at least temporarily, they depend on a chemical agent to function at a desired level. Clients must also consider that their previous coping skills may have been insufficient to manage certain thought or mood problems. Although clients may be relieved to have a means to regain a higher level of stability, their sense of psychological efficacy may nevertheless be diminished.

Adverse Social Effects

Adverse social effects refer to the interpersonal and organizational barriers clients face daily as identified consumers of psychotropic medications. Auge and Herzlech (1998) outlined aspects of the "sick role." In receiving the diagnosis of a mental disorder and accepting treatments for it, including medication, an individual acknowledges that he or she has a condition that requires the help of experts. Regarding social norms, the client may be temporarily excused from certain interpersonal and occupational responsibilities if he or she agrees to participate actively in the treatment for the illness. Of course, a few clients refuse to take medications, because they do not want to acknowledge a sickness or accept the stigma that accompanies that role. As noted earlier, clients may not agree that they have a problem, may not agree with the details of its assessment, or may not believe that it is serious enough to require certain treatments, including medication. However, if clients with mental illness reject the sick role and also fail to maintain work, family, and other social responsibilities, they will be labeled irresponsible. They may, for example, lose a job rather than be given temporary leave if they fail to manage ordinary work responsibilities.

Of course, acknowledging a mental illness may foster a social stigma. For example, many employers may be reluctant to hire people with mental disorders if this becomes known or if they note medications and illnesses on job applications, despite the legal implications of the Americans with Disabilities Act (Corrigan, Lawson, & Kuwabara, 2010). Further, because of the chronic nature of some disorders, a person's development of new skills and strengths may go unacknowledged by those around him or her who assume that serious problems will inevitably follow. The adverse social effects of taking medication are serious and may be addressed by the social worker in the roles of advocate (in the case of job discrimination, for example), monitor, and educator.

SUMMARY

Psychotropic medications produce changes in a client's emotions, thoughts, and behaviors, theoretically, by altering existing processes in the central and peripheral nervous systems. They interfere with natural neurotransmitter processes— increasing or decreasing the levels of those chemical substances in nerve pathways—to produce change. Although the details of how these systems work still lie beyond the full comprehension of scientists, enough is known about the structure of the brain and its neurons that reasonable hypotheses exist to account for the actions of medications. Because drug actions are not specific enough— that is, because they affect sites in the brain beyond those that are targeted as the source of mental illness—adverse effects are common.

The social worker must be able to assess and monitor all medication effects as they affect the client's overall physical, mental, and emotional well-being. A prescriber may prescribe medications as a primary or secondary method of intervention, but in either case, drugs do not represent the entire problem-solving process in the treatment of mental illness. The social worker must be prepared to use other interventions to fully enhance a client's social functioning. A basic knowledge of pharmacokinetics and pharmacodynamics does, however, equip the social worker to understand the major positive and negative effects of drugs on clients, to explain such effects to clients and their families, and to make informed decisions about intervention from a biopsychosocial systems perspective.

TOPICS FOR DISCUSSION
AND LEARNING ACTIVITIES

1. Research the Internet and professional literature for information about one or more of the major neurotransmitters with regard to their influence on the development of symptoms of mental illness. Evaluate the evidence for claims made by researchers regarding this influence.

2. Research the professional (particularly psychiatric) literature to determine how members of diverse client populations (based on age, sex, culture, ethnicity, and race) may differ with regard to the physical functions of absorption, distribution, metabolism, and excretion of substances. Tie this information to a specific psychotropic drug as it might pass through the body.

3. Research two psychotropic drugs with respect to their typical pharmacodynamic properties (therapeutic index, potency, dose response, lag time, tolerance, and adverse physical effects). Compare drugs along these dimensions with those researched by your classmates.

4.   Search the Internet for two examples of first-person accounts of psychotropic medication consumers who have experienced major problems with adverse effects. How would you work with these clients about their ongoing or future use of medications?

5.   Interview a prescriber about her or his preferred drugs from one of the five medication classes discussed in this chapter. Ask how these preferences developed over time with regard to their perceived pharmacokinetic and pharmacodynamic properties with a range of clients.

4

✳

The Five Classes of Medication

Learning Objectives

Upon completion of this chapter, the reader will be able to:

1. Describe five classes of psychotropic medication.
2. Describe subcategories of medication within each class (two types of antipsychotics, three types of antidepressants, two types of mood stabilizers, two types of anti-anxiety drugs, and two types of psychostimulants).
3. Describe five types of medication from each drug category.
4. Articulate the major therapeutic effects associated with each class of medication.
5. Articulate the major negative physical effects of each class of medication.
6. Articulate two possible psychological and social adverse effects of medication use.

Having examined the structure of the body's nervous system, the characteristics of neurotransmitters, and the actions of psychotropic drugs within the body, we now turn to the range of drugs used in the treatment of mental, emotional, and behavioral disturbances. We describe in some detail the symptoms that the five classes of medication are intended to treat, as well as their adverse physical, psychological, and social effects. In Chapter 8 we focus particular attention on the social worker's management of their adverse effects. We emphasize again that the social worker is in an ideal situation to mediate among the physician, the client, and her or his significant others to monitor both the positive and negative effects of medications.

The primary sources we used to research this material include the American Psychiatric Association (2000), Doran (2008), Ingersoll & Rak (2006), Janicak, Marder, & Pavuluri (2011), Julien (2011), Sadock and Sadock (2009), Saija and Mortimer (2011), Schatzberg and Nemeroff (2009), and Stahl (2008). Additional sources are cited within the chapter.

MEDICATIONS THAT TREAT SYMPTOMS
OF PSYCHOSIS

Mental states that feature symptoms of psychosis, which the antipsychotic medications target, are generally characterized by the person's misperceiving sounds, smells, sensations, and activities in the outside world or in his or her own mind. These disturbances of thought greatly impair one's reality testing or ability to evaluate the outside world objectively. The individual with psychotic symptoms is at least temporarily unable to evaluate the accuracy of his or her perceptions and thoughts and makes many incorrect inferences about the outside world, even in the face of contrary evidence. While our focus is primarily on psychotic symptoms, the mental disorders that feature these symptoms include the schizophrenias, delusional disorders, schizoaffective disorder, bipolar disorder, and (some) major depressions. Other types of emotional trauma that produce high anxiety may also produce transient psychotic symptoms.

The Symptoms of Psychosis

We describe the symptoms of psychosis using schizophrenia as the primary example. Schizophrenia is a mental disorder characterized by a person's abnormal patterns of thought and perception, as inferred from his or her language and behavior. Schizophrenia includes two types of symptoms (American Psychiatric Association [APA], 2000). *Positive symptoms* represent exaggerations of normal behavior. These include hallucinations, delusions, disorganized thought processes, and tendencies toward agitation. *Hallucinations* are sense perceptions of external objects when those objects are not present. These may be *auditory*, *visual*, *gustatory* (the perception of taste), *tactile* (feeling an object), *somatic* (an unreal experience within the body), and *olfactory* (a false sense of smell). *Delusions* are false beliefs that a person maintains even though overwhelmingly contradicted by social reality. They include *persecutory* (people or forces are attempting to bring one harm), *erotomanic* (another person is in love with the individual), *somatic* (pertaining to body functioning), and *grandiose* (an exaggerated sense of power, knowledge, or identity) beliefs, *thought broadcasting* (one's thoughts are overheard by others), *thought insertion* or *withdrawal* (others are putting thoughts into or taking thoughts out of one's head), delusions of *being controlled* (thoughts, feelings, or actions are imposed by an external force), and delusions of *reference* (neutral events have special significance for the person). The *negative* symptoms of schizophrenia represent the diminution of what would be considered normal behavior. These include flat or blunted affect (the absence of expression), social withdrawal, noncommunication, anhedonia (blandness) or passivity, and ambivalence in decision-making.

Besides these symptoms, people who experience psychosis sometimes neglect hygiene and personal appearance. When present, these behaviors generally indicate a preoccupation with mental processes at the expense of social and self-care concerns. They do not indicate a willful disregard for self-care but rather an impairment in one's ability to focus thoughts on the normal activities of daily living.

SPECIFIC MEDICATIONS

Origins

The field of psychopharmacology did not generate much interest among researchers until after World War II. Drugs such as opium, morphine, bromide derivatives, chloral hydrate, and other barbiturate compounds were used only for the sedative control of the symptoms of mental, emotional, and behavioral disturbances in state hospital settings from the beginning of the nineteenth century. After the war, however, the great successes of the new antibiotic drugs led to a strong faith in the power of medications to treat diseases of all types. It was in this context that the first antipsychotic medications were introduced.

The story of the development of chlorpromazine is a fascinating example of how science and serendipity governed the early days of psychopharmacology (Swazey, 1974). The drug's parent compound, phenothiazine, was synthesized in Germany in 1883 as the basis for a new blue dye. The field of organic chemistry was new at that time, and, like other discoveries, phenothiazine was investigated for other possible uses. It was found to be ineffective as an insecticide and antimalarial agent, but in the latter experiments it demonstrated antihistaminic qualities.

By 1900 it had been discovered that in humans histamine substances caused shock (characterized by a rapid drop in blood pressure and a loss of fluid from the circulatory system), and research was initiated to develop antihistamines for treating shock in medical patients. From the beginning it was observed that these substances had a strong sedative quality, but this was considered to be an adverse effect. Synthetic antihistamine research was undertaken during the 1930s in Germany and France in response to the demands of treating World War II casualties, and it was discovered that the phenothiazine-derived compounds were most efficient for this purpose.

Interestingly, as a side note, these drugs were used as early as the 1940s in some settings for the sedation of manic and other agitated psychotic persons. In the populous laboratories of the state hospitals, it had been observed that persons in acute psychotic states did not seem to suffer from allergic diseases; they seemed to have a decreased histamine sensitivity. Through a curious reverse logic, this led to the experimental use of antihistamines as a means of reducing the symptoms of psychosis.

In the early 1950s antihistamines such as chlorpromazine were utilized in medicine as presurgery anesthetics, pain medication, and treatment for shock. During its testing, alert researchers observed that chlorpromazine lowered the body temperatures of animals. Because cold water and cold packs had long been used as a means of sedating mental patients, it was hypothesized that the new drug might have the same effect. It failed to lower body temperatures but was effective in controlling agitated behavior. By 1952 a series of papers appeared in the medical literature, noting the positive impact of chlorpromazine on a range of mental disorders.

Between 1952 and 1954, chlorpromazine was formally tested as an antipsychotic drug with positive results. In March 1954, the Food and Drug Administration (FDA) formally approved it for the treatment of nausea and vomiting and in neuropsychiatry. The American drug company Smith, Kline, and French had difficulty with its marketing because of psychiatry's adherence to the psychodynamic model of treatment and the problem of public financing of the drug for state hospital use. Through aggressive lobbying, the company was able to persuade state legislatures to invest money in the drug, arguing that the resulting deinstitutionalization would lower the total cost of public mental health. Eventually chlorpromazine became widely used, and, despite what we now know to be its extreme limitations, was proclaimed as psychiatry's first wonder drug.

Current Medications

There are many drugs available for treating the symptoms of psychosis (see Table 4.1). Although all of them are associated with a reduction or elimination of symptoms, not all are suitable in every case. Consumers respond to them differently because of variations in body chemistry, metabolism, and other personal characteristics. For reasons that are not clear, antipsychotic medications are generally more successful at treating hallucinations than delusions. Further, they tend to control the positive symptoms of psychosis (bizarre thinking and behavior) more so than the negative symptoms (apathy, withdrawal, and poverty of thought), although there is evidence that the newer medications have a stronger effect on negative symptoms. Most of the medications are thought to work by blocking dopamine receptors in the brain. The half-lives of all the antipsychotic drugs are relatively long (10 to 20 hours), so in many cases they can be taken once daily.

All of the medications produce, or carry the potential for, adverse effects. Although some are more serious than others, they all cause the consumer discomfort, so it is important to evaluate all effects throughout the treatment period. Table 4.2 summarizes the adverse effects of the antipsychotic medications. As defined earlier, sedation refers to the degree of drowsiness caused by the drug. The anticholinergic effects (ACE) include dry mouth, constipation, blurred vision, and urinary retention. Hypotensive effects involve the lowering of one's blood pressure. Extrapyramidal symptoms (EPS) include muscle spasms, stiffness, tremor, reduced movement in the facial muscles, and restlessness. These factors vary predictably between the low- and high-potency medications. High-potency medications are those prescribed in lower milligram dosages (such as risperidone), while low-potency drugs are given in high milligram amounts (such as clozapine). Potency is unrelated, however, to effectiveness.

Two other types of potentially serious adverse effects of the antipsychotic drugs include tardive dyskinesia and neuroleptic malignant syndrome. Defined earlier in this chapter, these are summarized in Table 4.3, along with other types of adverse effects and information about their treatment. Neuroleptic malignant syndrome, although rare, is the most severe because it represents an immediate life-threatening reaction to a medication. Symptoms evolve over a period of 1 to 3 days; the untreated course of the syndrome unfolds over

Table 4.1 Antipsychotic Medications

Drug	Trade Name	Preparation*	Usual Daily Dosage
First-Generation Drugs			
Acetophenazine	Tindal	T	60–120 mg
Chlorpromazine	Thorazine	T, C, S, I	300–800 mg
Chlorprothixene	Taractan	T, S, I	50–400 mg
Cyamemazine	Tercian	T, S, I	25–600 mg
Fluphenazine	Prolixin	T, I	1–40 mg
Haloperidol	Haldol	T, S, P, I	6–20 mg
Loxapine	Loxitane	C, S, I	60–100 mg
Mesoridazine	Serentil	T, S, I	75–300 mg
Molindone	Moban	T, S	50–100 mg
Perphenazine	Trilafon	T, S, I	12–64 mg
Pimozide	Orap	T	2–20 mg
Prochlorperazine	Compazine	T, S, I, Suppository	15–40 mg
Thioridazine	Mellaril	C, S, I	200–600 mg
Thiothixene	Navane	C, S, I	6–30 mg
Trifluoperazine	Stelazine	T	6–20 mg
Triflupromazine	Vesprin	I	100–150 mg
Second-Generation Drugs			
Aripiprazole	Abilify	T, S	10–30 mg
Clozapine	Clozaril	T	400–600 mg
Iloperidone	Fanapt	T	12–24 mg
Lurasidone	Latuda	T	40–80 mg
Olanzapine	Zyprexa	T	10–20 mg
Paliperidone	Invega	T, I	6–12 mg
Quetiapene	Seroquel	T	50–750 mg
Risperidone	Risperdal	T	4–6 mg
Ziprasidone	Geodon	C	40–80 mg

*T - Tablets, C - Capsules, S - Solution, I - Injectable

© 2013 Cengage Learning

2 weeks. Consumers with these symptoms must immediately stop taking the medication and receive medical treatment.

Tardive dyskinesia, also extremely serious, can be a long-term adverse effect of the antipsychotic medications. Although there is some controversy regarding its prevalence, its incidence increases by about 4% per year after 5 years of anti-psychotic medication treatment (Howland, 2011). Tardive dyskinesia tends to

Table 4.2 Adverse Effects of Antipsychotic Medications

Drug	Typical Adverse Effects
Aripiprazole Ziprasidone	Insomnia, headache, agitation, nausea
Chlorpromazine Chlorprothixene Clozapine Quetiapine Thioridazine	Sedation, blurred vision, constipation, urinary impairment, dry skin, weight gain, gastrointestinal discomfort, lowering of blood pressure (orthostatic hypotension, or lightheadedness), salivation
Acetophenazine Haloperidol Perphenazine Thiothixene	Moderate levels of muscle spasms (in tongue, face, neck, and back); restlessness and anxiety
Fluphenazine Molindone Olanzapine Trifluoperazine	Sedation; greater possibility of spasms in tongue, face, neck, and back; restlessness and anxiety; weight gain, orthostatic hypotension
Loxapine Mesoridazine	Sedation, blurred vision, constipation, urinary impairment, dry skin, weight gain, gastrointestinal discomfort, orthostatic hypotension; possibility of spasms (as described above; restlessness and anxiety
Risperidone	Sedation, blurred vision, constipation, urinary impairment, dry skin, weight gain, gastrointestinal discomfort, reduced sex drive
Triflupromazine	Sedation; blurred vision, constipation, urinary impairment, dry skin, weight gain, gastrointestinal discomfort, orthostatic hypotension spasms, restlessness

© 2013 Cengage Learning

Table 4.3 Types of Side Effects of Antipsychotic Medications

Reaction	Features	Treatment
Acute dystonia	Spasms of tongue, face, neck, back; mini-seizures	Antiparkinsonian drug
Akathisia	Restlessness with anxiety or agitation	Reduce dose, change drug, propranolol, benzodiazepines, antiparkinsonian drug
Anticholinergic effects	Blurred vision, confusion, constipation, dry skin, delayed urination, sweating, gastrointestinal discomfort, sexual dysfunction, weight gain	No medical treatment; specific symptoms may be alleviated with diet, exercise, use of fluids
Malignant syndrome	Catatonia, stupor, fever, unstable pulse and blood pressure	Stop medication
Parkinsonism	Motor slowing, retarded facial movement, rigidity, gait disturbance, resting tremor	Antiparkinsonian drug
Tardive dyskinesia	Involuntary rhythmic movement in mouth and face, spastic movements in limbs	No treatment; gradual remission is possible

© 2013 Cengage Learning

occur after long-term use and tends to strike older adults and people with mood disorders. Its symptoms become more apparent when consumers take reduced doses of the responsible medication. The potential for permanent damage continues with higher doses, however, even though the observable symptoms may remit. The prognosis is variable. The more acute dystonias occur early on and strike younger people, males, and people with mood disorders. Anticholinergic (also known as antiparkinsonian) drugs may ameliorate the condition.

We will now describe the antipsychotic medications in more detail by separating them into two categories—the first- and second-generation drugs.

The "First Generation" Antipsychotic Drugs

Once known as the "conventional" antipsychotics, the drugs developed prior to the mid-1980s are associated with symptom improvement for over two-thirds of people who use them. They are also available at a relatively low cost, and many are available in a variety of preparations (tablet, capsule, and injection). The bothersome adverse effects of the first-generation drugs are one of the disadvantages of their use. These effects have a notable influence on adherence and often contribute to a poorer quality of life for persons who experience symptoms of psychosis. Because EPS effects are often more easily managed, the high-potency medications are more frequently prescribed. They can also be administered intramuscularly when a peak blood concentration is reached in as little as a half hour (versus 2 to 3 hours when taken orally). In addition, finding the therapeutic dose occurs more quickly with high-potency drugs.

For the average consumer, there is general agreement that, on average, 300 to 750 mg of chlorpromazine or its equivalent dosage of another medication is needed to achieve a therapeutic effect. In the maintenance phase of treatment, exacerbation of symptoms occurs within a year in about 55% of clients receiving a placebo versus 14% to 21% of those on conventional antipsychotic medications. While this decrease in the risk of relapse supports the use of antipsychotics in the later phases of treatment, there is more debate about appropriate dosing and medication management strategies in these phases. The minimally effective dose to protect 50% of persons with psychosis is typically between 50 to 150 chlorpromazine (CPZ) equivalents (the number of milligrams of chlorpromazine that are equivalent to the dose of the other drug). While higher doses may be needed by 25% of consumers, the final 25% can be maintained on even lower doses.

A maintenance strategy called "continued low-dose" is often utilized with stable persons with long-term psychotic symptoms because of its demonstrated preventive effects on relapse and reduced side effects. This strategy is characterized by dose reductions below the standard (mean ratio of standard- to low-dose is 3.3 to 1). Doran (2008) recommends reducing dosages about 20% every six months during the maintenance phase until a minimum dose is established. "Targeted" or "intermittent" dose strategies, on the other hand, have lost favor. This strategy calls for the administration of medication on some fixed schedule and making changes when the warning signs of relapse first appear. Subsequent relapse rates may be too high to justify widespread use of this strategy. A consensus also exists that oral medication is the first-choice route of administration for adherent consumers because of its ease of administration and respect for one's sense of autonomy. Nevertheless, injectible medications are always an option for reducing the risk of relapse, especially for consumers who have difficulty with adherence.

There are no substantial differences in efficacy among the first-generation antipsychotics. As with all prescriptions, prescribers select a specific medication for a client based on factors including previous treatment response, the desired side-effect profile, the consumer's preference, and the phase of the illness. Advances in pharmacogenetics may help prescribers make more informed decisions about differential responses. Psychiatrists often develop preferences for certain medications. Individualized titration is key in decisions regarding drug choice, dosage, and maintenance strategies. This is one of the most important points for social workers to understand as they collaborate with clients, families, and other providers around medication issues.

Adjunctive and Adverse Effect Medications.   A number of adjunctive medications are used with consumers of first-generation antipsychotic drugs to treat adverse effects and sometimes to enhance the efficacy of the primary medication. These agents do not dramatically affect the consumer's functioning beyond what is experienced with the antipsychotic drug, but modest additive improvements or a reduction of adverse effects can improve the quality of life for some persons. Unfortunately, some of the adjunctive treatments also have adverse effects; thus, decisions regarding their use takes place in a cost–benefit context. Depending on whether the physician is trying to reduce adverse effects or reduce residual symptoms, this might include reducing dosages, changing to a lower potency conventional drug, or moving to a newer antipsychotic. Table 4.4 provides a list of the generic names, brand names, classes of medication, and usual dosages of the common adjunctive and side-effect medications.

Under the category of antiparkinsonian medications, several types of agents are used to reduce the EPS experienced with antipsychotic medications. Trihexyphenidyl, a drug first used to treat Parkinson's disease, is a commonly used anticholinergic (an antagonist of acetylcholine) drug. Benztropine, another anticholinergic, is available in tablet and injectible forms and is effective in controlling tremors, spasms, and rigidity. Because of associated euphoria, anticholinergic drugs can be abused or combined with street drugs for enhanced effect. Diphenhydramine is the primary antihistamine used as an antiparkinsonian drug.

Other medications can also be used to treat EPS. Beta blockers, first used to treat hypertension and cardiovascular problems, have been found effective in treating akathisia. The anti-anxiety benzodiazepine drugs are sometimes used with antipsychotic medications to treat EPS, especially akathisia. In the absence of controlled research, controversy about the use of all antiparkinsonian drugs persists. Areas of uncertainty relate to the appropriateness of their prophylactic use, the appropriate length of treatment, and procedures for withdrawing the medications.

Some research supports the use of lithium as an adjunct to antipsychotic drugs with persons who experience depression, tend to be aggressive or agitated,

Table 4.4 Adjunctive and Side-Effect Medications Used with Antipsychotic Medications

Generic Name	Brand Name	Type of Medication	Usual Daily Dose
alprazolam	Xanax	benzodiazepine	0.5–4 mg
amantadine	Symmetrel	dopaminergic	100–300 mg
benztropine	Cogentin	anticholinergic	0.5–8 mg
biperiden	Akineton	antiparkinsonian	2–20 mg
carbamazepine	Tegretol	anticonvulsant	800–1200 mg
clonazepam	Klonipin	benzodiazepine	0.5–10 mg
clonidine	Catapres	antihypertensive	0.3 mg
diazepam	Valium	benzodiazepine	2–60 mg
diphenhydramine	Benadryl	antihistamine	25–200 mg
ethoprozapine	Parsidol	anticholinergic	50–600 mg
lithium carbonate	Eskalith	antimanic	900–2100 mg
lorazepam	Ativan	benzodiazepine	2–6 mg
metoprolol	Lopressor	antihypertensive	150–300 mg
orphenadrine	Norflex	antiparkinsonian	50–300 mg
procyclidine	Kemadrin	antiparkinsonian	5–20 mg
propranolol	Inderal	antihypertensive	60–120 mg
trihexyphenidyl	Artane	anticholinergic	2–20 mg
valproate	Depakote	anticonvulsant	1200–1500 mg

© 2013 Cengage Learning

or have residual negative symptoms. Anticonvulsant medications have been found in some studies to have usefulness in clients with electroencephlogram (EEG) abnormalities or a coexisting seizure disorder and with hostile, agitated, or violent persons with psychotic symptoms.

The Second-Generation Antipsychotics

The newer antipsychotic medications were initially categorized as "atypical," although they have now been on the market for up to 25 years (see also Table 4.1). Some suggest they do not seem to cause the same levels of EPS that are associated with the earlier medications, although they do include adverse effects. While their precise mechanisms of action are not fully known, the newer medications tend to have broader action on neurotransmitters, apparently impacting serotonin, acetylcholine, and norepinephrine, in addition to subtypes of dopamine receptors. While a major advantage of these medications was thought to be their improved adverse-effect profile for some consumers, a clear disadvantage is their cost. Many can exceed $4000 a year. At 20 mg a day, the first-generation drug haloperidol costs $10 a week compared to $106 a week for clozapine at 400 mg a day.

Clozapine was developed in the 1960s, but only since the publication of an impressive study by Kane and associates (1988) has the drug gained wide recognition and use in this country. They reported positive results for 30% of subjects in reducing both positive and negative symptoms in a relatively short time (2 weeks) when compared to treatment with chlorpromazine. Given the fact that all of the subjects were those for whom a number of trials with older antipsychotics had failed, this was a major step forward. A number of well-controlled studies since then indicate that 40 to 60% of people with schizophrenia who are treated for at least four months with clozapine will have a positive response. One of the highly touted aspects of clozapine is its seemingly superior impact on negative symptoms, although this may be related to the fact that it does not produce EPS, which often mimics negative symptoms.

The typical daily dosage of clozapine is between 300 and 600 mg, with a maximum allowable dose of 900 mg. Common adverse effects and the range of percentages of people who experience them include sedation (20 to 50%), hypersalivation (30%), weight gain (13 to 23%), tachycardia (12 to 25%), and seizures (in 6 to 8% of those on doses above 600 mg). Ironically, weight gain also correlates with a clinical response; those who gain the most weight experience the greatest benefit. Agranulocytosis, a dangerous health condition in which white blood cells become depleted, is said to occur in approximately 1% of cases; thus, mandatory regular blood counts are required. Because agranulocytosis is most likely to occur during the first six months of treatment (up to 80% in the first 18 weeks), consumers in the United States can reduce the frequency of blood tests from weekly to biweekly after six months. Other minor adverse effects include dizziness, constipation, nausea, orthostatic hypotension, and a transient fever during the first few weeks of treatment.

The development of risperidone, marketed in 1994, as a first-line resource—not just for those deemed "treatment resistant" like clozapine—was in part related to the concern about agranulocytosis. Risperidone has shown to be a highly effective medication (Komossa et al., 2011), and it is among the most prescribed antipscyhotic medication as well, due to its comparatively mild side-effect profile. The most effective dose of risperidone for the typical consumer is 4 to 8 mg; larger doses are associated with the same EPS typically associated with the older antipsychotics. A recent systematic review noted the following adverse effects, however: weight gain, sedation, orthostatic hypotension, and decreased sexual drive (Hunter, Kennedy, Song, Gadon, & Irving, 2010). Because risperidone elevates prolactin levels, disturbances in menstruation are possible. A few cases of neuroleptic malignant syndrome (NMS) have been reported, but the risk for consumers developing tardive dyskinesia is unknown.

Olanzapine was approved for use in the United States in 1996. It is similar to clozapine in chemical structure. The drug is believed to have a regionally selective effect on dopamine, affecting those neural pathways which go to the limbic system and frontal cortex. Olanzapine is effective in the acute phase of psychosis when administered in daily doses of 10 to 20 mg. Research on the maintenance phase of long-term psychotic disorders or for those who are deemed treatment-resistant is lacking. Weight gain, sedation, and a decrease in standing blood pressure are the most common adverse effects. The drug is said to produce about 50% fewer motor side effects than the first-generation medications. Its half life of just over 24 hours makes olanzapine amenable to a single daily dose.

Quetiapine, a strong serotonin blocker, was cleared for marketing by the FDA in 1997. It affects the dopamine pathways most associated with psychosis rather than those associated with EPS. Initial double-blind studies demonstrate its effectiveness in reducing positive and negative symptoms, although its impact on negative symptoms is less consistent. It produces anticholinergic side effects but these are said to be relatively mild except for the sedation effect. Quetiapine's short half-life of 7 hours necessitates several doses over the course of a day.

Ziprasidone, FDA approved in 2001, is a potent blocker of a number of serotonin, acetylcholine, and dopamine receptor subtypes, and it may be one of the only antipsychotic drugs to act presynaptically to moderate dopamine release and reuptake, rather than changing post-synaptic binding mechanisms. It is said to be weight-neutral and less sedating than many other medications of its type, although insomnia and agitation have been observed as side effects.

Aripiprazole, FDA approved in 2003, appears to be a potent agonist of D2 receptors, a partial agonist of serotonin a receptors, and an antagonist of serotonin 2a receptors. It, too, has a relatively mild side-effect profile but does produce insomnia, headache, and nausea in some consumers.

All of the second-generation antipsychotic drugs have been compared to each other and to the first-generation drugs in randomized trials that have been systematically reviewed. While they are comparable in effectiveness to the first-generation medications, their side-effect profiles are thought to be much milder (Bhattacharjee & El-sayeh, 2010; Hunter et al., 2010; Srisurapanont et al., 2010.) They are also comparable in effectiveness to each other but demonstrate variable adverse effects with regard to extraparamydal symptoms, anticholinergic effects, weight gain, insomnia, headache, and increased heart rate (Komossa, Rummel-Kluge, Schwarz, et al., 2011; Komossa, Rummel-Kluge, Hunter, et al., 2010; Komossa, Rummel-Kluge & Schmid, et al., 2010; Lobos, et al., 2010).

Psychopharmacology researchers are currently working to understand the effects of antipsychotics on the D3 and D4 receptors and the possible role of the neurotransmitter glutamate in producing psychotic symptoms. At least two trends seem to have special relevance to social work: first, the increasing appreciation of the diversity of people with psychotic symptoms, and second, improvements in the assessment of pharmacotherapy outcomes.

Table 4.5 outlines the effects of other drug interactions with antipsychotic medications. The impact and effectiveness of any medication, psychotropic or otherwise, depends on many factors, including the concomitant use of additional substances. The social worker's educator role is essential in making the client aware of these possible interactions. Although combining drugs is unavoidable in many circumstances, the client must be encouraged to discuss such combinations with the treatment team to evaluate potential risks fully.

Table 4.5 Drug Interactions with Antipsychotic Medications

Drug	Possible Effect
Alcohol	Nervous system depression
Anesthetics	Hypotension
Antacids	Decreased absorption of antipsychotic drug
Anticholinergics	Decreased absorption of antipsychotic drug
Anticoagulants	Increased bleeding time
Antidepressants	Increased blood levels of both drugs
Antihypertensives	Hypotension
Barbiturates	Decreased blood level of antipsychotic drug, increased depressant effect
Beta blockers	Hypotension
Caffeine	Reduced antipsychotic drug effect
Carbamazepine	Decreased blood level of antipsychotic drug
Cigarette smoking	Decreased blood level of antipsychotic drug
Diuretics	Hypotension
Estrogen	Increased blood level of antipsychotic drug
Lithium	Possible additive toxic effect
Narcotics	Decreased ability to experience pain, increased respiratory depression
Sedatives/Hypnotics	Additive depressant effects

© 2013 Cengage Learning

CASE EXAMPLES

Brad was a 30-year-old, single Caucasian male, living alone, who had experienced schizophrenia since the age of 18. Highly delusional, he believed he was a central figure in a religious war taking place between God and Satan. He had frequent visual hallucinations, some of which represented real people in his life while others represented historical religious figures. Atypically, he had few auditory hallucinations. Despite the severity of his symptoms, Brad's level of social functioning was surprisingly strong, indicating some interpersonal skills. He managed his own apartment and finances and worked responsibly as a newspaper carrier that required him to rise at 5:00 a.m. each day. He had few relationships outside his family, but he did make occasional efforts to cultivate friends. Unfortunately, his bizarre ideas interfered with long-term friendships. His mother was his primary support.

Without medication, Brad was a social recluse, staying in his basement apartment for weeks at a time, staring into space and talking to himself. After entering treatment, his behavior did not improve because he refused to take his oral medications. He did not believe that he had any problems. The social worker could not initiate any psychosocial rehabilitation activities because Brad was unconcerned with most routine activities of daily life. However, the worker eventually engaged Brad in treatment through careful partnership building with Brad and his mother. Brad eventually saw the agency physician and agreed to take injectable fluphenazine, which the physician chose because of its effectiveness and the possibility that Brad, with his general distractability, would not take oral medication. The social worker educated Brad's mother about the actions and limitations of the medication and counseled the client on his full range of treatment options.

Brad's symptoms improved dramatically. With the medication, his anxiety level decreased, his preoccupation with delusions abated (but did not disappear), and he more fully attended to his interpersonal needs. Eventually, at Brad's request, and after he seemed well engaged with his treatment team, his medication was changed to include the low-potency oral medication seroquel. The physician believed that the new medication was both effective and relatively safe and that its sedating quality would help control Brad's anxiety and allow him to sleep. He began with a low dose, gradually increasing the dosage until it reached a point of perceived maximum effectiveness. The social worker continued educating Brad and his mother about the expected actions and possible side effects of these medications, and he monitored Brad for evidence of adverse effects.

The drugs worked well for Brad until several years later, when he began complaining that sedation was interfering with his ability to manage his job and social activities. Reluctant to change an effective medication regimen, Brad's doctor agreed to place him on a high-potency medication, risperidone, which would not be as sedating. This eliminated Brad's drowsiness but increased his extrapyramidal symptoms of hand tremor and general anxiety. In fact, he became hypomanic, indicating that the new medication was not as effective in controlling his symptoms as the former one. In the roles of consultant/collaborator and monitor, the social worker helped evaluate and reflect on these effects over time.

Brad reluctantly agreed to go back to the seroquel because the doctor felt that, all things considered, this would be the most effective plan. Although not happy, Brad came to accept that all medications have side effects and the best he could do was make decisions about them based on the overall profile. Interestingly, Brad never agreed that he had a mental disorder, believing instead that the medication was prescribed merely to control his anxiety.

Jackson was a 25-year-old African American male, sentenced to 10 years in prison at the Mechanicsburg Correctional Institute (MCI) for possession of drugs, armed robbery, and assault. MCI was a large state facility with more than 500 inmates. Five years previously Jackson had been diagnosed with schizophrenia and was on the caseload of an Assertive Community Treatment Team at a community services board located several hundred miles away. He was highly symptomatic upon his admission to MCI, stating that he was on a religious mission from God to save humankind and was being "persecuted." Jackson refused to shower for fear of being poisoned by fumes coming from the showerhead, and he complained of odors in the prison that were brainwashing his mind. Jackson was quite loud with his pronouncements and as such alienated the other inmates.

He was immediately referred to the mental health team, consisting of a social worker, psychiatrist, and nurse practitioner.

Shawn was the prison's full-time social worker and organized Jackson's comprehensive assessment, which involved securing his records from the previous mental health agency, conducting a new psychosocial assessment, referring him to the nurse practitioner for a medical examination, and scheduling an appointment with the part-time psychiatrist. The team wanted to help Jackson stabilize not only for his own benefit but because in his psychotic state he was vulnerable to physical abuse from the other inmates. Shawn learned that Jackson had been previously well stabilized on the antipsychotic medication olanzapine, and following his assessment the psychiatrist decided to continue with that same regimen. A problem developed, however, in that Jackson, while a generally pleasant man, adamantly declined to take any medications, believing they were poison. Shawn worked with him over a period of days, patiently encouraging him through counseling to consider accepting the medication, but it became clear that Jackson would not budge on this point.

As an ethical social worker, Shawn was uncomfortable with the idea of forced medication, but in this case he felt that it might be in the client's best interest to be adjudicated for incompetence on this point, since he was being isolated, taunted, and threatened with physical violence by some other inmates. That is, the alternative to Jackson's not taking medication would be either significant physical danger or isolation from the rest of the population. Still, prison policy dictated that forced medications were not permissible at MCI. (Only about 30 inmates there were taking such medications.) There was one prison in the state, however, the Canton Correctional Center (CCC) that was appropriately staffed to house and work with persons who had serious mental illnesses, and it was the only facility where an inmate could be required to take medications. With the approval of the other members of the treatment team and with the full knowledge of Jackson's family, Shawn arranged for the transfer (which took 6 weeks to process). Jackson would serve out his sentence at CCC and, at least for the time being, be mandated to take antipsychotic medications, requiring him to take them in the presence of a nurse on a daily basis or by injection. Jackson perceived his transfer as further persecution, but Shawn felt good about his actions because it got Jackson into a safer environment where he would have an opportunity to receive more comprehensive mental health interventions.

ANTIDEPRESSANT MEDICATIONS

A *mood* can be understood as a pervasive, sustained emotional state that colors an individual's perceptions of the world. There is no truly "normal" mood, and all people deal at times with feelings of depression. Furthermore, even a depression that occurs frequently and interferes to some degree with effectively managing daily tasks may not signify a problem requiring professional intervention. The line between a "normal," or manageable, depression and a situation requiring intervention is not clear and will be defined differently by laypersons and professionals alike. The type of depression that may indicate a need for medications goes beyond mere feelings of sadness in relation to certain conditions of living. It consists of a low mood often accompanied by difficulties in thinking and psychomotor changes (either excessive physical activity from tension or slowed physical movements and reactions). Furthermore, depression can be masked by symptoms of anxiety, agitation, and obsessive thinking. However manifested, significant depression tends to persist and impair one's ability to deal with daily life and relationships.

Symptoms of Depression

A range of symptoms characterize depression. They include a depressed mood or loss of interest in almost all normal activities, which persists for several weeks or more and represents a significant change in the person's usual quality of functioning. Associated symptoms include weight gain or loss, sleep disturbance (insomnia or hypersomnia), psychomotor changes (physical agitation or retardation), decreased energy level, feelings of worthlessness, a general sense of guilt, concentration problems, and recurring thoughts of suicide or death. Although not every person experiencing a major depression will exhibit all of these symptoms, most will exhibit at least five of them. Episodes of depression may occur only once or be recurrent. Before diagnosing depression, the social worker must rule out physiological causes.

SPECIFIC MEDICATIONS

Origins

The story of the development of antidepressant medications is unique from that of some other psychotropic drugs, in that the process was based on at least tentative pharmacological predictions (Kline, 1970). By the mid-1950s it was suspected that agitated and depressed mental states were accompanied or perhaps caused by changes in biogenic amine concentrations in the brain. Low levels of some of these amines appeared to be associated with depression. It was also understood that the inhibition of monoamine oxidase (MAO) in the nervous system enhanced amounts of biogenic amines and thus might stabilize some depressions.

Physicians and medical researchers observed that iproniazid, a drug introduced in 1951 to treat tuberculosis, seemed to have mood-elevating effects on those patients. Based on those findings the drug was studied for its potential in treating mental patients. Researchers in the United States first combined iproniazid with reserpine, an early antipsychotic drug, for their combined effects and found that the former drug seemed to energize experimental animals and thus counter the bothersome sedative effects of the latter. It was eventually determined after further trials that the mood-energizing effect was specific to iproniazid. The drug was found to act as an MAO inhibitor, thus supporting the tentative biological theory of depression.

Already on the market as a treatment for tuberculosis and with the pent-up demand for antidepressant medication, iproniazid was widely prescribed after its antidepressant efficacy was reported in 1957. Approximately 400,000 persons had been treated before iproniazid was withdrawn from the market when reports of negative effects on liver function surfaced. This complication prompted the search for safer and more effective MAO inhibitors and led to the introduction of tranylcypromine, another drug with a different chemical composition but a similar mechanism of action.

Imipramine, another antidepressant drug introduced in 1957, was not an MAO inhibitor. It was the first cyclic antidepressant (so called because of its chemical structure), and it quickly took over as the most widely used such drug in the world. Kuhn (1970) initially developed and tested imipramine in Switzerland as an antipsychotic medication; it was in fact synthesized as a phenothiazine derivative, similar to chlorpromazine in structure. Kuhn had previous research experience in sleep therapy, and it is a testament to his creative intellect that he also tested this new neuroleptic drug as a potential antidepressant. In its trials, the drug demonstrated a strong antidepressant but a weak antipsychotic effect. Its popularity was due to its effectiveness and also its lesser side-effect profile in comparison with the MAO inhibitors. The tricyclic drugs were widely used to treat depression until the introduction of fluoxetine, which will be described later.

Current Medications

Today there are four general types of antidepressant medications: the monoamine oxidase inhibitors, cyclic antidepressants, selective serotonin reuptake inhibitors (SSRIs), and atypical antidepressants. The established medical practice with each is to begin by prescribing a low dose and then build to a level that seems optimally therapeutic, alleviating symptoms while limiting adverse effects. All of the medications require 2 to 6 weeks to produce their antidepressant effect.

Montgomery's (2006) review provides guidelines for drug selection with clients who experience depression. Appropriate drug treatment is likely to shorten the duration of a person's depression as well as its severity. Two-thirds of consumers respond to any of the three classes of medications, but up to one-third of consumers using placebos also demonstrate improvement. While this may seem to be an unimpressive evaluation of drug efficacy, almost half of nonresponders to one drug show positive response to an alternative drug (although it is possible that improvement could be related to a remission of the depression). Further, medication seems to impact the "vegetative" symptoms of depression (including insomnia and appetite loss) more dramatically than the person's level of social functioning.

Most persons who experience an episode of depression will experience a subsequent episode. The risk of recurrence, however, declines with the increasing duration of recovery. On the other hand, the depression-free period is thought to decrease with each subsequent episode. Approximately 20% of those who use cyclic antidepressants will experience a relapse within six months, even if they are taking medications. Over a 5-year period, 60% of consumers of antidepressant medication will experience a recurrence of depression, although it may be mild.

There have been few studies on the preventive potential for antidepressant medications in the recurrence of depressive episodes, so no statements can be made about this issue with any confidence. It is difficult to differentiate the effects of medication in the context of "natural" remission, particularly because the medications require time to take effect. With so much individual variation among depressed persons, one's improvement or decompensation with or without medication may be due to internal as well as drug-related factors. Most physicians will tend to lower doses of any of the antidepressants if a client has been symptom-free for 8 months or longer. A dose from the low end of the average therapeutic range may be continued as a preventive intervention.

Each of the first two classes of medication described below has a low therapeutic index, which means that there is not a great difference between the amounts required for therapeutic effect and overdose. This is a particular problem for physicians because these drugs are often prescribed for clients who exhibit self-destructive tendencies and who may use the drugs in suicidal gestures.

The MAO Inhibitors

The MAO inhibitors (see Table 4.6) are effective medications, significantly relieving symptoms of depression in 52 to 70% of consumers (Bainbridge, Page, & Ruscin, 2008). At present the primary MAO medications marketed in the United States are phenylzine, tranylcypromine, and selegiline. Phenylzine has been studied more extensively. Structurally different from the antidepressant medications that have followed them, the monoamine oxidase drugs inhibit action on enzymes that metabolize norepinephrine and serotonin. The medications also have an inhibitory effect on dopamine. In addition to their antidepressant effects, these drugs have utility in treating panic and other anxiety symptoms, as well as the types of depression that feature somatic and other anxiety symptoms. Tranylcypromine is structurally related to amphetamine and has a stimulant effect on some persons. The MAO inhibitors are often effective with some clients who do not respond to the other antidepressant medications and are sometimes the drug of choice for older adults who tend to have an excess of MAO in their nervous systems.

Table 4.6 Monoamine Oxidase Inhibitors

Drug	Trade Name	Usual Daily Dose
Isocarboxazid	Marplan	45–90 mg
Moclobemide	Manerix	150–600 mg
Phenylzine	Nardil	10–30 mg
Selegiline	Eldepril, L-Deprenyl	10 mg, 12mg/24 hrs (patch)
Tranylcypromine	Parnate	10–30 mg

© 2013 Cengage Learning

The MAO inhibitors are not usually prescribed first because consumers must observe extensive dietary restrictions to avoid potentially serious adverse reactions. The MAO inhibitors react with foods rich in the amino acid derivative tyramine, prompting a hypertensive condition that can be fatal. Many popular foods including cheeses, wines, and some meats contain tyramine. Table 4.7 includes a list of their predictable side effects, and Table 4.8 presents many of the foods to be avoided when one takes MAO inhibitors. Because the consumer

Table 4.7 Side Effects of MAO Inhibitors

Common	Less Common
Constipation	Agitation
Dizziness	Blurred vision
Dry mouth	Headache
Hypotension	Hypertension
Insomnia	Hypomania
Nausea	Impaired muscle coordination
Sexual difficulties	Muscle cramps
Skin reaction	
Weakness	
Weight gain	

© 2013 Cengage Learning

Table 4.8 Foods and Drugs to be Avoided When Taking MAO Inhibitors

Foods	Drugs
Aged cheeses	Amphetamines and other stimulants
Banana skins	Cocaine
Beer	Decongestants
Broad-bean pods	Dental anesthetics containing epinephrine
Caffeinated beverages	Fluoxetine
Canned figs	L-Dopa
Chocolate	Meperidene
Non-fresh, fermented, or preserved fish, liver, and meats	
Pickled herring, sardines, and anchovies	
Red wine	
Yeast extracts	
Yogurt and sour cream	

© 2013 Cengage Learning

must exercise a significant amount of discipline to avoid all of these foods consistently, some people do not wish to take MAO inhibitors or are not good risks for taking them. The social worker should engage in problem-solving and explore the cost–benefit ratio with clients using these medications, reviewing dietary habits regularly, making sure the client keeps a written record of foods to be avoided, and quickly referring the client to a prescriber if the client, knowingly or by accident, consumes any prohibited foods.

During the 1980s it was discovered that there are two types of MAO inhibitors, type A (which breaks down norepinephrine and serotonin) and type B (which breaks down dopamine) and that medications that selectively impact type B would not produce the side effect of tyramine deamination. The two newest MAO inhibitors in the United States are selective and thus may not produce the potentially severe adverse effects described above when taken in small doses. One of these is meclobemide and the other is selegiline, the latter of which is available as a tablet and also as a small patch that adheres to the skin. These medications, being rather new, are more expensive than the older products, but they represent a safer and effective alternative to the older MAO inhibitors.

In addition to dietary precautions, care must be taken in combining the MAO inhibitors with other drugs. Table 4.9 includes a list of the drugs most commonly taken with MAO inhibitors. In the role of educator, it may be important for the social worker to ensure that the consumer of MAO drugs has this information in writing.

Cyclic Antidepressants

The cyclic drugs, so named because of the number of "rings" in their chemical structures, were the most commonly prescribed antidepressants from the late

Table 4.9 Drug Interactions with SSRI Antidepressants and MAO Inhibitors

Drug	Effect
Alcohol	Hypertensive crisis
Antiasthmatic drugs	Hypertensive crisis
Antihistamines	Hypertensive crisis
Antihypertensive drugs	Hypertensive crisis
Anesthetics with epinephrine	Hypertensive crisis
Cyclic antidepressants	Nausea, confusion, anxiety, hyperthermia, hypotension
Diuretics	Hypertensive crisis
Fluoxetine	Nausea, confusion, anxiety, hyperthermia, hypotension
Sinus, cold, hay fever medications	Hypertensive crisis
Stimulants	Hypertensive crisis

1950s through the 1980s. The first antidepressant of this class was imipramine. A meta-analysis (Storosum et al., 2001) indicated that these medications produce a therapeutically significant response in 46% of consumers.

While the mechanism of action for these drugs is not clear, they are believed to work by blocking the reuptake of norepinephrine and serotonin. Their metabolites also have antidepressant action. Unlike the antipsychotic medications, daily dosage does not vary much among these drugs and thus does not distinguish them. Only protriptyline is manufactured in a comparatively small dose, but it does not have different side effects than the others in its class. All the cyclic medications have relatively long half-lives, so they can be prescribed in once-daily doses. Most produce significant anticholinergic effects. These effects, described in the section on antipsychotic drugs, account for most of the unpleasant effects of the medications. Many consumers develop tolerance to certain of these adverse effects but not to the therapeutic effects. The drugs, described in Table 4.10, all of which have a demonstrated effectiveness, require 2 to 6 weeks to achieve therapeutic impact. The anticholinergic effects, unfortunately, can begin at the time of first administration. The drugs can also have an immediate sedative effect which, while troubling to some consumers, may provide relief to depressed persons with insomnia.

The cyclic antidepressants are generally initiated for a consumer at dosage levels below those considered optimal. The dose is rather rapidly increased, however, for a period of 1 to 2 weeks until the usual therapeutic range is achieved. Because their optimal therapeutic effect may not occur for 2 to 6 weeks, a prescriber may ask the client to continue with a particular regimen for 6 weeks before either settling at that level or making another adjustment. Some clients

Table 4.10 Cyclic Antidepressants

Drug	Trade Name	Preparation*	Dosage	Sedation	ACE
Amitriptyline	Elavil, Endep	T, I	100–300 mg	High	Low
Amoxapine	Asendin	T	200–400 mg	Low	Low
Clomipramine	Anafranil	C	150–200 mg	High	High
Desipramine	Norpramin	T, C	150–300 mg	Low	Low
Doxepin	Adapin, Sinequan	C, I	100–200 mg	High	Moderate
Imipramine	Tofranil	T, C, I	150–300 mg	Medium	Moderate
Maprotilene	Ludiomil	C	150–250 mg	Medium	Low
Nortriptyline	Aventyl, Pamelor	C, I	75–150 mg	Low	Low
Protriptyline	Vivactil	T	15–40 mg	Low	High
Trimipramine	Surmontil	C	150–300 mg	High	Moderate

*T - Tablets, C - Capsules, I - Injectable

may benefit from higher-than-usual dose levels, but it is also possible that another drug will be initiated as a replacement at that point.

Table 4.11 also summarizes the adverse effects of the cyclic antidepressants. Although these effects tend to be strongest in the first few hours after a person takes the medication and some remit completely within a few weeks, many persist. The side-effect profiles of these medications vary. For example, amoxapine, desipramine, and nortriptyline are all comparatively low in both sedation and ACEs. One might assume, on this basis, that these drugs would be prescribed more frequently than the other medications. However, the medications are not equally effective in reducing symptoms in all consumers. Therefore, a medication with positive therapeutic benefit may be prescribed, even if it has a greater amount of adverse effects. Remember, too, that physicians tend to prescribe certain medications with which they have a history of success. If necessary, however, prescribers will usually experiment with several medications until they find one with a high therapeutic benefit. Because the medications can be taken once daily, it is often desirable for clients to take the medication at night. Although they will be asleep when the side effects most prominently appear, the medication will remain in their systems the entire next day.

Table 4.11 Drug Interactions with Cyclic Antidepressants

Drug	Possible Effect
Alcohol	Sedation, decreased antidepressant blood level
Amphetamines	Increased antidepressant blood level
Antihistamines	Sedation, additive anticholinergic effects
Antiparkinsonians	Additive anticholinergic effects
Antipsychotics (all)	Sedation
Antipsychotics (low potency)	Hypotension, additive
Antispasmodics	Additive anticholinergic effects
Beta-blockers	Hypotension
Carbamazepine	Decreased antidepressant blood level
Cigarette smoking	Decreased antidepressant blood level
Dilantin	Decreased antidepressant blood level
Diuretics	Hypotension
Fluoxetine	Decreased antidepressant blood level
Oral contraceptives	Increased antidepressant blood level
Phenobarbitol	Decreased antidepressant blood level
Thyroid hormones	Increased antidepressant blood level
Sedatives	Increased sedation, decreased antidepressant blood level

Decisions about discontinuing an antidepressant medication should be made by the client in consultation with the prescriber and social worker, as relevant to the setting. In every case the drug should be tapered gradually, over a period of 2 to 4 weeks. An abrupt discontinuation may cause short-term but distressing effects of anxiety, insomnia, and a rebound depression, particularly with the cyclic antidepressants. Other possible withdrawal symptoms include cardiac arrhythmias, nausea, anorexia, diarrhea, sweating, muscle soreness, headache, chills, fatigue, anxiety, and insomnia.

Table 4.11 lists possible adverse drug interactions in people taking cyclic antidepressant medications with other substances. All these effects are negative in that they either interfere with the targeted amount of medication that reaches clients' bloodstreams or else may cause clients to be unenthusiastic about taking their medications. Besides providing face-to-face education, the social worker should make sure that the client receives a written list of these interactions. The social worker might also help the client monitor certain routine practices, such as eating habits, that may interfere with the drug's effectiveness. For example, some clients experience stomach distress if they do not take their medication with meals.

The Serotonin Reuptake Inhibitors and Other New Drugs

A variety of drugs from a class known as the selective serotonin reuptake inhibitors (SSRIs), have been available in the United States since 1987 (see Table 4.12). Fluoxetine was the first of these. The fact that these drugs are selective for serotonin adds to the uncertainty about the relevant actions of antidepressant drugs on those neurotransmitters that correlate with depression. The actions of these drugs may include the stimulation of certain neurotransmitter building blocks in the cell body in ways that are not yet understood. The SSRIs have become standard medications within this drug category. The medications are more potent than the cyclic drugs and also have a long half-life. Two of their major attractions are their reduced overdose potential and the fact that they have fewer adverse effects than other antidepressant groups. Some are used to treat symptoms of anxiety as well (see that section in this chapter).

Table 4.12 SSRI Antidepressants

Drug (Tablets)	Trade Name	Usual Daily Dosage
Citaprolam	Celexa	20–40 mg
Escitalopram	Lexapro, Sarafem	10–20 mg
Fluoxetine	Prozac	20–40 mg
Fluvoxamine	Luvox	50–300 mg
Paroxetine	Paxil	10–60 mg
Sertraline	Zoloft	50–200 mg

© 2013 Cengage Learning

The SSRI medications demonstrate effectiveness rates of 60 to 70% across studies. Some of the serotonin–reuptake inhibitors differ chemically from each other as well as from bupropion. Much of their appeal comes from their side-effect profiles (see Table 4.14). Markedly less characterized by anticholinergic activity than other antidepressants, these drugs are often more agreeable to clients. Additionally, their overdose potential is much lower than that of other antidepressant drugs. Their potency varies somewhat, particularly that of fluoxetine and paroxetine, which are given in relatively low milligram doses. Unlike MAO inhibitors and cyclic antidepressants, the SSRIs do not need to be gradually introduced to the consumer; they can be initiated at a therapeutic dose, although this may be adjusted upward or downward by the physician, depending on the client's response.

There is another group of newer antidepressant medications that do not fit neatly into any category (Table 4.13). While different from each other in chemical structure, they all act on neurotransmitter systems in addition to serotonin. Venlafaxine, mirtazepine, nefazodone, and duloxetine are all known to act similarly on norepinephrine and are thus sometimes called "serotonin-norepinephrine reuptake inhibitors." It is hypothesized that both of these neurotransmitters have an impact on mood. Bupropion is believed to act on norepinephrine and dopamine. These are equal to the other antidepressants in effectiveness and again tend to differ in side-effect profiles from each other and from other drugs.

Table 4.14 outlines the adverse effects of the serotonin–reuptake inhibitors and other new drugs, and although the range of these effects overlap with the other antidepressant medications already discussed, the ACEs of the newer drugs are much less pronounced. Common side effects include anxiety, weight loss, headache, and gastrointestinal discomfort, but many consumers tolerate these without serious complaint. The most common side effects of bupropion are headaches, restlessness, and nausea. Although agitation and irritability may also occur, this medication is not associated with hypotension, weight gain, drowsiness, and ACEs. There is a possibility of seizures with very high doses. Table 4.15 includes a short list of drug interactions with the atypical antidepressants, demonstrating again that using drugs in combination tends to inhibit the effect that each drug might have by itself and may in fact produce additional unpleasant or even dangerous effects.

Table 4.13 Atypical Antidepressants

Drug (Tablets)	Trade Name	Usual Daily Dosage
Bupropion	Wellbutrin, Zyban	200–400 mg
Duloxetine	Cymbalta	40–60 mg
Mirtazepine	Remeron	15–45 mg
Nefazodone	Serzone	200–600 mg
Trazodone	Desyrel	150–400 mg
Venlafaxine	Effexor	150–375 mg

© 2013 Cengage Learning

Table 4.14 Side Effects of Serotonin-Reuptake Inhibitors and Related Drugs

Common	Less Common
Anxiety and restlessness	Diarrhea
Constipation	Dizziness
Dry mouth	Excessive sweating
Headache	Memory impairment
Nausea and vomiting	Sexual dysfunction (impotence)
Sedation	Weight loss

© 2013 Cengage Learning

Table 4.15 Drug Interactions with SSRI Drugs

Drug	Effect
Benzodiazepines	Increases effect
Buspirone	Decreases effect
Carbamazepine	Changes levels unpredictably
Cyclic antidepressants	Increases effect
Lithium	Changes levels unpredictably
L-Tryptophan	Toxic effect

© 2013 Cengage Learning

There is some evidence that atypical depressions, or those characterized by mood reactivity with transient remissions, may be particularly responsive to the MAO inhibitors. Delusional symptoms in depression may require a combination of antipsychotic and antidepressant medication for successful treatment. For treatment-resistant consumers, lithium may potentiate the antidepressant effect of a medication although it is not generally effective as a maintenance drug and, for persons with bipolar disorder, may initiate a manic episode (Sussman et al., 2012).

CASE EXAMPLES

Sara is a social worker employed as a case manager at a hospital-affiliated medical agency known as Care Connections for Children. Her agency accepts referrals from physicians to provide active and ongoing monitoring and social services interventions for children and adolescents with multiple health concerns. One of Sara's clients was Albert, a 14-year-old Rwandan male who had suffered a severe spinal cord injury following a car accident at age 10. Albert experienced head trauma that affected his learning potential, and he was tragically rendered a quadriplegic, limited to minimal use of his hands. Secondary to his injury, Albert experienced a disorder that produced brittle bones. It was Sara's responsibility to facilitate the family's attendance at their frequent appointments with a variety of doctors and to help them manage the stresses of raising a physically and mentally impaired child. The family did not have many financial or support resources available to them. Albert had been born when his mother was 14, and she had developed a substance abuse problem since the accident. Albert's stepfather had spent time in jail on several occasions. Sara once had to involve Child Protective Services for the parents' noncompliance with Albert's health care plan.

Albert was depressed and intermittently suicidal because of his physical condition and loneliness and the tensions around the house (which included 4- and 7-year-old stepsiblings). He was prescribed an SSRI antidepressant to help with his mood, and, interestingly, he was also prescribed gabapentin for relief of physical pain. The latter medication is generally used as a psychotropic drug to treat unstable moods and anxiety, but it also works as a pain reliever in some persons. Sara monitored Albert's subjective responses to these medications, as well as reports from his parents so that she could report them to the prescriber. As a monitor and educator, it was Sara's responsibility to make sure the family understood the rationale for, and importance of, Albert's medications and to answer their questions about the medications when she could. Because of the complex medical problems faced by her client, Sara carried medical reference books with her and often referred her clients to their physicians for more information.

Jinny was an 86-year-old married Caucasian female who had experienced Alzheimer's disease for almost 10 years. She lived in a nursing care facility and had an extremely poor short-term memory. Related to the organic brain disorder, the most common observable symptoms other than memory loss for Alzheimer's disease are apathy, agitation and aggression, anxiety and depression; 10 to 20% of such persons qualify for a diagnosis of a major depressive disorder (Henry, Rendell, Scicluna, Jackson, & Phillips, 2009). As her memory declined, Jinny became increasingly agitated and depressed. As part of her medication regimen, Jinny was prescribed risperidone, an antipsychotic drug that in small doses reduces agitation, and a moderate dose of sertraline for her depression. Her social worker Eli met regularly with the family to assure them that, according to the medical doctor, Jinny's "unpleasant" mood states were related to her dementia rather than a focused anger toward them. Eli shared literature with the family that described how such anger was often directed at the people closest to a person with dementia. Jinny continued on these medications until her level of functioning worsened to the point that she was mostly bedridden and unaware of her surroundings.

MOOD-STABILIZING MEDICATIONS

Bipolar disorder is a disorder of mood in which, over time, a person experiences one or more manic episodes, usually accompanied by one or more major depressive episodes (American Psychiatric Association, 2000). The disorder is associated with chemical imbalances in the nervous system; thus, mood-stabilizing medica-tions are almost always utilized as a major (and sometimes only) means of inter-vention. There are two types of bipolar disorder: Bipolar I disorder is characterized by one or more manic episodes, usually accompanied by a major depressive episode. Bipolar II disorder is characterized by one or more major depressive episodes accompanied by at least one hypomanic episode. For both types of the disorder, the duration between episodes tends to decrease as further cycles occur (Geller et al., 2008).

A person with bipolar I disorder does not necessarily swing from mania to depression with equal frequency. Fifty percent of persons with the disorder move through alternating manic and depressed cycles. A majority of persons (70 to 90%) return to a stable mood and level of social and occupational func-tioning between mood episodes. Approximately 10% experience "rapid cycling," which means that over a 12-month period they will experience four or more manic or depressive cycles. Additionally, 40% have a "mixed" type of the disor-der, in which a prolonged depressive episode features bursts of mania, as brief as a few hours in duration. This type is associated with a poorer prognosis. Although the antidepressant medications work toward elevating a low mood into the nor-mal range and although this action may seem synonymous with that of the "mood-stabilizing" medications, the actions of the latter are not the same. Mood-stabilizing medications are unique in that they also lower mood levels from a manic state.

The symptoms of depression described earlier characterize the depressive phase of bipolar disorder. What follows is a description of the symptoms of mania and a description of how mood-stabilizing drugs can help to stabilize them.

Symptoms of Mania

A *manic episode* is a distinct period in which a person's predominant mood is elevated, expansive, or irritable to a degree that there is serious impairment in occupational and social functioning. Manic episodes may be characterized by any of the following symptoms (at least three must be present): unrealis-tically inflated self-esteem, a decreased need for sleep, pressured speech, rac-ing thoughts, distractibility, an increase in unrealistic goal-directed activity, and involvement in activities that have a potential for painful consequences. Manic episodes are rapid in onset and may persist for a few days up to several months. Symptoms of major depression were described earlier in this chapter.

There are two types of bipolar disorder (APA, 2000). *Bipolar I disorder* is char-acterized by one or more manic episodes, usually accompanied by a major depressive episode. *Bipolar II disorder* is characterized by one or more major depressive episodes accompanied by at least one hypomanic episode. In other words, bipolar I disorder features a mix of mood episodes, whereas in bipolar II disorder depressive episodes predominate.

SPECIFIC MEDICATIONS

Origins

Lithium is the oldest effective medication used to treat bipolar disorder (Johnson, 1984). Discovered as an element in Sweden in 1817, the substance was found to be highly soluble in uric acid. Its initial medical uses (beginning in 1859) were to treat bladder stones and gout (an excess of uric acid in the joints). Coincidentally, a "uric acid diathesis" theory of medical and emotional illness became widely accepted in the United States and Europe by the 1870s. A variety of ailments such as arthritis and rheumatism were treated with lithium and other alkaline waters because these were believed to clear one's system of harmful uric acid.

The first report of lithium being used to treat depression appeared in 1886. Hydropathic spas became popular as well, and, at the turn of the century, wealthy patrons traveled to resorts to bathe in mineral waters claimed to possess quantities of lithium. By 1900 a variety of lithium products (waters, salts, tablets, and even beer) were marketed for the treatment of various physical and nervous disorders. These products fell out of public favor by 1910, after the cardiac side effects of lithium were noted and the uric acid diathesis began to be discounted. Still, established ideas die hard, and, in the 1920s a lithium bromide was developed as a sedative.

In the late 1940s an Australian physician named John Cade was investigating the organic causes of mental disorders. He was comparing the urine toxicity levels of persons with various disorders by injecting guinea pigs with the substance, and he discovered that the urine of manic–depressive persons was the most toxic. In order to refine his experiments (because the differences in toxicity were small), he searched for a substance that would make uric acid more soluble and chanced upon lithium. The guinea pigs injected with the solution containing lithium became markedly lethargic. Cade correctly hypothesized that lithium might thus be effective in stabilizing persons with mania, but initially for the wrong reason. (His guinea pigs had likely experienced toxic reactions to high lithium levels.) Still, he conducted successful lithium trials with 10 human subjects, and physicians in Europe began using lithium for treating bipolar disorder. It was not approved for use in the United States until 1970, partly because of the negative impact of the hypertension and deaths experienced by some persons who used a salt substitute containing lithium during the 1940s and 1950s. As American medical researchers argued for the safety of the controlled distribution of lithium, John Talbot in 1950 developed the important practice of monitoring lithium levels.

Current Medications

The Food and Drug Administration (FDA) has approved a number of medications for the treatment of bipolar disorder (see Table 4.16). Most prescribers recommend that clients take medication even after their moods stabilize to reduce the risk of recurrence of another mood episode. Generally a single mood-stabilizing

Table 4.16 Mood-Stabilizing Medications

Drug	Trade Name	Preparation*	Usual Daily Dosage
Lithium Carbonate	Lithium	C, I	900–2100 mg
	Lithobid	T	900–2100 mg
	Eskalith	C, T	900–2100 mb
	Lithium Citrate	I	8mEq (mg equivalents per 5 ml)
	Lithonate	C	900–2100 mg
	Lithotabs, Lithane	T	900–2100 mg
Carbamazepine	Tegretol	T, I	400–1600 mg
Divalproex sodium	Depakote,	T, C, S	1200–1500 mg
Gabapentin	Neurontin	C	1800–3600 mg
Lamotrigine	Lamictal	T	100–400 mg
Oxcarbazepine	Trileptal	T, S	600–2400 mg
Topiramate	Topamax	T, C	200–400

*T - Tablets, C - Capsules, I- Injectable, S – Syrup

© 2013 Cengage Learning

drug is not effective indefinitely, and a combination of medications is often used (Hamrin & Pachler, 2007). It must be emphasized that while older adults may benefit from the same medications as younger populations, they are more susceptible to adverse effects (Young, 2005).

Lithium

Lithium is relatively inexpensive because it occurs naturally. With a shorter half-life than the antipsychotic and antidepressant drugs, it must be taken more than once per day (unless in time-release form) to maintain a consistent blood level. Lithium takes 2 or more weeks to establish a therapeutic effect. Table 4.16 indicates the drug's availability in various preparations and dosage levels. After a consumer's manic episode recedes, lithium (or another mood-stabilizing medication) must still be taken as a prophylactic agent to guard against recurrence. Frequently, consumers want to terminate the medication once they feel normal again. Stopping medication can put the individual with bipolar disorder at risk for the recurrence of a manic episode, however, because the mood swings are unpredictable and alternate with long periods of normal mood.

Lithium is the best studied of the mood-stabilizing drugs. Pooled response rates from double-blind studies of lithium indicate significant improvement in 70% of consumers. In these studies, improvement is defined as a sufficient remission of symptoms to permit the client's attending to activities of daily living. Lithium reduces manic symptoms by 50% in 50% of clients after 3 weeks of treatment; within 2 weeks, 20% of clients are completely free of symptoms

(Grof & Muller-Oerlinghausen, 2009). It is effective for stabilizing both manic and depressive episodes in bipolar disorder, although it is more effective for treating manic than mixed or rapid cycling episodes (Huang, Lei, & El-Mailach, 2007). As a maintenance drug, lithium has been shown in a meta-analysis to be effective in preventing all types of relapses, but again, it is most effective with manic relapses (Geddes et al., 2004). Lithium also has a positive effect on clients' suicidal ideation. A meta-analysis documented an 80% decrease in such episodes for consumers who have used the drug for 18 months (Baldessarini et al., 2006). Still, lithium is less effective at preventing relapses after about 5 years of use (Coryell, 2009). Medications from other classes may be used in conjunction with lithium, particularly to treat acute psychosis or agitation (as described below).

Like other drugs, lithium is only effective as long as a steady blood level of the drug is maintained. Because the blood level equals the amount in the nervous system, lithium levels are more easily monitored than those of most other medications. People who take this drug must become accustomed to getting blood drawn regularly. The difference between therapeutic and toxic levels is narrow, so monitoring lithium is particularly important. In the absence of adverse effects, routine monitoring of lithium levels can be performed monthly for 4 to 6 months. For the remainder of the first year, these measures can be obtained every 2 to 4 months and every 6 months thereafter. A measurement of 1.0 to 1.5 mEg (milligram equivalents per liter of plasma fluid) is considered therapeutic. At lower levels, the medication has no effect, and the physician may increase the dosage. Levels higher than this amount indicate toxicity, requiring at least a temporary tapering of the medicine or a lowering of the prescribed dose.

When a consumer is asked to get a lithium blood level drawn, a prescriber's order is required, and the person should not take any lithium for 12 hours prior to the test. Taking it would cause a misleading elevation in the blood level at the time of the test. Prescribers usually ask clients to have their blood drawn in the morning before taking that day's first dose. This way their schedule of usage will not be disrupted.

After the remission of acute symptoms and a 6- to 12-week continuation stage, lithium treatment of acute mania may be gradually tapered. Still, physicians usually recommend permanent prophylactic use. Maintenance blood levels of lithium range from .6 to 1.2 mEq and can be maintained with doses of 300 mg 3 or 4 times daily. Still, its use does not preclude the possibility of a recurrence of mania. Clients experience 50% fewer recurrences of mania with the drug compared to a placebo (Burgess et al., 2009). A 5-year study of clients who had been symptom-free for 2 years indicated an 83% probability against relapse after 1 year, 52% after 3 years, and 37% after 5 years (Peselow et al., 1994). Combination treatments of lithium and other medications (antidepressant, antipsychotic, and anticonvulsant drugs) produce an improved long-range outcome, but it is clear that bipolar disorder cannot be fully stabilized with lithium or any other drug.

Relapse in bipolar disorder is due in part to the person's biology but other factors include adverse life events, the nature of one's social supports, and participation in psychotherapy (Altman et al., 2006). The social work roles of counselor, monitor, and educator are crucial in alerting clients to the possibility of relapse, even with long periods of normal functioning, and assessing any symptoms that may signal its recurrence. Clients should be informed that one of the most common reasons for relapse is discontinuing an effective medication regimen against medical advice.

Lithium should not be prescribed for women during pregnancy because it is associated with fetal heart problems. During the first trimester there is a potential for birth defects, and, if used in the late stages of pregnancy, the infant may be born with lithium toxicity. Lithium is excreted in breast milk and thus should not be used by women while breast-feeding. Further, a pregnant woman's blood volume increases during pregnancy, making the monitoring of lithium levels difficult.

Lithium seems to have antiaggression effects on children and adolescents. It is not advised for children under age 8, as its effects on them have not been adequately studied. When used by older children and adolescents, who have naturally high clearance rates, a higher dose may be required to achieve a therapeutic effect. Adolescents appear to tolerate long-term lithium treatment well, but there are concerns about its accumulation in bone tissue and its effect on thyroid and kidney function.

Their decreased kidney clearance rates put older adults at a higher risk for toxic blood levels. Older adults are particularly susceptible to the side effects of any drug, particularly cardiac effects. They may be prescribed a smaller dose of lithium because they metabolize it more slowly but also to guard against its side effect of lowering the heart rate.

Most of the common side effects of lithium, listed in Table 4.17, are thought to be transient and benign. However, they need to be carefully monitored, particularly with the introduction of the medication or any dosage changes, because serious symptoms may develop. Thirst and weight gain are often experienced; other effects are less common. The potentially serious side effects listed in the table may result from the toxic effects of a buildup of lithium in the blood. Table 4.18 includes a listing of symptoms associated with mild, moderate, and

Table 4.17 Side Effects of Lithium Carbonate

Common	Less Common	Potentially Serious (Toxic)
Confusion	Acne	Diarrhea (severe)
Diarrhea	Edema (swelling)	Dizziness
Fatigue/lethargy	Hair loss	Drowsiness (severe)
Hand tremors		Muscle weakness
Increased thirst		Nausea/vomiting (severe)
Increased urination		Slurred speech
Muscle weakness		Marked tremors/twitching
Nausea/vomiting		Spastic movements in limbs or face muscles
Weight gain		

severe toxicity. The social worker should assume that all side effects are serious and should arrange for a client's evaluation by a health care professional. Severe toxicity can be deadly, implying that a dangerous overdose can also occur with lithium. When lithium toxicity is suspected, the social worker should advise the client to discontinue the medication immediately, contact a physician or other provider, and begin ingesting large amounts of fluids to reduce the lithium blood level. The client should be taken to an emergency room. Medical staff will complete a physical examination, including a lithium level, and initiate hydration and electrolyte balancing interventions. Hemodialysis, or the extraction of lithium with an "artificial kidney," may be initiated and be repeated until lithium levels reach a stable range.

Table 4.19 lists drug interactions between lithium and other substances. It is a given that any effect that increases the lithium blood level is potentially serious

Table 4.18 Signs of Lithium Toxicity

Mild/Moderate (1.5–2.0 mEq per L*)	Moderate/Severe (2.0–2.5 mEq per L)	Severe (Over 2.5 mEq per L)
GASTROINTESTINAL		
Abdominal pain (persistent/severe)	Anorexia	Coma
Dry mouth	Decreased urination	Kidney failure
Nausea or vomiting (persistent)		
NEUROLOGICAL		
Dizziness (severe)	Blurred vision	
Drowsiness (severe)	Confusion (severe)	
Lethargy or excitement (severe)	Convulsions	
Marked tremors or twitching	Coordination impairment	
Muscle weakness (severe)	Delirium	
Slurred speech	EEG (electroencephalogram) changes	
Fainting		
Hyperactive muscle reflexes		
Spastic movements in limbs, face		
Stupor		
CIRCULATORY		
Arrhythmia (irregular heartbeat)		
Lowered blood pressure		

*Milligram equivalents per liter

Adapted from "Psychopharmacology and Electroconvulsive Therapy," by J. M. Silver, M. D. & S. C. Yudofsky. In J. A. Talbott, R. E. Hales, & S. C. Yudofsky (Eds.), The American Psychiatric Press Textbook of Psychiatry, 2nd Edition, p. 970. Copyright ©1994 American Psychiatric Association Press, Used with permission.

Table 4.19 Drug Interactions with Mood-Stabilizing Medications

Drug	Effect
LITHIUM	
Antibiotics	Increased toxicity
Antidepressants	Possible mania, tremors
Anti-inflammatory drugs	Increased toxicity
Antipsychotic drugs	Increased toxicity
Cardiovascular drugs	Possible toxicity
Diuretics	Increased excretion
Loop/distal-tube diuretics	Increased concentration
CARBAMAZEPINE	
Benzodiazepines	Decreased effect
Cyclic antidepressants	Decreased effect
Dilantin	Unpredictable
Valproic acid	Decreased effect
VALPROIC ACID	
Alcohol, other depressants	Increased effect
Antidepressants	Increased effect
Aspirin	Increased anticoagulance
LAMOTRIGINE	
Oral contraceptives	Reduces lamotrigine levels
Phenobarbital	Decreases levels
Phenotyn	Decreases levels
Primidon	Decreases levels
Valproic acid	Increases blood levels, side effects

because such an increase can produce a toxic effect. Note that antidepressants used with lithium may prompt a manic phase, which is why antidepressants should not usually be taken with lithium. If the client has bipolar II disorder, lithium may be considered as a means of enhancing the effect of the antidepressant.

Anticonvulsant Medications

Another class of medications, the anticonvulsants, is also effective for the treatment of bipolar disorder. Three of these are FDA-approved for bipolar disorder: valproate, carbamazepine, and lamotrigine (Melvin et al., 2008). Others include gabapentin, topiramate, and oxcarbazepine. These medications offer an advantage over lithium in that they usually begin to stabilize a person's mood in 2 to

5 days. These drugs are equal to, but not more effective than, lithium in preventing relapses (Hirschowitz, Kolevzon, & Garakani, 2010).

The antimanic effect of carbamazepine was discovered in the 1960s, when it was observed that the drug improved mood in many persons who used it for seizure control. Carbamazepine, a potent blocker of norepinephrine reuptake, inhibits the repetitive firing of sodium channel impulses by binding to them. It may also function as an inhibitor of central nervous system enzymes that break down the neurotransmitter gaba aminobutyric acid (GABA). The GABA neurotransmitter may have antimanic properties, and thus its increased prevalence in the nervous system may enhance mood stability. Carbamazepine was once a leading alternative to lithium and valproate, but its side effects tend to be more discomfiting than those of the other drugs, and only about 50% of clients who use the medication are still taking it one year later. The common and generally transient side effects of carbamazepine include dizziness, sedation, short-term anorexia, constipation, diarrhea, and gastric distress resulting in nausea (see Table 4.20). Acute confusional states, double vision, and impaired muscle coordination may also occur but are less common. Extremely rare but serious adverse effects include anemia and agranulocytosis (lowered white blood cell count). Carbamazepine decreases the effect of benzodiazepine (anti-anxiety) medications and other anticonvulsant drugs when used in combination with them. No fatalities have been reported from overdoses of carbamazepine.

Valproate is the most thoroughly tested of the anticonvulsants for bipolar disorder. It was FDA approved as an anticonvulsant medication in 1978, and in 1995 it received approval as a mood-stabilizing medication. Valproate also has pre- and postsynaptic GABA receptor effects. It increases levels of GABA by blocking the convulsive effects of GABA antagonists. Data suggests that valproate is as effective as lithium in treating the symptoms of bipolar disorder but may be even more effective in mixed-state or rapid-cycling types of the disorder. Additionally, it works well as a preventive agent. Common and short-term adverse effects include nausea, sedation, weight gain, tremor, and hair loss. Less common effects include anxiety, depression, hand tremor, headache, and impaired muscle coordination. Rare but more serious side effects include damage to the pancreas and liver. When used in combination with antidepressant medications and alcohol, valporate increases their effects. It increases the effects of sedation and muscle stiffness when used with antipsychotic medications. Finally, valproate should not be used with another anticonvulsant medication because of the risk of significant additive side effects.

Lamotrigine is a well-established anticonvulsant agent that has shown efficacy in the prevention of mood episodes in adults with bipolar I disorder (Goldsmith et al., 2004). Its mechanism of action may be related to the inhibition of sodium and calcium channels in presynaptic neurons and subsequent stabilization of the neuronal membrane. In two large, randomized double-blind trials of 18 months duration, lamotrigine significantly delayed the onset of any type of new mood episode compared with a placebo (Goodwin et al., 2004). Additionally, it was significantly superior to a placebo at prolonging time to intervention for depression, but it was less effective than lithium in treating manic episodes. Lamotrigine

Table 4.20 Side Effects of Other Mood-Stabilizing Medications

Common	Less Common
CARBAMAZEPINE	
Confusion, memory disturbance	Anemia
Dizziness	Cardiac conduction
Lower white blood cell count (benign)	Double vision
Nausea	Dulling of vision
Sedation	Hepatitis
Skin rash	Impaired muscle coordination
Tremors	Lower white blood cell count
	Speech impediment
VALPROIC ACID	
Hair loss	Anxiety
Nausea/vomiting	Depression
Sedation	Hand tremors
	Headache
	Hepatitis
	Impaired muscle coordination
	Pancreatitis
LAMOTRIGINE	
Dizziness	Nausea
Double vision	Sleepiness
Fatigue	Rash
Headache	Blurred vision
Unsteadiness	Liver failure
Vomiting	

is generally well tolerated, does not appear to cause weight gain and, unlike lithium, generally does not require monitoring of serum levels (Licht et al., 2010). Its major side effects include sedation, weight gain, and blurred vision, and others include nausea, fatigue, and problems with muscle coordination.

Other anticonvulsant drugs used with persons who have bipolar disorder include oxcarbazepine, topiramate, and gabapentin, although none is FDA-approved for that purpose. Oxcarbazepine is a derivative of carbamazepine, and, in a review of seven studies, the drug was found to be comparably effective to other antimania drugs and to have similar side-effect profiles to other anticonvulsants (Vasudev et al., 2011). Topiramate augments the activity of gamma-aminobutyric acid

(GABA) at a subset of its receptors and thus potentiates the activity of that neurotransmitter. It is also a glutamate receptor antagonist. Still, topiramate has been researched very little as a treatment for bipolar disorder and little can be said at this time about its effectiveness (Vasudev et al., 2009). Gabapentin has a different composition than the other anticonvulsant drugs. It is structurally related to the neurotransmitter GABA, but it does not interact with GABA receptors. Its mechanism of action with bipolar disorder is unknown and, like topiramate, few studies have been done on its effectiveness with those symptoms.

Like lithium, the mechanisms of action of the anticonvulsant drugs in controlling mania are not clear. One theory holds that, in limbic system neuron tracts, they control a "kindling" process that contributes to the development of manic states (see Chapter 3). Like lithium, these medications need to be taken more than once daily to maintain a therapeutic level. Their prescription does not require frequent blood tests, however, since they do not share lithium's characteristic of being evenly distributed throughout the circulatory and nervous systems. An advantage that these medications have over lithium is that, when effective, they begin to stabilize the consumer's mood in as few as 2 to 5 days. Table 4.16 includes the trade names, preparations, and average daily dosage requirements for the anticonvulsant medications.

The anticonvulsant drugs are all used in the treatment of children with bipolar disorder, but few studies have been done to establish long-term safety (McIntosh & Trotter, 2006). The same qualifications that apply to lithium for pregnant women, children, and older adults also apply to the anticonvulsant medications. Carbamazepine is used more cautiously with children, as it can precipitate aggression (Ginsberg, 2006), and it has also been associated with developmental and cranial defects in newborns (Swann & Ginsberg, 2004).

The anticonvulsant drugs do have one additional major limitation. A meta-analysis of clinical trials involving a variety of those drugs indicated that persons who use them develop an increased risk of suicidal thoughts or behavior (Patorno et al., 2010). While researchers debate the validity of those findings, the FDA initiated a requirement in 2008 that manufacturers of these drugs include a written warning to that effect and that health care professionals inform consumers verbally.

Many clients are prescribed antipsychotic medications on a short-term basis to control the agitation and psychotic symptoms that may accompany their mood episodes. Approximately one-third of persons with bipolar disorder use small doses of these drugs during the maintenance phase of treatment as well, because they tend to experience periods of intense agitation (Faravelli et al., 2006). Among the newer antipsychotic medications, aripriprazole, olanzapine, risperidone, quetiapine, and ziprasidone have been tested as treatment adjuncts. In a meta-analysis of 18 studies, all of these drugs were superior to a placebo in treating bipolar mania, with no significant differences among them (Perlis et al., 2006). These medications may be effective for acute bipolar depression as well.

Antidepressant medications (usually the SSRIs) are not generally used for the treatment of bipolar I disorder. They have been shown to induce mania in as many as one-third of all clients, and one-fourth of consumers experience the activation of a rapid-cycling course (Vieta & Suppess, 2008). In bipolar II disorder, however, the antidepressants may be used along with an antimania drug for mood stabilization (Sussman et al., 2012). After a first episode of bipolar depression, antidepressant therapy is typically tapered in 2 to 6 months to minimize the possibility of the development of a manic episode.

Drugs from several other classes appear to have potential as antimanic agents, by themselves or as adjuncts to the primary drugs. However, research on these agents is limited. Several benzodiazepine drugs, primarily used as anti-anxiety medications, have been tested for antimanic effect. Clonazepam has received the most attention as an adjunctive drug for use with lithium, particularly in acute mania, because of its rapid onset, long duration of action, and anticonvulsant effects that may impede kindling (Winkler et al., 2003). Lorazepam has similar characteristics but has not been tested as thoroughly. These drugs may eventually provide a viable alternative to the adjunctive use of antipsychotic drugs in stabilizing manic persons because the adverse effects of the latter drugs discourage some clients from adherence.

The calcium channel blockers (verapamil is the best known), used primarily in the treatment of cardiovascular disorders, are also under investigation as antimanic drugs. They have effects on intracellular calcium ion concentrations similar to those of lithium. Preliminary findings with nimodipine, one calcium channel blocker, have supported its utility as a mood stabilizer against both manic and depressive episodes (Robb & Joshi, 2008). If effective, the relatively mild side-effect profiles of these drugs, including safety during pregnancy, will make them attractive treatment alternatives.

CASE EXAMPLES

Sharon was a single, 23-year-old Puerto Rican college student referred for outpatient care following hospitalization for treatment of a manic episode. She had been psychotic during her mania, characterized by sleeplessness, hyperactivity, racing thoughts, hypersexuality, paranoid delusions, and alcohol abuse. Sharon, who had never lived away from her parents, was well stabilized on lithium and aripiprazole at the time of her referral. An initial trial of haloperidol had to be discontinued because in combination with the lithium it had produced severe muscle stiffness, particularly in her arms and neck. Sharon was seen monthly, or more often as requested by the agency psychiatrist. The social worker always participated in these meetings to ensure collaborative continuity of care. Maintained with periodic adjustments throughout her agency involvement, the medications kept Sharon's mood stable. The aripiprazole was gradually eliminated but had to be reintroduced in small doses on a few occasions when her anxiety level escalated because of environmental stress. Her bothersome side effects included weight gain and a mild tremor in one hand.

Sharon's mood symptoms were exacerbated by environmental stresses that required regular attention from the social worker. While outwardly successful,

Sharon's father was alcoholic and physically abused his wife. Although most of the children had detached themselves from the family turmoil, Sharon remained materially and emotionally dependent on her parents. She became uncontrollably anxious whenever they left town, even for short weekend trips. With only two semesters remaining in her college curriculum, Sharon had begun to fail her classes; she later speculated that this was an effort to postpone the onset of adult responsibility.

The course of Sharon's bipolar disorder was connected to these issues. As a result, the social worker met with her weekly to help her develop strengths for coping with various age-appropriate responsibilities and to become less reliant on her parents. They worked on her fears, lack of confidence, poor self-image, and awkward interpersonal patterns, including her family and siblings in the process. To keep from driving the parents away, the social worker did not confront them about certain family problems. Instead, the worker educated them about medications and the impact of mental illness on family systems. The worker invited the family to the agency's education and support group, which they did attend, although irregularly. The worker also validated Sharon's feelings of dependence, of which she was ashamed but which she needed to accept and work through. Because Sharon tended to be passive, the worker acted as an advocate for her regarding vocational training and clubhouse involvement.

Sharon made steady progress in her treatment, although it came slowly, and she suffered some setbacks. She experienced two additional manic episodes over the next 4 years. The first occurred when she secretly stopped taking her medications, which prompted a regression, to avoid a planned but dreaded move into an apartment. The second episode took place 1 year later when Sharon was beginning a new job and her parents were out of town for several weeks. This time, she needed short-term hospitalization to get stabilized. Because the course of Sharon's bipolar disorder was closely related to her self-image, family situation, and management of stress, all these factors needed to be addressed in a holistic manner that included but was not limited to her medication treatment.

Ina Katsev is a 76-year-old single Israeli woman who has been residing in a publicly run assisted living facility (ALF) for 7 months. She was recently deemed incompetent to care for her financial affairs for reasons of mental instability (being diagnosed with bipolar disorder) and was granted a guardian, a former friend. Prior to moving into the ALF, she had lived alone in a rented townhouse for 18 years.

Ms. Katsev is a retired pediatrician, has never been married, and has no children. She immigrated to the United States 30 years ago to be near her older brothers. She says that during college, she experienced periods in which she thought she could accomplish anything and that everybody loved her, but then she would slide into a depression for several months when "blackness" came upon her. Despite these mood swings, she functioned with some success. She went to a prestigious university to undertake her premed coursework and attend medical school. Throughout these years Ms. Katsev felt at times, usually when depressed, that the "authorities" were watching her closely as a suspected spy.

During medical school Ms. Katsev sought psychiatric help and was given medication for "anxiety," but she does not recall what this was.

Ms. Katsev's depression and mood swings continued into her medical residency, immediately following which she took $5000 from her father's savings account without permission and traveled to Europe, where she met "the most interesting people" of her life. Ms. Katsev remembers being "very talkative" at this time and sleeping little. She was briefly hospitalized upon her return. She was stabilized with anti-anxiety medication and shortly thereafter began her career in pediatric public health. Her mood swings, primarily characterized by depressive episodes, continued until about 10 years ago. They lasted between 2 weeks and 6 months. Her behavior featured impulsive and reckless acts. Ms. Katsev was never rehospitalized, but over the next 20 years she held 15 different medical positions, and she attributes the volatility of her career to her moodiness. She retired from medical practice 15 years ago.

Ten years ago Ms. Katsev first started receiving lithium, which helped to control her mood symptoms. The ALF social worker asked Ms. Katsev what that was like and she said, "It was as if the blinders had been taken off, the shades had been lifted, and my eyes had been dusted." When asked how often she experienced these feelings, Ms. Katsev said, tearfully, "Only a few times." For the last 3 months Ms. Katsev has felt useless and that she is not accomplishing anything. She lacks the ability to concentrate, often thinks "black thoughts," and is unsure she wants to continue living. Ms. Katsev feels she cannot safely eat or sleep during her "dark" periods, because she wonders if she is "being watched."

Although Ms. Katsev has no difficulty making friends, keeping them is more of a challenge. After a few weeks of friendship, Ms. Katsev suggests that her new friend has some incurable disease and needs a nursing home or hospice care. The same scenarios play out with her roommates, and three of them have asked for transfers. Ms. Katsev has two outside friends. One is 45 years old, on dialysis, and calls Ms. Katsev every night. The second friend is 62 years old and in good health, and she seems to take Ms. Katsev's pronouncements in stride. Her two brothers, aged 82 and 86, both live in the vicinity but are frail and have infrequent contact with her.

Ms. Katsev has a variety of medical diagnoses including glaucoma, peripheral vascular disease, hypertension, osteoporosis, hypothyroidism, allergic rhinitis, and gastroenteritis reflux disease. While these conditions are serious, they are controlled with medical care and do not incapacitate her. The ALF employs a medical treatment team including a physician, nurse, and social worker, and they regularly consult about the effectiveness of these medications and the quality of her life.

Prior to her latest depressive episode, Ms. Katsev participated in activities at the ALF, including a book club, arts and crafts, walks, resident council, a political discussion group, and recreational outings. She now participates in only a few activities. She has recently said, "I think there'll be a time when I'm going to feel desperate. I don't have enough money to live anywhere else, and I don't want to live here. There's not enough for me here. I'm not being challenged or stimulated, and I don't know what to do."

The social worker was asked to take the lead in implementing the treatment plan for Ms. Katsev's bipolar disorder. The goals included her maintaining stable moods, and the desired actions toward that end were participating in weekly cognitive therapy with the social worker to correct her negative thinking and developing and practicing interpersonal skills to improve her relationships with others. The social worker participated in monitoring Ms. Katsev's moods and behaviors while providing her with regular psychosocial therapies.

ANTI-ANXIETY MEDICATIONS

Anxiety is an unpleasant but normal and functional affect that provides us with warning signs about perceived threats. It includes physiological and psychological symptoms that prepare us to confront or avoid a threat (Marks, 1987). The anticipated danger may be internal or external in origin. Anxiety is best understood from a biopsychosocial perspective. Our genetic endowment, psychosocial development, past experiences, and cognitive appraisal of internal and external events all influence its regulation. Four neurotransmitters, including noradrenaline, serotonin, dopamine, and gaba aminobutyric acid (GABA), are believed to be significant in regulating anxiety.

Anxiety begins as the body's physiological reaction to a threatening stimulus, but the emotions that follow our appraisal of that stimulus can be varied. The experience can be either positive or negative. An anxiety-producing situation may be perceived as a challenge when we appraise it as an opportunity for growth. Anxiety may be perceived negatively as a threat when we apprehend the possibility of harm. Excessive anxiety can be understood as the reaction to an event in that environmental or internal demands exceed our perceived ability to cope with the threat. Anxiety is problematic when it creates in us a sense of powerlessness, suggests a danger that is unrealistic, produces an exhausting state of alertness, produces a level of self-absorption that interferes with our problem-solving or creates doubt within us about the nature of reality.

Symptoms of Anxiety

1. *Motor tension*. Trembling, twitching, feeling shaky, muscle tensions, muscle aches and soreness, restlessness, easy fatiguability

2. *Autonomic nervous system hyperactivity*. Shortness of breath, the feeling of being smothered, accelerated heart rate, sweating or feeling cold, clammy hands, dry mouth, dizziness, lightheadedness, abdominal distress (including nausea and diarrhea), hot flashes or chills, frequent urination, difficulty swallowing, the sensation of a lump in the throat

3. *Hypervigilance*. Feeling edgy or keyed up, an exaggerated startle response, difficulty concentrating or feeling that the mind is going blank, trouble falling asleep or staying asleep, irritability.

SPECIFIC MEDICATIONS

Origins

The anti-anxiety drugs, like others we have already described, were discovered serendipitously (Berger, 1970; Cohen, 1970). In the mid-1940s, drug researchers in London were investigating new antibacterial agents that might supplement or improve upon the actions of penicillin. Frank Berger examined the toxic potential of one such compound by injecting it into mice. He noticed that the substance produced an unusual short-term reversible paralysis of their muscles. The mice were sedate but maintained consciousness with no disturbances to their autonomic functions (respiration, heartbeat, etc.). Further, when the drug wore off, the mice demonstrated a complete recovery. After clinical trials on humans, this substance, mephenesin, was introduced as a muscle relaxant. It had the drawbacks of weak action and too-rapid metabolism, however, and Berger soon undertook research for a similar but more effective compound. This resulted in the introduction of meprobamate, the first popular muscle relaxant and anti-anxiety agent, which had a duration of action 8 times longer than the former drug.

By the mid-1950s, psychopharmacology drugs included meprobamate and chlorpromazine, but there was much demand among prescribers for drugs of "intermediate" potency, not as strong as the antipsychotic drug but more tranquilizing than the new anti-anxiety agent. Leo Sternbach had done research on the chemical properties of "benzophenome" drugs during his postdoctoral studies in Poland in the 1930s. At that time his work was theoretical; he was not interested in developing active biological agents. In 1954, however, while working as a drug company chemist in New Jersey, Sternbach was inspired by developments in psychopharmacology to revisit those compounds for their potential as medicines. He synthesized new compounds from his original products but their effects as pharmacological agents was disappointing, so he abandoned the project. Ironically, he left one untested compound on his shelf. In 1957, during a routine cleanup of his laboratory, a chemist found this last compound and suggested that it be submitted for testing since its chemical analysis was complete. Two months later, its utility as a minor tranquilizer was established—the compound had hypnotic and sedative effects similar to meprobamate, but was significantly more potent. The benzodiazepine substance became the focus of intense research by his drug company and was introduced into medical practice as chlordiazepoxide in 1960. At present four types of medication are primarily used to treat anxiety: benzodiazepines, beta-blockers, the SSRIs, and several atypical medications.

CURRENT MEDICATIONS

Benzodiazepines

The benzodiazepines comprise the largest class of anti-anxiety medications and were the most frequently prescribed from the late 1950s into the 1990s. Compared to their barbiturate predecessors, the benzodiazepines (see Table 4.21) have

Table 4.21 Benzodiazepine Medications

Drug	Trade Name	Preparation*	Usual Daily Dosage
Alprazolam	Xanax	T	0.5–6 mg
Chlordiazepoxide	Librium	T, C, I	15–100 mg
Clonazepam	Klonopin	T	0.5–10 mg
Clorazepate	Tranxene	T, C	7.5–60 mg
Diazepam	Valium	T, C, S, I	2–60 mg
Estazolam	ProSom	T	1–2 mg
Flurazepam	Dalmane	T	15–30 mg
Halazepam	Paxipam	T	60–160 mg
Lorazepam	Ativan	T, I	2–6 mg
Midazolam	Versed	I	7.5–45 mg
Oxazepam	Serax	T, C	30–120 mg
Prazepam	Centrax	T, C	20–60 mg
Quazepam	Doral	T	7.5–30 mg
Temazepam	Restoril	T	15–30 mg
Triazolam	Halcion	T	0.125–0.25 mg

© 2013 Cengage Learning

*T -Tablets, C - Capsules, S - Solution, I - Injectable

a lower (but still real) potential for abuse, dependence, and tolerance, and a higher therapeutic index (the difference between therapeutic dose and overdose). The benzodiazepines are anxiety-reducing in lower doses and sedating in higher doses. As noted earlier, chlordiazepoxide was the first such drug; the second, diazepam, was for a time the most prescribed medication in the world. Six percent of the American population reported using benzodiazepines at least once in the late 1980s, but the percentage has dropped since then (Olfson & Pincus, 1994). More women use the drugs than men, probably due to gender differences in help-seeking and treatment traditions among physicians.

The benzodiazepine medications are thought to achieve their therapeutic effect by increasing the efficiency with which GABA binds with its receptor sites, thus blocking central nervous system stimulation in areas associated with emotion. They are quickly absorbed in the gastrointestinal tract and have a rapid effect—usually within 30 minutes. There is variation in the dose range but most have relatively short half-lives. Unless taken on an as-needed basis, the medication must be taken 2 or 3 times per day to maintain a therapeutic effect.

The benzodiazepines achieve a therapeutic effect within 1 week, and 75% of consumers demonstrate moderate to marked improvement. Their therapeutic benefit appears to peak after 4 to 6 weeks of use, but some consumers use the drugs for months or years without developing a tolerance. Longer-term use of the drugs is indicated in cases where the anxiety is likely to be long-term in duration, but short-term use is indicated for clients who have experienced trauma (where psychotherapy usually plays a more significant role), older adults (who have lower rates of metabolism and a greater sensitivity to side effects), persons with insomnia (who can learn alternative means of resting), and those who abuse substances (during the withdrawal process).

Most adverse effects of the benzodiazepines are described as mild and transient (see Table 4.22). Dizziness, drowsiness, and impaired muscle coordination are most frequently reported. Sometimes consumers experience gastrointestinal distress. The medications may also produce a transient amnesia and a diminished quality of task performance, both of which remit after several weeks. These effects make the drugs less practical for persons whose jobs or lifestyles require fine muscle coordination. Less common adverse effects include vision impairment and decreased sexual drive. Depending on the duration of and level of discomfort with these adverse effects, the consumer may be advised to try another type of medication.

The benzodiazepines have a serious disadvantage in that they may become physically addicting over time. There is no clear rule about the time required for a person to become at risk of dependence, and many clients use the medication safely for years. It is estimated that only 6% of consumers abuse the

Table 4.22 Adverse Effects of Anti-Anxiety Medications

Substances	Common	Less Common
Benzodiazepines	Confusion	Allergic skin reactions
	Dizziness	Blurred vision
	Drowsiness	Depression
	Headache	Dry mouth
	Impaired muscle coordination	Nausea/vomiting
	Irritability/restlessness	Sexual impairment
	Memory impairment	Weakness
Beta-Blockers	Hypotension	Abdominal pain, diarrhea
	Insomnia	Depression (mild)
	Nausea, vomiting	Dizziness
	Sedation	
	Sexual impairment	
	Slowed heart rate	
Buspirone	Dizziness	Insomnia
	Headache	Nervousness
	Nausea	Skin rash
	Sweating	

Table 4.23 Benzodiazepine Withdrawal Symptoms

Transient	True Withdrawal
Agitation	Delirium
Anxiety	Depression
Blurred vision	Enhanced sensory perceptions
Diarrhea	Hypothermia
Dizziness	Nausea
Headache	Paranoia
Insomnia	Seizures
Muscle aches	Tinnitis
	Tremors

medications and only 15% of users take the drugs for longer than 1 year (Carter, Swift, & Turnbull, 1996). Still, addiction should always be considered a possibility. Clients who abruptly discontinue the benzodiazepine drugs may experience the withdrawal symptoms of nausea, loss of appetite, depression, depersonalization, irritability, insomnia, headache, trembling, sweating, dizziness, and impaired concentration (see Table 4.23). It is recommended that benzodiazepines be tapered weekly at a rate of 25% of the previous week's dose. Complete discontinuation for long-term users may require 6 to 7 months.

The benzodiazepines interact with some substances to produce a differential response (see Table 4.24). The presence of any type of food decreases absorption time in the stomach and intestines. Some medications, including most antidepressants, increase blood levels of the benzodiazepines by slowing the client's metabolism. This enhances the drug's anti-anxiety action but also its adverse effects. Anticonvulsant drugs increase metabolism and thus decrease the blood level of the medicine. Alcohol use increases the effects of intoxication and sedation.

Some researchers stipulate that there are four subtypes of benzodiazepine drugs. The high-potency drugs, which may be short- or long-acting (alprazolam and clonazepam, among others) have the highest relative withdrawal potential but are well suited for the treatment of disabling anxiety states such as panic attacks. The low potency benzodiazepines, such as chlordiazepoxide and temazepam which also may be short- or long-acting, are indicated for the control of milder anxiety states and muscle relaxation. The short-acting drugs are appropriate for the short-term treatment of insomnia and anticipatory anxiety.

Buspirone

Several other classes of medication are used to control anxiety (see Table 4.25). Buspirone is a newer drug classified as an "azapirone," a term that refers to its chemical structure. It has an impact on serotonin receptors, which are believed

Table 4.24 Drug Interactions with Benzodiazepines

Drug	Effect
Alcohol and other sedatives	Increased nervous system depression
Antacids	Decreased absorption efficiency
Antibiotics	Increased blood levels
Anticonvulsants	Decreased blood levels
Antihistamines	Increased nervous system depression
Barbiturates	Increased nervous system depression
Cimetidine	Increased blood levels
Cyclic antidepressants	Increased nervous system depression
Disulfram	Increased blood levels
Estrogen	Increased blood levels
Fluoxetine	Increased blood levels
Isoniazid	Increased blood levels
Tagamet	Increased blood levels

© 2013 Cengage Learning

Table 4.25 Other Anti-Anxiety Medications

Drug	Trade Name	Preparation*	Usual Daily Dose
GABA AGONISTS			
Zaleplon	Sonata	C	5–20 mg
Zolpidem	Ambien	T	5–10 mg
BETA-BLOCKERS			
Atenolol	Tenormin	T, I	50–100 mg
Metoprolol	Lopressor	T, I	150–300 mg
Nadolol	Corgard	T	80–240 mg
Propranolol	Inderal	T, C, S, I	240–420 mg
AZAPIRONES			
Buspirone	Buspar	T	15–30 mg

*T - Tablets, C - Capsules, S - Solution, I - Injectable

© 2013 Cengage Learning

to be anxiolytic in the hippocampus and limbic areas. It balances serotonin levels, lowering them in persons who have too much (anxious persons) and raising levels in those who have too little (some persons with depression). Buspirone is quickly absorbed and must be taken regularly to achieve and maintain its effect. An average daily dose is 5 to 15 mg, 3 times per day, but this may be higher when the drug is used as a primary treatment for depression. Part of its attraction to prescribers is that buspirone is not addictive. Frequently, clients who have taken benzodiazepines are changed over to buspirone. It does not have anti-convulsant effects or does not produce psychomotor impairment, withdrawal, or cardiac problems. It is thought to be suited for elderly clients, who are susceptible to the adverse effects of the benzodiazepines.

Buspirone seems particularly effective in treating "generalized" anxiety disorders and mixed anxiety and depression states (Chessick et al., 2009). It requires 2 weeks or more to achieve full effect because, like the antidepressant drugs, it is initially resisted at its sites of action. It is thus not useful for crisis intervention or the treatment of panic disorder. It is sometimes used as an adjunct to other anti-anxiety, antidepressant, and antipsychotic drugs.

Buspirone has recently been found to have additional therapeutic benefits (Egger & Hebert, 2011). It reduces aggression and irritability in persons with brain injuries and organic disorders, such as dementia, and in children with developmental disabilities, mental retardation, and autism. It can be an effective adjunct to antidepressant drugs in treating obsessive-compulsive disorders. Buspirone appears useful in the treatment of alcohol abusers with anxiety because of its low abuse potential. It may also retard one's desire to return to alcohol consumption.

Buspirone does have limitations. Common adverse effects include dizziness or lightheadedness that occur shortly after ingestion, but these rarely persist for more than 20 minutes. Less common adverse effects include headache, nausea, nervousness, and insomnia. Drug interactions have been reported with clients also taking the antipsychotic drug haloperidol, the MAO inhibitors, and anta-buse. Adherence is an issue for some clients who prefer the sedation produced by the benzodiazepines. Buspirone's lack of sedative effect precludes its use in treating insomnia. Further, persons who have taken benzodiazepines seem to respond less well to buspirone than others. Cost must also be considered a limitation, as the drug is not yet available in generic form.

Other Anti-Anxiety Medications

The beta-blockers (see Table 4.25) inhibit norepinephrine receptor sites in the brain and peripheral nervous system. These drugs were originally developed to lower blood pressure in persons with hypertension but are also fast-acting and effective in treating anticipatory anxiety (specific situations in which unmanageable anxiety will be encountered). They lower anxiety by reducing the consumer's physical symptoms of rapid heartbeat, muscle tension, and dry mouth. The consumer's capacity to experience the physical symptoms of anxiety is thus diminished. The beta-blockers are not addicting but are prescribed less often than the benzodiazepines because they have a brief effect, only a few hours. Their adverse effects tend to be minimal and include sedation, hypotension, and dizziness. Beta-blockers are generally not prescribed for persons with cardiac problems or asthma.

The antihistamines are still occasionally prescribed as anti-anxiety agents, particularly with children and adolescents. These drugs block histamine receptors in the nervous system that are associated with anxiety and agitation. Antihistamines are rapidly absorbed and maintain a therapeutic effect for approximately 24 hours. Antihistamines tend to be highly sedating, however, and are effective for only a few months before a tolerance develops. They are not addictive and are most frequently used as relatively safe sleep-inducing agents.

The newest anti-anxiety drugs available in the United States are zolpidem and zaleplon (Dang, Gard, & Rataboli, 2011; Hindmarch et al., 2001). Zolpidem has been marketed as a short-term hypnotic to treat insomnia. It is chemically different from the benzodiazepines but works in a similar manner, binding at the benzodiazepine receptor but inducing sleep rather than wakeful calmness. It has the same side-effects profile as the same pattern of potential tolerance and dependence. Zolpidem is an atypical drug and affects a smaller subset of GABA than the benzodiazepines. Consumers of zolpidem, which is also available in time-release form, must be careful to go to sleep immediately after taking the drug or they may experience short-term psychotic symptoms. Zalepon is similar to zolpidem in chemical structure and effects, although it has a shorter half-life and thus is less likely to produce tolerance and dependence.

Almost all of the medications initially developed as antidepressants are used at times for the primary or adjunctive treatment of anxiety disorders (Skolnick, 1997). In fact, these drugs tend to relieve anxiety prior to the onset of their antidepressant effect, which requires 2 to 6 weeks. There seems to be an overlap between the biological causes of depression and some anxiety disorders, probably related to the serotonin neurotransmitter. The medications may also stimulate other neurotransmitters in ways that are not yet understood. The selective serotonin reuptake inhibitors also have great utility for treating anxiety. Most of the SSRIs are thought to be useful for treating persons with obsessive compulsive disorders. Additionally, fluoxetine is sometimes used to treat persons with bulimia and panic disorders; paroxetine is used for persons who experience generalized anxiety disorders (GADs), social anxiety disorders, panic disorders, and posttraumatic stress disorder; Lexapro is used with GAD.

The MAO inhibitor phenylzine is useful in treating panic and anxiety, and tranylcypromine has a stimulant effect on some persons. The cyclic drug imipramine has been found effective in the treatment of panic, although 3 to 5 weeks of use is required to achieve its effect.

CASE EXAMPLES

Lynne was an unemployed 43-year-old divorced Hispanic female with two adult children and a history of labile moods and dependent relationships. Several months after divorcing her husband of 20 years, she entered counseling with a psychiatrist for help with anxiety and panic attacks. She was having great difficulty living on her own and coped with stress by withdrawing to her bedroom in states of high anxiety. Lynne was hospitalized for several weeks after becoming suicidal. Her psychiatrist initiated treatment with both antidepressant and anti-anxiety medications, but soon after discharge she was tapered to a moderate dose of the benzodiazepine alprazolam. This became Lynne's standard medication regimen, which persisted through her transfer to a mental health facility.

Lynne received psychosocial intervention from a social worker and medication from a physician. After 1 year of intervention, during which she reached many of her psychosocial goals, including a successful employment experience, her physician and social worker became concerned that she was psychologically dependent on the medication. Although the drug served a therapeutic purpose, Lynne discounted the need to make further adjustments in her coping strategies and relationships with family, friends, and employers.

Fearing a return of anxiety attacks, Lynne initially resisted the suggestion to change medication but eventually agreed to a gradual 1-year plan to transfer from the benzodiazepine to the nonaddictive drug buspirone. The social worker, who met with Lynne much more frequently than the physician did, assumed a crucial monitoring and consultant role through this process. Every month or two, the physician decreased the alprazolam by 0.25 mg daily and increased the other drug. The social worker also increased her visits with the client. If Lynn experienced high anxiety, she could call her social worker between their biweekly visits. These instances usually came about because of Lynne's ambivalence about the change in medications rather than her primary psychiatric disorder. The social worker was careful to validate rather than discount Lynne's reactions to the change so that she would not feel a need to either hide or exaggerate them. The transition proceeded smoothly. Eighteen months later, the client was functioning well with a modest dose of buspirone. She did not report any bothersome side effects from the medication.

Dennis was a 10-year-old Hispanic male in the fourth grade at a public school in a large midwestern city. The oldest of three children, Dennis had always been described as an "anxious" child by his parents. He had difficulty developing interpersonal skills and tended to be both fearful and controlling of his siblings and peers. His parents hoped he would grow out of those tendencies, but they persisted into his school years, and it was noticed that Dennis was being teased and excluded by the other students. Dennis's parents had him tested at their doctor's suggestion, and he was found to have "high functioning autism" or Asperger's disorder. Dennis thus qualified for a multidisciplinary Individual Education Plan (IEP), which was helpful, although in the third grade he began to demonstrate strong obsessive-compulsive behaviors, characterized by extreme needs for neatness, cleanliness, and predictability. Dennis was a stubborn child and efforts to help improve his behavior through behavioral means was not successful. Dennis's parents asked the school social worker (with whom they had regular contact to monitor his school functioning) if he should be on medications. The social worker referred the family to a child psychiatrist in the area, who felt that the child might benefit from a moderate dose of paroxetine to compliment the rest of his intervention program. The medication did seem to reduce Dennis's agitation and extreme need for structure, although the child was unhappy about taking medication.

During one IEP meeting the team decided to limit Dennis's use of the drug to a 6-month trial. The social worker kept in contact with the family to answer their questions about how to interact with Dennis behaviorally, how to talk with him about medication, and monitor the referral.

PSYCHOSTIMULANTS

The psychostimulant medications produce states of wakefulness, mood elevation, alertness, initiative, and enhanced competence. They are primarily used to treat persons with attention deficit hyperactivity disorder (ADHD). Ironically they do not produce a subjective effect of stimulation for those persons, instead enhancing their ability to maintain concentration and self-control. The medications are controversial because most are controlled substances with abuse potential and are primarily used to treat a disorder that is itself ambiguous to many professionals. The social work profession is extensively involved with clients having ADHD in a variety of child care settings, particularly schools, where the condition tends to be diagnosed. Social workers participate as members of treatment teams with physicians, nurses, family members, psychologists, and teachers on behalf of their clients with ADHD. The persistence of ADHD symptoms into adulthood for many persons has also been identified.

Attention Deficit Hyperactivity Disorder

Attention deficit hyperactivity disorder (ADHD) is characterized by a persistent pattern (6 months or more) of inattention and/or hyperactivity and impulsivity in behavior that is more frequent and severe than what is typically observed in others at a comparable developmental level (APA, 2000). Symptoms of ADHD are present by the age of 7 years and continue in attenuated form into adulthood for 10 to 60% of persons with the disorder (Hallowell & Ratey, 1994), although adult estimates have been increasing since the adult form of the disorder has received greater attention (Montejano et al., 2011). In children, ADHD is characterized by a lack of self-control and ability to sustain direction. Children with ADHD are distractible, often do not finish what they start, and are irritable and impatient, often interrupting and pestering others. Physical hyperactivity may be quite pronounced (boys with the disorder are more likely to be hyperactive than girls). Adults with the disorder are usually not hyperactive but are impatient, restless, and moody, and have difficulty managing their time and setting priorities. The severity of the disorder is variable and likely to worsen in situations that demand sustained effort or high levels of structure. To receive the diagnosis, the person must be impaired in at least two settings, such as school, work, and home. The disorder may be predominantly hyperactive/impulsive, inattentive, or combined in nature.

There is controversy among professionals about the validity of the ADHD diagnosis. This is due to the purely observational criteria of DSM-IV, the inconsistency of symptoms (a child may function well in one setting but poorly in another), the belief that the condition is often designated by frustrated adults who cannot manage active children, and the lack of knowledge about a biological basis of ADHD. The decision to medicate should be based on the conclusion of a physician and other involved professionals that the symptoms are severe enough to preclude age-appropriate social, academic, or occupational functioning.

Ethical Issues in the Drug Treatment of Children

We have noted throughout this chapter that medications from all five diagnostic categories may be prescribed for children and adolescents. However, we focus here on the ethical issues related to this practice because children are the primary recipients of psychostimulant medications. Concerns include the appropriateness of medication (rationale for use, alternatives, toxicity), the dangers of inadequate clinical management, the general problem of child and adolescent non-adherence in health care (fears of peer ridicule and a reluctance to accept being labeled as "ill"), the possibility of negative effects on physical development, and ethical issues in decision-making and the rights of minors (Petr, 1998).

There are also concerns related to iatrogenic effects, or what children may learn from the process of taking medications. Children and adolescents may learn to attribute adjustment problems to factors beyond their control and thus become less receptive to behavioral interventions. They may fail to acquire adaptive behaviors because their symptoms are suppressed and caregivers do not recognize the need to teach other coping strategies, may learn to take medication as a way of coping with a variety of adjustment difficulties, and may become more likely to abuse psychoactive substances (Koelch, Schnoor, & Fegert, 2008; Singh, 2007). These effects are possible within any age group, but children and adolescents have not yet had the opportunity to develop a range of healthy habits for coping with stress.

The social worker should view the absence of active parental or caregiver interest with the child using psychostimulant medications as a major treatment concern. With the developmental issues of this life stage, including beginning needs for separation from the family, drug management requires a strong social worker–family alliance to ensure that the young client's needs are addressed holistically.

As a consultant, the social worker is likely to have a major role in the medication assessment process. It was noted earlier that the diagnosis of ADHD requires a thorough social history as well as medical examination of the client. The social worker may have primary responsibility for conducting the necessary interviews with family members, teachers, and significant others, and also providing the client and family with formal testing materials. In this process the social worker must also assess the attitudes of the client and family, including what they expect from medication and its possible impact on the consumer's self-esteem and sense of competence. This information will be important in the ultimate decision about whether or not to prescribe medication. The social worker's relationships with the client and family may increase the likelihood of compliance with whatever plan is adopted.

It is suggested that the social worker begin serving as an educator in describing the actions, benefits, and risks of the psychostimulants before they are prescribed. This may be the physician's primary responsibility, but the social worker should have sufficient knowledge to provide the client and family with verbal and written information. Of course, these activities may result in the client's decision not to take medication, and thus the process of education should be coordinated among members of the treatment team. The educator role will continue after the client begins using the medication because the social worker must put the client's unique responses into a context of what tends to occur for most clients who take the medication, as discussed earlier.

As a counselor and advocate, the social worker can ensure that the needs and preferences of the client and family are made clear to all who participate in the intervention, both before and after medication is prescribed. This is particularly crucial in that the client may be a minor whose preferences are not given priority by adults involved in his or her care. The social worker often spends more time with the client and family than others on the treatment team; he or she may be best informed about their perspectives regarding medication and other interventions.

SPECIFIC MEDICATIONS

Origins

The first known stimulant, cocaine, was isolated in 1860 as a chemical salt, but it had been used for centuries in South American cultures via the coca plant to fight off fatigue, lessen hunger, and increase endurance. The chemical extraction is more powerful than the plant and was used by soldiers in eastern Europe as early as 1884 to decrease fatigue. The prototype of the current psychostimulant drugs is amphetamine, a substance of medical interest and controversy since it was synthesized in 1887. A California chemist named George Alles first developed this substance for clinical use in the 1930s while conducting drug experiments for the treatment of allergies (Leake, 1970). Specifically he was studying ephedrine, a chemically active agent derived from a plant long known to Chinese herbalists as an effective treatment for asthma. This substance is structurally similar to the neurotransmitter epinephrine. Because supplies of ephedrine for research were limited, Alles made successful efforts to develop synthetic compounds. He named two of these benzedrine and dexedrine. The first of these amphetamines was marketed to treat asthma orally and to raise low blood pressure. Because its side effect, central nervous system stimulation, was obvious, use of the drug was soon expanded to treat narcolepsy and obesity. It had also been noted in early trials of amphetamine that the drug had a paradoxical effect on some consumers; that is, it produced states of relaxation instead of alertness and excitation.

Amphetamines were used in the 1930s as bronchial dilators, respiratory stimulants, analeptics, and to treat parkinsonism. They were widely used by British, Japanese, and American soldiers during World War II. This was actually encouraged by American physicians, but was controversial because of concerns about the toxic effects of overuse. It was only after the war, however, that the amphetamines became well-known drugs of abuse. Japan had large stocks of the drugs that could be purchased without prescription. The drugs were later utilized for the treatment of various conditions, including depression, until the development of the MAO inhibitors.

Amphetamines were first used with children in the 1920s by Dr. Bradley, a Rhode Island physician, in a successful effort to help survivors of an influenza epidemic who developed neurological impairments become less agitated and more teachable. Stimulants have been used to treat ADHD since 1936, when it was found that the paradoxical effects of amphetamine drugs on some persons could be effective in controlling hyperactivity.

Current Medications

The primary psychostimulant drugs include methylphenidate, the amphetamines (including dextroamphetamine and methamphetamine, which are more potent substances), and pemoline (see Table 4.26). Except for pemoline, all are classified as Schedule II drugs by the Drug Enforcement Agency (DEA) because of their abuse potential. This is the most restrictive classification for medications, prohibiting both their prescription by phone and the writing of refills. The psychostimulants are currently approved for the treatment of ADHD, narcolepsy,

Table 4.26 Medications for ADHD

Drug	Trade Name	Preparation	Usual Daily Dose	
Stimulants				
Amphetamine	Adderall	T	5–60 mg	3 and older
Dexmethylphenidate	Focalin	T	5–20 mg	
Dextroamphetamine	Dexedrine	T, C*	10–60 mg	3 and older
Methamphetamine	Desoxyn	T	20–40 mg	
Methylphenidate	Ritalin	T, patch*	20–40 mg	6 and older
Pemoline	Cylert	T, patch	37.5–112.5 mg	6 and older

Drug	Trade Name	Preparation	Usual Daily Dose	
Non-Stimulants				
Atomoxetine	Strattera	C	0.5–1.2 mg	6 and older
Clonidine	Catapres	T, patch	0.2–0.6 mg	
Guanfacine	Tenex	T	1–4 mg	

*Available in time-release form

© 2013 Cengage Learning

and obesity. At present they account for 95% of ADHD medication therapy in the United States. In this country 90% of children with ADHD take methylphenidate because it is effective, has been available the longest, and has been tested most thoroughly. Five percent take dextroamphetamine and 2% take pemoline (Lawrence, Lawrence, & Carson, 1997).

While the entire mechanism of action of these drugs is not known, they release norepinephrine, dopamine, and serotonin from presynaptic terminals in the frontal portion of the brain where attention and impulsivity are regulated. They also inhibit norepinephrine and dopamine reuptake. Approximately 70% of consumers respond positively to any one of the drugs, and 20% of those who do not respond to one of the drugs will respond positively to another. Moderate doses appear to improve attention, concentration, and cognitive functioning in adults as well, although ADHD in adults has not been studied as thoroughly.

The common adverse effects of the stimulants are generally transient and include loss of appetite, weight loss, irritability, insomnia, and abdominal pain (see Table 4.27). Less common adverse effects include depression, increased blood pressure, tachycardia, nightmares, tics, skin rashes, toxic psychosis, and liver toxicity. All of the drugs except pemoline carry a "rebound" effect, meaning that the symptoms of ADHD tend to recur dramatically after the medication is eliminated from the consumer's body. They may stunt physical growth among children and adolescents, but there is a rebound growth to normal height during drug holidays or after the drug is discontinued. Further research is needed on the impact of these medications on the physical growth and rebound growth of children.

In most cases consumers are given periodic drug holidays of at least 2 weeks as a means of assessing the status of their condition. These holidays are most practical when children are out of school and have fewer persistent demands on their attention. Studies of drug effectiveness beyond puberty is not extensive, but there is evidence that treatment in childhood leads to better outcomes in adulthood. Steele, Jensen, and Quinn (2006) found that children using psychostimulants for 3 years or longer had better outcomes relative to further psychiatric treatment, levels of education, independent living, and aggression. Because many children experience a natural reduction in the symptoms of ADHD as

Table 4.27 Side Effects of Psychostimulant Medications

Common	Less Common
Anxiety	Itching, skin rash
Insomnia	Fever
Loss of appetite	Dizziness
Gastrointestinal pain	Headache
Cardiac arrythmia	Blood pressure changes

© 2013 Cengage Learning

they grow through adolescence, physicians attempt to taper and eliminate the medication at intervals; generally every few years.

Methylphenidate, the most widely used and studied psychostimulant, was introduced as a treatment for children with hyperactivity in 1958 (Jacobvitz, 1990). It is approved by the FDA for children 6 years and older. Methylphenidate releases stored dopamine, decreases dopamine reuptake, and inhibits monoamine oxidase activity. It is quickly absorbed into the bloodstream, requiring only 30 to 60 minutes to take effect and reaching peak blood levels within 2 hours. Its half-life is 2 to 3 hours, which necessitates that it be taken 2 to 4 times daily. It does not typically impair sleep. A time-release form of the drug is available, but there is some evidence that this preparation is less effective than the standard form. Its slower absorption results in delayed onset and also increases sleep and appetite disturbances. One advantage of methylphenidate relative to other stimulants is its lesser appetite suppression effect.

Dextroamphetamine is approved for children 3 years and older. It is believed to work by increasing dopamine and norepinephrine transmission and inhibiting monoamine oxidase activity. Dextroamphetamine, the least expensive of the psychostimulants, is also fast-acting, and with a half-life of 6 hours, the medication needs to be taken only twice daily. It does have disadvantages, including a potential for abuse and diversion to the illicit drug market. Its adverse effects, including a higher likelihood of anorexia, insomnia, and cardiovascular effects, are slightly more pronounced than those experienced with methylphenidate.

Adderall is an amphetamine; it is not a new medication but has recently been FDA-approved as a treatment for persons with ADHD aged 3 years and older. It is composed of a unique mix of amphetamine isomers. Adderall has a rapid onset and with a 2- to 6-hour effect can be given once or twice daily in most cases. Because it is composed of different substances than other amphetamines, Adderall may be useful for consumers who do not respond to amphetamines.

Methamphetamine is rarely prescribed for ADHD because it is a stronger amphetamine substance with greater abuse potential, but it can be effective as an alternative medication. It is also long-acting, needs to be taken twice daily, and has fewer systemic side effects than dextroamphetamine. It is, however, more expensive.

Pemoline is structurally different from methylphenidate and amphetamines. It seems to act through dopamine mechanisms in ways which are not well understood. Pemoline has a half-life of 12 hours (slightly longer for adults) and an 8-hour duration of action. It only needs to be taken once daily and is available in a chewable tablet; thus, it may be easier for children (6 years and older) and families to manage. The lesser stimulant effect of pemoline reduces its abuse potential and produces less anorexia and insomnia. Further, it is the only psychostimulant drug that apparently produces no rebound effect on discontinuation. As a Schedule IV controlled substance, it must be prescribed in writing but may include refills. Pemoline does have drawbacks. It may require up to 6 weeks of use before demonstrating a therapeutic effect, and it is more expensive than other stimulants. Most seriously, pemoline has not been researched as extensively as methylphenidate. There are reports in the literature of some deaths from liver toxicity, which has recently placed the drug out of favor with physicians.

Atomoxetine is approved for use with persons age 6 and older. It is not a stimulant, but a norepinephrine/dopamine enhancer. This medication is particularly attractive as an ADHD medication because it lacks abuse potential and street value. The drug has shown to be comparable to methylphenidate in effectiveness in a recent meta-analysis of nine studies (Hanwella, Senanayake, & de Silva, 2011). Common adverse effects include gastrointestinal discomfort, fatigue, and dizziness. Unfortunately atomoxetine produces suicidal ideation to an extent beyond a placebo, which is a major drawback of the medication.

Other Drugs Used to Treat ADHD

While the stimulants are the drugs of first choice in treating symptoms of attention deficit and hyperactivity, alternatives are available. Many clients will either not respond to the primary medications or experience intolerable adverse reactions. Evidence for the effectiveness of other medications for treating these symptoms is emerging. These other drugs have not been extensively evaluated, but some clinical studies have demonstrated their promise.

Clonidine was originally developed to lower blood pressure but is also used to treat such conditions as opiate withdrawal, Tourette's syndrome, and smoking cessation. It has recently emerged as an alternative for treating ADHD symptoms. Clonidine decreases certain types of arousal by decreasing the activity of "alpha-2" receptors in the central nervous system (and thereby promoting the release of norepinephrine). The drug is quickly absorbed, reaches peak plasma levels in 1 to 3 hours, and has a half-life of 6 to 20 hours. Clonidine has been effective with children who have severe problems with mood, activity level, cooperation, and frustration tolerance, but it is reportedly less effective at improving attention. It is sometimes prescribed along with a stimulant for a combined effect. One unique feature of this medication is that it can be dispensed with a 7-day patch. Common adverse effects include dry mouth and eyes, fatigue, irritability, sedation, dizziness, hypotension, and constipation. Less common adverse effects include insomnia, anxiety, and depression.

The antidepressant drugs are differentially effective for persons with ADHD symptoms (Spencer, Biederman, & Wilkins, 1998). The cyclic antidepressants, including imipramine, desipramine, and amitriptyline, have shown effectiveness and are particularly useful for adult consumers who have a family history of depression or anxiety. The cyclic drugs should not be used with children, however, because their effectiveness has not been adequately demonstrated, and they produce adverse effects of dry mouth, blurred vision, constipation, and sedation, all of which many children cannot tolerate. On the positive side, cyclic drugs have longer-lasting effects, allow greater dose flexibility, and carry a lower risk of abuse. Bupropion is an antidepressant with a pharmacological profile somewhat similar to the stimulants but without abuse potential. One review concluded that the drug was effective in treating ADHD, although there was a slightly greater improvement for subjects using the stimulants (Paykina &

Greenhill, 2007). The newer serotonin reuptake inhibitors have not yet been adequately tested as treatments for ADHD.

CASE EXAMPLES

Tracy was referred to the elementary school's Child Study Committee by her fifth-grade teacher. It was early in the school year, and the teacher had noted that the 12-year-old child (who had once been held back) was not motivated to do schoolwork, could not focus on classroom tasks, made inappropriate noises, was distracting to others, and had poor peer relationships. Tracy's mother attended the committee meeting, which included a social worker, guidance counselor, psychologist, nurse, and the teacher, in addition to Tracy. This was a single parent who worked full-time to raise her family, which included a younger son as well as Tracy. The mother admitted that Tracy demonstrated the same problem behaviors at home and at the day care center that she attended after school. Her mother added that Tracy could not relax and go to sleep at night and may have been getting only 5 hours of sleep. All members of the committee agreed that, despite her behaviors, Tracy was a warm child with an engaging sense of playfulness about her actions, problematic as they might be.

The social worker, noting that the child exhibited the same behavior control problems in a variety of life settings, recommended that the mother take Tracy to their physician to get an assessment and to get more information for later problem-solving at the school. In the school setting, all problems were framed as educational in nature. While Tracy's mother followed up on the referral, the social worker, teacher, and guidance counselor constructed a behavioral intervention for the classroom. This plan was based on the child's strengths of wanting to be helpful and having a particular desire to work with younger children at school as a mentor for their class projects. If Tracy would do her required work and not talk so much with her peers, she could be assigned to work with the younger children on a regular basis, deliver the teacher's notes to the office when needed, and be permitted to stay after school to help clean the room.

Tracy was assessed by her physician; she referred her to a pediatric psychiatrist who diagnosed the child with ADHD symptoms. A mid-range dosage of methylphenidate was prescribed for the child, and the mother agreed to support Tracy's regular use of the drug. Within 4 weeks, significant positive changes were noted in the classroom, and the mother also reported positive changes at home and the day care center. It was not clear to what extent the school behavioral program, medications, and parent support (by the social worker) each contributed to the changes, but this ambiguity is often true of children with ADHD. The significance of the changes in all spheres led the social worker to conclude that the medications were a major contributor to Tracy's improvement. The social worker monitored Tracy's medication adherence through weekly phone conversations with her mother. She also helped the parents maintain a structured behavior modification plan for the home via problem-solving skills training. The

Child Study Committee reviewed the case every 2 months, in accordance with its policies. Six months into the intervention plan, Tracy was still functioning satisfactorily in the classroom and elsewhere and appeared to be a reasonably happy child. She was also getting along better with her classmates.

How long would Tracy take the medication? The social worker knew that she could not make specific recommendations on that issue but could only encourage her mother to keep in regular contact with their treating physician and to use the social worker as a consultant and counselor. The social worker knew that, in many cases, parents tend to stop focusing on the medications as long as the child is behaving well, and sometimes they stop making doctor's appointments. And what did Tracy think about taking medicine several times per day? She seemed to take it in stride. She complained of stomachaches for the first few weeks, but these stopped when she learned to take the medicine with food. "Mom didn't say too much about what the medicine was for," Tracy once said to the social worker. "She said it was just something I need, like glasses."

Patrick came to the attention of the school social worker at an earlier age than Tracy—he was only 7 years old and in the second grade. A new student at the school, Patrick had already been diagnosed with ADHD and was taking a high dose of methylphenidate. His parents had sought help from the Child Study Committee because they had been frustrated for several years with Patrick's hyperactivity, poor attention span, and apparent lack of positive response to medical interventions.

Patrick was an adopted biracial (African American and Caucasian) child of this achievement-oriented professional couple. He had two brothers, aged 4 and 8, both of whom were also adopted. Of the three he was the only child who demonstrated behavior problems to his parents or the school. His parents reported to the Child Study Committee that Patrick had been diagnosed with ADHD at age 3, after they became concerned about his general unruliness and lack of self-control. They believed that Patrick had been born drug-addicted and wondered what effect that might be having on his physical condition. His parents reported that Patrick could never focus on his homework and was not social. He seemed to prefer being by himself and loved computers, as many children do, for the colorful stimulation they provided.

During the family assessment, the social worker noticed that Patrick's parents were extremely anxious, almost frantic in their efforts to see that something more be done for their child. They had taken Patrick to several psychologists who specialized in the treatment of ADHD and were told that some of his behaviors were "just his personality." "He is an energetic child" was a comment from another. His parents' comments that "something is terribly wrong with Patrick," and "we want him to become a true member of our family" made the social worker concerned that Patrick might be feeling badly about himself. She was also concerned that the parents admitted to favoring high doses of methylphenidate, although it was apparently not working well. This could be contributing to his poor sleep quality. With this information the Child Study Committee suggested that Patrick continue seeing a physician and perhaps have his medications reviewed. They also included the family in planning a classroom behavioral management program.

Patrick was soon evaluated by a physician who changed his medication to an amphetamine and also moderated the dose. His parents explained the ongoing need for medication to Patrick, saying "You have an illness that we have to treat. It's like having allergies." With the change in medication, there was some improvement in Patrick's behavior. It was more controlled, and he was sleeping marginally better, but he also became more irritable and defiant of authority figures. The social worker understood that this might be a manifestation of ADHD, but it could also be either Patrick's interpersonal style or due to the medication's side effect of anxiety.

The social worker, teacher, and guidance counselor implemented a behavioral program that addressed Patrick's low self-esteem by including much praise for his positive and social behaviors. His parents were encouraged to do the same. Still, Patrick continued to be a management challenge for the school and family. The social worker consulted regularly with Patrick, his parents, and his teacher. She tried to provide the parents with education about a comprehensive approach to helping a child with ADHD. She also focused on their own needs to relax and try to acquire some detachment from Patrick's presenting problems, as doing so might benefit them as well as their son.

Robbie, age 27, came to the mental health agency for counseling because his 5-year marriage and new career were falling apart. His wife Susan was threatening to leave him because he was sullen and irritable around the house, blaming his bad moods on work stress, and paying little attention to her. She was also concerned that, while Robbie had always enjoyed drinking several beers every evening, he was increasing his alcohol intake. Susan had always been attracted to Robbie's physical energy and playful sense of adventure, but she was concerned now that he lacked any career focus. She wanted to start a family but felt that Robbie was not emotionally stable enough to do so.

The social worker spent several meetings assessing Robbie's present situation and background. Robbie had never experienced emotional problems in the past. He had been an energetic child and young adult who particularly loved outdoor activities such as camping and climbing. He had been a fair student but never a scholar; he was one of the average kids who tended to be bored in the classroom but produced satisfactory work. It was hard to get interested in reading, he said. He was more the athletic type. Robbie had attended community college (initially to prepare for a social work career) but did not finish. He had held several jobs as a recreation leader but was thrilled to be hired 1 year ago as the Youth Director of his Methodist church. Robbie had always been a participating church member and loved working with kids. He particularly enjoyed planning and participating in their evening and weekend outings.

Robbie's current problems surfaced when he began this new job. He was great with the kids but was extremely disorganized in tending to the administrative demands of the job. Robbie could never focus on more than one office project at a time. Further, if he was interrupted from completing a task by a phone call or visitor, he could not remember later what he had been doing or where he left off. Robbie purchased a sophisticated "pocket organizer" and began sticking Post-It notes to his left hand and wrist, each one listing his tasks for the day so that he could remind himself of what he needed to accomplish. These efforts did not work. Robbie became increasingly frustrated and tense, which greatly affected his marriage. His pastor warned him, while being support- ive of his talents, that he might need to leave the job if he could not manage the department better. Robbie started drinking more. He always liked to drink beer to relax himself at the end of a day, and now it was harder to relax.

The social worker suggested a medical evaluation, wondering if Robbie might have ADHD. She recognized that while he had never been diagnosed with the disorder as a youth, his classroom behaviors indicated that he may have had a disorder of the inattention type, rather than the more noticeable impulsive/hyperactive type. This might also account for his present inability to manage the fairly basic administrative responsibilities of his job.

Robbie would not consider the evaluation at first—he called the physician only after his wife insisted he do so as a condition of their staying together. The doctor did make a diagnosis of ADHD, inattention type, following a consultation with the social worker. He wanted to prescribe methylphenidate, but Robbie refused this because he was wary of all medications but also because he did not want to give up drinking. The social worker provided additional counseling and support to Robbie and his wife before he could concede that he had in fact been medicating himself with alcohol. It had been his means of reducing his anxiety and tension for 10 years but the prescribed medication might be a more effective sub- stitute. Robbie agreed, with the support of his wife, to stop drinking and try the medication. He demonstrated a remarkably positive response, and this helped him keep both his job and his marriage. Robbie has been on the medication for 1 year. He hopes to be able to discontinue it, but he is careful to add that he would only do so if his physician supported the idea.

SUMMARY

This chapter has consisted of discussions of five major classes of medication, the symptoms they treat, the types of medication within those classes, and their effects, positive and negative, on clients who use them as part of their interven- tion strategies. In the next chapter we turn to special issues with psychotropic medication as they apply to specific populations of clients.

TOPICS FOR DISCUSSION
AND LEARNING ACTIVITIES

1. Choose two psychotropic medications and conduct an Internet search of websites devoted to them. Report on the nature of the website, the chem- ical description of the medication, and the drug's acknowledged therapeutic

and adverse effects. Identify the website's sponsor and discuss whether there seems to be a bias in how the information is presented.

2. Choose *any* specific mental disorder in which you have a particular interest. Research the medications used to treat that disorder. Look for rationales for the use of these medications as well as summaries of their therapeutic and adverse effects. Present this information in a two-page single-spaced report, including a reference list of four to five major sources. Make a copy of the report to share with each of your classmates.

3. Divide into three groups and articulate examples of physical, psychological, and social adverse effects of medication based on your work or field placement experiences. Share your examples with the entire class. The instructor may select one example of each type of adverse effect and lead a discussion about how social workers can assess and intervene with these over time.

4. Choose one "newer" and one "older" medication from each of the five categories of drugs and investigate their monetary costs to consumers. Next, consider information presented in this chapter about the therapeutic and adverse effects of these medications. Is there an apparent relationship between cost and perceived effectiveness? What does this suggest about social work role activities?

5

Intervention Concerns with Special Populations

Learning Objectives

Upon completion of this chapter, the reader will be able to:

1. Articulate the physical differences among members of special populations that contribute to differential effects of psychotropic medication.

2. Summarize the differential effects of psychotropic medication among women, older adults, children and adolescents, African Americans, people of Hispanic cultures, and people with a dual diagnosis of mental illness and substance abuse.

3. Articulate strategies for approaching members of special populations about their potential to benefit from using psychotropic medications.

A major strength of the social work profession is its appreciation of human diversity; its understanding that all persons are unique, but members of different genders, age groups, and racial and ethnic populations tend to display some biological as well as social differences. This appreciation of diversity impacts psychopharmacology as much as any other aspect of social work intervention.

In the previous two chapters we outlined the actions of psychotropic medications and their implications for the social worker's seven roles. Besides those general actions, however, distinct actions occur among members of some special populations. Because few other professions are as extensively educated about issues of diversity, social workers have a particularly important responsibility to understand these differences and communicate their implications to the client, prescriber, and others involved in client care. Keep in mind, however, there is not universal agreement about these specific effects; much remains to be learned about how different populations react to psychotropic drugs. In this chapter, we will focus on the following groups: women, the elderly, children and adolescents, members of several racial and ethnic populations, and people experiencing symptoms of both mental illness and substance abuse.

Unless otherwise cited, our general information about pharmacokinetics and dynamics is drawn from Doran (2008), Ingersoll & Rak (2006), Janicak, Marder, & Pavuluri (2011), Julien (2011), Sadock and Sadock (2009), Saija and Mortimer (2011), Schatzberg and Nemeroff (2009), and Stahl (2008).

GENDER DIFFERENCES

General Considerations

Women have always outpaced men in their consumption of psychotropic medications, and this gender difference has become even more pronounced in the past 20 years, specifically with regard to antidepressant medications (Paulose-Ram et al., 2007). This is not to say that women necessarily have a greater need for medications. Men tend not to accurately report their own medication use because of a "pharmacological Calvinism," or a reluctance to admit use even when drugs are helpful (Stein, 2012). Casper, Belanoff, and Offer (1996) found in a sample of 497 students from three high schools that girls were significantly more likely to report emotional distress than boys on a standardized instrument. This may indicate a valid difference in distress levels but just as likely points to a greater proclivity among girls to be open about their emotional concerns. Finally, in Western culture, prescribers, most of whom are male, may subtly encourage females to fit into a mythical model of the "ideal woman" by suggesting medication when their patients complain about such issues as an unfulfilled marriage, demanding children, and a boring job (Farmer, 2003). The psychological and social factors of drug prescription and use, discussed in Chapter 4, suggest that learning why women are prescribed a disproportionate amount of drugs is an important area for ongoing study. As researchers, social workers might productively monitor their own caseloads for trends in medication use and response along gender lines.

Considering their usage patterns, it is ironic that women have been underrepresented in pharmacological research. Incredible as it may seem, it was not until 1993 that the Food and Drug Administration began to include women in the clinical evaluation of drugs and announced guidelines for the study and evaluation of gender differences in medication response. This lack of comparative data presents serious limitations in our ability to understand the effectiveness and risks of medication for women.

Women have a lower ratio of lean body mass to body fat, differences in hormone levels through the life span (including changes during menstrual cycles, pregnancy, lactation, and menopause), and some differences in brain chemical composition (Ghaemi, 2002). These differences may affect a given drug's therapeutic efficacy, adverse effects, and interactions with other drugs. We will now review the implications of these differences in more detail.

Neurotransmitters

There are some known neurotransmitter differences between the sexes that are at least in part related to variations in levels of sex steroids that interact with neuro-transmitters (Clayton, 2005). As examples, estrogen modulates serotonin function and a metabolite of progesterone acts as an agonist of GABA. Both estrogen and progesterone stimulate the release of dopamine. Some internalized sex steroids, such as those found in hormonal contraceptives and hormone replacement thera-pies, may lead to a reduction in an enzyme used in serotonin production. It is also speculated that serotonin levels play a role in the production of affective disorders related to the menstrual cycle (Rubinow & Schmidt, 2003). Although the practi-cal effects of these differences are not great in most cases, they provide evidence of sex-specific medication effects about which social workers should be aware.

Further, the experience of stress affects biological responses that differentially affect neurotransmitter production. Certain sex steroids may be affected by stress in such a way as to decrease serotonin-mediated activities. This may help to explain the increased frequency in women of some stress-related conditions, such as anxiety and depression. On the other hand, bipolar disorder and schizophrenia are experienced with equal prevalence by men and women, but women often present later in life with these disorders and experience a more benign course. Region-specific gender differences in serotonin functioning may mediate differ-ences in the expression of characteristics, such as aggression, suspiciousness, nega-tivism, and verbal hostility (Soloff et al., 2009). These (and other) biological differences suggest a basis for differential response to medication treatment by gender. As examples, men appear to respond equally well to SSRIs and tricyclic antidepressants TCAs, while women preferentially respond to SSRIs. Further, women may require lower doses of medications than men, even when adjusted for body weight, due to hormonal influences on blood levels.

Absorption

Women empty their stomach contents at a slower rate than men, which has an effect on a drug's systemic absorption. This does not affect a drug's effectiveness, but it does slow the rate at which some drugs begin demonstrating a therapeutic effect. At the same time, women have higher overall absorption rates for many medications, including the cyclic antidepressants, benzodiazepines, and antipsy-chotic phenothiazines. During their premenstrual cycles, women have a lowered ability to absorb and to clear medications, which means they are prone to higher blood levels and greater sensitivity to adverse effects at those times.

Distribution

A drug's concentration in a woman's body tissues is affected by her higher per-centage of body fat. Women maintain a higher volume of distribution for fat-soluble drugs; they have more body space available to contain such drugs. In the case of fat-soluble medications, a higher percentage of body fat also accounts for the relatively smaller blood plasma concentrations in proportion to dosage and half-life. Conversely, water-soluble drugs have a lower volume of distribution in women, which increases plasma concentration and explains, for example, why women have less tolerance for alcohol than men. Increased body fat also affects drug elimination rates (in either direction, depending on the nature of the drug). A lower binding capacity for numerous drugs, including chlordiazepoxide, diazepam, imipramine, nortriptyline, and lithium, has been established for women, and a larger amount of a drug that is free from binding increases its toxicity. Any medication of this type that has a low therapeutic index is more likely to become toxic, such as lithium and the antidepressant nortriptyline.

Metabolism

Women and men metabolize medications differently. Several variables that influence liver metabolism and clearance include hormones, pregnancy, race, food, and circadian rhythms (one's biological cycles). Hormonal fluctuations in the menstrual cycle result in a higher clearance of a drug. Oral contraceptives inhibit the metabolism of several medications, including some benzodiazepines and the antidepressant imipramine. Other benzodiazepines, however, have an increased clearance rate in the presence of oral contraceptives.

Drug metabolism is related to the actions of certain enzymes; one relevant set of enzymes (cytochrome) has been found to be more active in younger women than in older women or men. This results in shorter half-lives for several benzodiazepines and thus may increase their addictive potential. Some women become dependent on these anti-anxiety medications and experience withdrawal upon their termination.

Classes of Medication

Some gender differences have been observed with regard to the symptoms of schizophrenia and the actions of antipsychotic medications. Women are more likely to experience late-onset schizophrenia than men, and across age groups they tend to show more pronounced positive symptoms than negative symptoms with fewer cognitive deficits (Torniainen et al., 2011). Women tend to respond more positively to antipsychotic medications, which is good, but they also experience more severe side effects, including extrapyramidal symptoms and tardive dyskinesia. Even with similar dosing, age, and weight, females maintain higher blood levels of antipsychotic medication than men (Smith, 2010). The hormone estrogen is said to be responsible for these differences because it acts as a dopamine antagonist. Since most antipsychotic drugs act as dopamine receptor antagonists, the presence of estrogen may accentuate the effect of antipsychotic drugs.

Some gender differences also exist in the experience and treatment of affective disorders. Regarding bipolar disorder, women are more likely to experience bipolar II disorder, and they experience more rapid cycling and mixed episodes with bipolar I disorder (Diflorio & Jones, 2010). A variety of studies have recommended guidelines for the drug treatment of women with affective disorders. One study recommended that women be treated with lower doses of antidepressants when taking oral contraceptives and higher doses when experiencing a premenstrual exacerbation of depressive symptoms (Jensfold, 1996). Symptoms of remenstrual dysphoric disorder, a type of depression, has been successfully treated with all types of antidepressant medications. Oral contraceptives may contribute to the development of depressive symptoms because their effect on amino acid metabolism results in a deficiency of serotonin in the brain. The SSRIs are the medication of choice in these situations

PREGNANCY

Most research about the effects of medications on women focuses on pregnancy. This is because some psychotropic drugs are *teratogenic*, or potentially harmful to the fetus. In addition, no controlled studies on the safety of psychotropic medications in nursing mothers have been done. Still, when considering potential risks and benefits, many prescribers conclude that some drugs can be safe for women when carefully monitored (Ergaz & Ornoy, 2010; Miller et al., 2008). In fact, some psychiatric disorders, such as the mood and anxiety disorders, tend to cluster in women during their childbearing years (Dennis, 2010; Stowe, 2007). The prescriber must consider four general issues when deciding which medications, of all types, to give a pregnant woman:

1. The risks and benefits of taking medication with regard to the mother's overall mental status.
2. The effects of medication on the fetus.
3. The long-term physical effects on the newborn (some of which may not become apparent for years).
4. The overall effects on the mother and newborn if a current mental disorder is inadequately treated (Janicak, Marder, & Pavuluri, 2011).

In general, it is considered best for a pregnant woman not to take *any* psychotropic medications, particularly during the first trimester when the fetus faces its highest risk of damage. The blood–brain barrier, as well as the blood–placenta barrier, is the layer of fatty tissue that serves as a boundary between the circulatory system and other organs; medication must penetrate these barriers to produce an effect within the enclosed structures. Medications cross the blood–placenta barrier as well as the blood–brain barrier, thus becoming part of the fetus's bloodstream. Additionally, prescribers are reluctant to prescribe medications during breast-feeding, because most drugs pass through the milk, directly affecting the infant. Although abstinence from drugs is always the physically safest strategy for the fetus or newborn, it cannot always be implemented, because the prescriber, social worker, and client must carefully weigh all four of the above considerations in making decsions about medication. Avoidance of medication is based largely on the possibility of adverse effects rather than their inevitability. Nevertheless, the social worker as educator can fully inform the expectant mother and her significant others about special risks in pregnancy.

The Food and Drug Administration has created category labels for drugs that may be used during pregnancy, as follows (Cooper, Hickson, & Ray, 2004):

A. Controlled studies show no risk (e.g., folic acid, vitamin B6, thyroid medicine)
B. No evidence of risk in humans (some antibiotics, acetaminophen, prednisone, insulin, ibuprophin)
C. Risk cannot be ruled out (some antidepressants, prochlorperazine)
D. Positive evidence of risk (alcohol, lithium, phenotyn)
E. Contraindicated in pregnancy (the sedative thalidomide)

By implication, it is usually helpful to increase the intensity of interventions other than psychotropic medication during pregnancy to offset any precautionary drug measures taken by the prescriber. These interventions may include cognitive behavioral, individual, or family therapy; client and family education; assistance with mental status monitoring; and client participation in psychosocial rehabilitation programs. The social worker may also need to link the client with community agencies that provide prenatal services.

Classes of Medication

When the risks of not taking medication, including unmanageable symptoms and self-care limitations, appear to be more serious than those of using it, prescribers follow several principles. For psychotic disorders, it may be safer to use the high-potency medications, such as haloperidol and risperidone, which have fewer negative effects on the fetus than other medications, effects such as sedation, hypotension, gastrointestinal slowing, and tachycardia. The prescriber may discontinue all medications several weeks before delivery so that the newborn will not experience problems related to withdrawal and other adverse effects. Unless the client has chosen to breast-feed, she should resume psychotropic medication immediately after delivery, particularly because there is always the possibility of postpartum psychosis. Furthermore, the prescriber may avoid or minimize antiparkinsonian drug treatments because this presents a further risk to the newborn. The nursing baby may experience infant extrapyramidal effects if his or her mother consumes these medications.

Antidepressant medications are also best avoided during pregnancy when possible. A systematic literature review concluded that while these drugs are relatively safe, some significant areas of concern exist, particularly the elevated risk of preterm birth, neonatal adaptation difficulties, and congenital cardiac malformations (Udechuku, Nguyen, Hill, & Szego, 2010). Taking a newly pregnant mother off medications must be done gradually so as to not cause withdrawal in either the mother or the fetus. The social worker should consider increasing educational and family support roles through this process so that the client and family understand the rationale for these changes and can actively help to maintain an environment conducive to a healthy pregnancy.

Mood-stabilizing medications are considerably more risky than those in other classes for the pregnant client (Cohen, 2007). Lithium use may cause fetal heart problems, specifically the development of the large vessels of the heart. If lithium is prescribed, lower doses may be used to avoid high peak levels. Further, because a pregnant woman's blood volume increases and lithium levels become more unstable, the drug is more difficult to monitor during pregnancy. Here again, the social worker's roles need to expand to provide alternative services and to help the client monitor effects for the prescriber and treatment team. Carbamazepine has been associated with various developmental delays and cranial defects in newborns (supplemental folic acid is believed to reduce the risks of some of these). Valproate can also be teratogenic. Although the studies on which these findings are based are inconclusive, the possibility of serious negative effects makes the use of mood-stabilizing medications an extremely delicate problem. Lamotrigine and oxcarbazepine have shown significant risk factors but are too new to have been extensively studied in this regard. When they are used, the fetus should be monitored with sonography to detect any adverse changes. The social worker may need to assume responsibility for planning and advocacy so that such procedures occur promptly and regularly.

The effects of anti-anxiety medications in pregnancy are also a concern. Benzodiazepines have been reported to cause fetal abnormalities in the first trimester of pregnancy (Masud, Sobhan, & Ryals, 2002). Further, a fetus can develop benzodiazepine dependence and experience withdrawal after birth. Diphenhydramine should be avoided because it may cause withdrawal complications for the newborn. Because this medication is available without prescription, the social worker can help to ensure that the client is aware of pregnancy risks even with these types of drugs. Buspirone has a relatively benign side-effect profile for pregnant women (Choy, 2007).

It is worth noting that, in general, the newer medications from each class have not been tested with pregnant women as much as the older medications. Thus, even though the newer medications have fewer overall adverse effects for general populations, their effects on a fetus are less well known.

SEXUAL ADVERSE EFFECTS OF MEDICATIONS

Psychotropic medication may adversely affect the sexual functioning of both men and women, and in the case of the SSRIs, this kind of adverse effect is now known to be greater than previously asserted (Clayton & Balon, 2009). Symptoms may include a decreased sex drive for both, an impaired ability to ejaculate or maintain erections for men, and an inhibition of orgasm for women. Serotonin-enhancing drugs, which increase prolactin release (a hormone that affects several aspects of sexual functioning), tend to produce a decrease in sexual desire. Prescribers can make medication adjustments that may alleviate these side effects. On the other hand, dopamine reuptake inhibitors may actually enhance sexual arousal and desire. In each drug category, some medications may have fewer of these potential adverse effects than others, although research is not extensive in this regard. With the newer antidepressant drugs, for example, it appears that venlafaxine, nefazodone, bupropion, and mirtazepine are likely to cause less sexual dysfunction than paroxetine, citaprolam, fluvoxamine, sertraline, and fluoxetine.

Because of the complexity of decision-making in the pregnancy and postpartum periods and the fact that many clients are uncomfortable discussing these issues with professionals, part of the prescriber and social worker's task is to create an environment where these concerns, if present, can be shared (Price & Bentley, 2012). The social worker can also help the client decide if the possibility of these side effects is worth the risk of increasing the client's anxiety. If the client is not sexually active while using medications, some of these effects may not be problematic; however, they may still impact a client's sense of self. In any case, the social worker can explore this area of the client's life as well as others to provide a relevant assessment in the event that psychotropic medications will be used.

OLDER ADULTS

General Considerations

Older adults (people age 65 years and older) are subject to the same mental health concerns as any other age group (Patterson et al., 2009). They experience more physical health problems, however, than younger populations. Older adults comprise 13% of the population but consume 33% of prescribed medications and 50% of all over-the-counter medications. In collaboration with other providers, social workers need to continuously help assess the extent to which psychiatric symptoms in the elderly result from psychological problems, medical illnesses, using multiple medications, or all of these.

The normal physiological changes that come with aging are relevant to decisions about the prescribing of any medications. These include changes in the following areas:

1. *Rate of gastrointestinal activity.* With the aging population, gastrointestinal tract activity slows, affecting medication absorption and distribution, so in most cases medications will not take effect as quickly.

2. *Body mass and weight.* Older adults have less total body water, less lean body mass, and more body fat (particularly women). As a result, the distribution efficiency of water-soluble drugs is reduced, while that of the fat-soluble drugs is increased. A lower body weight implies that the prescriber may determine dosage levels on a "milligram by weight" basis rather than strict milligram dosages, although this occurs in some other cases as well, such as for people who weigh more than average.

3. *Reduction in serum protein levels.* It should be recalled from Chapter 4 that a significant amount of many drugs is rendered inert in one's system because of binding with protein in the bloodstream and thus remaining unavailable to

the desired site of action. In older adults with a reduction in serum protein levels, there are higher levels of the free drug available for therapeutic action. As a result, a smaller dose of a given drug is required for a desired effect. Drugs with active metabolites should be avoided when possible to improve clearance.

4. *Metabolism.* As people age, there is a gradual decline in the quality and efficiency of their liver and kidney functions. Both therapeutic responses and side effects may occur at blood levels lower than expected with other age groups. As metabolism slows, the half-lives of all psychotropic medications increase, some of them doubling or tripling. A general prescription strategy is thus "start low, go slow." The social worker must also be aware that toxic amounts of medication may build more quickly in an older client's bloodstream. Toxicity (see Chapter 4) also becomes problematic because of decreased rates of renal clearance (up to 50% less by age 70). Clearance is also less efficient in older men because prostate enlargement causes greater urinary retention.

5. *Cardiovascular efficiency.* The aging process impacts cardiovascular system functioning as cardiac output and blood perfusion into other organs diminishes. Kidney function is therefore slowed and liver function is compromised.

6. *Sensitivity of certain nervous system receptors.* Certain neurotransmitters in the brain become more sensitive in older people, another reason why the same amount of medication may have a greater effect.

Studies have been done regarding age-related changes in serotonin availability (Pacheco et al., 2012). A decrease in serotonin levels in older adults is associated with enhanced memory, and thus serotonin-antagonist medications may actually help some elderly people with memory problems. Older adults also experience a reduction in naturally occurring cholinergic neurons. As a result they are more sensitive to the anticholinergic effects of some antipsychotic and antidepressant medications.

In addition to these changes are the dangers of polypharmacy, or prescribing more than one medication to treat the same or other physical or mental problems. These dangers include problems related to misuse of over-the-counter drugs, alcohol abuse, and the impact of multiple drugs on their clearance from one's system. In the roles of consultant, educator, and monitor, the social worker can continuously update the prescriber about the client's physical status and changes in usage of other medications and help ensure adherence by offering medication education.

As a means of managing issues related to polypharmacy, social workers can ask themselves the following questions (Doran, 2008):

- How many prescription medications does my client take?
- How many non-prescription medications does my client take?
- With how many health professionals does my client consult?

- Is my client impaired in any way that will affect his or her ability to manage the prescription schedule?
- Does my client live alone?
- Can my client self-administer the medications?
- Is special packaging required?

Classes of Medication

When psychotic symptoms appear for the first time in older adulthood, it should be presumed that the causes are medical (Patterson et al., 2009). Once these are ruled out, general drug treatment strategies for older adults resemble those used for other age groups, but prescribers may implement them differently (Meeks & Jeste, 2008). Two significant concerns include the heightened sensitivity of older adults to anticholinergic effects and the risk of falls owing to hypotension. The high-potency antipsychotic medications (such as risperidone) have fewer anticholinergic effects but produce uncomfortable extrapyramidal effects and hypotention; the opposite is true for the low-potency drugs (such as clozapine). With their increased sensitivity to the anticholinergic effects of any drug, the elderly may experience "central anticholinergic syndrome," characterized by problems with short-term memory, confusion, and, occasionally, visual hallucinations. The effects of this syndrome resemble those of Alzheimer's disease. The newer antipsychotic olanzapine represents a promising alternative. Further, members of this population sometimes exhibit a serious problem with agitation that is not related to symptoms of a mental disorder, but is still responsive to low-dose antipsychotic medications.

Older adults experience an increased risk of tardive dyskinesia (TD). Although the overall prevalence of TD for persons using antipsychotic medication is about 24% (Jeste & Caligiuri, 1993), the risk increases with age. The onset of TD may be related to a cumulative effect of medications over time as well as their interactions with normal physiological changes in parts of the brain. With this movement disorder, older adults also demonstrate fewer instances of spontaneous remission. Fortunately, studies of the second-generation antipsychotic medications thus far suggest that those drugs produce the effect only 50% as frequently (Dolder & Jester, 2003). As with other risks, careful monitoring is essential; the social worker should report any evidence of TD to the prescriber and help determine appropriate interventions. Tardive dyskinesia can be treated when it occurs, with varying degrees of success, with dosage lowering or the introduction of additional medications (Howland, 2011).

Because of their need to cope with medical disorders, physical pain, increased overall drug use, social isolation, and cumulative bereavement issues, older adults are more predisposed to depression than younger persons. It is a mistake to assume that it is normal for older adults to feel depressed or that they can tolerate it any better than younger people. Late-onset depression is frequently characterized by higher levels of cognitive impairment, insomnia, agitation, and mortality rates. Suicide rates are in fact highest among the older adult population (Patterson et al., 2009). Unfortunately, because of their multiple health concerns, these clients often receive too much, or sometimes too little, antidepressant medication. The social worker's challenge is to assess levels of depression and help to sort out the various physical and emotional issues contributing to it.

The typical side effects of the cyclic antidepressants are particularly troublesome for older adults (Gonzalez, Mustelier, & Rey, 2005). They include sedation, hypotension, anticholinergic effects, and cardiac effects. Prescribers generally do not use them for persons with cardiac conditions or those at risk of falling. The anticholinergic effects of constipation and urinary retention can go unrecognized until they cause significant problems for the elderly client. The MAO inhibitors, and phenelzine in particular, so difficult to manage in younger populations, present certain advantages for older adults. They do not produce anticholinergic effects and, in fact, may counteract the production of natural but potentially harmful increases in monoamine oxidase in the aging brain. Of course, the risks of hypotension and dietary reactions remain. In short, the MAO drug class may be more suitable for the elderly than some younger populations.

The serotonin reuptake inhibitors do not appear to pose any special risk for elderly clients. In fact, the absence of sedation, hypotension, and anticholinergic and cardiovascular effects make them particularly attractive. However, the side effects of nausea, nervousness, and insomnia will be troublesome to those persons already experiencing related problems. These drugs are also more expensive, which is often a concern for all consumers but sometimes more so with older adults who live on restricted incomes.

Lithium is the only psychotropic medication that is water soluble, making age-related changes in response to it predictable. These changes are associated with alterations in the renal system and the increased sensitivity of some nervous system receptor sites. Decreased clearance rates put older consumers at risk for higher therapeutic and toxic blood levels. In recent years the anticonvulsant medications have been used more often as mood-stabilizing drugs of first choice but they feature several problematic side effects for older adults, including dizziness, sedation, and others (Doran, 2008).

Anxiety is highly prevalent among older adults and may be manifested differently than in younger people (El-Gabalawy et al., 2011). Phobic disorders and generalized anxiety disorder are the most common among older adults. Simple phobia is the only type that has been commonly found to have an initial onset after age 60. Panic disorder is relatively rare, but sleep disturbances are common, experienced by over 50% of older adults. The benzodiazepines, while effective medications, produce side effects of sedation, cognitive impairment, reduced psychomotor coordination, and falls due to hypotension, all of which are serious. Further, with a reduced clearance rate, older adults more quickly experience a toxic amount of these drugs. Many of these problems may be minimized by using benzodiazepines with shorter half-lives and less active metabolites (Benitez et al., 2008). Generally, the short-acting, low-potency drugs such as lorazepam, oxazepam, triazolam, and temazepam are well tolerated by older adults, while longer-acting drugs such as diazepam and clonazepam are best avoided. Unfortunately, these drugs can be abused, with their overprescription being a major problem in nursing homes. Prescribers are becoming more reluctant to prescribe benzodiazepines at all, and more often use buspirone, which has been shown to be effective in the treatment of anxiety. The social worker may also use nondrug cognitive-behavioral interventions for anxiety, such as encouraging clients to sleep well, maintain good hygiene, avoid stimulants, reduce environmental agitation, and exercise regularly.

CHILDREN AND ADOLESCENTS

General Considerations

We have already addressed aspects of this issue in the previous chapter but will make additional, more fundamental observations here. The use of psychotropic drugs in children and adolescents has often produced controversy. Most issues pertain to either the appropriateness of medication (rationale for use, alternatives, toxicity) or inadequacies in their clinical management (Wolraich, 2003). Further, children and adolescents experience rapid physical, emotional, and cognitive development processes, and there is concern that any of these may be adversely affected by the introduction of psychotropic medications. New drugs are rarely studied in children and adolescents before marketing. In fact, 80% of the medications used by children and adolescents have not been extensively tested with that population (Patterson et al., 2009). While there is evidence that medications can be helpful for members of this population who experience ADHD and depression, evidence for other problems is not extensive (Johnston & Frehling, 2008). There is a dearth of studies on the medication of children and adolescents and that any drug prescription must be done with extreme care and caution.

According to a work group of the American Psychological Association (APA) (2006), most of the evidence for the effectiveness of psychotropic drugs for children and adolescents is limited to acute symptomatic improvement with only limited attention paid to functional outcomes. Very few studies have considered issues of diversity within this population. Further, the benefits of some behavioral treatments are well documented. Thus, for most of the major mental, emotional, and behavioral problems of children and adolescents, psychosocial interventions can be effective as stand-alone interventions.

The symptoms for which psychotropic drugs are prescribed can be generally categorized as either behavioral inadequacies or excesses. Besides the symptoms already discussed in this book, children and adolescents may receive psychotropic medications for pervasive developmental disorders, Tourette's syndrome, sleep disorders, enuresis, and conduct disorder. With this population, two special concerns arise: the child's often reluctant participation and the possibility that otherwise effective medications may harm physical development. Ranked from least to most troublesome with respect to side effects, the most commonly prescribed psychotropic drugs for children and adolescents are stimulants, cyclic antidepressants, and antipsychotic medications. Other drugs, such as beta-blockers, lithium, carbamazepine, and the atypical antidepressants, are more difficult to evaluate because of the relatively short time they have been available for research.

The psychopharmacological assessment and management of children and adolescents is more complicated than that of adults (Floersch et al., 2009). This is due to (1) the need for comprehensive family involvement to ensure that the perspectives of all members are represented in decision-making, (2) wide differences in physical development among children and adolescents, (3) the diagnostic ambiguity of emerging first episodes of mental illness, (4) ethical issues in decision-making and the rights of minors, and (5) the impact of drug treatment on the child's self-concept. Social workers should view the absence of active interest by parents or caregivers as a major treatment concern. When one adds psychosocial developmental issues (such as the adolescent's need to separate from the family) to the complications of prescribing medications, drug management requires a strong partnership between social worker and family to ensure collaboration. Because of fears of peer ridicule and a reluctance to participate in therapies that label clients as "ill," non-adherence with most interventions is a general problem in child and adolescent health care. The prescriber will usually start low, aiming for the lowest possible effective dose. Monitoring and laboratory follow-up may need to be more frequent than with other age groups.

School-age children metabolize and clear psychotropic drugs rapidly, but paradoxically, they are also more sensitive to their therapeutic effects, which complicates the issue of appropriate dosing. This is particularly true before puberty, after which sex hormones increase and compete with drugs for enzymes, slowing metabolism rates. Typically, children and adolescents can tolerate a higher ratio of milligrams to body weight. Young female clients seem to achieve higher blood levels than young male clients and experience more side effects from the same weight-adjusted dose. Children tend to have a greater level of fluid intake than adults, which produces a shorter half-life with water-soluble drugs such as lithium.

Classes of Medication

Antipsychotic medications, especially the second-generation drugs, can produce symptomatic improvement in members of this age group, although this is less marked in children under age 15. The FDA has approved the use of antipsychotic medications with children for some behavioral disorders as well as psychotic symptoms. Overall prescriptions of these medications for children have risen five-fold since the mid-1990s (Harrison, Cluxton-Keller, & Gross, 2011), although they have not received extensive testing (Ben Armor, 2012). Both children and adolescents experience the adverse effect of sedation more often than adults do. They may complain less about these effects, so the prescriber and social worker should inquire about this effect regularly. Without consumer feedback, the social worker can also help to monitor indicators of "behavioral toxicity," including diminished activity, apathy, withdrawal, cognitive dulling, and sedation. Long-term adverse effects of these drugs may include interference with the client's natural physical growth. An increased risk of tardive dyskinesia (TD) with ongoing use of medications also requires close monitoring. Some prescribers assert that the risk of TD may be greater because the consumer's brain is still developing (Farrel, Fischer, & McCabe, 2010). The reduced risk of movement reactions (i.e., dystonia, akathisia, or parkinsonianism) among young persons using antipsychotic medications is offset by more pronounced anticholinergic effects. Extrapyramidal symptoms, including dystonic reactions and parkinsonianism, appear to be more prevalent among teenagers, especially males, than all other age groups. High-potency antipsychotic medications probably interfere less with learning than low-potency types, and the lower anticholinergic activity of the high-potency medications minimizes the risk of delirium, which can occur in young populations.

During the 1980s, an outpouring of research on mood disorders in children and adolescents resulted in the widespread use of antidepressants with this group. Besides uncomplicated depression, common syndromes these drugs are used to treat include hyperactivity (when stimulants are not effective), separation anxiety, and obsessive-compulsive behaviors. Several difficulties, however, arise in the use of antidepressants with adolescents (Ahn, Yakutis, & Frazier, 2012). First, hormonal changes make measuring effectiveness very difficult. High levels of sex hormones modulate the developing neurotransmitter systems in ways that diminish antidepressant efficacy. Second, nonpharmacological aspects of treatment are more difficult to control in this population than in others. Finally, as adolescents confront identity stressors, peer relationships, and independence issues, they may be tempted to misuse medication in an attempt to take control of their lives. Amazingly, many studies indicate that antidepressant drug treatment is often no more effective than a placebo. In fact, the placebo effect in children is so profound in research on antidepressant drugs that the social worker and prescriber should always be cautious about attributing signs of clinical improvement to the biological effect of a medication (Scahill, Solanto, & McGuire, 2008).

Side effects common among younger people but uncommon among adults include cardiovascular toxicity (arrhythmia) and neurological symptoms (the possibility of seizure). The cyclic antidepressants produce dry mouth, nausea, constipation, dizziness, blurred vision, drowsiness, appetite changes, headaches, fatigue, and sleep disturbances, including insomnia and nightmares. The adverse effects are the same as those in older populations except that the medications are more likely to increase blood pressure in younger people. Although a common cardiovascular effect is mild tachycardia, serious hypotension is rare.

There is growing evidence of the effectiveness of SSRI antidepressants, however (Taurines, Gerlach, Warnke, Thome, & Wewetzer, 2011). These drugs may be preferable because of their relatively well-tolerated side-effect profiles and their reduced potential for intentional overdose. These atypical antidepressants appear relatively safe for children, although they may experience the same side effects as older persons. These side effects can sometimes be minimized by "halving" adult doses for children (splitting tablets in two and taking one of the halves as a full dose). Popper (1995) cautions, however, that the new antidepressants may be changing attitudes too quickly about prescribing such drugs; they are being used rather extensively without a background of research on which to base judgments about their benefits and risks. It must be emphasized, however, that the FDA has introduced strong precautions against prescribing SSRI drugs to people younger than age 18 because of some reports of increased suicidality among those consumers (Gibbons et al., 2007). This evidence suggests that adolescents may have a higher risk of a manic episode while on cyclic or atypical antidepressant drugs. Finally, some evidence suggests that adolescents may have a higher risk of a manic episode while on either cyclic or SSRI drugs. Because of their high elimination rates, abrupt withdrawal of antidepressants may cause children to develop gastrointestinal complaints and fatigue, which may be confused with continuing depression.

There is a significant body of literature on the effectiveness of antimanic agents on children and adolescents with bipolar disorder, and it indicates that such treatment can be effective, although the range of adverse effects is considerable (Liu et al, 2011). Because children rapidly clear lithium, the prescriber may prescribe higher doses than those for adults to achieve therapeutic effect. Children may experience the same side effects that adults do, but they seem to tolerate long-term treatment well. The most serious concerns in children and adolescents are the long-term consequences of lithium accumulation in bone tissue and lithium's effect on thyroid and renal function. Nonetheless, lithium appears to be somewhat better-tolerated overall than the antipsychotic medications.

Relatively few studies of drug therapy for anxiety symptoms in children and adolescents exist. Many prescribers believe that anxiolytic drugs make hyperactive and psychotic children worse, so SSRI drugs have become the first-line treatment options for this population (Rynn et al., 2011). The state of the evidence is that while cognitive-behavioral therapy CBT may be the best initial treatment for anxiety disorders, this may be augmented if necessary by the SSRI drugs. The FDA recommends that prescribers meet with the child or adolescent client weekly for the first 4 weeks following medication initiation, every 2 weeks for 4 weeks, and then monthly for 12 months.

Tourette's disorder, an inherited biological disorder characterized by tics, noises, and coarse speech, does respond positively to medication. Haloperidol is the best-known and longest-used drug to treat this disorder, but others, such as pimozide and clonidine, are available as alternatives. Haloperidol has also been effective with persons having autistic disorder, although such children are at a high risk for tardive dyskinesia and other adverse effects. Alternative medications for autism include naltrexone, propranolol (for aggression and agitation), and fenfluramine (for hyperactivity).

With children, there is an additional concern related to iatrogenic effects, or new developmental problems the child acquires as a result of taking medications. Concerns have been raised in the literature (Barnett, 2012) that children may (1) attribute adjustment problems to factors beyond their control and become less responsive to behavioral interventions, (2) fail to acquire adaptive behaviors because their symptoms are suppressed, and caregivers thus do not recognize the need to teach coping strategies, (3) come to regard medication as the primary or only effective way to cope with adjustment difficulties, and (4) become more likely to abuse psychoactive substances. Although these effects can occur within any age group, children and adolescents have not yet formed overall coping and adaptation styles.

ETHNOPHARMACOTHERAPY

The racial and ethnic demographics of U.S. citizens have undergone tremendous changes during the past 50 years (Fong & Furuto, 2001; United States Census Bureau, 2012). Until 1965, two-thirds of all legal immigrants to the United States came from Europe and Canada. In 1965, a new immigration act allowed for an annual immigration quota per country. The effect of this act, along with an increase in ethnic self-identification and a slowing of the birth rate of whites, has been striking. The percentage of immigrants from Asia rose from 6% in the 1950s to 44% in the 1980s, and the percentage from Europe and Canada fell from 65% to 14%. The percentage of immigrants from Mexico and other Latin American countries grew from 25% to 40%. Overall, the percentage of the U.S. population composed of ethnic minorities grew from 11% in 1960 to 26% in 2010. In addition, there is great diversity within these ethnic and racial groups. For example, Asians residing in the United States speak more than 100 different languages, African Americans are being joined by immigrants from the Caribbean, South America, and Africa, American Indians belong to more than 500 tribes, and Hispanics come from countries throughout Latin America.

Research is only beginning to focus on the area of racial variations in medication response. Some evidence exists that such differences do exist, but findings must be considered tentative. Perceived differences in symptomatology and treatment response among racial and ethnic groups may occur because of differences in treatment-seeking behavior and differential presentation of symptoms (Shim, Compton, Rust, Druss, & Kaslow, 2009). Further, it is difficult to claim that any sample is representative of a racial or ethnic group, given the mixed lineage of so many consumers (Pena, 2011). Some cultural trends do exist, however, in the ways individuals cope with stress, express emotion, and conceptualize and treat mental problems.

The range of biopsychosocial factors that influence psychotropic drug metabolism and response among ethnic groups include the following.

1. Diet and nutritional factors (influence on metabolic activity)
2. The actions of certain enzymes
3. Differences in consumption of cigarettes, caffeine, alcohol, herbs, and other psychoactive substances (influence on drug metabolism or response)
4. Sleep or activity and rest patterns (effect on other physiological events)
5. Environmental exposure to toxins or pollutants
6. Differences in exposure to psychological stress
7. Prescribing practices among health care providers
8. Patterns of illness behavior among cultural groups
9. Cultural attitudes toward medication usage (Turner & Cooley-Quille, 1996)

An important perspective that the social work profession can bring to ethnic understanding is what health and illness mean within a culture (Kirkcaldy, Furnham, & Siefen, 2011). In addition to a client's physical characteristics, a prescriber should take into account the psychological and social factors noted above when he or she considers what medications to prescribe. The social worker's person-in-environment perspective places him or her in a sound position for helping to assess and evaluate the social and cultural contexts of mental illness. Social workers can coordinate the actions of the interdisciplinary team in educating both clients and professionals, eliciting treatment expectations from clients and their significant others, and enforcing an affirming emotional tone in communications among workers, clients, and families.

The study of the relationship between an individual's genotype (reflected in racial and familial differences) and his or her ability to metabolize drugs is known as *pharmacogenomics* (Leckband, Bishop, & Ellingrod, 2007). Introduced in Chapter 3, this is the study of how a person's genetic inheritance affects his or her response to medications. While it is true that environment, diet, age, lifestyle, and health status all influence a person's reactions to medication, genetic factors are considered to be a major determinant of the normal variability in drug effects. Important work has been done identifying *polymorphisms*, naturally occurring variants in the structures of genes, and enzymatic differences among the races. Polymorphisms in drug metabolism genes are important to study because they act across classes of drugs. The best-known polymorphisms at this time affect the metabolism of antidepressants, antipsychotic medications, and benzodiazepines. For example, tricyclic antidepressants have a narrow therapeutic index, and poor metabolizers may have problems when these drugs are taken at usually prescribed doses due to their elevated blood concentrations.

Most oxidation processes that govern metabolism are performed by one of three enzyme systems associated with the cytochrone (CYP) P450 enzyme. These are responsible for breaking down more than 30 different classes of drugs and 80% of current prescription drugs. DNA variations in genes that code for these enzymes influence the person's ability to metabolize certain drugs. Less active or inactive forms of CYP, which are unable to break down and efficiently eliminate drugs from the body, can cause overdose in some consumers.

Research in the past 35 years has uncovered significant differences among racial groups in their rates of drug metabolism. As examples, Asians are poor metabolizers of many drugs and thus have a higher incidence and severity of drug-related side effects. Hispanic persons have been reported to require lower doses of antidepressants and to experience more side effects compared to Caucasians. African Americans show higher blood levels and faster therapeutic response. Compared with whites, Asians respond to lower doses of antipsychotic drugs and develop toxic side effects at lower doses. Flockhart and Oesterheld (2000) classified all psychotropic drugs specifically by the six enzymes from the CYP system that metabolizes them. They noted that 3 to 4% of Caucasians and 15 to 20% of Asians are poor metabolizers of one of these enzymes (2C19). A second enzyme (2C9) is poorly metabolized by 1 to 3% of Caucasians, and a third (2D6) is poorly metabolized by 5 to 10% of Caucasians. Still, precisely how to adjust dosages of a medication is unclear to prescribers because of the small amount of research done on the topic thus far. Complicating the process is the fact that we have limited knowledge of what genes are involved with each drug response, and millions of DNA sequence variations must be identified and analyzed to determine their involvement (if any) in drug response (Caley, 2011).

African Americans

African Americans are more likely to be diagnosed with schizophrenia than any other racial group (Neighbors et al., 2003). This seeming overdiagnosis may be related to a higher perceived prevalence of positive vs. negative symptoms in African Americans. Potter et al., (2009) found that this trend held among older adults with dementia, as African Americans were more likely to present symptoms of psychosis than depression. This difference in presentation may be due to family members not bringing their loved ones to the attention of mental health professionals until the symptoms became relatively extreme. African Americans are also less likely to receive lithium, anti-anxiety, and antidepressant medications. They are more likely than Caucasians to experience adverse effects with "standard" doses of lithium, because it appears to be excreted more slowly. African Americans may experience a worsening of hypertension if that condition exists before lithium is prescribed.

Caucasians experience higher lifetime rates of major depression but African American persons experience dysthymic disorder more often (Riolo et al., 2005). African Americans demonstrate a higher risk of depressive disorders resulting from medical illness, a higher prevalence of phobic disorders, higher rates of adjustment disorders with mixed emotional features, and episodes of delirium from drug interactions (Breslau et al., 2006). The latter finding may be related to the fact that African Americans are also more likely to experience polypharmacy than other racial groups.

The apparent higher use of some medications among African American adults is troubling in that they are at a higher risk for adverse effects with some medications. Burroughs, Maxey, & Levy, (2002) note that African Americans are "poor metabolizers" for antidepressant and anti-anxiety drugs. That is, they required lower doses with smaller increases than other races for the same effects. As another example, African Americans seem to have low baseline white blood cell counts, which prevents them from meeting minimum levels required for the antipsychotic drug clozapine. On the positive side, African American clients tend to have a faster response than other racial groups to benzodiazepine drugs and to the cyclic antidepressants when given an appropriate dose.

Regarding treatment-seeking behavior, it has been noted that African Americans are less inclined to self-disclosure than Caucasians (Consedine et al., 2007). Further, African American families are less likely to seek help from mental health professionals for their children, and individuals of all ages are less likely to perceive themselves as having a mental illness (Kranke et al., 2012).

People of Hispanic Cultures

Medication-related studies of Hispanic people (from Spain, Mexico, Cuba, Puerto Rico, Central America, and South America) are far fewer than those of other racial and ethnic populations. Still, the large and rapidly growing Hispanic population in the United States mandates the social worker's need to understand their orientation and response to medications. The reliance of this ethnic group on traditional social supports rather than on professional intervention suggests that the social worker may have problems in maintaining contact with clients over time (Woodward, 2011). Interestingly, in one large study, Mexican Americans were less likely to have a psychiatric disorder that non-Hispanic whites, but their greater acculturation in the United States was associated with a greater risk of a mental disorder (Ortega et al., 2000). Acculturated Puerto Ricans had a greater risk of substance abuse. At the same time, the percentage of Hispanic persons seeking professional help for emotional problems has actually decreased in the last 20 years (Blanco et al., 2007). More aggressive outreach activities, as is typical with case management practice, may be necessary to ensure a positive outcome with Hispanic clients.

People of Hispanic descent have certain enzyme differences compared with other populations that affect their metabolic processes, causing slower drug metabolism. Doctors in Latin America typically prescribe lower doses of medication than their counterparts in the United States. Evidence indicates that all Latin Americans tend to respond better to lower doses of the antipsychotic drug risperidone and have a higher rate of adverse effects from the medication (Lawson, 2000). Further, clients in Argentina and Chile respond well to 300 mg per day of clozapine, which is less than the amount typically used in the United States (Mendoza & Smith, 2000). Some evidence exists that Hispanic clients require less antidepressant medication and have more side effects at lower dosages than Caucasians (Turner & Cooley-Quille, 1996). Their particular liver enzymes make them more susceptible to alcohol toxicity as well (Kail, 1989). There are no reports of differences among members of this ethnic group with regard to lithium response. One study of 50 Hispanic people with schizophrenia (Dassori et al., 1998) indicated that they may experience a higher level of negative symptoms than Caucasian or African American people, more specifically, cognitive deficits. Still, like African Americans, Hispanics are reluctant (particularly younger people) to participate in formal intervention programs (unless the professional is Hispanic), so little is known about their special characteristics regarding medications (Hosch et al., 1996; McMiller & Weisz, 1996).

Asian Americans

The term *Asian* refers to Chinese, Filipino, Indian, Korean, Vietnamese, Japanese, and other groups from the continent of Asia. These people have the *lowest* use of formal mental health services of any ethnic population because of stigma, shame, lack of financial resources, and conceptions of health and intervention that differ from Western culture (Tung, 2011). Further, Xu et al. (2011) found in a national study that Asian Americans have a lower prevalence of mental, emotional, and behavioral problems than Caucasians. Asian traditions of viewing the body and mind as unitary result in their focusing on physical discomfort more than emotional symptoms. Because of their reluctance to seek professional help, Asian Americans who do present for services tend to have serious disturbances.

Fewer than half of Asian American clients adhere to psychotropic medications when they are prescribed, largely due to cultural beliefs (Fancher et al., 2012). In working with Asian clients, it may be important for the social worker to elicit beliefs in traditional Asian medical practices and to involve family members in diagnosis and treatment planning, given the especially strong family orientation of Asians. Further, some Asians use herbal treatments for a variety of problems (Fang & Schinke, 2007), and this can result in adverse reactions when psychotropic drugs are prescribed. Asian populations tend to expect Western medications to exert effects swiftly, to carry a high likelihood of severe adverse effects, and to be effective only for superficial manifestations of a problem (Lin & Shen, 1991).

Asian people demonstrate pronounced pharmacokinetic and pharmacodynamic differences from other ethnic groups (Ramirez, 1996). They have a smaller body size than many other groups; they also metabolize antipsychotic, antidepressant, and anti-anxiety medications more slowly. Comparatively lower dosages can be effective but still carry the potential for greater toxicity. Researchers have suggested that for all psychotropic medications, prescribers begin with half the standard dose. Asians may be at an increased risk for acute dystonic reactions from antipsychotic drugs. Conversely, some studies report a lower prevalence of tardive dyskinesia among some Asian clients, depending on where the client lives. That is, Koreans living in China have a higher rate than Koreans living in Seoul, and Chinese and Korean clients living in the same region have similar rates. These differences indicate how ethnic characteristics interact with other factors, such as diet and lifestyle, in producing medication effects. There are mixed reports about lithium; some research indicates that it is cleared at a similar rate in Asian and Caucasian groups, whereas other studies have found smaller doses necessary for Asian groups (Wing et al., 1997). Asian refugee groups show a high prevalence of posttraumatic stress disorder, for which MAO inhibitors have been demonstrated to be useful, as well as of depression and panic disorders.

Asian Americans experience lower rates of most anxiety disorders (Asnaani et al., 2010). Interestingly, benzodiazepines are widely prescribed in Asian countries, and in some areas they are available without a prescription. Long-term tolerance may thus exist among people who have recently emigrated to the United States.

PEOPLE WITH A DUAL DIAGNOSIS OF MENTAL ILLNESS AND SUBSTANCE ABUSE

In the past 30 years, attention has increasingly focused on the prevalence of substance abuse among people with symptoms of mental illness and the difficulty in providing effective treatment for them, medication and otherwise. Substance abuse is probably most common among those with depressive disorders (Renner et al., 2011). It occurs in as many as 50% of people with long-term mental illnesses (Doran, 2008) but unfortunately is underdiagnosed by mental health professionals in approximately 20% of cases (Schulte et al., 2010). The substances most frequently cited as exacerbating psychotic or affective symptoms include alcohol, cocaine, marijuana, stimulants, and hallucinogenic drugs. If inclined to use alcohol or other drugs, people with mental illness tend to use what is available in their environments rather than any particular substance. Although each substance has unique effects, many, including cocaine, nicotine, marijuana, and caffeine, directly affect dopamine, serotonin, and other neurotransmitters that are relevant to the symptoms of various disorders (Ziedonis et al., 2000).

Clients with dual diagnoses experience higher levels of anxiety than clients who have similar symptoms but not a co-occurring substance abuse problem (Curtis, 2004). They tend to be younger, male, at a higher risk of experiencing episodes of mental illness and to have a poorer long-term prognosis for recovery (Rassool, 2006). When intoxicated, they are more disinhibited and aggressive. They are also at greater risk for relapse, hospitalization, family problems, and residential instability. Of most immediate concern to social workers is their tendency not to adhere to their medication and to mix prescription medications with alcohol or street drugs. People with schizophrenia and a substance abuse problem have a higher likelihood of tardive dyskinesia. When going through withdrawal from substance abuse, these clients, as with all people, may experience tremors, hallucinations, seizures, and delusions, which complicates their existing symptom profile.

With manic conditions, substance abuse can impair a client's already poor impulse control. To help themselves relax, people with bipolar disorder and anxiety disorders often use self-medicating agents (Weinberger & George, 2009). Self-medication is also sometimes seen when clients try to reduce the side effects of neuroleptic medications with such drugs as alcohol and marijuana. Stimulants may increase a client's affect and energy levels that are diminished by some medications. Nicotine reduces some of the muscular side effects of neuroleptic drugs, but it also impairs the drugs' therapeutic potency. A longitudinal study of New Hampshire Medicaid beneficiaries found that, across all diagnostic groups, clients with dual diagnoses used benzodiazepine drugs at a significantly higher rate than clients without a substance abuse problem (Clark, Xie, & Brunette, 2004).

Some of the psychotropic drugs themselves can be abused (Baird, 2011). We have discussed the potential for abusing benzodiazepines, which treat anxiety, the hypnotic drugs that promote sleep, and the psychostimulants. However, the anticholinergic drugs can also produce a "high" when taken in larger amounts than typically prescribed. Prescription drug abuse has risen significantly since 1991, probably due to the increased overall prevalence of these medications (McCabe, Cranford, & West, 2008).

All helping professionals who treat clients with dual diagnoses face a major problem: Substance abuse makes accurate diagnosis extremely difficult, therefore hampering the development of appropriate interventions (Crawford, Crome, & Clancy, 2003). In one controlled study among professionals using a structured interview format, the diagnosis of mental illness was significantly less reliable in the presence of substance abuse (Corty, Lehman, & Myers, 1993). In this study of 47 dual-diagnosed clients assessed by nine skilled interviewers, with each client assessed separately by two interviewers, the lowest frequency of agreement occurred with clients who had either mood or psychotic disorders. There was only a slightly higher frequency of agreement about clients with anxiety disorders.

A major concern for treatment providers is the negative interactions of these substances with psychotropic drugs (see Chapter 4). For instance, many substances can make the symptoms of schizophrenia more pronounced or promote a resurgence of psychotic symptoms. One of our clients, for example, liked to drink beer. Because he knew that it might interact with his antipsychotic medications to produce a high level of sedation, he decided not to take his prescription drugs on nights when he drank beer. The alcohol still interacted with his medications in a potentially dangerous way, and, without a consistent blood level he was at a greater risk for decompensation.

A further problem for treatment providers is the great difficulty in treating either of the two disorders (mental illness and substance abuse) when they coexist. Professionals in the mental health and substance abuse fields have tended to work apart over the years, holding different philosophies and areas of expertise. Social workers have complained at times that substance abuse counselors are too rigid, whereas the counselors have thought in turn that social workers do not confront clients and set firm enough limits about substance abuse. Today there is increasing agreement that collaborative interdisciplinary work in this area of intervention can be well coordinated in the best interest of the client. Recent research indicates that clients do respond well to structured interventions; in fact, their gains in social functioning are comparable to those of non-dual-diagnosed people with mental illness (Drake, O'Neal, & Wallach, 2008). Successful programs are characterized by intensive case management and integration of the mental health, substance abuse, and legal systems.

The bottom line is that both disorders need to be treated; the social worker should not assume that if one of the client's disorders is brought under control, then the other can be more easily addressed or perhaps will disappear. Before intervening, the social worker first needs to understand whether the client has two truly coexisting disorders, is medicating him- or herself with substances for the primary disorder, or has a drug-induced psychotic state that may abate with rapid intervention. Although drug-induced psychoses are transient, tending to resolve themselves in several hours or days, they do require intensive interventions at times and perhaps a brief regimen of psychotropic medications. If the client is self-medicating, the social worker needs to understand why. Finally, however serious the adverse effects of prescribed medications are, clients should negotiate with the prescriber the most appropriate means to alleviate discomfort.

In summary, intervention with clients who have dual diagnoses should include the following principles (Ulus, 2001):

- Using caution in prescribing any psychotropic medications to a substance user.
- Assessing the risks and monitoring the effects of drug interactions.
- Continuing to recommend abstinence and offering substance abuse intervention.
- Being aware of the specific ethical and legal risks involved in the practice of prescribing medications to a substance user.

Intervention issues in this area are still being debated. Minkoff (2001) asserted that the risk of side effects resulting from drug and drug or drug and alcohol interactions for clients is small compared to poor outcome resulting from medication discontinuation. He believes that it may be unethical to deny treatment to dual-diagnosed clients even when they do not adhere to all recommendations of the treatment team.

Mental Illness and Alcohol Abuse

Polypharmacy, or combining different types of psychotropic drugs, has become a norm in psychopharmacology, but it can be a risky practice because drug interactions can have negative effects on the consumer. However, in treating clients with the dual diagnosis of mental illness and substance abuse with the goal of abstinence from alcohol, there are indications at times for polypharmacy. The adjunctive medications described here generally work by stabilizing the client's mood and anxiety levels, thus facilitating the physical and psychological processes of alcohol withdrawal. All the findings in this discussion are based on a small number of studies (Schatzberg & Nemeroff, 2009), so the social worker should be cautious in assuming their general validity.

For people with schizophrenia, some evidence exists that, although disulfram (Antabuse), a medication used to make alcohol physically distasteful to the consumer, it may increase symptoms of psychosis; a similar drug known as naltrexone may help the client both resist alcohol and experience a decrease in hallucinations. For clients with depressive disorders, the cyclic antidepressant imipramine and the SSRIs have been shown in a few studies to reduce the client's craving for alcohol, but only during the first 3 weeks of use. For clients with bipolar disorder, lithium appears to have no utility as a deterrent to alcohol use, but the anticonvulsant drugs may have some beneficial effect. At the least, the anticonvulsants can help stabilize the physical condition of alcohol abusers who risk experiencing seizures during the process of withdrawal.

The anti-anxiety medications are well-established adjunctive drugs for clients with dual diagnoses who are going through withdrawal from alcohol dependence. They are effective as a short-term treatment for 20 to 50% of such persons (Doran, 2008). These drugs increase treatment adherence and days of abstinence while decreasing anxiety and the risk of relapse. Finally, it is useful to encourage clients who abuse alcohol to take vitamins B and C, because alcohol depletes these substances in the body.

SUMMARY

Medical science, like other fields of science, is only beginning to appreciate the variability of effects that people demonstrate in response to all types of intervention. For years, social workers have faced a major challenge in determining which treatments work for which clients under which circumstances. It has become clear that this same challenge applies to drug treatments, which at one time were assumed to be more universal and predictable in their outcomes. Although not typically experts in chemistry, social workers offer an advanced perspective about individual and group differences in terms of the factors that contribute to their psychosocial functioning. With this professional strength, they can contribute important insights into the client's experience of taking medication in a social as well as a physical sense.

TOPICS FOR DISCUSSION
AND LEARNING ACTIVITIES

1. Search the literature (medical, psychological, sociological, and self-help) for articles related to one or more special populations and their physiological reactions, psychological reactions, and cultural attitudes regarding psychotropic medication. Share the information from one especially good article or report with the class.

2. Develop a holistic assessment strategy for one special population related to its potential to benefit from psychotropic medication. This strategy should include attention to the relevant biological characteristics of members of that population as well as their common psychological concerns, social customs, and spiritual practices. Incorporate into this process the list of nine biopsychosocial factors that influence psychotropic drug metabolism and response among ethnic groups.

3. Interview several parents of children and adolescents who do not take psychotropic medication. Ask what their reactions would be if a prescriber recommended a prescription to their son or daughter to address a hypothetical emotional problem. What do the parents' responses reveal about sensitive issues related to medicating children and adolescents?

4. Select one or more of the special populations discussed in this chapter. Create a case scenario in which the client is highly reluctant to consider using medications because of a concern related to his or her sex, age, overall health status, or culture. Develop a procedure that will help the social worker decide whether to pursue the use of medications or rely instead on alternative interventions.

PART III

Knowledge and Skills for Embracing Psychosocial Roles

Chapter 6

Referrals, Decision-Making, and the Meaning of
Psychiatric Medication

Chapter 7

Medication Education for Clients and Families

Chapter 8

Medication Monitoring and Management

Chapter 9

Medication Adherence

6

✳

Referrals, Decision-Making, and the Meaning of Psychiatric Medication

Learning Objectives

Upon completion of this chapter, the reader will be able to:

1. Discuss professional challenges related to parallel and integrated care.
2. Discuss five elements of excellence in making referrals and real-world strategies for addressing obstacles to their implementation.
3. Identify seven themes related to the meaning of psychiatric medication and the social worker's role in helping clients manage issues of identity and meaning.
4. Define shared decision-making and detail how to enact its principles in real world practice.

In the large national survey of clinical social workers discussed throughout this text (Bentley, Walsh, & Farmer, 2005a), the most frequent medication-related activity reported by practitioners was discussion with clients about their feelings about medication. Eighty percent of the sample of almost 1,000 NASW members reported "very frequently or often" talking to clients about their feelings with respect to medication. Ninety-six percent believed this was an appropriate role for social workers and 91% felt "quite competent" in performing this role. The next most frequent activity by the respondents was "making referrals for a medication assessment with a client" with 72% of practitioners reporting they do this very frequently or often. At the same time, only 38% actually reported "preparing clients for interview" with a prescriber, even though over 84% thought this was quite appropriate for social workers to do. Discussing the "combined effects of medication and psychosocial interventions" was also reported frequently or often by over 70% of these social workers. Fifty-two percent of respondents said they frequently or often helped clients consider the pros and cons of taking medication. This chapter attempts to expand on common social work roles of decision-making and referrals and present content on how social workers can more fully respond to the feelings, reactions, and meaning that making decisions to take psychiatric medication can elicit. These notions of shared decision-making, meaning-making, and referrals that support collaborative and parallel approaches to care are an important foundation for the other social work roles related to psychoeducation, problem-solving, medication monitoring and adherence, and advocacy that are covered in the chapters that follow. We will start with a discussion of integrated and parallel care across settings, which provides an important contextual discussion of the varied roles of the social worker in psychopharmacology.

Parallel and Integrated Care across Settings

As we noted in Chapter 2, a third strategy that undergirds effective collaboration with clients, families, and providers is the successful integration of psychosocial interventions with psychopharmacotherapy. Social workers need not only recognize the intrinsic power of combined treatments but also appreciate the ideological and practical challenges that emerge, especially in managing parallel treatment or services; that is, care in which one professional provides psychosocial treatment at the same time a prescriber provides pharmacological or other services to the same client. A comprehensive edited volume published by the American Psychological Association provides but one example of the dissemination of knowledge related to using psychosocial strategies in conjunction with medications (Sammons & Schmidt, 2001). Updating the work of psychiatrists Beitman and Klerman (1991) more than two decades ago, the psychologists show that either solid empirical research or decades of clinical experience support combining treatments in persons diagnosed with such mental disorders as depression, obsessive-compulsive disorder, phobias, binge eating, substance dependence, and schizophrenia. In our own field the late Gerard Hogarty, a social worker who devoted much of his career to understanding the interactions between psychotropic drug use and psychosocial treatments among people with schizophrenia in particular, concluded that the effects of medication and psychosocial treatments combined were additive; that is, the effects of each seem to contribute to the other's effectiveness. Nonetheless, even though social workers know that it may be very productive to offer both kinds of treatments to clients, clients too often are not afforded the opportunity.

One important barrier to combining treatments is the ideological conflict stemming from certain schools of thought. For example, those trained in psychoanalytic, interpersonal, or behavioral techniques may place less emphasis on medication than on psychosocial treatment. Those trained in biological psychiatry, on the other hand, place tremendous emphasis on pharmacology. Thus, some professionals conclude that medication merely covers up symptoms and avoids the "real" issues, while others deride psychosocial interventions as "psychobab-ble" or "soft." Some assert that this split reflects the historical separation of body and mind (Bradley, 1990). Saleeby (1985) speculates that the historic lack of bio-logical content in social work curriculums is related to professional suspicions about the medical model. He suggests that, rather than allowing biological con-tent to narrow their perspective and contribute to reductionist thinking, social workers should see how knowledge about human biology and medication allows them to be more holistic. Others have called for, and we are certainly seeing, a similar integration of biology and psychology in mental health, as we presented in Chapter 1. One example, relating to the treatment of people with bipolar disorder, captures this idea well: "Although biologic variables underlie the etiol-ogy of this disorder, its primary manifestations are behavioral and psychological, with profound changes in perceptions, attitudes, personality, mood and cogni-tion. Psychological interventions can be of unique value to the client" (Jamison and Akiskal, 1983, p. 185). Similarly, Hoffman (1990) pleads with readers to reject the "two-track" model of treating depression, in which persons receive treatment as if they have two distinct disorders, biological depression (treated with medication) and psychological depression (treated with psychotherapy). He calls for a "unitary approach" that recognizes the complexities of treating dis-orders that have both biological and psychological components. "We have to take care to keep both the baby and the bath water in the same tub" (p. 371). Since social workers cannot prescribe medication or medically monitor its thera-peutic effects, working toward an integrated approach means working toward open and productive partnerships with prescribers and the effective management of parallel treatment.

For social workers in various settings, collaboration around parallel and inte-grated care can look very different. In school settings, for example, social workers may collaborate with guidance counselors, psychologists, and nurses, all employed by the school system and who may or may not be under one roof. Professionals who are prescribing medication for the children and adolescents under the care of school social workers may be private family care physicians or community-based child psychiatrists. Child welfare social workers and even social workers in private practice may be interacting with providers across public service arenas including public mental health centers, university hospitals, or not-for-profit agencies. In mental health settings, social workers assume roles as both therapists and case managers. Kanter (1989) has written extensively on the clini-cal case manager's role in collaborating with physicians, especially in maintaining effective medication regimens. A number of other authors have also commented on the increased frequency and need for so-called three-party treatment relation-ships. Pilette (1988), for example, attributes this rise to the expansion of the pri-vate practice marketplace and the increasing access of social workers and psychologists to insurance reimbursement, among other things. Historically, community mental health centers and HMOs have relied on nonmedical profes-sionals to provide psychosocial treatment and relied on physicians to provide drug consultation. While the client may benefit from the respective strengths of each clinician and the providers may benefit from covering all the clinical bases, the problems inherent to the arrangement raise many difficult questions. For instance, who has the ultimate authority over and responsibility for the client's treatment? How will disagreements be handled? Who will decide about major changes in treatment? Questions about confidentiality (how much sharing is too much?) also arise. Bradley (1990) contends that the client's "entry route" is an important factor in answering those questions, that is, how the client came to the three-party relationship. Was she or he a client of a psychiatrist who referred the individual to a social worker or vice versa?

Goldberg, Riba, and Tasman (1991) examined psychiatrists' attitudes toward prescribing medications for persons being treated by nonmedical psychotherapists. In this study, of the 60 respondents who prescribed such medication, 73% worked with master's-level social workers (MSWs). Three-fourths of the medication services were initiated by the nonmedical provider. Over two-thirds of the psychiatrists were satisfied with their current level of involvement in the cases; in fact, 25% said they wished they did less with clients, whereas 8% wished they did more. Interestingly, one of the concerns that psychiatrists raised most often was their need to know more clearly how they were to be available after hours or for emergencies.

Kelly (1992) advises pharmacotherapists (physicians, psychiatrists, and other prescribers) to work only with people they know and trust and to make it clear they are not just a medication dispenser but a consultant. Kelly says the pharmacotherapist should consider the psychotherapist to be a responsible professional and a reliable informant but "not a medical colleague, supervisee or competitor" (p. 779). According to Kelly, the psychotherapist should also use a pharmacotherapist who appreciates the complexity of parallel treatment and considers her- or himself as a consultant, not a co-therapist or competitor. Balon (2001) comprehensively reviews the positive and negative aspects of so-called split treatment. For example, these arrangements may be cost-effective, allow for fuller quality of care, increase adherence, and add to the support perceived by professionals. On the other hand it may cloud both legal and clinical responsibilities.

Cathie Gray (1998), a social worker who has shared her own joys and struggles of collaborating with psychiatrists about medication, uses a line, a triangle, and a circle as symbols of her personal reflections. The line represents the hierarchies that exist in three-party arrangements, especially with respect to the "who's in charge" question. She jokingly confides that sometimes when things are going well, she is more than willing to see herself as responsible and "in charge," but when things are not, she figures it is easy to conclude it must be the medicating physician's responsibility! When thinking about the triangle, which represents the client, herself, and the physician, she says that she sometimes questions who is really the "third party," and frequently wonders about how to best manage information sharing. The circle is a metaphor for the interconnectedness of all the relationships among providers and the client and the recognition that when all the lines and triangles are removed, we are all working toward the same goal in collaboration. Bradley (2003) has also used the triangle as a metaphor in the "psychology of psychopharmacology," noting that both clinicians should be aware of transference and countertransference issues that emerge in three-party relationships. According to Bradley, these issues can emerge from the client, the clinician, and the prescriber. For example, the addition of a second clinician can be experienced as either "narcissistic injury" for the client ("I must be sicker than I thought") or evidence of a lack of interest or competence on the part of the referring clinician. Likewise, physicians must avoid being the "all-knowing doctor" or letting clients idealize them, thus devaluing the clients' psychosocial treatment. Interestingly, while stressing collaboration and frequent communication between the nonmedical provider and the prescriber, several authors warn against the collaboration becoming overly close, making role distinctions unclear or skewing appropriate differences in approaches (Busch & Gould, 1993; Kelly, 1992).

Also, in collaborating with other providers, social workers need to be aware of the potential influence that psychosocial treatment and medication can have on each other. For example, while psychosocial treatments may actually help a client adhere to a medication regimen, medication may in turn help clients become more cognitively or emotionally "ready" for psychosocial treatment. Although medication may heighten the client's confidence in treatment on the one hand, it may also encourage magical thinking, increase the dependency on the clinician, decrease motivation for psychosocial treatment, or somehow derail progress (Bond & Lader, 1996).

Excellence in Making Referrals for Psychiatric Medication

The suggested foundation of partnership, balance, and integration has implications for how and when social workers make referrals to physicians. We know that when making referrals to prescribers, social workers may have to face their own discomfort about exposing their work to another, while the prescribers who receive referrals have to deal with sharing power and avoiding competition (Busch & Gould, 1993). Indeed, Bentley, Walsh, and Farmer (2005b) noted that the literature on referral practices tends to focus on referrals from a primary care provider to a psychiatrist, and often addresses such issues as lack of follow-through, reasons for, or appropriateness of; and initial referral or attitudes of one medical discipline toward another. Because few studies exist about the referral process in social work and psychopharmacology, not much is known about it even though it is a common activity among clinical social workers. An exception, Littrell and Ashford (1994) examined the impact of treatment settings on the medication referral practices of social work field instructors and have found that in cases of major depression, the field of practice setting did not affect the sense of obligation to refer. On the other hand, with clients whose symptoms were less severe, those in mental health settings were more likely to make referrals than those in family service settings. How long clients had been in treatment had no effect on the obligation to refer. Perhaps one of the biggest contributions that Littrell and Ashford make is to raise this question: "Are social workers legally and ethically culpable should they fail to raise the possibility of medication referral?" (p. 123). We will revisit this question in the last chapter.

In spite of the limited research, Bentley, Walsh, and Farmer (2005b) note that existing studies and professional consensus suggest that a good referral is one in which the social worker takes responsibility for the quality and results of the connection between the client and prescriber. (Gilmour et al., 2011, p. S182) go so far as to say that when a clinician refers a client to another provider, "he or she is assuming some level of moral responsibility for the outcome of that referral." They note that implicitly the client is being given the message: "I trust this person and you can too." We define "excellence" in referral practice as having several dimensions addressed in relation to their global relevance to medication management throughout the text. These include establishing and maintaining collaborative relationships with prescribers, knowing when and how to refer, preparing clients and families for the actual medication evaluation, following up the results of the referral, and effectively managing legal and ethical concerns related to referrals:

Establishing and Maintaining Collaborative Relationships with Prescribers.   The first part of this chapter presented content on the collaborative context of medication-related parallel practices outlined in the book. Thus, to perhaps state the obvious: In order to make excellent referrals for medication, social workers need to have contacts with helping professionals who are licensed to prescribe medication. Physicians, physician's assistants, nurse practitioners, dentists, some psychologists, and some pharmacists have this privilege in various settings around the country. Some settings have built-in access, seeming to make the referral process less complicated. However, wait lists and limited resources may influence actual access. Hospitals typically have a psychiatry department, and a referral may simply be a written request on a chart with a face-to-face follow-up in the hallway. On the other hand, the psychiatry department may prioritize people admitted to the psychiatric unit over those on medical or surgical floors, for example, and there may be frustrating waiting lists. Community mental health centers and residential facilities will likely have psychiatrists on staff, even if part-time, and coordination of appointments and consultations may not be overly difficult. However, some resources may be overworked or have limited availability. Schools and public child welfare agencies typically do not have full-time prescribers on staff, but nurses, case managers, or other helping professional staff may keep lists of resources or have contracts with local prescribers. Long-term care facilities, as well as jails and prisons, have their own challenges with respect to accessing specialized mental health care of any kind. These issues speak to the need for social workers across settings to develop and maintain relationships with prescribers from many local resources.

If one's setting does not have built-in access, for example, private practice, then one way to ensure access to prescribers is to develop referral networks and nurture opportunities to develop cross-referral "highways." For social workers this means teaching a network of prescribers about one's own practice and learning more about the prescriber's practices. Lawless and Wright (2000) suggest well-planned approach to marketing oneself to potential prescribers via mailings, videos, brochures, or newsletters. They note the importance of maintaining name recognition and interacting more extensively and directly with prescribers in ways that they want in terms of types and depth of information. These ideas seem to ring true no matter what setting. In the Bentley, Walsh, and Farmer study (2005a), over half of the respondents noted the number one thing they would do to improve their response to clients who take medication was to interact more frequently and closely with prescribers, including visiting them at their offices, increasing accompanying clients to face-to-face appointments with prescribers, and following up with referrals. The key, however, to maintaining good relationships with prescribers may be for the social worker involved in parallel care to communicate relevant and complete client information in a timely and professional manner.

Knowing When to Refer, Who to Refer to, and What to Say to the Prescriber.   It seems reasonable to consider referral whenever a client experiences symptoms for which there are known useful drug treatments. This is particularly true when the client has only partially responded to psychosocial interventions. In deciding the timing of the referral, social workers must consider the severity of the client's symptoms and the extent to which the client's life is disrupted. Research, on the initiation of antipsychotic medication in particular, showed that a failure to start medication early on was associated with an overall poorer treatment response over the long haul (Haas, Garratt, & Sweeney, 1998).

Buelow, Hebert, and Buelow (2002) also offer some solid guidance on when non-medical practitioners should refer to a prescriber. These include times when the client does not seem to be in a position to fully benefit from any psychosocial interventions the social worker might provide because they are simply too depressed, too manic, too anxious, too confused, or too out of touch with reality. Clients may have relapsed or be assessed to be at high risk of suicide or any form of self-harm, including serious self-neglect. Clients may self-disclose that medication has helped in the past and they wish to revisit the option. But admittedly, a very basic and humane questions for those considering referring clients to a prescriber: Could medication help my client? Could it help over and above what we may accomplish together? Is there a reasonable chance that medication will be of benefit, based on all I know from current research and standard practices as well as their own past experiences with clients in similar situations?

The setting may have implications for who precisely the social worker refers the client to and how the logistics of the referral happen. The client may very well have preferences as well. We know that 70% of psychiatric medications, for example, are prescribed by family physicians. Collaborative care will be enhanced if the prescriber, no matter who it is, is given timely, salient information about the client's clinical situation, including a brief overview of their mental status, physical functioning, recent changes in sleeping or eating habits, recent changes in social functioning, including at work, in school or in their relationships and family life, and current mood and affect. The social worker might use an email or a letter or create some sort of standardized form to institutionalize communication between themselves and prescribers at the initiation of a referral or to ensure follow-up. It is especially important for social workers who embrace partnership practice to compassionately convey to the prescriber the impact of symptoms and struggles on the client's "lived experience" and quality of life.

The intended nature of future collaboration needs to be shared with the prescriber as well. Is this a complete transfer of care or simply the addition of an additional service component toward parallel treatment? How will the collaboration among all stakeholders (clients, families, social workers, prescribers, others) be nurtured and maximized?

Preparing Clients and Families for the Actual Medication Evaluation.   In Lynn Videka's (1988) meta-analysis of mental health interventions, she concluded that client preparation, that is, working with clients to ready and orient them for the helping processes, was one of the most effective known intervention techniques and, regrettably, one of the least utilized. We have already noted that our 2005 study bears that out with respect to preparation of clients for referrals. While making referrals for medication evaluations was the second most frequent activity, preparing clients for meetings with prescribers was dramatically less frequent. An excellent referral emerges when a social worker and client openly discuss the rationale for the referral and its connection to the client's goals. In order to demystify the referral process and increase the client's confidence in its potential usefulness or desirability, the social worker should share how specific choices were made about specific agencies, providers, or resources, and offer any "insider" information and insights about the history, philosophy, community context, or even the general personality of a referred resource. It is important to remember that any referral a social worker makes to a physician is really a referral for an evaluation of possible treatment with psychotropic medication. Therefore, any discussion with clients about such a referral should begin with an overview of what to expect in the evaluation process, including a review of the pros and cons of merely seeking an evaluation. Does the idea itself impact self-esteem, stimulate fears of social stigma, or elicit notions of self-stigma (Bursztajn & Barsky, 1985)? What could be the positive outcomes of seeking a medication evaluation? What could be the unwanted consequences? What does it mean to the client that the social worker suggested or wanted to explore a possible referral? What does it mean to the social worker to seek external consultation on medication? Clients will probably also want to discuss what they will do if either offered or denied a prescription. If they seek an evaluation and no medication is offered, will they be angry, disappointed, relieved? If the prescriber does indeed offer a prescription, which happens in most cases, what might be the emotional fallout? Is the client's reaction dependent on the type of medication, for example, an antidepressant versus a mood stabilizer versus a stimulant or even an antipsychotic medication?

What do typical medication evaluation interviews with prescribers look like? While wide variability exists between prescribing providers and settings, clients can expect prescribers to use a series of direct questions to gather information on the length and severity of symptoms, the impact on the quality of life, and previous coping methods. Many prescribers will delve into client's developmental history and may suggest or require paper and pencil or formal computer-based assessments and scales. The prescriber is looking for information to help her or him make decisions about diagnosis, the likelihood of benefits from medication, medication type, and dosage. Social workers can and should coach clients about asking the prescriber questions about their questions so that decision-making is more transparent, as we discuss later in our section on shared decision-making. Clients and social workers can generate a list of questions or concerns for prescribers and even role-play possible clinical scenarios (see Chapter 8 on skills training) in order to boost a client's confidence in the encounter. Importantly, armed with a primer on biological aspects of psychopharmacology, social workers can do much to help clients appreciate not only the complexity of the prescriber's decision-making around medications, but also the "trial and error" nature of finding the "right" medication regimen.

Sharing up-to-date information on what is known and not known about a medication's effectiveness, the known potential interactive or additive effects with psychosocial treatments, and fully discussing alternative treatments and options are integral to the preparation process. The spirit of informed consent underlies these conversations, which may include sharing what is known about relapse rates and about possible placebo effects. Social workers should use all their clinical skills to elicit thoughts and feelings and help clients practically and emotionally manage decisions to seek a prescriber's evaluation and treatment and to do so in a spirit of cautious optimism. After the medical evaluation, the client and social worker will continue to address client reactions and responses on a number of levels. Helping clients and families manage the meaning of medication will be especially important when making referrals but because of its keystone place in the array of social work roles in psychopharmacology, an entire section of this chapter is devoted to that topic.

Consistent with the position of maintaining "balance," when it comes to preparing clients for referrals for psychiatric medication, it is argued that social workers should reject both the roles of cheerleader for medications or a naysayer against them. The task for social workers in making referrals around psychiatric medication is to "translate complex information into understandable, useful knowledge for living" (Bentley & Walsh, 1998, p. 310). They should be in a position to dispel myths yet also provide realistic cautions.

Following Up the Results of the Referral. An excellent referral exceeds "steering" clients to resources. Steering is simply directing a client to a resource by, for example, just writing down the name of an agency and a contact person's name and phone number or email. Following up to ascertain the usefulness and impact of a referral is an important check on the quality and results of a referral and, again, is an underutilized strategy in practice today. "Cementing" is a term given to activities where the social worker is trying to ensure a strong, stable connection between the client and a resource, in this case a client with a prescriber. Reinforcement might be as simple as a phone confirmation with the client and/or the prescriber. As with all three party arrangements, prior discussion of confidentiality parameters is needed. An important element to assess in the follow-up contact, in addition to general satisfaction levels, is to ascertain the actual impact of the referral versus the expected impact. For example, clients may need reminders that "psychiatric medication are not magic bullets. They do not go to the center of the problem and destroy it" (Buelow, Hebert & Buelow, 2002, p. 7). Medications are one intervention strategy known to help many people, but their possible impact on any one individual is simply not knowable in advance. All the other social work roles discussed in this book, such as educator, monitor, consultant, counselor, and advocate have relevance in the follow-up to referrals.

Managing Legal and Ethical Concerns in Referrals.   Social workers experience several important dilemmas and conflicts that seem to have special relevance for referral processes (Walsh, Farmer, Taylor, & Bentley, 2003). Where is the line between encouragement and coercion with respect to discussing medication options? What client experiences and perspectives should be shared with families, if any? To what extent do we question a prescriber's decisions and recommendations? And perhaps the most difficult of all, how can we respect self-determination when clients choose to decline medication in the midst of heartbreaking symptoms? What do we do when we are just not sure about the quality of psychopharmacological care with our clients? Are they misdiagnosed? Being overmedicated? Under-medicated? And in terms of the larger context of care as it relates to referrals, what can we do about long waiting lists in public mental health settings? How do we confront the impact of managed care on prescription writing? How do we address the rising costs of psychiatric medication and the availability of new generations of medications?

Some research has also noted that psychiatrists often have ethical concerns about treating clients being followed mainly by others providers (Goldberg, Riba, and Tasman, 1991), specifically related to ambiguities of liability and responsibility, especially in emergencies. Some professionals in our sibling disciplines may not embrace collaboration as we would hope. Potential loss of autonomy may be at the center of concerns there and intensify the turf battles that take place in the real world. For example, one study showed that while social workers accounted for 20% of the claims in one managed care company (not counting psychosocial support services), 79% of clients saw only one provider. Psychiatrists tended to see more severely disabled clients (Sturm & Klap, 1999). This data, however, was presented as a way to allay fears that nonmedical providers are "taking over" behavioral health care. Another article acknowledged that when brief psychotherapy was called for, social workers did provide the least expensive care; however, the authors also argued that three-party arrangements represented "fragmented" services and implied that care by nonphysicians was poor (Dewan, 1999).

The Meaning of Psychiatric Medication

The "meaning of medication" relates to what people who use psychiatric medications think and feel about their medication, what impact it has on their identity and sense of self, and what taking it symbolizes to them about themselves as human beings. "Meaning" is about the subjective significance of something, in this case the subjective experience of taking psychiatric medication. Indeed, many years ago it was said that "(f)ew human experiences are so universal and have such symbolic overtones as the ordinary acts of prescribing and ingesting medicines" (Pellegrino, 1976, p. 624). In this book, we argue that social work is in an ideal position to respond to clients with empathy, understanding, and compassion to the plethora of meanings that may emerge in the midst of receiving referrals for medication, actually picking up the prescription, being administered medication, ingesting medication on a regular basis, and relying on it as in some way a part of one's life. We can help translate and convey meanings to other providers and to families when called for and use what we know to improve our responsiveness to client's medication-related dilemmas no matter how they present themselves.

Symbolic interactionism is a useful theory for social work in general (Forte, 2004; Walsh, 1995) but especially when thinking about the meaning of medication. A school of thought in sociology and social psychology, the major premise is that we act toward all things—that is, people, events, objects we see or own, including "social objects," like psychiatric medication—on the basis of the meaning they have for us, what they symbolize to us about ourselves. These meanings form the basis of our action and may change over time due to changes in the interpretation of our interactions with our physical, social, and cultural environments. In the review of the literature on the meaning of medication (see Bentley, 2010), it is noted that metaphors and symbols have been important in the research on the meaning of medication because our interpretations of our interactions with the environment involve symbolic communication such as language and ritual. For example, a researcher in London in the early 1980s offered the metaphors of "tonic," "fuel," and "food" to summarize the meanings that his study subjects gave to their medications (Helman, 1981). In his view, these meanings seemed to relate to the degree of control over the drug experienced by the patient, its actual effects, and their beliefs about medication. Similarly, after examining the transcripts of staff and patient interviews, another researcher Rhodes (1984, p. 58) generated a typology of seven different and contrasting types of images and metaphors used to describe the negative and positive role and effects, or meaning, of psychiatric medication:

1. *blockage/release* ("cuts me off at the neck," "keeps the lid on my thoughts")
2. *clearance/fogging* ("clears my mind," "clouds my mind")
3. *distortion/straightening* ("distorts my mind," "keeps my thoughts straight")
4. *poison/nurturance* ("contaminates my mind," "a godsend")
5. *breakage/remediation* ("contaminates me," "like insulin")
6. *immobility/mobility* ("like a zombie," "wakes me up")
7. *up/down* ("brings me down," "evens out the highs and lows")

More recently, Rosenfeld (2007) used the familiar metaphors of "poison" versus "cure" in describing the differential perceptions of both consumers and prescribers of antipsychotic medication in particular. He, like us, will conclude that the entire historical and scientific context of care and treatment influences the meaning of medication, including the nature of the relationship between client and prescriber. As eloquently put by Shoemaker and de Oliviera (2008, p. 86), the medication experience "is an encounter that is given meaning before it occurs." Their meta-synthesis of three qualitative studies on the meaning of medication conclude that even the initial "encounter" with medication sends messages to the self that involve such things as losing control or stigma. Many other researchers urge us to embrace research into the subjective experience of pharmacotherapy and more fully use what we know in our clinical encounters (Awad et al., 1996; Carrick et al., 2004; Jenkins et al., 2005; Rappaport & Chubinsky, 2000; Usher, 2001) They all present a compelling case that a person's interpretation of physical, cognitive, and emotional changes that can occur while taking psychiatric medication influences medication adherence, side effects, and clinical outcomes.

More recently in social work, Jerry Floersch's research addresses meaning, identity, and body image among children and adolescents who take psychiatric medication. Findings from his NIH-supported research with 20 adolescents suggest youth take on different points of view to make sense of (and make decisions about) their medication experience, such as perceptions around the need for medication or ideas about how medications work. Importantly, in this study "the theme of expectation and hope" was "particularly central" to the experience of these youth (Floersch et al., 2009, p. 170). Chubinsky and Rappaport (2006, p. 112) have also written extensively about the "significant psychological meaning of medication" to children, adolescents, and families. They make a compelling case for clinicians to understand how recommending medication for a child or adolescent has great meaning for the family as a whole, and parents themselves will attach many meanings to that action, including some powerfully negative meanings. These may include feeling ashamed of their child or angry with her or him, feeling like a personal failure, being suspicious of the prescriber's motivations, or guilty for transmitting something to their child. They may also feel hopeful or be overly optimistic. Children may very well have significant reservations about taking psychiatric medication and even doubt the accuracy of their diagnosis or its connection to biological factors. They may likely have fears of stigma, being seen as crazy or stupid, and worry about weight gain and acne, for example.

Interestingly, these recent studies of meaning are noted to be in sharp contrast to those in the 1960s and 70s on the meaning of medication that emphasized purely psychodynamic interpretations of the pill as a symbol of nurturance and as a power dynamic in the psychiatrist–patient dyad (see, for example, Adelman, 1985; Brody, 1988; Hausner, 1985–86; Levy, 1977; Nevins, 1990; Sarwer-Foner, 1975). As Bentley (2010, p. 481) noted, borrowing some from Gutheil (1977), while reliance on some of these psychoanalytic interpretations now seems a bit dated and off-base to many, a central point summed up is that "we can no longer hold to the 'comfortable delusion' that giving medication and taking it are 'uncomplicated processes'."

Bentley (2010) describes her own community-based qualitative research study with 21 adults with serious mental illness at a residential treatment facility. She conducted semi-structured interviews, then did a thematic analysis of the transcripts to generate a seven-dimension typology (see Figure 6.1). In addition to interviewing clients of the residential facility, Bentley had each participant draw pictures depicting their own "meaning of medication." Figure 6.2 through Figure 6.8 are seven examples of those drawings, one associated with each dimension in the typology (21 complete drawings are available at http://blog.vcu.edu/kbentley/2008/07/a_typology_of_the_meaning_of_p.html). Importantly, these seven themes emerge from a central overarching message about psychiatric medication in these people's lives: Medication is something that:

- *Incites meaning*
- *Influences identity, and*
- *Impacts life.*

That is, taking psychiatric medication is not some benign, insubstantial, or trivial act. And there is a conundrum: medication is "an avenue to full humanness and a more positive life experience, but also can be the source of felt

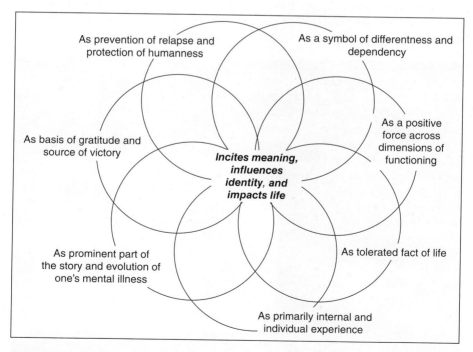

FIGURE 6.1 A Typology of the Meaning of Psychiatric Medication.

Used with permission from: Bentley, K. J. (2010). The meaning of psychiatric medication in a residential program for adults with serious mental illness. *Qualitative Social Work, 9*(4), 479–499.

differentness and resignation" (Bentley, 2010, p. 488). The seven themes suggest that psychiatric medication is:

1. **A pervasive positive force.**
2. **A tolerated fact of life.**
3. **An internal and individual experience.**
4. **A prominent part of the story and evolution of one's mental illness.**
5. **A basis of gratitude and source of victory over past struggles.**
6. **A necessary protection of a personal sense of humanness.**
7. **A symbol of differentness and dependency.**

Psychiatric Medication as a Pervasive Positive Force across Several Dimensions of Experience. This theme was meant to capture the fact that the participants in the study noted that medication was good for them for *many* different reasons. Presuming neurological effects of medication, they said things like the medications "fixes" their brains, helps them with "chemical imbalances," and helps their bodies deal with their illness. They also noted more direct symptom reduction, specifically a decrease in their self-injurious impulses, voices, anxiety, racing thoughts, lethargy, and paranoia. They talked about improved cognitions like having clearer thoughts, improved focus and concentration, and a better outlook on life. In addition there were positive psychological and emotional effects like providing a sense of comfort and calm or helping to regulate

Rainbow Glider

- A horse with wings means freedom, flying
- Freedom is to feel good, to be able to do what you want to

© 2013 Cengage Learning

FIGURE 6.2

mood. Medication not only helped them achieve their goals of being happy, pursuing hobbies, or going to school, for example, but helped them avoid unwanted outcomes such as going back to the hospital, getting cranky or angry, or being over-reactive or self-absorbed. The other important positive effect was supporting their identity as a normal person. Many reported being more alive, coping better, being more aware and in control, having more energy, and interacting more with other people.

Psychiatric Medication as Tolerated Fact of Life. This theme tries to capture the idea that while there is general acceptance of medication use by most, there is also great resignation. For most this is mainly due to side effects and other negative aspects of medication use. Only a few residents have never experienced side effects, while a few others reported lifelong struggles with severe side effects. By far most residents report widely ranging experiences of both minor and moderate side effects, including headaches, increased appetite and weight gain, palpitations, tremors, sleeplessness, dry mouth, drooling, reduced sex drive, twitching, restlessness, and "klutziness," to name a few. Side effects are something that must be endured and tolerated.

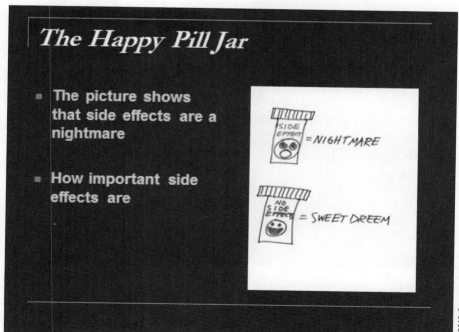

FIGURE 6.3

Psychiatric Medication as Primarily an Internal and Individual Experience.   This theme is meant to capture the idea that for these residents the experience of taking medication is both a real, visceral, and palpable internal physiological experience and a psychological experience. It is both physical and emotional, a very personal, subjective, individual-lived experience. While family and friends' perspectives and pressures, as well as those of the larger society, play into their experience, they are more of a backdrop to their experience. Positive reactions to medication and positive attitudes about them are, not surprisingly, connected to positive therapeutic effects, and negative reactions and attitudes are associated with negative experiences, particularly bothersome side effects. It seems then that the most important modifier of meaning is the nature of medication's effects. Floersch (2003) discusses this meaning being related to the gap—or lack thereof—between desired and expected effects of medication.

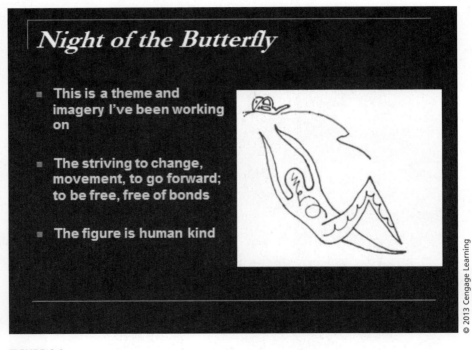

© 2013 Cengage Learning

FIGURE 6.4

Psychiatric Medication as a Prominent Part of the Story and Evolution of One's Mental Illness.   This theme is meant to capture the idea that the initial "meaning of medication" for people is very much intertwined with their own stories of coming to grips with having a mental illness. Their own narratives about their early days of psychosis, for example, include heartbreaking stories of withdrawal, depression, anxiety, panic, stress, violence, repeated hospitalizations, suicide attempts, job and relationship setbacks, and encounters with the law. However, these stories are almost always connected and interlaced with details about what medication they were on, how there were so many "trial and error" changes, and how difficult it was to tolerate side effects. The parallel life experiences of both mental illness and medication use continues to emerge as they share current stories about their lives.

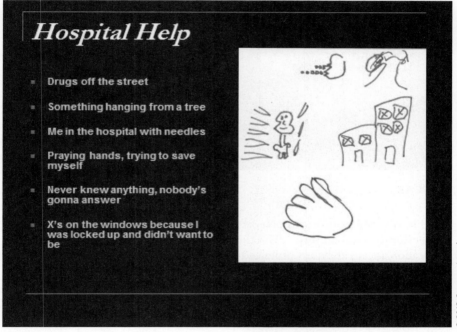

Hospital Help

- Drugs off the street
- Something hanging from a tree
- Me in the hospital with needles
- Praying hands, trying to save myself
- Never knew anything, nobody's gonna answer
- X's on the windows because I was locked up and didn't want to be

FIGURE 6.5

Psychiatric Medication as a Basis of Gratitude and a Source of Victory over Past Struggles.   This theme tries to capture the idea that, not only are many experiences with medication over time generally positive, but medication is seen as something that helped to win hard-fought battles in the past and is helping them to develop insight, growth, and tenacity. Residents vividly recount dramatic movement from severe symptoms, instability, and chaos to their current status of being relatively stable and safe. They describe the movement away from anger and denial and away from thinking of medication as "stupid." Rather, medication is something that gives hope.

Violet Blue

- The sun's rays, the colors and the life force they represent

- Live life as colorful and there is hope for everyone; doesn't matter who you are

© 2013 Cengage Learning

FIGURE 6.6

Psychiatric Medication as Necessary for Prevention of Relapse and Protection of Humanness.   This theme tries to capture the idea that for many, medication means they are protected against the much-feared negative, indeed intolerable, consequences of relapse. Significant non-adherence to psychiatric medication is simply not seen as an option because of dreaded consequences (real or anticipated) of symptom return or relapse and the accompanying lack of control in their lives. They do *not* want to *not* feel like a 'regular' human being. If medication is effective, a clear sense of their own identity is somehow preserved—apart from being mentally ill or taking medication. Medication helps them see and better appreciate their unique selves, personal qualities, their likes and avocations.

Psychiatric Medication as a Symbol of Differentness and Dependency.   This theme tries to capture the idea that frequently residents report resistance to feeling a lifelong sense of differentness and dependency. This seems to be related and the reliance on an external entity—a pill or shot—and having to do something that most other people don't have to do in order to function more normally. This feeling is also undoubtedly connected to the stigma of mental illness and the moments where residents admit some denial about their diagnoses. There was "clear acquiescence to the possible reality of taking medications for the rest of their lives and deference to its power in their lives" (Bentley, 2010, p. 492). Some expressed a sense of melancholy and loss about these matters, while for others it was more of an "it is what it is" matter of fact reality about it without any sadness.

My Mind

- My medication is like rods of cadmium and uranium, to keep me from a runaway fission reaction

- My medication keeps my mind from exploding

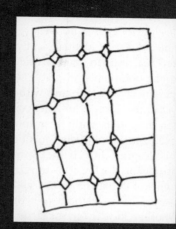

© 2013 Cengage Learning

FIGURE 6.7

Moods of a Psychiatric Mind

- These are brain waves, thought processes

- The meds are the round circles

- The waves are even keeled

© 2013 Cengage Learning

FIGURE 6.8

The agency where the research was conducted considered how to really use what was learned to improve their program. Several of those activities have relevance for expanding social work roles across settings in helping clients manage the meaning of medication. For example, social workers should consider how can they:

1. *Give greater voice to the client's medication-related experiences.* After the research was completed, the residential facility started a reading club where clients gathered and shared reactions to short articles and clippings about psychiatric medication. This was just one highly adaptable way to create opportunities for clients to share their experiences with you and with each other. Clients of any age, in individual, group, or family settings can be encouraged to find articles in magazines and newspapers for discussion with their social worker or in groups with other clients. Alternatively, social workers can find short research articles to share with clients or with colleagues. Just as the participants in the study did, social workers can also invite clients to draw pictures depicting their experience with medications. Prompt clients to draw "before and after" pictures of themselves or their life's experiences. Challenge them to write a short story or poem about their experiences. Another idea is for social workers in group settings to organize a "speak out" around some medication-related question. The question is what can social workers do in school settings, in child welfare settings, in inpatient and outpatient mental health settings, in acute care hospitals, to "give voice" to the lived experience of clients? Armed with a typology of meaning, the hope is that social workers will do more to solicit the narratives of clients' experiences, invite more shared dialogue among clients, and design creative avenues for expression.

2. *Work with agency staff to find ways to do things more proactively with residents about their medication concerns.* At the residential facility where the research was conducted, skills training programs were conducted with staff to teach them how to instruct clients on how to talk more openly and assertively with prescribers about their medication experiences. Using simple modeling and role playing as described in the skills training model presented later in the text (see Chapter 8), clients can easily be taught to confidently raise questions with prescribers about the type of medication they are taking, the rationale for decisions around dosage, expected side effects, or lag time, for example, and especially share with prescribers the impact of those decisions on them as it relates to the "meaning" psychiatric medication has for them. Another idea is for social workers or other agency staff to examine intake forms to ensure there are appropriate and relevant questions about client's medication-related experiences, both positive and negative. Social workers as individuals or in a collaborative could generate a list of possible open-ended questions that would allow clients to talk about issues related to identity, felt "difference," and fears of relapse, for example.

3. *Expand residents' knowledge, curiosity, and support for using psychiatric medication.* The chapter on psychoeducation (see Chapter 7) will argue that social workers should take a larger role in proactively providing medication-related education to clients. However, there are other things social workers can do to support the exploration of meaning and give greater voice to the role of medication in the lives of clients. For example, social workers could teach clients how to search the

web for reliable, trusted information about psychiatric medications and connect with other client chat rooms or listservs that relate to psychiatric medication use. Another idea is to organize a field trip to a pharmacy so clients could directly chat with pharmacists about their life experiences related to filling and refilling prescriptions, therapeutic and side effects, half-lives and drug interactions.

Alicia Powell, agreeing that medication-related issues are clinically underexplored, stated: "(T)he medication life is rich in detail that may be fruitfully used to gain information about the patient's experience, strengthen the alliance, and improve treatment outcome" (2001, p. 217). Increasing our own knowledge about the meaning and impact of medication, as well as trying to give voice to clients' experiences in as many ways as possible, is likely to not only help us deepen the clinical relationship but improve the client's own self-recovery.

Shared Decision-Making and Collaboration with Clients and Families

The term "decision science" is gaining familiarity and popularity and is being applied widely. It is one that appears to have emerged out of the field of business and the interest in predicting consumer behavior and choices. A web search of the term "decision science" today yields a fascinating and disparate array of websites that include a link to a manuscript on the general role of uncertainty in decision-making to one on neuroeconomics and the role of the brain in decision-making to a site advertising a consultation service to improve a litigator's prediction of juror decisions! In recent years, however, there is a growing interest in "decision science" and health care in particular, both decisions of health care consumers as well as health care providers. New organizations have sprung up like The Society for Medical Decision Making, which describes its mission as improving health outcomes "through the advancement of systematic approaches to clinical decision-making and policy formation in health care" (http://smdm.org/mission_values.shtml). Their vision includes the promotion of an "integrated approach to health care decision-making" that rests in "multiple perspectives and expertise from multiple disciplines." New textbooks in health behavior and health promotion focus on the range of theories that inform health care choices like stages of change theory, reasoned action, health belief models, naturalistic decision-making, and numerous communication theories. Another group, the Society for Participatory Medicine, emerged that "encourages and expects active involvement by all connected parties (patients, caregivers, health care professionals) as integral for the full continuum of care." They publish their own journal in hopes of advancing a model of health care where "patients shift from being mere passengers to responsible drivers of their health, and in which providers encourage and value them as full partners" (http://participatorymedicine.org/).

And that brings us to the topic of decision-making as it relates to psychiatric medication, which is also discussed elsewhere in the text. For example, in Chapter 9, there is a discussion of motivational interviewing and the importance of "being where the client is" when it comes to intervening with clients around issues related to adherence and refusal. In Chapter 8 on medication monitoring and management, there is content on problem-solving, which is a systematic way of making decisions about taking action. In this chapter focusing on the parallel care, referrals, and the initial interface of clients and social workers with respect to medication, the topic of shared decision-making is introduced.

Shared decision-making is defined as "a person centered alternative to traditional notions of medical compliance" (Deegan, 2007) and an explicit rejection of paternalism. It "can be seen as emancipatory praxis" (p. 64), where the client is seen as an expert on his or her experience and the entire emphasis of health care is put on client choice. Shared decision-making "is a collaborative process between a patient and provider to share information, perspectives, and responsibility for decisions" (Mistler & Drake, 2008, p. 334). Shared decision-making is sharply contrasted not only with "the medical model" but with the "informed choice model." Informed choice suggests the client is a passive recipient of health care information that is provided in a one-way style of communication by an unbiased and essentially silent health care provider (Hamann, Leuct, & Kissling, 2003). Shared decision-making, on the other hand, by definition demands active participation by all involved, bidirectional communication and information flow, joint participation in decision-making, and a final consensus regarding treatment choice. It has been explored and applied to such decisions regarding care of atrial fibrillation, stroke, prostate cancer, diabetes, heart disease, breast cancer, and more.

In psychiatry, shared decision-making has been described as an "ethical imperative" and part of the larger evidence-based medicine movement (Drake & Deegan, 2009). Researchers acknowledge research on shared decision-making in psychiatry is not as well developed as in other areas of medicine. Much of the research concerns patient and provider attitudes toward shared decision-making and preferences for involvement in decision-making. In psychiatry, it seems to be an aspirational concept that is not as fully enacted in the real world as might be hoped for. In that regard, it has been noted that psychiatrists philosophically embrace the notion especially for well-informed and compliant patients and as long as they don't have doubts about the patient's decisional capacities (Hamann et al., 2009). Others have pointed out the fact that rigorous studies show that decisional incapacity is in the real world "exceedingly rare" (Drake & Deegan, 2009). Psychiatrists also admit they have concerns that sharing information about adverse effects of medication discourages some of their patients from consenting to treatment. They admit to using "strategic dishonesty" and being "economical with the truth" (Seale et al., 2006, p. 2861, 2866). They also are not clear about the appropriateness of including the patient in decisions around some topics, such as involuntary commitment and the use of restraints (Mistler & Drake, 2008). Research on patient preferences in shared decision-making affirm their desire to get up-to-date, accurate information about their health and to generally participate in decisions. There is much variability and complexity, however, in patient preferences in terms of their desired extent of involvement, depending on such factors as age, type or stage of illness, or level of trust in the provider–patient relationship (Adams & Drake, 2006).

What does shared decision-making look like in practice? Most frequently, shared decision-making is operationalized by following a series of "steps," the use of decision aids, information sharing practices, and communication training for practitioners. Elwyn and colleagues, for example, suggest eight skills and steps for shared decision-making (Elwyn et al., 2000) that look very much like problem solving in the context of a partnership model of practice. Indeed, it starts with developing a partnership with clients, then moves on to establishing their preferences for participation in decision-making, ascertaining expectations, identifying choices and evaluating evidence, negotiating and agreeing on an action plan. There is a growing body of literature on the use of decision aids in medical decision-making including a developing consensus on what makes for high-quality tools. These can be something as simple as unbiased information booklets, balance sheets, or graphic displays of medication choices to software packages or web-based applications that guide a client through the process on a laptop, as is the case with Pat Deegan's Decision Support Program for use with consumer-run programs (Deegan, 2007).

Interestingly, research to date has not shown a consistently robust relationship between participation in shared decision-making around medication and medication adherence. Although one small qualitative inquiry into why people with serious mental illness stopped taking their medication revealed a "noticeable lack of shared decision-making" and "no sign that their values and preferences were taken into consideration" (Roe et al., 2009). Even satisfaction with care may or may not be effected by shared decision-making. Some speculate that if satisfaction with care is the goal, this may relate more to their relationship with the provider rather than their role in decision-making (Adams & Drake, 2006). Nevertheless, shared decision-making is thought to be associated with increased empowerment of clients and the assurance of basic consumer rights (Hamann, Leuct, & Kissling, 2003). Interestingly, the literature on shared decision-making focuses almost exclusively on the "patient" and physician experience with little connection to its interface with contemporary, interprofessional practice, or, for that matter, family-centered care (Stacey et al., 2010) as we have discussed in this chapter. Clearly, however, there is congruence with the principles and strategies of shared decision-making and the partnership model of practice and interventions presented throughout this text.

SUMMARY

This chapter presents several foundational roles for social workers with respect to medication management, including making excellent referrals to prescribers, helping to give voice to the meaning and impact of taking psychiatric medication for clients, and helping clients make basic decisions around medication use, especially initial use. Implicit in these roles is the imperative of compassionate partnership practice, as well as the management of parallel care across settings.

TOPICS FOR DISCUSSION
AND LEARNING ACTIVITIES

1. How can social workers effectively educate members of interdisciplinary teams about social work's unique knowledge, skills and values?

2. Share with a peer your most satisfying referral experience? Your most negative? What reflections do you have now on what contributed to the success and lack thereof of each?

3. Interview a client about their experiences with various service providers? Can they differentiate roles? How do they conceptualize the domain and sanction of various helping disciplines?

4. How well are medication and psychosocial interventions integrated at your placement or agency? What types of interventions are most commonly integrated, and why?

5. You believe, based on symptoms and signs, that one of your clients may be overmedicated. How might you approach the prescriber and phrase a question about this to her or him?

6. Have you ever been helped by medication of any kind? Draw a picture to capture your experience. What might someone draw who was not helped by medication?

7. Create or propose some other way to give voice to a client's "lived experience" with psychiatric medication in your practice in your specific agency setting.

7

✳

Medication Education for Clients and Families

Learning Objectives

Upon completion of this chapter, the reader will be able to:

1. Provide three rationales for the medication education of clients and families by social workers.
2. Articulate five leadership qualities that can facilitate effective medication education programs.
3. Identify special learning needs of clients, families, children, and older adults.
4. Identify four common deficits of patient education programs.
5. Articulate three benefits to clients of participating in peer-run education programs.
6. Describe 13 common topics found in comprehensive medication education programs.

There are many excellent reasons for providing mental health clients and perhaps their families with education about psychotropic medications, including the human rights of clients, the increasing demands by clients and their families for up-to-date information, and the hope of increased adherence with medication plans. Many professionals have discussed medication education in the context of human rights of consumers (Cohen, 2011). With growing legal pressures to provide all health care clients with full and accurate information about their diagnosis and treatment as a matter of right, a consensus has arisen that client safety and security is also a right. These rights closely relate to the notion of informed consent, the idea that to be able to make choices about treatment, clients need complete knowledge about the benefits and risks of all available treatment options, including medication.

Similarly, one can see medication education in terms of supply and demand. That is, the increased emphasis on such education is related to the growing demands from clients and families for current knowledge. In addition to society's consumer orientation, this increased demand may be related in part to the renewed emphasis on biological factors in mental, emotional, and behavioral problems and their relationship to medication as a major treatment strategy. Data support the perception of high demand for information. For example, a survey conducted in St. Louis of 86 psychoeducation participants (family members, clients, and service providers) found that, while some differences emerged between the groups in terms of their rankings of problems and desired topics, issues around medication, compliance, and perceived "denial" emerged as most important (Pollio, North, & Foster, 1998).

In another survey of mental health clients, Goldbeck, Tomlinson, and Bouch (1999) documented low levels of medication knowledge among 59 mental health center clients with psychotic, mood, and personality disorders, including positive effects, adverse effects, and rationale for use. MacPherson, Double, Rowlands, and Harrison (1993), in a random sample of 100 long-term hospital patients on psychotropic drugs, found that only 8 named all their medications and 23 named only one. Many could describe the drug's color and shape, but most showed no understanding of the therapeutic action. A different study of 253 inpatients on the day of discharge found that 37% of respondents did not know why they were taking their medication, even after receiving some individual and group instruction. While the good news is that 63% could name their medication, 47% did not know when to take it (Clary, Dever, & Schweizer, 1992). A nationally representative sample of mental health insurance claims shows very little family intervention activity in general, a mere 1% of claims (Dixon, et al., 1999). A field test follow-up showed that only 8% of families attended any education or support groups, much less education specifically geared to medication-related issues. This research again points to the tremendous gap between what professionals know is needed ("best practices") and what they provide ("standard practices"). In our own research (Bentley, Walsh, & Farmer, 2005b) we found that 24.7% of social work respondents "very frequently" or "often" talked with a client's family about medication issues, while 60.8% believed that the activity was "quite appropriate."

Perhaps the most often cited rationale for providing medication education is the hope that increased knowledge and support will increase the client's adherence to the prescribed drug regimen. While strong evidence supports the connection between noncompliance and relapse (Julius, Novitsky, & Dubin, 2009), the evidence regarding the actual impact of medication education on adherence is less certain but still encouraging. Professionals also hope that medication education helps clients and families to participate more responsibly in the treatment process. For example, many have noted that education provides a flexible and empowering means of engaging clients in the treatment process and that, even if they forget the actual information, the educational efforts remain worthwhile. Clients and families must build competence and take charge of their medication situation. To do this, they need medication education to increase their knowledge and skill. In any case, medication education is seen as promoting cooperation, strengthening coping skills, enhancing clients' acceptance of their mental or emotional disorder, increasing hope for change, providing emotional support, reducing the family's burden, and helping clients acquire new skills. All are considered protective factors in the stress–diathesis model (see Chapter 1).

Before proceeding with our discussion, we note that the term *psychoeducation* is often used interchangeably with education, although the former term is broader, describing a range of individual, family, and group interventions that are focused not only on *educating* participants about a significant challenge in living, but also helping participants develop *social and resource supports* in managing the challenge, and developing *coping skills* to deal with the challenge (Griffiths, 2006).

THE EFFECTIVENESS OF
MEDICATION EDUCATION

Studies that have evaluated medication education programs over the years offer good reason to be optimistic about its potential impact on clients' understanding of medication, adherence, symptomatology, attitudes, fears, and ability to negotiate with clinicians. In fact, psychoeducation is said to be among the most effective of the evidence-based practices that have emerged in clinical trials and practice settings (Lukens & McFarlane, 2006). Many single-subject and quasi-experimental designs have been utilized to test the effectiveness of these interventions on client populations, and some experimental studies have also been conducted. Most studies show that psychoeducation is equal to or superior to alternative interventions. One review found that there is an increasing body of evidence showing education to be an effective component in a comprehensive treatment approach to mental illness (Landsverk & Kane, 1998). This review revealed that educational interventions can be beneficial for a wide variety of populations and problems in living. It also found that psychoeducation can empower participants and that the process allows them to collaborate more fully with their health care providers. In addition, this review revealed the importance in psychoeducation of the skills and attitudes of leaders and peer-to-peer interactions. Psychoeducation is most effective when it includes educational content that is specifically targeted to its recipients.

Psychoeducation research regarding schizophrenia and bipolar disorder is extensive with a number of meta-analyses, systematic reviews, and literature reviews having been performed. In one meta-analysis of randomized, controlled trials, it was found that family education resulted in greater medication adherence and significantly decreased relapse rates for the client relative (the family member with mental illness) at 9 to 18 months follow-up, compared with standard care (Pekkala & Merinder, 2007). The general characteristics of family groups that appear to produce positive outcomes include longer durations (10 sessions or more), including families with relatives who have a similar disorder (including the ill relative in some or all meetings), and focusing on education and support rather than "therapy." A literature review showed that family intervention designed to reduce expressed levels of criticism, hostility, or over-involvement decreased relapse and increased compliance with medication (Pharoah, Rathbone, Mari, & Streiner., 2003). Another review noted that single-family interventions reduced the impaired relative's readmission rates in the first year and that after two years the interventions lowered relapse and readmission rates as well as increasing medication compliance (Pilling, et al., 2002). A fourth review of 40 randomized, controlled studies identified four significant outcomes, including (1) education improved members' knowledge of mental illness, (2) behavioral instruction helped members ensure that their ill relative took medications as prescribed, (3) relapse prevention skills development reduced the ill relative's relapses and rehospitalizations, and (4) new coping skills development reduced the distress associated with caregiving (Mueser, et al., 2002).

Psychoeducation has an important role in educating persons with bipolar disorder about the illness and its repercussions (Rothbaum & Austin, 2000). The chronic nature of bipolar disorder is difficult for people to come to terms with, and psychoeducation can help them deal with the effects of past episodes on their lives, comprehend the impact of the disorder on their self-image, and make plans to minimize future problems. The more that a person and those in his or her environment understand about the disorder, the better able they will be to manage it (Miklowitz & Goldstein, 1997; Rouget & Aubrey, 2007). Literature reviews consistently bear this out. Along with cognitive-behavioral intervention, psychoeducation is the most effective means of preventing recurrences of manic and depressive episodes (Colom & Vieta, 2004). Other researchers add that interpersonal, family structure, and social rhythm therapies should be included in these programs (Geller & Goldburg, 2007; Zaretsky, Rizvi, & Parikh, 2007). Psychoeducation helps individuals become active, informed participants in the management of the disorder and promotes a collaborative relationship between persons and their caregivers (Vieta, 2005). Researchers in one study found that persons most likely to participate in a psychoeducation program were young adults with relatively high education levels, a shorter duration of the disorder, a better initial knowledge of medication, and a lesser external locus of control orientation (Even, Richard, & Thuile, 2007).

Persons with depression who attend psychoeducational programs experience a lower rate of relapse than those persons who do not attend such groups (Franchini, et al., 2006). Specifically, interventions based on cognitive-behavioral theory have been clearly documented as effective treatments for major depression in a meta-analysis of 56 studies (Lewinsohn, Clarke, & Hoberman, 1989). Such interventions offer participants new behavioral skills and new ways of thinking about themselves. Treatments derived from a cognitive perspective are aimed at depressive thought processes, whereas those derived from behavioral positions are aimed at increasing pleasant activities and time management skills and improving social, relaxation, and problem-solving skills.

In summary, medication education appears to rest on solid logical and ethical grounds supported by encouraging empirical data. Before detailing the content of specific medication education programs, we will present some of the principles and structural issues underlying the implementation and evaluation of some of these programs for both adults and children.

ISSUES IN IMPLEMENTING AND EVALUATING MEDICATION EDUCATION

Medication education may be provided to clients on an individual basis, but it is often done in formal programs that run a wide structural gamut. Psychoeducational programs are not a "one size fits all" approach to service delivery. Programs may be provided in one hour (Clemens, 2004) or one day (Pollio, North, & Reid, 2006), up to 15 sessions or more (Brennan, 1995), and with open or closed-ended structures (Botsford & Rule, 2004). Some programs for youth are integrated into school curricula (Dore, Nelson-Zlupko, & Kaufmann, 1999). Human service professionals have leadership in most psychoeducation services, but consumers or family members of consumers lead some groups, and others are co-led by professionals and consumers (Ruffolo, Kuhn, & Evans, 2006). Social workers need not be "experts" when providing medication education to clients, but certain practices must be addressed when taking on the role of educator. One social worker has developed a set of principles for educational practice (Stromm-Gottfried, 2009). We summarize these six principles below and also elaborate on them.

Developing Clear and Appropriate Objectives

Goals and objectives for medication education may fall into three general categories: knowledge, skill, and insight advancement. Adult learners tend to apply what they learn, so medication education should address their individual hopes and dreams. Further, the more quickly the information can be put to practical use, the better the retention (Green, 1998). For people with symptoms of mental, emotional, and behavioral disorders, such dreams can include staying out of the hospital, getting or keeping a meaningful job, or feeling like a normal human being. Social workers must take care not to oversimplify the goals of the educational effort. This might occur in medication education, for example, when medication adherence becomes the entire goal, even though studies point to other powerful outcomes, such as helping clients feel validated and competent.

Understanding the Specific Needs and Abilities of the Learners

This range of needs includes understanding the client's sources of motivation, making the material relevant to the client, building on his or her existing knowledge, sequencing material from the familiar to the unfamiliar, identifying the client's learning styles, and expressing confidence in the learner's abilities.

People with symptoms of mental and emotional problems may experience certain learning challenges. For example, Torres, et al., (2011) list the potential challenge of impaired cognitive functioning among persons with psychosis and mood disorders. Other potential learning problems may include impairment in memory, intellectual functioning, cognitive processing speed, and nonverbal reasoning. People with depression show a poorer understanding of treatment explanations (Ghormley, et al., 2011).

Social workers should consider these facts not only when choosing content for medication education but when managing the dynamics of classroom interaction. At the same time, any educational effort should strive to debase myths, stereotypes, and misinformation about the limitations of the people who suffer from psychiatric conditions; it should reflect the social worker's sensitivity to real impairments of the population. Although some argue that inclusive education (such as with professionals, consumers, and families together) is the most desirable because it draws people together and enhances the empathy and appreciation of these groups for each other (Cubine, et al., 1999); the best way to respond to the specialized learning needs of each audience may lead to separate offerings or curriculums.

Social workers must also be careful not to make erroneous assumptions about the educational needs of the learners. In medication education, this might come up as underestimating clients' concerns about side effects or overestimating a family's need for information on brain biochemistry. One way to overcome this error is to simply ask and observe. For example, one researcher administered his own informal pretest survey at his 9-week family education and support group to gather information about family members' knowledge of medications and other issues related to mental illness (Walsh, 2010).

Creating an Atmosphere Conducive to Learning

This refers to both the emotional and physical environment. Regarding the former, educators should support the learner's participation and risk-taking in pursuit of knowledge and establish a climate of trust and safety. Clients and families sharing their experiences with other group members is a major mechanism of learning. Even if a great deal of content is delivered didactically, the sharing approach is built into most programs. Heyduk (1991) goes even further to suggest that programs must let participants guide the teacher in what they need to know. Green (1998) notes that direct participation in the learning process adds to a sense of control around health issues. Because life experiences, both positive and negative, tend to lead to strong feelings and beliefs, social workers must provide an atmosphere that validates and encourages sharing but also allows for the presentation of accurate and balanced information. Open discussions can help participants examine their attitudes, clarify their feelings, and dispel myths about psychotropic medications and their use. Adults learn more effectively if past experiences are explicitly integrated into the process of learning.

Knowledge of the Material

How much knowledge is required about a topic such as medication depends on the needs of the learners and the purposes of the educational program. While an appropriate level of knowledge is essential, the social worker need not be an expert. He or she need not be the "sage on the stage" so much as "the guide on the side" (Stromm-Gottfried, 2009 p.723). Social workers' training in group process and empowerment practice provides them with an excellent foundation for leadership. Further, interdisciplinary collaboration has become commonplace in the practice (e.g., Toprac, et al., 2006). Interestingly, in a survey of 159 families using social work services, most thought of the psychiatrist as the most desired source of information, even though the social worker was reported to be the most available and therefore most used information source (Thompson & Weisberg, 1990). This same study stated that those family members with the most education received most of their information from psychiatrists, while those with the least education received most of their information from nurses. In terms of information exchange in psychiatric care, this seems to suggest a sort of class structure worthy of further research. A similar survey of non-NAMI members found that 72% preferred a psychiatrist to lead medication education programs, but social workers were still in the top three professionals after psychologists (Ascher-Svanum, et al., 1997).

Should leaders get special training to do medication education beyond their usual professional preparation and clinical experience? Of course, the leader should be very knowledgeable about medications and especially those topics usually included in medication education programs. The leader should also embrace the partnership model of helping and feel comfortable with empowerment practice. In any educational intervention, this includes believing that clients and families can learn and can live more productive lives. It also means being able to tolerate frequent repetition and a slow pace. Even so, leaders may not need additional specialized training that can be expensive and time-consuming. One study compared the implementation of the Medication Management Module (MMM) between professionals who participated in an on-site, 2-day training program offered by their own staff with those who received only mail about their program and a brief telephone consultation (Eckman & Liberman, 1990). While those who participated in the on-site training were evaluated as most competent to use the model, those without training were also judged satisfactorily competent. Most important, the study cited no differences in client outcomes between the groups. We do not discourage participation in training programs but encourage any well-prepared social worker to forge ahead, even in the absence of training.

Skills for Selecting and Using Appropriate Teaching Methods

Appropriate teaching methods may include lectures, demonstrations, role-plays, case discussions, audio and video resources, and web-based technologies. All of these have their benefits and limitations because there are different types of learners. The educator does not need to assess the preferred learning styles of his or her participants in advance, but should integrate learning activities into programs that touch on each of them. Four general types of learners are described below (Kolb, 1984):

The *activist* learns best through experimentation of the type found in simulations, case studies, and homework assignments. This person learns best not by listening, but by doing. Appropriate educational approaches for this person include problem-solving activities, small-group discussions, peer feedback, and homework. When learning about medications, for example, the activist may want to participate in simulated "treatment monitoring" exercises to get a "feel" for which kinds of services might be most useful for the family member.

The *reflector* learns best through reflective observations and discussions about a topic. The use of learning journals and brainstorming activities are helpful for this person. The learner needs time to think about new material, to see how it fits with his or her view of the world. This person may try hard to get a "feel" for what it is like to take medications and deal with certain side effects (that perhaps might be simulated). Lectures are helpful toward this end, and the educator should also provide general commentaries about the material that the learner can ponder.

The *theorist* learns best through abstract conceptualization, through lectures and supplemental readings that link the material to other ideas. This person may best learn about the pros and cons of medication intervention, for example, by comparing the ideas formulated by professionals on different sides of the issue. Suitable educational approaches include theory readings and debates.

The *pragmatist* learns best with concrete experiences of the type found in fieldwork and personal observations. Peer feedback is helpful for this learner, and activities should be provided that help the learner apply new knowledge and skills. The educator serves as a catalyst for a self-directed, autonomous learning for this person. For learning about medications, this person may benefit from interacting with several prescribers and learning about the various interventions they utilize. He or she may be particularly interested in the empirical evidence that supports these interventions.

The Ability to Assess One's Performance and the Learner's Acquisition of Educational Outcomes

Most evaluations answer, or should answer, two questions: "Were the learning objectives achieved?" and "How effective was the instructor in helping them be met?" Both are critical and there are a variety of measures available to cover each. Key outcome measures include medication adherence and knowledge of medications. Other measures include satisfaction with health care providers, symptomatology, rehospitalization, and attitudes toward treatment. Chapter 8 summarizes several rapid assessment inventories used to monitor medications. The main point here is that researchers should assess the impact of medication education—and all interventions—using a number of measures. Agency-based single-subject designs offer a good option for practicing social workers to respond to the call for increased accountability and data-based decision-making. Program and practice evaluation efforts can be replicated, analyzed, revised, and replicated again. Two possible errors in evaluation include drawing conclusions about the effectiveness of education too soon after classes end or in conclusions based solely on whether the education was enjoyable to the participants.

Special Considerations for Children and Older Adults

Although research tends to focus on adult drug education, many of the principles of drug education apply to children and adolescents as well, even though they have unique needs. For example, families play a more critical role in the medication treatment of children and adolescents than they do in that of adults (see Chapter 5). Pescosolido, et al. (2007) offer specific suggestions about how to tailor medication education for children. Perhaps most important is that children feel particularly out of control in terms of decision-making around treatment in general and medication in particular. The authors suggest building on the principles of anxiety reduction in medication education programs. In addition, children do not retain information well and, depending on the developmental level of the children, techniques that will help address both concerns (retention and anxiety) are called for. These might include puppet play (having the child pretend to be a nurse dispensing medications or to be him- or herself talking to a physician), art (having children draw a "before and after" medication picture), and frequent use of audiovisual aids. All techniques should be used in the context of a supportive, reassuring environment. Adolescents, in particular, might benefit from the decreased isolation that a peer group may provide.

There is also a growing literature that speaks to the special medication education needs of the elderly. Fawzi, et al. (2012) encourage medication education planners to emphasize brevity, repetition, the avoidance of technical terms, and sensitivity to sensory deficits. Further, their findings strongly support challenging specific beliefs about medicines in adherence, in part by providing information about treatment, and discussing side effects. Still, the discussion of special learning needs of children and the elderly seems to speak to the broad area of relevance to all learners, and that's "learning readiness." Green (1998) stresses the leader's role in assessing barriers to learning, either in the patient receiving education or the environment where the education is going to occur. These could be language barriers, culture, psychomotor barriers, or a consumer's past experiences, denial, depression, symptoms, literacy, or even physical pain.

A Word about Recruitment Challenges

The first task in implementing a focused medication education program is recruitment. For inpatients, this may not be a problem; recruiting families, however, particularly minority families, may be a major challenge. One group of researchers found that 60 to 75% of families did not show up for their psychoeducational program, which suggested accumulated frustrations with or skepticism of the mental health system (O'Shea, Bicknell, & Whatley, 1991). In a large study of recruitment and retention of cancer patients for an education group, it was found that only 5% of persons initially screened were eligible, consented to participate, and completed the program, with participation "burden" being a leading cause of non-participation (Ransom, Azzarello, McMillan, 2006). In the former study, disinterest, a lack of resolve about the importance of the education, denial of the illness, family chaos, and the treatment setting may also contribute to this lack of involvement. However, family disinterest or a low priority of education has not been supported by the data reviewed earlier.

EXAMPLES OF MEDICATION EDUCATION PROGRAMS

In this section we describe a range of education programs in which social workers do or might participate. First we focus on several older programs to highlight practical ways in which content can be delivered, and then we describe a range of newer programs to illustrate options for how they can be structured.

Content of Medication Education Programs

One of the first successful education programs was developed by Falloon and his colleagues, including a social worker, Christine McGill, as part of their behavioral family therapy project (Falloon Boyd, & McGill, 1984). In their comprehensive psychoeducational program, designed for people with schizophrenia and their families, family members and clients participate together in sessions that take place in the family home. Following a session on the nature of the illness (symptoms, cause, course), the second educational session is completely devoted to medication. In this session the leader uses a handout to guide the presentation and discussion.

After reviewing the previous session's main points and answering any questions the participants might have, the leader begins the medication education by discussing the underlying rationale for medication. Using a stress–diathesis model of mental illness, medication is explained as a way of managing the chemical imbalance in the brain. A brief account of the introduction of antipsychotic drugs into psychiatric care is given, followed by a review of the types of medications, their chemical and brand names, dosage issues, and their benefits. Using simple graphs, the leaders highlight the reduced symptoms and relapse rates of those individuals who regularly take their prescribed medication. Throughout this presentation, they ask clients and families how this information relates to their own experience. For example, when presenting information on how individuals respond differently to various medications, the leader asks the client to describe her or his experience with such medications. When presenting information on relapse, the leader asks if the client has ever had a relapse related to the cessation of medication.

The session continues with a list and discussion of common "warning signals," those symptoms that usually precede a relapse, such as increased tension or restlessness, poor concentration, and sleep difficulties. With input from both the family and client, the leader creates an individualized list. Then, the leader reviews a "what to do next" set of options so that clients and families know how to respond if and when warning signals appear. Because most clients taking medication experience side effects (a major complaint), the Falloon program devotes a good bit of attention to this topic. Side effects are defined as unwanted, often quite unpleasant effects of medication. In terms of the ultimate benefit to clients, however, some side effects may be a necessary evil; thus, successful side effect management is a key to successful medication management. Common side effects, such as drowsiness, dry mouth, and muscle stiffness, are described along with brief advice on how to cope with them. The first overall strategy, for example, is to wait for a few days or even a week or two, because many side effects will wear off. Leaders give the client and the family opportunities to share how they have coped with side effects and to ask questions.

The Falloon program also includes a discussion of adherence issues. Reasons that people with mental illnesses stop taking their medication are outlined, including bothersome side effects, the medication serving as a reminder of the illness, and people searching for other cures. Clients and families can then share times when clients have stopped taking their medication, exploring why they did it and what impact it had on each person. At this point, the group discusses alcohol and drugs. This program presents the idea that street drugs frequently make things worse and that very small amounts of alcohol may be acceptable, although neuroleptics may intensify its effects. Providers conclude by pointing out that education is ongoing and that the professional keeps teaching and learning throughout the helping process.

Liberman and his associates have also developed an impressive medication education program that has been in use for several decades (see Eckman & Liberman, 1990; Eckman et al., 1990). Liberman's "stress-vulnerability-coping-competence" model of mental illness suggests that the use of psychotropic medication and psychosocial interventions to promote its use are protective factors that may forestall or prevent relapses in people with mental illness. His Medication Management Module (MMM) addresses four specific skills:

1. obtaining information on the benefits of antipsychotic medication,
2. knowing correct self-administration and evaluation of the medication,
3. identifying side effects, and
4. negotiating medication issues with health care providers.

This module is one of 10 or so modules developed by Liberman and his associates, each targeting a specific social or independent-living skill. Money management, food preparation, grooming, dating and friendship, and conversational skills are examples of others. Although designed for use with groups of mental health clients in inpatient or outpatient settings, these modules are readily adaptable. The MMM begins with a general introduction to the goals and rationale of the module. Each of the four skill areas entails learning a number of requisite behaviors. Skill number 4, for example, includes learning to greet the prescriber pleasantly and being able to describe side effects clearly. After viewing videotapes of people correctly demonstrating the specific skill, participants then do role-playing, receive feedback, and finally receive homework assignments.

The module also helps clients anticipate certain kinds of problems. Patients learn to handle their "resource management problems," which might include a lack of time to see the doctor or inadequate transportation to his or her office. "Outcome problems" are those disappointing or unexpected events that upset even the best-laid plans. To address this problem, a leader might teach the client how to figure out what to do if the psychiatrist is called away for an emergency and thus is unavailable.

Researchers evaluated the impact of their Medication Management Module in 28 field-test sites around the country involving 160 persons with schizophrenia (Eckman & Liberman, 1990; Eckman, et al., 1990). The field-test sites included both public and private settings, inpatient and outpatient facilities. A range of professionals participated, including social workers, nurses, occupational therapists, psychologists, and psychiatrists. Results indicated the program effectively increased clients' knowledge of antipsychotic medications and their side effects, improved clients' skill in negotiating with health care providers about their medication-related concerns, and improved medication adherence as reported by both psychiatrists and caregivers.

We now present information about several structured educational programs that may be used when working with individual clients or provided in groups.

The Patient and Family Education Program

The Texas Medication Algorithm (TMA) Project, a collaborative initiative involving state departments and universities in Texas, developed an educational program that can be incorporated into the day-to-day activities of mental health agencies (Toprac, et al., 2006; Toprac et al., 2000). The Patient and Family Education Program (PFEP) is suitable for clients who experience schizophrenia and mood disorders. TMA put together a committee of professionals and representatives from the major advocacy groups and designated the following primary content areas for PFEP: diagnosis of disorders, their symptoms and criteria, their etiology and course, the range of useful medication and other treatments, benefits and side effects of all treatments, how clients can self-monitor treatment and side effects, and other management tools. It was recommended that all educational materials be phased from simple to more in-depth and include repetitions of key concepts, messages of hope and recovery, and multiple learning modalities. The materials used in the program include written, pictorial, oral, videotaped, and interpersonal formats to accommodate different learning styles. Both individual and group formats are incorporated into the program with the groups featuring peer leadership. A key challenge in this program is that all agency staff must become aware of their unique roles in the process, because educational material is provided as part of their routine interactions with clients.

The educational focus in the initial visits with the psychiatrist and clinical staff is to explain the diagnosis, emphasizing its biological basis and key symptoms. Once a client's treatment plan is developed, staff explain the purpose of the medication, directions for use, and expected positive and adverse effects. Clients are provided with information to help them monitor symptoms and potential side effects. The physician assumes primary responsibility for explaining diagnosis and treatment options. The materials shared with clients in this stage include a series of prepared fact sheets about the disorder, medication (including possible adverse effects), symptoms and side effect monitoring and coping. After the first few visits, other involved clinicans provide enough additional information to ensure that the client understands the treatment plan and its rationale and has the tools to cope with managing his or her symptoms. As the client improves, more extensive and individualized educational interventions are provided. Groups are made available (but not required) for clients and their families for the delivery of additional information, an exchange of information about coping challenges, problem-solving, and managing perceptions of mental illness.

A follow-up test of seven community mental health centers in Texas, including 487 clients, had disappointing results, however. While nearly all clients (95.1%) had at least one educational encounter, only 53% met the study criteria for "minimum exposure to the available educational interventions." Further, only 31% participated in group interventions, and 42.5% had a family member involved in at least one encounter. The authors conclude that this was due to time constraints within the agency, not to client disinterest, and emphasize that the entire agency needs to "buy into" and support such an educational plan.

Multifamily Group Intervention for Schizophrenia

William McFarlane (2002) and his associates have developed and evaluated a Multifamily Group Intervention (MFI) that includes family members and their relatives with schizophrenia. This is a lengthy, 2-year program that integrates educational and behavioral interventions and is intended to compliment a client's individual interventions. MFI provides education about symptoms and their management and encourages the family's development of social support with the overall goals of decreasing symptoms, relapse, and hospitalization; and enhancing the client's social functioning. A minimum of three sessions is devoted to worker and family engagement that is conducted with single families. This is followed by a day-long, or two-to-three session, multifamily workshop consisting of four units (development of a working alliance between participants and professionals, a survival skills workshop, discussion groups about ways to utilize the didactic material, and planning for the ongoing use of workshop information).

Regular meetings are held every two weeks for one year and monthly thereafter, focused on social and vocational functioning.

The multiple family interventions are delivered by two mental health professionals to groups of 5 to 8 families, with 29 sessions during the first year and 12 sessions during the second year. After the joining and psychoeducational phases, which are completed in one month, the final, extended phase is delivered using a structured problem-solving group format. Through the 36 sessions, consumers and families are helped to set individual family and client goals and are then taught to use a systematic problem-solving strategy for overcoming symptom-related difficulties. MFI outcome studies have shown that the programs are successful in expanding the client and family's social network (a variable that is associated with lower client-relapse rates and fewer hospitalizations). Clients and families become more open, cooperative, and appropriately involved across family boundaries. Harmful intra-family interactions also diminish. The programs have been found best suited for young, community-based, relapse-prone clients and those who live in close proximity to their nuclear families.

The Family Survival Workshop for Schizophrenia

Pollio, North, & Reid (2002) have developed a 1-day intervention known as the Family Survival Workshop. This program features information about schizophrenia and its etiology, course, outcome, and treatments (including medication), and common problems faced by clients and families. The leaders make a point of allowing ample time to answer questions from participants regarding their specific concerns. The workshop is structured as follows:

- Leaders consult with families in advance to determine workshop content
- Families are surveyed in the morning about their specific areas of interest
- A "plenary" presentation is given on the nature of mental illness, the brain, and the treatment of mental disorders
- Family issues are discussed in groups at a midday luncheon at tables of 8 to 12 people, with placards drawing participants to particular topics
- Hour-long breakout sessions in the afternoon include education and discussion (about area resources, success stories, "ask the doc," religious resources, and legal rights)

This workshop provides family members with much information quickly, and thus participant follow-up with their treatment providers is necessary to build on and clarify this knowledge. The authors report in their program evaluation that there are gains from pretest to posttest in participants' feelings of control, ability to manage crises, knowledge of resources, and knowledge of the illness, along with reduced feelings of guilt.

Family-to-Family

NAMI, the National Alliance for the Mentally Ill is a large, nonprofit, self-help support and advocacy organization for people with mental illness and their families (NAMI, 2012). NAMI provides educational groups for several consumer populations, several of which are described here. NAMI provides skills-training programs for its group facilitators, reflecting its belief that consumers can become effective leaders in psychoeducation and may be more effective than professionals, given their firsthand experience with the array of challenges related to mental illness.

Family-to-Family is a 12-week program for NAMI members, with weekly meetings of 2 to 3 hours duration (NAMI, 2009). Two family members serve as instructors, and classes are held in community settings rather than mental health agencies. Its primary focus is on family member outcomes through better understanding of symptoms and reduced stress. Client well-being is a secondary goal, achieved through improved communication and the development of a calmer family atmosphere. The program is not diagnosis-specific; there is an emphasis on common issues, needs, and concerns of family members whose client relatives have a variety of mental, emotional, and behavioral challenges. Each class utilizes a combination of lecture, class participation, and interactive exercises and can include up to 25 members. Topics include:

- Stages of emotional reactions to the trauma of mental illness
- Diagnostic criteria of psychotic disorders, mood disorders, bipolar disorder, borderline personality disorder, and anxiety disorders
- Basic information about brain functioning
- Problem-solving skills development
- Medication review
- The experience of coping with a brain disorder
- Communication skills development
- Self-care
- The vision and potential of recovery
- Advocacy

Outcome studies indicate that Family-to-Family results in significantly improved caregiver satisfaction, decreased problem management information needs, and decreased social functioning information needs (Dixon, et al., 2010). Program participation is also associated with lower rates of psychiatric hospitalization. The positive changes appear to be maintained over at least 6 months.

Group Psychoeducation for Bipolar Disorder

Group psychoeducation in one program in Canada, conducted by a nurse, a social worker, and a psychiatrist, had a positive effect on the participants' quality of life, defined as a subjective state of well-being. This outcome variable was assessed in an 8-week time-limited psychoeducation program (Michalak, et al., 2005). The program addressed the following five goals, which were incorporated into all eight sessions, with emphases depending on the expressed wishes of the participants during the first meeting:

- To help participants identify the signs and symptoms of bipolar disorder and enhance their knowledge about the course of the disorder
- To raise awareness of the impact of bipolar disorder on psychological, cognitive, physical, emotional, and social functioning
- To improve participants' knowledge about medication treatments for bipolar disorder and their common side effects
- To provide guidelines for ensuring medication effectiveness and safety
- To provide cognitive strategies for coping with bipolar disorder

The researchers found that 57 program participants demonstrated a significant improvement in quality of life indicators in terms of reported physical functioning and life satisfaction. Colom, Vieta, Martinez-Aran, et al. (2003) conducted a randomized trial of the efficacy of a Barcelona Bipolar Disorders Group in the prevention of episode recurrences for 120 bipolar clients whose disorders were in remission (the controls attended nonstructured group meetings). Through 21 sessions, each of which was led by two psychologists and included the formal presentation of material and group discussion, the featured topics were medication adherence, coping with environmental stress triggers, and issues related to social and occupational functioning. With 2 years of follow-up, the researchers found that the experimental program significantly reduced the number of client relapses and increased the time span between recurrences of depressive, manic, or mixed episodes. Clients in the experimental group also experienced fewer and shorter hospitalizations. The authors concluded that the differences between the two groups were due to the experimental group's emphasis on early recognition of symptoms of relapse and modifications of participants' daily routines.

Family Focused Treatment

Family Focused Treatment (FFT) is a well-researched psychoeducational intervention that attempts to improve family functioning by focusing on the three topic areas of education, communication skills and problem-solving skills (Rea, et al., 2003). Two practitioners trained in the approach meet weekly with participants for the first 3 months, every other week for the second 3 months, and monthly for the final three sessions. The 21 individual sessions are an hour in length, and the leaders address all three program components during each meeting.

The program's educational component includes information about symptoms, course, causes, and treatment presented within a vulnerability-stress framework with attention paid to risk and protective factors. Communication skills training includes active listening, giving structured positive and negative feedback, and making positive requests about one another's behaviors. These activities include role-playing and between-session practice. Problem-solving training includes the structured cognitive-behavioral process with special attention given to family problem-solving around a "relapse drill." A variation of this FFT structure includes addressing each of the three major components separately for 2 to 9 sessions, depending on the assessed needs of the families (Miklowitz & Goldstein, 1997). The FFT intervention has been evaluated with regard to several outcome measures. In one control-group study (with controls receiving individual family intervention and medication management), the program led to a reduced risk of relapse and hospitalization (Rea, et al., 2003). Interestingly, this effect was strongest after, but not during, the year of active intervention. It was speculated that this is because experimental-group families had learned and retained skills they could utilize after the program ended, more so than participants in the control group. Additionally, the more symptomatic clients were better protected from relapse in the FFT group.

In another FFT evaluation study, 101 clients were randomly assigned to a 1-year program of FFT or to medication and crisis management services

(Miklowitz, et al., 2000). Results indicated that clients receiving FFT achieved longer periods without relapse than clients in the comparison groups. The greatest effects were found for depressive symptoms. Further, after 9 months of FFT, clients and family members were found to be using more positive communication skills that predicted later symptom amelioration, as in the earlier study.

Education for Adolescent Clients

Family-Focused Treatment for Adolescents.   Another FFT group was developed especially for families with adolescent ill members to see if outcomes were comparable to the adult groups (Miklowitz, et al., 2004). Since the presentation of adolescent bipolar disorder is different from that of adults, it is difficult for families to distinguish symptoms from "normal" behavior relative to one's stage of life. Program modifications include addressing the developmental issues common to adolescents and the unique clinical presentations of bipolar disorder in adolescents (a non-episodic, chronic, rapid-cycling mixed state featuring agitation, excitability, aggression, and irritability). Families are helped to understand the interactions of psychosocial development and biological illness and not to assume that all challenging behavior is indicative of a mental disorder. The program was successful, as participants reported improvements in depressive symptoms, manic symptoms, and behavior problems over a 1-year period. Another group of researchers determined that parents of children with bipolar disorder are more knowledgeable about mood symptoms than parents of children with depression and that children with bipolar disorder had greater histories of hospitalization, outpatient treatment, medication trials, and placement in special education classes (Fristad, Goldberg-Arnold, & Gavazzi, 2002). Both types of families expressed knowledge gains, skills, support, and positive attitudes during an FFT intervention.

The Multi-Family Psychoeducation Group for Depression

The Multi-Family Psychoeducational Group (MFPG) is an 8-session, manual-driven treatment for children with mood disorders that is designed as an adjunct to medications and psychotherapy (Cummings & Fristad, 2007). Its goals are to educate parents and children about medications and their management, increase communication with the prescribing physician, and manage adverse effects of medication. The MFPG targets 8- to 11-year-old children and is conducted in a series of 90-minute sessions. It trains families in communication, social problem-solving, and emotion-regulation strategies to address the management of their child's mood symptoms. Each session covers a specific topic. Children and parents are seen together for the first 15 minutes of the group and again for the last few minutes. Otherwise, parent and child group sessions occur separately. At 6-month follow-up, participants show increased parental knowledge about the child's mood symptoms, more positive family interactions, improvement in the child's perception of parental support, and a better service utilization rate.

CONTENT RECOMMENDATIONS FOR
ALL EDUCATION PROGRAMS

It might be useful at this point to summarize common topics found in any comprehensive educational program. Depending on the client's needs, social workers can present the content broadly or make it specific to certain mental or emotional disorders or particular medications.

Rationale for medication use. All medication education programs should contain information about why medication is used in the treatment of mental and emotional disorders. The stress–diathesis model provides a useful framework for presenting the rationale. Information on the effectiveness of medications in relation to psychosocial treatments might be useful as well. Many clients appreciate the analogy of the person with diabetes needing to use insulin regularly.

Benefits of medication. Clients and their families should receive accurate information about the benefits of medication, including its proven impact on certain symptoms and on relapse rates. Symptoms that tend to be less affected should also be reviewed.

Types of drugs. Depending on the audience, the curriculum might include a thorough review of one type of medication (antidepressants or mood-stabilizing medications, for example) or might review all the categories of drugs.

Side effects. Major and minor physical, psychological, and social adverse effects should be reviewed. Many programs describe creative or practical ways of coping with the range of side effects.

Dosage and equivalents. Information on the differences in dosage among medications helps clients understand such things as changes in medication orders and the importance of taking correct doses.

Forms of drugs. The pros and cons and general rationale for using various types of drugs (such as tablets, injectibles, and patches) should be included.

Absorption and predicted response. Discussion of the impact of individual metabolism on absorption rates helps clients understand better why individuals respond differently to psychotropic medication. Some programs present theories of drug action and teach clients appropriate expectations about a medication's effects at different phases of the illness.

Interactions. Common interactions, particularly those involving alcohol and drug use, should be taught to clients and families. Information on complex drug interactions is best left to an individual consultation with the physician, especially in light of increasing use of polypharmacy.

Addictiveness and withdrawal. Sometimes these fears of clients and families are unfounded. Nevertheless, strong cautions are usually in order, especially with certain types of tranquilizers and sedatives. There is developing knowledge about drug withdrawal with some antidepressant medications, for example.

Self-administration principles. Clients and families often need simple advice on how to take or store psychotropic medications, read labels, manage missed doses, or use reminders.

Adherence. A discussion of why people stop taking their medication is crucial to compliance, including issues of identity and body image. Clarifying the attitudes and beliefs of both the client and the family is important, as is anticipating both short- and long-term barriers to medication use, such as fears of toxicity, high expectations of efficacy, or fears based on cultural or societal influences.

Communication/negotiation. Although not enough programs include information on communication skills, many clients need help talking about medication to their social worker, case manager, therapist, or psychiatrist. Because clients often feel incompetent or intimidated in this area, teaching such skills is critical.

Emerging trends and research. Clients and families are interested in and often heavily invested in the latest medication research: what scientists are testing and what new trends or philosophies of care have evolved.

SUMMARY

This chapter has provided a rationale for medication education, reviewed issues related to the implementation and evaluation of medication education programs, and discussed the content of such programs. Implicit in the chapter is a call for social workers to embrace the role of educator. Even in the face of understandable doubts about their competence to do so, social workers in all settings can and should start or contribute to such groups or programs, either alone or in collaboration with other providers, clients, and families.

TOPICS FOR DISCUSSION
AND LEARNING ACTIVITIES

1. Consider the leadership qualities that are conducive to effective psycho-educational groups. How are these similar to or different from the qualities necessary for other types of intervention groups with which you have had experience? Might it be beneficial to have a family member co-lead such a group?

2. Assume that you work in an agency where social workers are discouraged from becoming involved in any discussions with clients related to medication. How might you organize a staff-development program for social workers (and perhaps other nonmedical professionals) that might reverse this position?

3. Develop in class a brief psychoeducational program for clients and their families that highlights the effects of psychotropic drugs on the body. Decide what material to include in that program and justify those decisions. Be aware that you will be presenting this body of difficult information to a lay audience.

4. Conduct a role-playing session with a client and family member immediately after a medication is prescribed for the first time. Any medication can be chosen for this purpose. One or two students can participate in the role of the social worker along with the students portraying the client and family member. Your goal is to articulate three or four major informational points about the medication in a way that is comprehensible to the consumers, including potential positive and adverse effects.

8

✳

Medication Monitoring
and Management

Learning Objectives

Upon completion of this chapter, the reader will be able to:

1. Define medication monitoring and list the range of social work activities it involves.

2. Understand five areas of competence required for effective medication monitoring.

3. Access formal instruments that can be used to assist in monitoring medication effectiveness.

4. Articulate three adverse psychological effects of taking psychotropic medication.

5. Teach problem-solving skills to clients and families with relevance to medication issues.

6. Teach assertiveness skills to clients and families for use when interacting with professionals.

7. Define advocacy with regard to psychotropic medication, and articulate five scenarios in which social worker advocacy might be required.

Monitoring both medication and the process of intervention is crucial to reducing client symptoms and enhancing psychosocial functioning. In this chapter we deal specifically with how social workers can help clients and families monitor and manage their medication in everyday life. Monitoring and managing medications for social workers means helping clients, families, and providers keep track of the medication's therapeutic effects and their impact on quality of life; cope with bothersome physical, psychological, and social side effects; solve any medication-related problems or dilemmas; and negotiate with each other about medication-related issues. In this chapter we also talk about the social worker acting as an advocate on behalf of clients and their families. Any discussion, with either clients or families, about the rationale, dosage, adverse effects, or effect of medications offers social workers an opportunity to clarify attitudes about treatment and to address these concerns. Even with full medication adherence, clients and families still need education and support as they learn how to manage their symptoms.

As stressed in the chapter on medication adherence (Chapter 9), "sophisticated and optimal treatment also entails careful attention to those psychosocial variables that may affect the ultimate outcome of the drug treatment regimen" (Docherty, 1986, p. 118). Docherty noted that monitoring drug response should also include monitoring the stress and activity levels of the client with an eye toward avoiding over- or under-stimulation. The social worker must first identify expected changes and then compare them to what actually occurs. Thus, as we have said, the role of the social worker in monitoring and managing medication is varied and complex and, as with all roles in psychopharmacology, is meant to be carried out in the context of a partnership model of practice.

There is good evidence that clients and their families can and do effectively participate in monitoring and managing medications. For example, families usually notice when their loved one's symptoms are increasing. McCandless-Glimcher and colleagues (1986) completed a literature review 25 years ago showing that by far most mental health clients and their families can and do recall changes in thoughts, feelings, or behavior before the onset or recurrence of symptoms. In their study, 98% of the clients with psychosis knew when their symptoms were getting worse. This means ample time often exists for social workers and others to help make decisions about what next steps can and should be taken. Furthermore, the ability to recognize an impending relapse has been associated with reduced hospitalizations among people with serious mental illness (Lang, et al., 2003) . Such awareness, along with the existence of a close confidant and positive feelings about treatment, can help social workers design useful interventions for clients and families. We emphasize, too, that for *some* clients with severe symptoms, this awareness correlates with a sense of despair (Hasson-Ohayon, et al., 2009).

Legal and ethical issues regarding adherence and refusal also arise in discussions about monitoring. Frequent questions that emerge in this arena include who makes final decisions about treatment planning and implementation, what is the "best interest" of the client, and how the rights of the individual on medication can be balanced with the responsibility of families, providers, and society. Because ethical conflict is intrinsic to monitoring and all aspects of social work, translating the lofty values of the profession into strategies for action will always be a challenge. For example, in a national survey of practicing social workers, perceiving that a client might be over- or under-medicated was the second most commonly identified dilemma, conflict, or struggle, and many social workers at least occasionally lacked confidence in the physician's ability to prescribe and monitor medications (Walsh, et al., 2003).

Another major ethical issue that arises in monitoring medication is subtle coercion. The most frequent ethical dilemma noted by practicing social workers in the Walsh survey was respecting a client's decision not to take medications in the face of continuing symptoms (Walsh et al., 2003). Likewise, a number of respondents felt internal or external pressure to support a prescriber's decisions even when they disagreed, and many reported feeling caught in the middle of clients and families regarding medication use. So the question is fair: If good evidence exists to encourage clients to use medication, where do social workers draw the line between coercion and encouragement? Despite a partnership model of practice that emphasizes equal power between social worker and client, vestiges of major power differentials persist. Because many agencies still strongly support these differentials, social workers and clients should watch for them, especially the ways they influence the client's perceptions of decision-making freedom. The principles of shared decision-making as discussed in Chapter 6 should be remembered. For example, Cohen (2009) believes that there can be no distinction between coercion and encouragement; therefore social workers should simply not be in the business of recommending psychotropic drugs. We believe that even though the line is difficult to draw, social workers should not abandon the task of trying to find the right place to do so.

Ethical issues and conflicts also emerge in the daily management of interdisciplinary relationships (see Chapter 2). For example, although we believe that social workers should actively assist in the medication-related dilemmas of clients and their families, we recognize that the prescriber holds the ultimate legal responsibility for choosing and adjusting the types of medication used, prescribing the actual dosages, and watching for precise therapeutic effects, physical side effects, and drug interactions. In addition, both nurses and pharmacists have a long and distinguished history related to distributing and explaining medications, a history that should be respected. Typically nurses see the administration and monitoring of medication as their "occupational territory" and one of the most important things that distinguishes them (Nash, 2011). However, nurses apparently mean something a little different by "monitoring" than what is described here. When nurses monitor, they look at weight, orthostatic hypotension, bowel movements, dental care, EEG data, heart rate, diet, and hydration and observe involuntary movements, tremors, and drowsiness. They also admit that such monitoring of physical effects is not sufficiently comprehensive or systematic. These acknowledged complementary roles of other providers underscore the desirability of interdisciplinary collaboration.

CLIENT SELF-MONITORING OF MEDICATION

If we look to the literature in such areas as diabetes care or asthma, we see the development of "self-management competencies" that may have relevance to understanding the full domain of needed skills and abilities of clients for facilitating their own recovery. Wilson (1993) characterized five different areas of needed competency that seem to capture the areas of concern in this chapter. We discuss them as they relate to people taking psychiatric medication:

1. *Preventive medication behaviors:* Making sure clients understand how to use their medications as prescribed.

2. *Precipitant avoidance behaviors:* Making sure clients and families know what things to avoid, such as things that cause stress or overstimulation or using substances that interact with medications.

3. *Symptom intervention:* Making sure clients and families recognize symptoms and other signs of difficulty and have a plan for when they reoccur.

4. *Communication behaviors:* Making sure clients have the knowledge and skills to optimize their interactions with health care providers and even to increase their capacity for self-management.

5. *Health promotion:* Working with clients to learn ways to prevent relapse or control symptoms and, in general, promote good mental and physical health (e.g., diet and exercise).

We know that by far most clients will change their behavior or engage in some kind of self-treatment in response to recognized signs of relapse and adverse effects. Kabat-Zinn (2003) has summarized the self-regulation strategies of people diagnosed with depression, including meditation, relaxation, and other techniques to reduce anxiety, often with good success. Contrary to the myth that people with mental illness always withdraw in response to such symptoms, these researchers found a high incidence of problem-solving efforts.

Self-monitoring involves two things: the client noting the occurrence of some behavior and then systematically recording it (Kopp, 1988). Clients who monitor their own use of medication must track (1) the taking of medication, (2) symptoms, and (3) physical and psychological side effects. Admittedly, clients and social workers can find it challenging to distinguish between symptoms and physical side effects. Client self-monitoring not only helps social workers collect information on which to base treatment decisions but also helps clients develop some level of self-awareness and increase their involvement and sense of power in the treatment process. Even clients who do not begin with much understanding of their illness or distress can develop it in the context of a caring therapeutic relationship (Diamond & Scheifler, 2007).

Perhaps the most common concrete strategy for self-monitoring medications is using a checklist of symptoms, either an existing one or an idiosyncratic one developed from the known experiences of the client. Identifying the warning signs of relapse and common adverse effects is almost always a part of comprehensive psychoeducational programs for mental health clients and their families (see Chapter 7). Although an existing checklist may have dozens of items with rather general categories, such as "trouble sleeping," "avoiding activities," and "confusion" (see Table 8.1), social workers can help clients and families create measures that are more precise and individualized and perhaps less overwhelming, such as "How many days last week did you wake up before 6:30 a.m.?" or "How much did you avoid contact with the members at Sunrise House today? A lot, a good bit, some, or not much?"

Table 8.1 Symptom Checklist

_____ Nervousness, tenseness
_____ Trouble sleeping (too much, too little)
_____ More than usual fatigue, no energy
_____ Depression
_____ Have difficulty thinking or concentrating
_____ Less active than usual
_____ Unable to get going (get up, go)
_____ Irritability
_____ Have difficulty doing work
_____ Avoiding activities with others
_____ Moodiness
_____ Trouble eating (too much, too little)
_____ Confusion
_____ Hearing voices
_____ Recurrent thoughts
_____ People are talking/laughing at you
_____ Others tell you that you are strange
_____ Get special messages (from television, radio)
_____ Lapses in memory
_____ Think someone is trying to hurt you
_____ Getting harassed by others
_____ Nightmares
_____ Religious concerns
_____ Headaches
_____ Think you have special powers
_____ Things look funny
_____ Think everyone can hear your thoughts
_____ Trouble talking so people can understand
_____ Feel like you are losing control of your thoughts
_____ Something is controlling or putting thoughts in your head
_____ Feel like hurting yourself
_____ Speech problems
_____ Sexual concerns
_____ You see things that others don't
_____ Heart pounding
_____ Feel like you are not really here
_____ Feel pressure in your head
_____ Feel something terrible or strange is happening to your body
_____ More active than usual
_____ Legal problems or trouble with the police
_____ Can't stop doing something over and over
_____ Have trouble getting along with other people
_____ Feel as though you are being controlled by a device (computer, electrodes)
_____ Feel like hurting others
_____ Everyone around you seems dead

SOURCE: Based on McCandless-Glimcher, et al. (1986).

Two examples may help to demonstrate this approach. A social worker helps "Bob" create a graph to monitor the adverse effects of his antidepressant medication as well as his depressive symptoms. On the graph Bob learns to keep track of his level of hopelessness, the number of hours he sleeps, the prevalence of dry mouth, and sexual dysfunction. The social worker also helps "Joan," a 62-year-old woman with a psychotic disorder and a history of numerous relapses who is currently taking risperidone. Together they create a simple checklist of Joan's unique warning signals, on which she can write yes or no, depending on whether or not she experiences the symptoms on a given day. Items include "Voices are using profanity," "Voices are getting louder," and "Can sit through all of *Jeopardy*." The sheet Joan fills out in the morning also has previously negotiated steps for her to take in case of problems. Obviously, as with any tool, clients and/or family members should be motivated and willing to use checklists that are easy to use and are periodically checked for accuracy and relevancy. One study, however, has suggested that an optimistic view of clients' ability to fairly assess their symptoms is in order. The self-reported positive, negative, and depressive symptoms of a group of 40 clients with psychosis were significantly associated with objective measures (Liraud, Droulout, Parrot, & Verdoux., 2004).

In their comprehensive review of self-management interventions, Ivanoff and Stern (1992) reported that individuals use a wide array of techniques to address their physical and mental health concerns, including chronic pain, insomnia, depression, anger, anxiety, agoraphobia, and lack of assertiveness. Although self-monitoring "was the single component most often associated with positive outcome" (p. 37), Ivanoff and Stern did not find a single study in the major social work journals that addressed the maintenance and generalization of self-monitoring skills. As such, social workers cannot assume that once clients have been taught to use self-monitoring techniques that they will do so indefinitely. The rationale for medication in general and for medication monitoring in particular may need regular revisiting and reinforcement. Clients need to see that what they do can powerfully affect clinical decision-making and the quality of their lives. Social workers can and should be a part of helping to make those connections.

Here we describe four medication-monitoring protocols that are at least partly client controlled:

The *Wellness Recovery Action Plan* (WRAP) is a structured system for client self-care developed in the late 1980s by Mary Ellen Copeland (2008). It offers a method for clients to reduce the severity and frequency of their symptoms. WRAP is offered as a psychoeducational program by trained mental health service consumers in group settings and incorporates the goals of promoting personal wellness. After a client develops his or her personalized WRAP plan, he or she can continuously review and update it with the assistance of a WRAP provider. The Copeland Center for Wellness and Recovery (2010) is the only organization that provides the training required to become a certified WRAP facilitator.

WRAP attempts to shift the focus in mental health care from symptom control to prevention and recovery. WRAP participants are encouraged to take responsibility for their own wellness by using a variety of self-help techniques provided in a workbook and reaching out for assistance to their network of family, friends, and health care providers. The intended outcomes of a client's WRAP involvement are life enhancement and gains in self-esteem and self-confidence and becoming a more fully contributing member of the community. The WRAP program topics include self-esteem, changing negative thoughts to positive thoughts, developing peer support, addressing work-related issues, trauma recovery, suicide prevention, and securing appropriate living space, life-style, and motivation. Courses may be offered through consumer organizations but WRAP is also a part of the programming of many social service agencies.

Through the time-limited group intervention (these often feature 2-hour weekly sessions for 8 weeks), WRAP promotes each consumer's development of a "wellness toolbox," or a list of resources he or she can utilize to stay healthy and deal with challenges. A client's WRAP plan consists of six parts, including:

- The daily maintenance plan (a description of the "well self" and lists of things one must do to maintain wellness).

- Triggers (things outside the self that can happen to make one feel worse).

- Early warning signs (subtle signs that let the person know he or she may be beginning to feel worse).

- "When things are breaking down" (signs that the person is feeling worse and in danger of experiencing a crisis, with tools for how to constructively respond).

- Crisis planning and "advance directives" (identifying symptoms for sharing with significant others that indicate they should take over responsibility for the consumer's care and decision-making, as well as a plan for staying at home and receiving appropriate support).

- Post-crisis planning (guidelines enabling the person to gradually resume life as it was before the crisis).

WRAP has proven to be a popular program nationally and has been evaluated numerous times. One recent quasi-experimental study with 114 participants examined the effects of WRAP participation on consumers' symptoms, hope, and recovery outcomes (Fukui, et al., 2011). WRAP sessions were facilitated by one staff person and one peer worker at five community mental health centers in a Midwestern state. Findings revealed significant group intervention effects for the variables of symptoms and hope for recovery. Group comparisons showed significant improvements for the experimental group with regard to symptoms and hope after the intervention, while nonsignificant changes occurred in the comparison group. In another study researchers assessed three dimensions of self-management (attitudes, knowledge, and skills) among consumers participating in WRAP programs representing two statewide (Vermont and Minnesota) initiatives (Cook, et al., 2010). Comparisons were made of reports from 381 participants on various outcome measures. Significant positive changes were observed in all three dimensions on 76% of items completed by Vermont participants (13 of 17 items) and 85% of items completed by Minnesota participants (11 of 13 items). In both states, participants reported significant increases in awareness of their early warning signs of decompensation, awareness of symptom triggers, having a crisis plan, having a plan for dealing with symptoms, having a social support system, and perceiving the ability to take responsibility for their own wellness.

The *Monthly Medication Journal* (MMJ) is a tool that clients can use to monitor their use and response to psychotropic medication (Finnell & Ditz, 2007). The MMJ has been developed in the format of a notebook that consumers can keep and carry with them to make daily recordings of their medication use and response. On each daily log a client records the date, time, dosage, and number of pills consumed, as well as times taken, doses missed, and reasons for missed doses. Each daily entry also includes a symptoms checklist covering the areas of mood, thinking, behavior, and activities of daily living. The client can make special checks about any persistent symptoms and ways of coping with them. There is also a template in the journal for obtaining thorough information from service providers about a medication (reason for prescription, anticipated benefits, possible adverse effects, etc.) and how to talk with a prescriber about medication concerns (a topic we cover later in this chapter). The client can review the journal on a regular basis with his or her service providers. Preliminary testing of the MMJ indicates that it promotes adherence rates of 83% (compared to 49 to 58% in most studies of standard care) and, more importantly, promotes holistic self-monitoring.

The *Cognitive Adaptation Training* (CAT) program is a manual-driven series of compensatory strategies and environmental supports for persons with mental illness who take medications to enhance their quality of life (Maples & Velligan, 2008). The psychosocial intervention seeks to bypass a person's symptomatic cognitive impairments and, as such, is most appropriate for clients with those features. Medication monitoring is a major part of this intervention. The CAT program attempts to enhance the client's environmental supports for medication monitoring through the use of such prompts as signs, calendars, pill containers, alarms, and reminder calls from relatives. Each client's treatment plan is personalized and is based on his or her assessed level of executive impairment and overt behavioral style. During the assessment, the practitioner makes a home visit to review the nature of the household as well as the neighborhood and other potentially supportive aspects of the client's life. Following the assessment, the practitioner helps the client develop any of the strategies described above to help him or her better manage the medications. The practitioner makes regular visits to the client's home (30 to 45 minutes, weekly or every 2 weeks) to monitor progress and make any adjustments in the plan. One version of this program, called the Pharm-CAT, is limited to medication monitoring, but it has been found that the intervention works best (that is, with the client's full cooperation) when the broader program is utilized.

The *Medication Event Monitoring System* is a computerized system for checking a client's medication adherence. Each medication bottle given to a client is equipped with a microprocessor that records data (the event and time) each time the bottle is opened (Lee, Kane, Sereika, Cho, & Jolley, 2011). When the client comes for another prescriber session, the data is downloaded onto a computer and printed out to summarize adherence patterns. While popular, this is not a process that encourages the development of self-management skills.

In addition to the monitoring procedures described already, social workers and clients can use one of the many existing rapid assessment inventories currently in use by clinicians and researchers for a range of disorders and symptoms. We present a few of the established instruments here, although we emphasize that we do not see social workers as relying heavily on these resources.

USING EXISTING MEASURES
TO GUIDE MONITORING

The *Psychiatric Symptom Assessment Scale* (PSAS), most often used for people with schizophrenia, includes 23 items, each rated from 1 to 7 for severity (Bigelow & Berthot, 1989). The PSAS provides an overall score as well as scores for the domains of anxiety and depression, positive behavior symptoms, positive verbal symptoms, deficit symptoms, and paranoia. The PSAS can be administered during the course of a 30-minute interview. All items and each point along the rating scale include assessment and rating guidelines.

The *Scale for the Assessment of Negative Symptoms* (SANS) and the *Scale for the Assessment of Positive Symptoms* (SAPS) are complementary instruments (Andreasen, 1982; Andreasen & Olsen, 1982). The SANS includes 25 items rated on a 6-point scale with five subscales (affect, poverty of speech, apathy, anhedonia, and impairment of attention). The SAPS includes 35 items, four subscales (hallucinations, delusions, bizarreness, and positive thought disorder), and one global assessment of affect. Both scales are designed for use in conjunction with client interviews, clinical observations, family member observations, and reports from other providers.

The *Barnes Akathisia Scale* measures the extent of movement disorder associated with the use of antipsychotic drugs. Clinician ratings are based on observations of at least 2 minutes of the person under two conditions: sitting and in conversation while standing (Barnes, 1989).

The *Simpson-Angus Neurological Rating Scale* involves clinician ratings on a 4-point scale of the severity of parkinsonian side effects, such as problematic gait, arm dropping, shoulder shaking, elbow or wrist rigidity, swinging of the legs, tremors, and salivation (Simpson & Angus, 1970).

The *Liverpool University Neuroleptic Side Effect Rating Scale* (LUNSERS) is a measure for assessing the side effects of antipsychotic drugs (Morrison, et al., 2000). It includes 51 items, 41 of which refer to known side effects of medications and 10 that are used as indicators of validity. Each item is rated by a mental health professional or client on a 5-point scale ranging from "Not at all" to "Very much." The scale can be completed in 5 to 20 minutes. A summary sheet enables the assessor to determine a total score and overall adverse effects level.

The *Brief Depression Rating Scale* (BDRS) (Kellner, 1986) is another practical tool for the clinical social worker. The format of the BDRS is similar to the Mania Rating Scale, which we describe in the next paragraph. Together the two scales can be used to assess clients with either bipolar disorder or depression.

The BDRS is an 8-item scale that measures depression by clinical observation. In this case the social worker rates the following observations on a 9-point scale that ranges from "incapacitating" to "absent"; the areas are depressive mood and feelings of despair; somatic symptoms; lack of interest, initiative, and activity; sleep disturbances; anxiety, worry, and tension; appearance; depressive beliefs; and suicidal thoughts or behavior. Individual items can be summed for a total score ranging from 8 (no depression) to 72 (high depression). The social worker can monitor specific symptoms as well. The BDRS has demonstrated high interobserver reliability and concurrent validity.

The *Young Mania Rating Scale* (MRS) is an 11-item clinician-administered instrument that can be completed by a clinician during a 15- to 30-minute interview (Young, et al., 1978). The scale items include mood, energy, sexual interest, sleep, irritability, speech rate and amount, language and thought disorders, speech content, disruptive and aggressive behavior, appearance, and insight. Scoring is based on both the client's report of his or her condition during the previous 48 hours and the social worker's observations during the interview (with an emphasis on the interview). Four scale items (irritability, speech rate and amount, speech content, and disruptive and aggressive behavior) are given greater weight to compensate for the anticipated poor reliability of manic clients. Each scale item includes five levels of severity, and a client receives an overall score of 0 to 60 from the summing of all item scores.

The *Child Mania Rating Scale-Parent* (CMRS-P) is a 10-item scale that has been shown to reliably differentiate bipolar disorder from ADHD and to discriminate among bipolar subtypes (Henry, Pavuluri, Youngstrom, & Birmaher, 2008). The scale includes descriptors adapted from the DSM-IV symptom criteria. Each item is answered on a 4-point scale (never/rare to very often), and the entire scale is designed to be completed in 10 to 15 minutes. The CMRS-P includes age-specific items. Each item is considered to be a problem only if it is causing trouble, is beyond what is normal for the child's age, and has been troublesome during the month preceding completion of the measure. The scale has an internal consistency reliability of .96. Validity evidence comes from correlations with other clinician-rated scales.

The *Hamilton Anxiety Rating Scale* (HARS) (Hamilton, 1959) is a practical monitoring instrument and the most widely used pharmacological outcome rating scale for anxiety. The HARS, which is completed by the clinician, consists of 14 items scored along a 5-point scale to yield total scores of 0 to 70. The scale includes two factors reflecting the psychological (anxious mood, tension, fearfulness, insomnia, intellectual and cognitive function, depressed mood, and behavior during the interview) and physical (muscular, sensory, cardiovascular, respiratory, intestinal, urinary, and autonomic functions) dimensions of anxiety.

The *Anxiety Rating for Children-Revised* (Bernstein, et al., 1996) uses the HARS as its basis. It consists of 11 items scored on a scale ranging from 0 to 4 and includes the same two anxiety dimensions. With these instruments, both of which demonstrate satisfactory validity and reliability, the social worker has a useful means to monitor a client's anxiety over time, including response to medications.

The *ADHD Rating Scale-IV* (DuPaul, et al., 1998) consists of 18 items taken directly from the DSM-IV list of symptoms for that disorder. Some items have been reworded for clarity and brevity. Nine items are devoted to each of the two subtypes of the disorder (inattention and impulsivity/hyperactivity). Two versions of the scale have been developed—one for school and another for home settings—but the versions are similar. The person completing the scale is instructed to read each item and consider to what extent it has been manifested in the client's behavior during the past 6 months. Each symptom is rated on a 4-point scale ("never/rarely", "sometimes", "often", and "very often"). The scale includes scoring norms for assessing whether the disorder of ADHD exists, but the scale can also be used to monitor symptom fluctuation in people who have already been diagnosed and may be taking medication. Social workers can complete either version of the instrument themselves; they can also provide family and school personnel with the form and review their responses.

A convenient instrument that social workers can use to monitor a client's overall level of functioning (beyond strict attention to the actions of medication) is the *Global Assessment of Functioning* scale (GAF) (American Psychiatric Association, 2000). This is, of course, Axis V of the Five-Axis diagnostic system utilized in this country by so many mental health practitioners. The social worker scores a client on a scale of 1 to 100 reflecting his or her overall occupational, psychological, and social functioning on a continuum of mental health and illness. Anchor statements are included at 10-point intervals to help the social worker make an accurate assessment. For example, scores from 90 to 100 document superior functioning in a wide range of activities, and scores from 0 to 10 indicate a persistent danger of severely hurting the self or others, a persistent inability to maintain minimal personal hygiene, or serious suicidal acts with a clear expectation of death.

We now turn to a series of specific recommendations that social workers can make to clients to help them manage their medications.

CONCRETE STEPS FOR COPING WITH ADVERSE EFFECTS

Clients cite bothersome adverse effects as a major reason for non-adherence to medication, and the severity of such effects is inversely related to their quality of life (Yen, et al., 2008). Thus, it is important that social workers respond to complaints and concerns about adverse effects in a way that supports the client's treatment goals, validates the client's experiences, and provides reasonable choices for action. When complaints about adverse effects emerge, social workers should first make sure that the medications are being correctly administered. Because many physical side effects abate after a few days to a few weeks, physicians usually first recommend encouraging the client simply to wait a while. Social workers should recognize that this advice may sound patronizing to clients asked to endure uncomfortable and meaning-laden physiological reactions.

The next piece of advice the prescriber usually gives is to reduce the dose, add another medication, or change the medication. Because management of dosages and schedules is largely an individual matter, relying on trial and error, adjustments in medication are common. Direct observation by others and blood tests provide two possible sources of information about the effects of medication. However, because clients' descriptions of their experiences with therapeutic and adverse effects usually provide the most important information for these adjustments, later in this chapter we discuss skills to help clients talk to and negotiate with their physicians and psychiatrists.

Client and family guides and manuals often provide the best sources of concrete and simple ways to live with some of the less serious physical side effects (e.g., Carter, 1999; Karp, 2001; Miklowitz, 2011). For example, advice to deal with drowsiness centers on taking the medication at or near bedtime and scheduling short naps during the day. Clients can reduce akathisia or internal restlessness as well as muscle stiffness by stretching or other physical activities. Dry mouth can be helped by sucking on sugar-free candy or sipping water; constipation can be alleviated by drinking 8 to 10 glasses of water daily, eating fresh fruits and vegetables, and using stool softeners or fiber supplements, if needed. With weight gain, clients may need to change medications or get advice about diet and exercise. Orthostatic hypotension, or dizziness upon standing, can be combated by helping the client practice getting up slowly from a lying or seated position. Sensitivity to sunburn responds well to sunscreens and avoiding peak sun exposure. For some physical side effects, such as hormonal changes, tremors, and rashes, there are usually no quick solutions. Other adverse effects, such as agranulocytosis, aplastic anemia, acute dystonias, and neuroleptic malignant syndrome, demand immediate medical attention. Tardive dyskinesia has created the most controversy to date about adverse effects (see Chapter 4). Treatments for that condition include vitamin E, calcium channel blockers, dopamine agonists, lithium, and benzodiazepines (Howland, 2011). Often the best advice offered by prescribers is to discontinue the drug or reduce the dosage, but because reducing or stopping medication is quite difficult for some individuals, social workers may need to make a careful assessment and review of risks and benefits.

Besides monitoring physical side effects, both clients and social workers should monitor the psychological, and social side effects of taking medication. It is true that some people may need to take medication for the rest of their lives. Still, social workers might be insensitive to how this idea affects the client's sense of identity as a self-determining human being (as discussed in Chapter 6). They may need to help the client come to terms with the need to take medication, to gradually incorporate this idea into his or her sense of self. Clients may need support in adjusting to a new self-image and the ways that they believe friends, family, and "society" may view him or her. It may take months, even years, before clients accept the reality of psychotropic medication in their lives; indeed, this may never happen. In the roles of consultant and educator, the social worker can work with clients, family members, and perhaps others in the client's social environment to help them come to terms with the anxiety, or even the normal ambivalence, generated by this identity issue.

As discussed in Chapter 2, a potential negative outcome of psychotropic medication use occurs when clients come to believe that only medication can help them function adequately, that they themselves and the providers in their lives are powerless to generate changes in other ways. By assuming helplessness with providers and peers, clients may fail to fully invest in other interventions. Many of the case examples in this book reflect clients' complex reactions to learning that they need medications to function acceptably in their social worlds. As a validator, the social worker can help to ensure that these clients maintain an awareness of their strengths and other resources that will help promote healthy social functioning.

Some clients may also develop a dependence on the prescriber or other providers, including the social worker. Clients may become unassertive with caregivers—that is, not disclose the full details of medication effects and life events—if they fear that doing so may disrupt any predictable patterns of daily functioning established with people in their lives (Walsh, 2000). It is certainly undesirable for clients to withhold information about medication or any other intervention issues from professionals who need to understand their reactions to these strategies. If social workers develop a relationship of trust with clients in accordance with the partnership model of practice, this situation can be avoided.

Another quite different adverse psychological effect is clients' anger at having to take medication, as noted in Chapter 6 when discussing parallel treatment and the meaning of medication. Their anger may center on the idea that they have been diagnosed with a disorder requiring medication, that they perceive providers to be promoting the notion that they are "ill" or that others in their environment, including family and friends, are stigmatizing them. These feelings may also represent a grief reaction. To accept that their situations can be dealt with constructively, clients may first need to be encouraged to experience and express these negative feelings so that they can eventually work through them. On the other hand, clients may disagree that they have an illness and never accept that there is a need to take medication. Again, the social worker can best address these issues through his or her relationship with the client and through collateral work with the client's significant others. Appropriate roles include that of the consultant who acknowledges the normalcy of the client's point of view. Medication education is another major component of this process.

In addition to regularly inquiring and helping clients articulate and reflect on these issues, depending on their level of functioning or interest, social workers might also encourage clients to express their feelings in art (as presented in Chapter 6). Although no art therapy program to date explicitly aims to help people monitor and cope with their own responses and adverse effects to medications, such therapy has helped people with such disorders as depression, bipolar disorder, schizophrenia, and ADHD (Dere-Meyer, Bender, Metzl, & Dias, 2011). In the field of social work, Potocky (1993) described the use of an art therapy group in a residential facility to help residents increase their social skills through self-expression and social interaction. Admittedly, these approaches for encouraging expression, ventilation, and developing insight are intuitively appealing but, in general, untested and might best be thought of as potential adjuncts to more traditional supportive techniques.

Interestingly, there is some evidence that people with certain personality characteristics may be more or less responsive to the effects of medications. These findings are believed to be related in part to expectations that people have about the effects, both therapeutic and adverse, of medications (Frank & Frank, 1993). People who exhibit high sociability tend to respond positively to medications compared to those who perceive themselves as more self-sufficient and independent. For naturally sociable people who are depressed, the use of medications may represent a social encounter; the person is particularly tuned in to opportunities for bolstering the sense of self on the basis of interactions with others (Quilty, et al., 2008). In other studies, people with the characteristic of acquiescence react more strongly to same-dose medications as non-acquiescent persons (Insel, Reminger, & Hsiao, 2006). The rationale for this finding is that the acquiescent person wants to interact with others and to transmit a willingness to be part of a social situation. Also, persons with depression who are self-critical tend to be poorer medication responders (Bulmash, et al., 2009). This is not an area of research that is being explored in depth today, but it is important to consider that the act of taking medications has different meanings for consumers with different personality types, and some of these may facilitate or inhibit the response to some medications.

PROBLEM SOLVING IN MEDICATION MANAGEMENT

One could argue that problem solving is the heart of social work practice. As such, many practice textbooks (for example, Hepworth, et al., 2012) present various models of the problem-solving process and encourage practitioners to work collaboratively through the steps with their clients. Other helping professions also value such training for clients as an avenue for increased social competence. For example, D'Zurilla and Nezu (2010) reviewed the effectiveness of problem-solving training across a variety of target groups, including people with alcohol dependency or psychiatric problems, depression, agoraphobia, stress, weight problems, marital and family problems, vocational indecision, and problems with academic achievement. They concluded that using problem-solving training as a clinical intervention can help clinicians move away from deficit models of psychopathology. Problem solving, then, becomes a portable self-management technique and coping strategy that serves as a buffer against future problems.

You can easily find specific examples of successful problem-solving training and coping skills programs for people with mental illness and emotional distress. Mueser and colleagues (2002) conducted a comprehensive review of over 10 of these programs and noted that despite a good bit of variability in actual programming, the programs had seen "uniformly positive results." In a meta-analysis of problem-solving interventions for persons with depression, Bell and D'Zurilla

(2009) found that the practice was equal in effectiveness to other active interventions. Problem-solving and coping skills are often also presented as the backbone of family psychoeducation programs (Walsh, 2010). Positive outcomes range from increased problem-solving knowledge and behaviors to more global measures of outcome, such as increased social functioning and decreased depression. Problem-solving training involves reviewing the six steps of the problem-solving process and then applying them to real situations. We have taken the following steps from Hepworth and colleagues (2012), and Mueser and Gingerich (1994).

1. *Define the problem:* The first step in problem solving involves determining what exactly the problem is, as specifically and concretely as possible. This is achieved through sharing perspectives, either in a group or with a provider. Mueser and Gingerich (1994) suggested providing a "Defining Problems Exercise" to help clients and families understand the challenges in defining problems. This involves offering a case vignette so clients and families could "practice" every step of the process before working with their own problems.

2. *Generate possible solutions:* In this step, participants share their ideas for solutions to the agreed-on problem in a nonevaluative environment. With such brainstorming, everyone should be encouraged to participate. Even outrageous ideas for solutions should be made welcome. When a client or family stops after producing five or six ideas, the social worker should encourage them to brainstorm further, as up to 10 possible solutions can be generated for any problem. It is in this step that creativity is encouraged, and clients are pushed out of their habitual ways of defining solutions.

3. *Evaluate the pros and cons of each solution:* This step involves evaluating the positive and negative aspects of each brainstormed idea. Mueser and Gingerich (1994) suggested moving through this step rather quickly by highlighting only the main strengths and weaknesses of each option while acknowledging that every idea has merit.

4. *Choose the "best" solution:* This step involves coming to a consensus on a solution or some combination of solutions based on the evaluation. The "best" solution is the one that is most practical for implementation at this time and with the (perceived) best chance for success. It calls for clear communication and a willingness to negotiate and compromise. The social worker must acknowledge that there is no guarantee that this solution will be fully effective.

5. *Carry out the solution:* Even the best of solutions cannot be implemented without some plan of action. In this step plans are broken down into manageable tasks; assigned to participants according to interest, time, resources, and ability; and have a time frame for completion. A discussion that anticipates potential negative consequences may also help. Participants should practice steps that require some overt skill or activity. Mueser and Gingerich (1994) provided a suggested "Action Planning Worksheet," much like a typical social work contract. It should specify the task, the person assigned to carry it out, the target date for completion, and a column to be checked off

upon completion of the task. Clients might want to place this worksheet on the refrigerator as a reminder.

6. *Review implementation and praise all efforts:* At some mutually agreed-on time, the group will evaluate the progress of task completion in particular and problem solving in general. Social workers should lavishly praise all efforts. When individual clients use the process on their own, they should be encouraged to reward all accomplishments, even partial ones. Of course, the chosen solution may not be successful, in which case the client and social worker return to step 3. Partial success is a useful way to describe the most common outcomes of problem solving. Failure should be reserved for those rare occasions when no efforts are made to achieve progress.

It may help to consider how such problem-solving efforts might help in an actual case taken from Chapter 1. Darlene is a 22-year-old single woman, unemployed and currently living with her sister in an apartment but financially supported by her parents who were involved in her treatment planning and care. Darlene suffers from bipolar disorder, which has required a number of hospitalizations in the last 3 years. Although stable on a combination of antipsychotic and mood-stabilizing drugs, Darlene stopped taking them. Her parents became furious with the social worker and the agency when they learned that the social worker did not know about it. Darlene finally revealed that she had not been honest about her adherence and was actually intentionally trying to prompt a regression out of her own fears of increasing responsibility. However, it was too late. The family decided to terminate care from this agency.

In this case the client and family might have come together to solve a number of problems to prevent the impending relapse and the major disruption in service to Darlene. For example, they could have examined Darlene's worsening symptoms, her covert noncompliance, her fears of independence, the family's anger at the agency, or even continuous care for Darlene in the transition to a new provider. In discussing Darlene's worsening symptoms, joint problem-solving would have afforded opportunities for the group to define the problem from each perspective, to express their feelings and disappointments, and to offer important reassurances. Darlene's non-adherence and her fears about becoming more independent would likely have surfaced. Brainstorming possible solutions might have yielded ideas such as increasing responsibility more slowly, adding psychosocial supports, arranging for additional counseling about her fears, learning more about medication, and adding tangible rewards for adherence. Each person in the group could have helped to evaluate alternatives and select and monitor a solution or combination of solutions.

Hepworth and colleagues (2012) offer guidance on how to prepare clients effectively for problem-solving. Their guidelines include laying the groundwork for the process early in the intervention phase; maintaining a positive, collaborative stance; and being sure to praise and highlight connections between problem-solving efforts and goal attainment. Problem-solving training begins with providing a rationale for the training to clients and families, which is the use of a step-by-step process to make oneself a better overall problem solver. Being specific when discussing problems and solutions, focusing on the present, breaking a problem into smaller parts, and listening actively are all keys to the successful use of problem-solving.

Teaching problem-solving skills works well in large audiences (with families, groups of clients in clinics, support groups, clubhouses, or residential facilities) but can be most specific when working with individuals. Formats may vary, however. For example, D'Zurilla and Nezu (2010) described different methods of presentation, including didactic presentations, slides, video demonstrations and taped practice, specially created games, and group exercises. Role-playing and homework are always crucial components of such programs.

Foxx and Bittle (1989) developed a program that addresses problem solving specifically for medication issues. They presented a curriculum for teaching people with mental illness what they call assertive problem solving, with similar curricula for people with developmental disabilities, brain injuries, and adolescents. The curriculum materials include trainee score-recording forms, a facilitator's scoring guide, and evaluation forms to make precise tracking of progress possible. Participants are taught to use a problem-solving "cue card" that provides guiding questions for the participants to solve case scenarios. By applying the following questions to each problem situation, participants build problem-solving competence:

1. When will the problem be solved?
2. Where would you (or a friend) look for help?
3. Would you talk to him, her, or them?
4. What would you say?

Participants receive 48 problem-situation cards with cases that deal with many topics such as obtaining professional help, stating one's rights, interpersonal issues, authority figures, community resources, and medication. Here are some examples of the problem situations that relate to medication, adapted from Foxx and Bittle (1989):

1. Every time you take your medication you become fidgety and can't concentrate on one thing for long. What should you do?
2. A friend of yours has been taken off her medication for some time and doesn't understand why her doctor has placed her back on it. She is thinking of not filling the prescription and not letting her doctor know. How would you help?
3. You believe that the treatment you've been receiving at the mental health center is not helping. What should you do?

In Example 1 the answers to the "cue card" questions might be:

1. The problem will be solved when I am not fidgety and stop losing my concentration after taking my medication.
2. I could look up my doctor or pharmacy in the phone book.
3. I could talk to my pharmacist, doctor, or social worker.
4. I could say, "Whenever I take my medication, I get fidgety and can't concentrate. I am taking [name of medication]. What should I do?"

Social workers could easily adapt or expand not only the case scenarios but also the answers to the questions for use with other medication-related problems. These might include the ambiguity some clients feel about the rationale for medication use, the impact of medication on the client's sense of self, adherence issues, the client's concerns about his or her relationship with the prescribing physician, and any agency policy that precludes effective psychopharmacology practice.

NEGOTIATING MEDICATION ISSUES WITH HEALTH CARE PROVIDERS

Social workers should never assume that their clients are confident enough to communicate their medication concerns to professionals. A recent study by Chewing, et al. (2012) concluded that 71% of respondents on a variety of types of medication desired shared decision-making roles with providers, while a related study found that relatively few clients either understood what pharmacists were saying or felt welcome to ask questions of them (Shah & Chewing, 2011). Clients and families need certain communication skills and tools to do this successfully. Similarly, as a foundation for a productive partnership, social workers must also have the knowledge and skills to negotiate with clients, families, physicians, and other health care providers. At the most basic level, providing clients and their families with a structured checklist of "agenda items" to be discussed with the prescribing physician might be extremely helpful. One approach (Chewning & Sleath, 1996) is for clients to be PREPARED for the meeting, that is, to discuss the

- **P**rescription
- **R**easons or indications for the prescription
- **E**xpectations or client-focused benefit
- **P**robability of benefits
- **A**lternative treatments available
- **R**isks of the medication
- **E**xpenses involved (both direct and indirect costs)
- **D**ecision

A few psychoeducational programs include how to negotiate with mental health providers. For example, Dow and colleagues (1991) stress principles of negotiation in their successful medication-management protocols. They suggest teaching clients to remain calm during all communication, to learn how to accurately describe their current problems, to jot down individualized questions about their medications to bring to their appointments, to write down the answers and repeat them back to ensure clarity, to make sure all information is clearly understood before they leave, and to be assertive, not aggressive.

In fact, assertiveness provides a solid base for the communication skills needed to effectively negotiate with health care providers. Watnabi (2006) reviewed a number of definitions of assertiveness and concluded that it includes four dimensions: open expression of thoughts and feelings, expression uninfluenced by emotion, flexible reactions based on the situation, and independent judgments of the behavior of others. This includes being able to say no, to ask for favors or make requests of others, to express positive and negative feelings, to initiate, continue, and terminate conversations, to accept and give compliments, to express personal opinions, and to stand up for one's rights. One can see how clients would need to be able to say, "No, I don't want to discontinue medication until after I start my new job" or "Please change my medication to one that does not increase my appetite, because I already have a weight problem" or "Dr. Smith, I'd really like to clarify your availability after-hours" or "I don't think the medication is helping."

Focused discussions with clients and families about assertiveness versus aggressiveness and nonassertiveness may serve as a helpful precursor to more specifically directed communication skills training. Clients can help articulate the differences in these three interactive styles and how their own and others' behaviors reflect them. Hepworth and colleagues (2012), for example, noted that assertive communication is characterized by a relaxed posture and direct eye contact with appropriately varied eye contact and moderately expressive gestures. On the other hand, aggressive communication features a glaring stare, pursed lips, rigid posture, and loud and sarcastic speech. Nonassertive communication is characterized by evasive eye contact, nervousness, and soft, whiny, hesitant speech.

Social workers can also help clients and families explore the feelings that each style elicits. How does it feel when someone points a finger and raises his or her voice? To understand how these differences relate to medication management, clients can generate examples (or social workers can create case scenarios based on their experience) of aggressive or passive behavior preventing some desired outcome, such as getting a timely appointment with the prescribing physician or getting the physician to agree to reduce the dosage. Social workers can also share examples of assertive behavior that helped to reach a goal, such as getting a "drug holiday" or trying one of the newer generation of antidepressants.

Liberman and colleagues (1987) detailed how to teach clients the skills of negotiating with their health care providers, one of the four skill areas in their Medication Management Module (see Chapter 7). They provide 11 specific requisite behaviors under the heading "Negotiating with Health Care Providers," behaviors that look remarkably like those needed for assertiveness. Effective negotiation means that clients should be able to demonstrate the following skills (adapted from Eckman & Liberman [1990]; Eckman, et al. [1990, 1992]; Meder, Morawiec, & Sawicka [1998]):

- Pleasantly greet the provider.
- Describe their problem specifically.
- Tell the length of its occurrence.
- Describe the extent of their discomfort.

- Specifically request some action.
- Repeat or clarify the doctor's advice.
- Ask about the expected time frame of effect.
- Thank the provider for her or his assistance.
- Establish and maintain good eye contact.
- Maintain good posture.
- Speak audibly and clearly.

These skills can be taught through the structured skills-training process described below, which can be used with individuals, groups, or families in six steps.

1. *Discuss the rationale for the skill:* The first step involves engaging the clients in the training process by building together a motivating rationale for learning the skill and each behavior required to perform the skill. Clients need to see, for example, the connections between effectively asking questions of physicians, understanding the physician's dosage rationale, and acquiring a generally greater knowledge of and motivation for using the psychotropic medication.

2. *Identify the components of the skill:* Every skill can and should be broken down into manageable components or steps that the client can help articulate. Thus, for example, clients who try to get clarification of medication orders should perform at least three steps: (a) looking at the physician/health care provider, (b) telling the provider what they heard her or him say about the medication orders, saying "I understood you to say …" or "Did you say that … " and (c) directly asking for feedback, such as "Is that right?" The extent to which components of any given skill are broken down depends on the functioning level of the client or family member.

3. *Model the skill:* In this step the social worker actually demonstrates each of the components outlined in the previous step. The client or another group member can play the part of the physician. Given what is known about the power of observational learning, this step is crucial. It also reinforces a partnership model of practice. The social worker might begin by saying, "If I were to ask for clarification of the dosage levels, I would sit up straight, look at Dr. Jones, and say, 'I hear you saying you are going to increase my dose because you want to see if it will lower my anxiety level faster so that I can get some better sleep. Is that right?' Now, if you were the physician, you would say, 'Yes, that's right, you haven't had any really bothersome adverse effects yet, so we'll try this and see how it goes.'"

4. *Role-play each component:* Role playing is a technique in which the client walks through the components in a situational exercise. Clients can help set the stage by providing examples from their own lives of situations where the skill might have been useful, obviously providing greater relevance.

5. *Evaluate the role play:* Next, the social worker offers much positive feedback that is behaviorally specific and then she or he provides some corrective

feedback. The social worker encourages the client to practice the role play again, incorporating the feedback that was just received. Feedback should attend to both verbal and nonverbal behaviors, and participants should receive an opportunity to share their feelings about the role play.

6. *Apply the skill in real life:* Hepworth and colleagues (2012) called this step the "ultimate test" of learning a skill because the client actually uses it in a real-life situation. For example, one skills-training program included having clients visit a local pharmacy to seek out possible remedies for bothersome adverse effects such as dry mouth and photosensitivity (Glynn, et al., 2002). Because application in real life usually entails some preparation, problem solving is almost always a useful and important adjunct to skills training. As in problem solving, social workers can help clients find the internal and external resources (i.e., the courage, the time, the money, the telephone) to carry out the skill. Anticipating problems and disappointments is also an important preparation. What if the pharmacist ignores or patronizes him? What will the client do if the physician ignores her requests for clarification? Debriefing and booster sessions can help consolidate learning and ensure proper credit. Praise is offered for successes, no matter how small.

Liberman's modules, as described in Chapter 7, often rely on video recorded case scenarios as part of the modeling step of skills training. Video recordings can also be used to provide effective feedback. These tools may become much more widely available in the future. In addition, more interactive and individualized computer-assisted instruction, video discs, and the like are being developed. Liberman and colleagues (1987), in their guidelines for providers negotiating with clients and families about medication, echoed the principles we have emphasized throughout the book, especially those discussed in relation to medication adherence and refusal. They suggest that all mental health providers do the following:

1. Use effective communication, including active listening, and acknowledge the client and family as "experts"; reinforce mutual collaboration; and encourage the expression of goals, needs, and wishes.
2. Acknowledge the rights and responsibilities of clients and families concerned about and actively involved in medication-related dilemmas.
3. Solicit their reactions and suggestions about medication management.
4. Maintain a nonpunitive stance.
5. Recognize and accept that not all treatment decisions will be accepted.
6. Be prepared for difficult negotiations.

Difficult situations may require compromise: restating your position while acknowledging the client or family member's position; ignoring provocation, criticism, and threats; focusing on benefits; and, when all else fails, politely terminating the interaction. All suggested responses begin with listening empathetically to clients and their families and exploring their reactions to medication issues.

ADVOCACY IN MEDICATION MANAGEMENT

Social work advocacy is a distinctive value in professional practice, with the purpose of improving the social status of persons who are considered vulnerable and oppressed. Still, it is underutilized in practice due in large part to issues of status and power in interdisciplinary teams and to a lack of clear roles in medication management. Connaway (1975) and Mailick and Ashley (1981) were among the first to ask questions about how advocacy and interdisciplinary collaboration fit (or do not fit) together. They both noted that although collaboration calls up notions of cooperation and cohesion, advocacy implies subtle coercion and potential conflict. A healthy dose of political acumen can thus help a social worker make judgments about when and how to advocate.

In defining the social workers' role of advocacy, Gerhart wrote that they "monitor the rights and entitlements of their clients" and "focus on influencing decision makers." Encouraging social workers not to equate routine brokering or linking services with advocacy, Gerhart described true advocacy as simply making persistent demands to decision makers on behalf of clients and families in cases where services have been "refused, resisted or inadequately offered" (Gerhart, 1990, pp. 271, 272; see also Gerhart & Brooks, 1983).

Regarding medication management, here are some examples of situations that might call for either social worker advocacy or client self-advocacy:

- A clinician refuses to refer clients for medication screening.
- An agency structures all medication–review appointments during the daylight hours on weekdays.
- A psychiatrist seems to be overmedicating a client.
- A family physician will not adjust the medication in response to continuing concerns about adverse effects.
- A hospital administrator opts not to participate in a free medication trial program.
- A treatment team will not allow a trial program of intermittent medication.
- An agency discontinues its medication education program when a key staff person resigns.
- An agency will not allow use of a certain drug reported to be effective.
- An insurance company differentially reimburses the cost of a drug depending on diagnosis.

As can be seen, advocacy is closely linked with client and family rights, particularly regarding access to quality treatment. In all mental health settings, clients' rights have long been a concern; certainly, regarding medication, these issues are even more pronounced (see Chapter 7). A statement of our views of client rights, adapted from "Every Person's Bill of Rights" (adapted from an undated, anonymous bill of rights), may be useful.

1. The right to be treated as competent health care clients.
2. The right to ask questions about the medication and its effects.

3. The right to express one's own opinions about medication.
4. The right to be listened to by the prescribing physician.
5. The right to be educated about one's medication.
6. The right to participate in psychopharmacological treatment planning and decision-making.
7. The right to make mistakes and to change one's mind.
8. The right to choose not to assert oneself.

Social workers perform two essential tasks that relate to medication management and their historic and ethical mandate to advocate for clients: (1) advocating directly for clients and families and (2) empowering and helping clients to advocate for themselves. Admittedly, deciding which approach is best can be challenging. For example, in Walsh and colleagues' (2003) survey of ethical dilemmas in medication management, "deciding when to advocate for your client yourself" or "push the client to advocate for him- or herself" was cited very frequently, often, or occasionally by just under half of the respondents. Willetts (1980) pointed out some time ago that clients themselves are often the most effective advocates because of their unique legitimacy and sensitivity to the issues. The rise of the consumer and family movements over the past 35 years has proven that point. All advocates, whether social workers or clients and families, should have a general knowledge of psychopharmacology, mental illness, and mental health law as well as an awareness of the interdisciplinary and sociopolitical challenges that emerge in the advocacy arena. Advocates must also have a foundation of good communication skills, some level of assertiveness, and a planned guide for action.

Social workers sometimes make a critical error when helping a client advocate within a system (Lens, 2004). Although social workers can apparently tolerate and forgive all sorts of behaviors on the part of the client and have little trouble finding strengths, they are often harsh to those with whom the client is trying to negotiate and can put clients at greater risk of being cut off by the system. To be an effective medium between the client and the mental health (or other) system, the social worker must first recognize and deal with his or her own feelings about other professionals until he or she can respond empathetically to them. Principled negotiation differs from approaches that view conflicts as win/lose situations. The social worker does not abdicate his or her role as an advocate to avoid conflict and maintain relationships, but observes four major principles in the process: separate the person from the problem, focus on interests not positions, invent options for mutual gain, and insist on using objective outcome criteria.

Gerhart (1990) outlined in detail six self-advocacy steps social workers should take on behalf of their clients. We have adapted these guidelines for use by clients and families.

1. *Identify the complaint:* Think about your complaint: Identify the facts and your feelings about them. Decide if this issue is worth fighting for. Forgive yourself if you decide it isn't. Psychologically prepare if you decide it is. Congratulate yourself no matter what you decide.

2. *Identify and minimize your risks:* Try to anticipate the consequences of your advocacy efforts without exaggerating or minimizing them. Look for allies in friends, organizations, and providers.

3. *Identify the appropriate decision maker:* In general, go to the first-line authority first. With medication-management issues most often the "decision makers" are prescribers, treatment teams, medical directors, commissioners, or even legislative bodies. Who is the person who really made the decision, and who has the power to change it?

4. *Prepare your requests:* Write an outline of your anticipated presentation to the decision maker, including any available information and a consideration of objections they are likely to have.

5. *Practice your presentation:* Rehearse the presentation of your claim or request in the mirror, with a friend or with your social worker, paying close attention to your demeanor. Calmness, politeness, and strength of conviction will make you seem the most credible. Always try to request rather than demand.

6. *Present your request:* Make an appointment with the decision maker and present your claim as practiced. Use negotiation, compromise, expression of feelings, and other communication skills to achieve the best outcome possible. Advocates should be prepared to pursue decision makers persistently and assertively, in a manner that does not generate unnecessary hostility. They must emphasize their needs, desires, and values and their relationship to the specific requested changes.

This plan of action is particularly relevant for "case advocacy" or advocacy on behalf of an individual client or situation, such as approaching a prescriber about changing a client's medication to an intermittent regimen. It is also useful for "cause advocacy." Hepworth and colleagues (2012) provide a list of techniques needed for advocacy and social action on a more global level to be used in conjunction with either the direct approach or, when this approach fails, an approach that includes the following: initiating legal action (e.g., suing for not referring for medication in the case of severe depression), forming interagency committees (e.g., for improving the quality of psychopharmacological care in a state hospital), providing expert testimony (e.g., on the psychosocial impact of long-term medication use), developing petitions (e.g., to request longer medication clinic hours), and contacting public officials (e.g., for ensuring that new effective medications will be covered by Medicaid).

SUMMARY

In this chapter we have presented social workers with a challenge to play a more active collaborative role with clients, families, and providers in helping clients manage and monitor their medication on a day-to-day basis. This means providing knowledge, skills, or insights to help keep track of client medication effects over time, to cope with adverse effects on a number of levels, to help make

Table 8.2 Dimensions of Partnership in Medication Management

Dimension	Typical Models of Care	Partnership Model
Goals of medication	Reduce symptoms	Improve quality of life; emphasis on client priorities
Who selects medication regimen	Physician provider	Client collaboration with providers to help define options
Education focus	Increasing compliance	Improving client's ability to understand and manage recovery
Monitoring and evaluating	Physician evaluates clinical status and levels of compliance	Client and providers evaluate range of outcomes and future options
Self-care by client	Largely ignored in mental health	Integrated into consultations with client and family
Control and status	Providers control processes and hold status positions	Emphasis on client control and the client's expertise and experiences acknowledged and valued
Refusal and reluctance	Seen as related to denial or paranoia	Seen as a right to be respected in all but emergency situations

tough decisions about treatment, and to negotiate, communicate, and advocate with all concerned as the desires and dreams of the client dictate. An important assumption in this context has been, of course, the social worker's embracing of the partnership model and what it means in terms of medication management and the social work role. Table 8.2, adapted from the work of Chewning and Sleath (1996), distinguishes between older ways of thinking about clients and medication and our partnership model that is more contemporary and client-centered.

Because we believe that many of the medication-related needs and dilemmas of the clients we serve too often go unmet, in this part of the book (Chapter 6 through Chapter 8) we have highlighted a range of psychosocial interventions and strategies to help social workers respond better to their clients' needs. It is about rolling up our sleeves and confidently using what we know.

TOPICS FOR DISCUSSION AND LEARNING ACTIVITIES

1. Locate several formal symptom-monitoring instruments. Bring them to class to share with other students. Discuss the pros and cons of using *formal* instruments to monitor medication effectiveness compared with using individualized means of doing so. Create your own symptom-monitoring

list for a particular disorder, using your own experiences, the professional literature, or both as a guide. Some of these instruments should be intended for client self-administration.

2. List examples of possible adverse psychological effects related to taking psychotropic medications. Develop one possible effect for each of the five types of medication and how it may be addressed through the social worker's intervention.

3. Role-play situations in which you help a family solve a problem regarding how to manage the adverse effects of a medication or some other concern. Three or four students can play the family and base their concern on a situation with which one student is familiar. A pair or trio of students can play the role of the social worker and collaborate among themselves and with the family during the problem-solving process.

4. Role-play situations with a client and then with a family in which they are helped to develop assertiveness skills with regard to a medication concern. Assume that the client is willing to take psychotropic medications for a mental illness but that adverse physical effects significantly impair his or her functioning. The client can be either nonassertive or aggressive by nature (role plays with *each type* of client will be useful).

5. Consider the five areas of competence required for effective medication management. Develop your own long-term (3-year) personal plan for achieving these areas of competence. Also develop plans for how you will help clients and families achieve this competence.

9

✳

Medication Adherence

Learning Objectives

Upon completion of this chapter, the reader will be able to:

1. Describe and identify the components of the self-efficacy model of medication adherence.
2. Articulate four conflicts that arise from ethical and legal dilemmas regarding clients with mental illnesses and psychopharmacology.
3. Articulate the positions of clients, professionals, and family members regarding the four conflicts.
4. Describe four strategies to assist a client with issues related to medication adherence.

The regularity with which health care clients in general do not comply with, or completely adhere to, their prescribed medication regimens is widely discussed in relation to diabetes, epilepsy, hypertension, AIDS, and especially mental and emotional distress. Even people who are not taking psychotropic or other medications can appreciate the idea of non-adherence. Most can remember those antibiotics they didn't quite finish or the times they took extra painkillers because they believed the dosages on the label weren't quite right for them. And for many, taking antibiotics or pain medications may not have the same underlying meaning, and certainly not the same side effects, as the psychotropic medications.

This chapter will focus on the social worker's need to address medication adherence and refusal holistically, including an awareness of related legal and ethical issues. Much of this chapter is devoted to helping social workers understand the theories and models used to explain adherence and non-adherence. We also present specific techniques, based on our own self-efficacy model, to help clients increase their adherence to medication regimens. We rely on the term *adherence* because the term *compliance* has lost favor in recent years with its perceived negative connotation of passivity and obedience. Furthermore, noncompliance implies that the client has done something wrong or is deviant, which "does not often reflect reality from the client's perspective" (Morris & Schulz, 1993, p. 603). The promotion of medication adherence, like all challenges in medication management, should be seen as the responsibility of both the client and the health care professional (Julius, Novitsky, & Dubin, 2009).

One of the most salient criticisms of the literature on adherence is that studies of clients' adherence are usually based on an ideal image of the client as a passive, obedient, and unquestioning recipient of medical instructions. In this context, divergence is seen as unreasonable in light of medical rationality. Fenton, Blyler, and Heinssen (1997), for example, noted that through the mid-1990s over 14,000 articles appeared in the medical literature about medication adherence, but almost none were directed toward the subjective experience of consumers or their decision-making processes. In fact there are many reasons why people do or do not do what a physician says. We encourage social workers to understand adherence in light of the clients' views of their illnesses, treatments, experiences, interactions, and expectations. This more active view of clients necessitates a greater focus on the social context in which symptoms are experienced and treatments used, which is an appropriate assignment for social workers. Conrad (1985) says social workers should reject the "doctor-centered perspective" of adherence and move toward a "patient perspective" that suggests greater emphasis on health beliefs, self-regulation, and the meaning of medication to clients.

Numerous authors have pointed out that adherence to medications is not usually all or nothing; rather, some degree of non-adherence can be expected up to 50% of the time (Grenard, et al., 2011). Medication non-adherence may be even lower among people with mental and emotional problems versus physical disorders (Cramer & Rosenheck, 1999). An outright continuous refusal of medications, most often discussed in the context of inpatient treatment of persons with psychoses, is rare (1 to 3%), even though much has been written on the right to refuse.

Non-adherence can include not filling the prescription or accepting medication at all, filling the prescription or accepting the medication but not taking it, taking only a part of it, or not following the prescribed dosage, either by not taking the proper amount of the drug or by not taking it at the desired frequency. Franson and Smith (1998) noted that 20% of all prescriptions are never filled, and only 50% of those filled are taken correctly. One major study found that 23.6% of persons in Europe with bipolar disorder were significantly non-adherent over a 21-month period (Hong, et al., 2011). Even though inadequately treated bipolar disorder can lead to a recurrence of symptoms (interpersonal chaos, substance abuse, financial crises, and personal anguish), many such persons are not satisfied with the physical side effects or the personal and social implications of the medication. Similarly, many people with depressive disorders stop taking their antidepressant medication after only a month, even before the full therapeutic effect is likely (Morris & Schulz, 1993). Estimates of non-adherence among people with psychotic disorders is, again, about 50% after 1 year and perhaps as high as 75% after 2 years (Weiden, et al., 1994). Unfortunately, most physicians see non-adherence as caused simply by their clients' denial of illness (Todman, Gordon-Leeds, & Taylor, 1997). We think the issue is more complicated than that.

Those with both psychiatric and substance abuse problems have an even harder time with adherence (Misdrahi, et al., 2012; Teter, et al., 2011). Non-adherence is especially serious among the elderly—up to 75% of older patients are estimated to be noncompliant, often due to underuse of a prescribed drug or inappropriate drug discontinuation (Gellad, Grenard, & Marcum, 2011). In one study of children, the rate of non-adherence at a 14-month post-discharge follow-up was 62% (Lloyd, et al., 1998).

In the social work profession, Cohen (1993) discusses the stigma that is associated with a consumer who is labeled noncompliant, which Cohen says often occurs because care providers fail to respond adequately to the expressed needs of the client. An emergency room visit that results in a prescription and an appointment card for a clinic visit in 2 weeks, for example, is not good crisis intervention. Labeling patients as noncompliant is "blaming the victim" for professional inadequacies. Obviously, we hope social workers will avoid this response and others like it.

Two caveats may be in order here. First, accurately measuring adherence to medications has been problematic. Even defining adherence, the necessary first step toward measurement, is difficult. For example, if adherence is not a dichotomous variable (i.e., yes or no), then is it an ordinal variable with such values as completely compliant, very compliant, not so compliant, and so on? Urine tests; pill counts; self-, collateral, and clinical reports; and even electronic tracking devices have all been criticized with respect to reliability and validity (Cassidy, et al., 2010). For example, several studies have found little correlation between physicians' assessments of their patients' adherence and the client's perspective (Goldberg, Cohen, & Rubin, 1998; Valenstein, et al., 1998). The Goldberg group found that physicians' judgment of adherence related to the seriousness of the condition and the effectiveness, or lack thereof, of the treatments. These problems make testing the impact of interventions difficult and call for the use of multiple measures when possible. They also speak to the importance of communication in the clinical encounter. Further, social workers need to be as interested in general adherence to treatment as in medication adherence.

MODELS FOR UNDERSTANDING ADHERENCE

In this chapter we will discuss various biological, psychological, and social influences on a consumer's medication adherence, but we begin with a model of working with clients that is consistent with the values of the social work profession.

The Self-Efficacy Model

The self-efficacy model draws upon an extensive literature review to inform the development of a coherent approach for social workers in addressing medication adherence. The model places the person with psychiatric symptoms as an active participant who is central to the process of medication taking (McCann, Clark, & Lu, 2008).

We will now consider some of the complex issues that affect a consumer's sense of self-efficacy and decisions about adherence. As we have said, decisions regarding medication use must be seen in their biopsychosocial and cultural contexts. Many have grouped the factors associated with medication adherence and non-adherence into "compliance domains" (e.g., McPhillips & Sensky, 1998; Weiden, et al., 1994) or some other model or framework (e.g., DeGeest, et al., 1994; Leventhal, Diefenbach, & Leventhal, 1992). We will organize our discussion of these factors around the following four dimensions: characteristics of the client, aspects of the treatment, aspects of the social environment, and the actual symptoms. It is important to emphasize that although more than 30 years of research into over 200 variables has not produced consistent information in these areas, the following review can help social workers appreciate the complexity of adherence and, we hope, design multidimensional strategies and techniques for addressing it.

Characteristics of the Client

The health belief model states that people base health care decisions on their understanding of some desired outcome, their motivation to seek it, and how they understand that a recommended "treatment" will help them realize the desired outcome (Youssef, 1984). Thus, people experiencing severe anxiety will more likely take their prescribed anti-anxiety medication if they understand what a lack of anxiety would be like for them, they are motivated to try to reduce their anxiety, and they appreciate the connection between taking the medication and achieving or maintaining a reduced state of anxiety. Clearly, this model calls for medication education (see Chapter 7). With some exceptions (e.g., Beck, et al., 2011), a number of studies of persons with serious mental illness have found a clear relationship between clients' understanding of their symptoms (that is, a recognition that a problem exists and requires medical intervention) and the perceived benefits of medication and medication adherence (Crowe, Wilson, & Inder, 2011; Dassa, et al., 2010).

Clients receiving medications may or may not place medical outcome or clinical efficacy at the top of their list. Instead they usually evaluate and balance a range of competing physical, economic, psychological, and social outcomes (Gearing, et al., 2011). To understand a client's decisions about medication, practitioners must try to ascertain what outcomes an individual values most. One study shows that the desired outcomes of medication use reported by psychotic clients were mostly indirect; that is, desired outcomes did not relate directly to symptom reduction but rather to keeping them out of the hospital or out of trouble (Adams & Howe, 1993). People with depression or anxiety may adhere to their medications because they simply want to "get back on track at work" or "be a better parent." On the other hand, clients may opt against using medications because the most compelling outcomes are to not be labeled "crazy," to remain sexually responsive, or to continue to enjoy fine red wine. These cost–benefit analyses are complex.

Self-regulation models of medication management (Reynolds, et al., 2012) suggest that what might appear to be noncompliance may actually be a form of asserting control over one's condition. Self-regulation includes both the client's perception of the health threat and his or her management of coping devices and emotional processes. Conrad (1985) notes that people with epilepsy take their medication, often in spite of absolutely hating it, not just to control seizures, but to reduce their own worrying and to ensure a sense of normality. This again demonstrates why the use of analogies, such as diabetes or hypertension, with psychotropic medication can be useful.

Clients may regulate their own medication by increasing or decreasing doses or stopping the medication altogether. Some authors claim that clients do this because they want to

- Test whether or not their symptoms are still there or just to see what will happen;
- Control their perceptions of dependence, because they may see taking medications as a threat to their self-reliance;
- Manage stigma, because the act of taking medication relays certain information to other people and at some level acknowledges the client's differentness; or
- Manage their symptoms or side effects, or regulate the disruptions of their lifestyle.

Reducing the dose to decrease a bothersome side effect is said to be the most common example of self-regulation of medication. Increasing the dose during times of stress is also common (Velligan, et al., 2009). Thus, the meaning that medication has for clients and their interpretation of being medicated is of utmost concern to the social worker trying to understand adherence issues (see Chapter 6).

Almost all research of factors associated with adherence and non-adherence has tested demographic and other variables, such as age, gender, socioeconomic status, level of education, type of symptoms, and the length of time the symptoms have existed. A few studies have found significant relationships; for instance, Draine and Solomon (1994) have found that older consumers with fewer symptoms and a greater array of daily activities have greater adherence, but that sensory or memory impairments, impaired dexterity, and the complexity of drug regimens and cost concerns may place elderly persons at risk for non-adherence. Researchers have begun to explore the role of visual memory and cognitive function as a factor in medication adherence (Gellad, Grenard, & Marcum, 2011). In addition, research has begun to uncover whether adherence is affected by differential perceptions that stem from clients' racial or ethnic backgrounds regarding drug toxicity and addictiveness. In general, however, no demographic variables seem consistently related to adherence or non-adherence (Frank, et al., 1992).

Aspects of Treatment

A number of factors related to the actual treatment itself are associated with adherence and non-adherence, including those that relate to the medication regimen, intended effects and side effects, the treatment system, and professional attitudes and behaviors. A study of male veterans in the general health care arena found that patient perceptions of being overmedicated were associated with non-adherence. The authors add that these perceptions turned out to reflect reality (Fincke, Miller, & Spiro, 1998).

Complex regimens are also associated with greater non-adherence. Clients with more than one medication or with challenging dosing schedules (such as more than once a day) are at higher risk of non-adherence than others (Haynes, et al., 2005). Some have even speculated that the physical aspects of a pill—the shape, size, color, and even taste—may contribute to adherence or non-adherence (Buckalew & Sallis, 1986). In addition, the cost of medication, perceptions of affordability, and general accessibility may each play a role (Gearing, et al., 2011). It seems obvious that if out-of-pocket costs for medication exceed the clients' budgets or if they cannot physically get the medications from a clinic or pharmacy, some non-adherence is likely. On the other hand, Morris and Schulz (1993) note that those who receive free medications are less compliant with those medications, leading to the speculation that free medications are not as highly valued as those that require some personal sacrifice.

Not surprisingly, the quality and timing of drug effects also play a role in compliance. The delay between the time the client commences medications and the time when any significant therapeutic effect is discernible may frustrate the client and weaken the perceived link between the treatment and its benefit. Similarly, when medications leave the body's system slowly, depending on half-life, a client may become discouraged (see Chapter 4). However, adherence improves when the actual effects of a drug most closely match the client's expectations for symptom improvement, which the prescribing physician may or may not share.

Non-adherence may be most heavily associated with negative physical side effects. While some providers and families argue that "illness-related" reasons figure most heavily in non-adherence, and especially refusal, clients most often point to unwanted side effects as the most important factor, because they are considered to be more troublesome than the symptoms (Loffler, et al., 2003). The adverse effects most likely to lead to non-adherence include extrapyramidal effects, dysphoria, sedation, weight gain, and sexual dysfunction. Weiden, Mackell, & McDonnell (2004) found a significant positive relationship between non-adherence and subjective distress from weight gain and obesity. Side effects can adversely affect one's perception of body image and how they think others perceive them.

Aspects of the larger treatment system itself may also contribute to non-adherence. For example, a system of services or a treatment plan that inadequately educates or prepares clients and families or one that structures an unfriendly aftercare environment, may foster non-adherence. The attitudes and behaviors of the clinical staff, especially psychiatrists and social workers, play a crucial role in shaping medication adherence of clients. Marked ambivalence, antagonism toward medication itself, or an attitude of "oversell" on the part of providers is associated with non-adherence (Franson & Smith, 1998). A lack of empathy toward medication-related dilemmas of clients and families is also problematic. Acknowledging medication issues as a serious concern and allowing clients and families to express and clarify their feelings about medication is a first step for social workers or any mental health care provider (see Chapter 2). One program went even further. Morse, Simon, & Balson (1993) describe a program in which 20 physicians and nurses took placebos on the same pill schedule as their HIV patients to better understand and empathize with them. This meant taking three pills 5 times a day at 4-hour intervals and keeping a diary of reactions. Although this part of the study lasted only 1 week and involved no physiological changes or side effects, long-lasting changes occurred in provider attitude and empathy. The diaries revealed intense frustration with rigid schedules and stigma felt from the need to take pills in public.

The nature of the social worker–client and physician–client alliance is a major factor in securing client adherence to medications. The "therapeutic alliance" is defined in a variety of ways but refers to a positive relationship between the client and provider, one that is characterized by empathy and open communication. It is consistently correlated with client adherence (Dassa, et al., 2010). This factor was found to be significant in two studies (Byrne, Deane, Lambert, & Coombs, 2004; Misdrahi, et al., 2012). Further, Gellad, Grenard, & Marcum (2011) found it to be one of three major predicators of adherence (along with client characteristics and drug-related factors). Another set of researchers found that a positive therapeutic alliance is associated with a client's enhanced "illness representation" (or awareness) much more than social support and that the alliance was a positive predictor of adherence (Rungruangsiripan, et al., 2011). Julius, Novitsky, and Dubin (2009) solidified this claim in a literature review, summarizing that the therapeutic alliance was central to client adherence, along with the assessment of client motivation and potential barriers to adherence.

Aspects of the Social Environment

The societal and community culture of medications, the extent of family and social support, and general cues and contingencies in the environment all tend to influence adherence to psychotropic medications. Public attitudes about the use or acceptance of psychotropic medication relate to various ideas about the causes of mental illnesses and emotional distress. Today, tremendous variability exists in society's acceptance, or lack of acceptance, of psychotropic medication use. People have many questions, such as, is the medication for "situational stress" or a long-standing "illness"? Is the medication addictive? It seems people more easily accept certain medications under certain circumstances with certain people and certain problems. To complicate matters further, the individuals whom the public will accept as users of medication is subject to change. People may fully support a coworker's daughter on risperidone for schizophrenia or a distant relative on lithium for bipolar disorder. People may completely accept a best friend on sertraline (Zoloft) for depression, but they do not want their spouses taking fluoxetine (Prozac) to increase productivity at work.

In popular culture, people often see psychotropic drugs portrayed in an intensely negative way, such as forced on people with mental illnesses. In addition, newspapers headline horror stories about acts allegedly committed by people because they use Prozac (fluoxetine), and best-selling books warn of continued psychiatric and psychopharmacological expansionism (e.g., Breggin, 2008; Breggin & Cohen, 2007; Szasz, 1994). However, countervailing influences also exist, and in the past 20 years there has been a growing understanding of the biological basis of many mental illnesses and their treatment. Therefore, social workers must appreciate this larger societal context of psychotropic medication use, including their own vulnerability to popular culture's manipulation and influence.

Families can also exert positive or negative influences on medication adherence. If the family agrees with the prescribing physician, understands the rationale underlying medication use, or somehow "believes" in it, and supports and perhaps even offers concrete help in achieving adherence or monitoring the effects of the medication, the family obviously has a positive influence. This has been shown to be important in studies of both children (Dean, et al., 2011; Hamrin, McCarthy, & Tyson, 2010) and adults (Le Quach, et al., 2009) who take psychotropic medications. However, if the family presents undue pressure or competing beliefs, such as "All she needs to do is pull herself up by her bootstraps" or "If she would just turn it over to God, everything would be okay," then the outcome is likely to be less positive. Interactions with friends, coworkers, and others can similarly affect decisions about medication use.

A recent literature review postulates that psychotropic medication initiation and adherence for children and adolescents can be understood from the perspective of social exchange theory (Hamrin, McCarthy, & Tyson, 2010). Rewards experienced from medication treatment include improvements in symptoms, school performance, family relationships, and levels of parenting stress. Identified costs include adverse side effects, social stigma, lack of response to a medication, fears of addiction, and changes in the child's personality. The authors summarize that positive family attitudes, beliefs, and perceptions of treatment play a large role in adherence decisions, in addition to a trusting relationship with a provider.

Aspects of the Symptoms

The last dimension in this framework for understanding adherence concerns factors related to the symptoms themselves, such as depression, anxiety, paranoia, grandiosity, hostility, and cognitive impairment. Studies consistently show that certain kinds of severe mental disorders, such as bipolar disorder and schizophrenia, are associated with noncompliance (e.g., Crowe, Wilson, & Inder, 2011; Gonzalez-Pinto, et al., 2010). For example, if an individual does not take his or her medication because of a delusion that the drug is part of some germ warfare plot, this symptom will clearly influence non-adherence. Perhaps a man in a manic phase simply believes he does not need his medication because he is king of the hill and can overcome his illness on his own. Or perhaps a woman is too depressed to get out of bed to go to the medicine cabinet or so depressed that she believes there is really no use, that treatment of her devastating illness is futile.

Everyone who has devised an explanatory model for adherence includes illness-related factors. Most psychiatrists—although not most clients—attribute medication refusal to these factors. Denial is usually discussed in this particular context. But denial is not always seen as an understandable and rather typical human protective response to be addressed with compassion and patience (Aldebot, de Mamani, & Weisman, 2009); rather it may be seen as an unacceptable symptom of an illness that must be broken down. Importantly, if providers heavily emphasize client symptoms or "illness" as a cause of non-adherence, the logic of forcing medication against the client's will is set up, all in the name of her or his best interest.

A restatement may be useful here. To more holistically address various forms of non-adherence, as well as more effective help with medication monitoring, social workers should draw from the wealth of knowledge that exists about factors that influence adherence, especially the complex physical, social, psychological, and emotional responses to medication. Table 9.1 summarizes a list of potential risks and protective factors for medication non-adherence as drawn from a range of resources cited previously or others (e.g., Agarwal, et al., 1998; Budd, et al., 1996; Dixon, et al., 1997; Duncan & Rogers, 1998; Heyscue, Levin, & Merrick, 1998; Marder, 2003; Swartz, et al., 1998). The risks and

Table 9.1 Possible Risks and Protective Factors for Medication Non-adherence

Possible Risks	Possible Protective Factors
Bothersome or adverse side effects	Belief that one has a mental illness
History of substance abuse	Adequate education and preparation of client and family
Severe positive symptoms	
Client ambivalence, anger, or grandiosity	Use of injectible medications
Forgetfulness	Positive subjective response to medication
Delay in achieving therapeutic effect	Good client-clinician relationship
Poor client-clinician relationship	Provider and family empathy with client
Unfriendly aftercare environment	Insurance coverage for medication
Complex medication regimen	Respected client autonomy
Episodic course of illness	Broad array of daily activities
Challenging dosing schedule	Fewer symptoms
Multiple providers	Client participation in assertive community treatment
Use of long-term maintenance medication	Consistent outpatient care
Young in age	Strong internal locus of control
Living alone	Positive perceptions of affordability
Unsupportive family	
Free medication	
Perception of being overmedicated	

protective factors are listed roughly in order of the frequency of their discussion and their prominence in the literature.

LEGAL AND ETHICAL ISSUES IN ADHERENCE AND REFUSAL

Even though overt refusal of medication is rare in mental health practice, a well-developed body of literature exists on the topic. Social workers should become familiar with this literature for two reasons. First, experience shows that social workers who work in a variety of settings will likely encounter medication non-adherence regularly, depending on the characteristics of the clients and the agency environment. Second, the themes that emerge from the literature on refusal offer insight into the range of clients' rights issues in relation to medication adherence.

As Lefley (1993) states, "The question of involuntary treatment embodies some of the most basic philosophical, clinical, and political issues in any society.... These issues are framed within the meaning of mental illness and any given time in history" (p. 7). We do not accept all of Lefley's positions on the role of forced medication, but she correctly identifies some of the important conflicts that emerge from this debate:

- The rights of the individual versus the rights of the group
- Civil liberties versus survival needs of people
- The rights of the disabled versus the rights of caregivers
- The obligation of society to protect its citizens

The true portrait of a client's right to refuse may be best exemplified by what occurs in inpatient facilities for people with mental illness. A study in Virginia found that 45 of 348 admissions to a state hospital refused medication (12.9%). However, because a clinician in Virginia can easily override a patient refusal, in this case 100% of those inpatients, almost all within 4 days, were administered medication anyway; 56% were treated involuntarily and 44% changed their mind and accepted the treatment (Kasper, et al., 1997). Clearly those clients never had a true right to refuse. Their refusal simply kicked in the process designed to override their wishes. In Louisiana, out of 1969 patients admitted to a psychiatric unit in New Orleans, all 40 "refusers" were also subject to an administrative review. A total of 29 were later medicated: 22 involuntarily, 7 changed their minds and took the medication, and 11 were not medicated and their initial wishes were allowed to stand (Urrutia, 1994). Further, in a recent large-scale survey of European psychiatric hospitals, it was found that 38% of involuntarily admitted clients received some form of coercive treatment, with forced medication (56%) being the most common (Raboch, et al., 2010).

Perhaps the two biggest questions that relate to the right-to-refuse issue are these: What is in the "best interest" of the client? Who decides? We believe that social workers should advocate the client's right to decline medication. The sole exception to this principle is a true emergency, such as when clients are at imminent risk of physically harming themselves or others. One of the issues that social workers must confront is that some providers and family members define "emergency" rather broadly, even to the point that any refusal or reluctance on the part of the client that conflicts with either the provider's or the family's judgment is grounds for forced medication (Bassman, 2005). Arguments to limit the client's right to decline medication assume that people with mental illness, especially those who refuse medication, also have impaired judgment and that they need and truly want outside intervention.

A published debate between a social worker and a physician highlights the intensity of emotions around this topic. Remler, a physician, argues that restricting the right-to-refuse medication is a reasonably pragmatic approach for clients with such disorders as schizophrenia, brain damage, and mental retardation because they "simply can not be allowed to determine their behavior.... They do not want their behavior changed.... They must be coerced" (Remler & Cohen, 1992, p. 304). Cohen, a social worker, argues that Remler "transforms disturbed and disturbing men and women from moral agents into brain-disordered organisms" (p. 306). We also believe that automatically equating mental disability or, for that matter, involuntary hospitalization, with incompetence that leads to a global indictment of the population that is destructive and stigmatizing. Presuming competence is an important check and balance in any due process procedure because doing so helps to establish the extent and direction of proof, much as presuming innocence does in criminal cases.

Indeed, evidence simply does not support the argument that most people who decline psychotropic medications are irrational (Joyal, et al., 2011). Nevertheless, two factors seem to keep the issue of violence and medication adherence in the forefront of provider's minds. First is recent research noting higher rates of violence for a specific subset of clients: young males who have both psychosis and substance abuse and are receiving improper or insufficient treatment (Van Dorn, Volavka, & Johnson, 2012). Second is the continued exposure to sensational high-profile media events in which violence and mental illness are linked.

The two preeminent value positions of the social work profession, self-determination and respecting the dignity and uniqueness of individuals, call for a more client-centered response. An authority on social work ethics, Barsky (2010) emphasizes that clients who either decline or withdraw consent for treatment should be considered legally and mentally capable. The fact that clients may be taking psychotropic medication or may be disabled to some degree by symptoms does not in itself provide grounds for denying them the right to refuse or withdraw consent. Wilk's study (1994) of clinical social workers has found that although social workers generally support a range of client's rights issues, they show the least support for the right to refuse treatment. Only 30% supported a client's right to refuse medication, while 57% opposed it.

If social workers are serious about respecting the dignity and uniqueness of individuals, they must advocate strongly for the fair due-process procedures now required by law in the case of refusal. This advocacy recognizes that "forced drugging of a patient absent a determination that a person is not capable of rationally deciding what is good for himself" cannot exist (United States District Court, 1980, p. 936). Social workers can also advocate for real procedural safeguards, those that honor either what clients say they want or, in cases where substituted judgment is called for, those that honor what the client would have articulated if she or he were competent. Thus, the expressed preference of the client should be the center of all deliberations.

Note that this position differs from that in which the provider or family can ultimately determine "the best interest" of the client. As indicated earlier, deciding on the client's best interest is a complicated task, influenced by issues of power and paternalism. For example, should "best interest" be legally determined or clinically determined? Lawyers and psychiatrists have fought about that question for years. Should family caregivers decide? Brown (1985) points out that the more providers or others can portray themselves as acting in the client's best interest, the more they can expand their power base. Others argue that it is the families who "really care" about the patients and that civil libertarians and advocates are often overly concerned with autonomy issues (Rosenson & Kasten, 1991). Social workers, too, must avoid any professional arrogance that they really know what "best interest" is, given their historical commitment to client rights and their holistic perspective.

Some view the recent initiation of client "advance directives," a legal process of allowing persons with mental illness to document their preferences for particular medications and other interventions if they temporarily lose capacity, as a positive step toward preserving client rights. In one study it was shown that such directives do result in clients being prescribed their requested medications some of the time (a 27% increase in the number of medications that had been requested), and this in turn results in significantly greater client adherence (Wilder, et al., 2010). Still, Bassman (2005) documents that physicians can (and do) legally override advance directives if they believe that the client is at imminent risk of harm to self or others. Thus, problems in adhering to the value of client self-determination persist.

Social workers can look to the courts to provide a number of other "causes of action" that have provided a legal and ethical basis for allowing clients to refuse their medication. These include the right to privacy, prohibitions against battery, and freedom of religion. As with all health care decisions, the bottom line is that respect for the autonomy of clients should be the basis of treatment and should only be "subverted," as Brabbins, Butleer, and Bentall (1996) describe it, in the face of the strongest of arguments. They suggest clinicians use a three-prong proforma to record their efforts: (1) make note of the shared information on the reasons for prescribing, the costs and benefits of the medication, and alternative treatments, (2) make note of the client's capacity to consent and the steps taken to ensure the client was able to understand the treatment and weigh her or his options, (3) note the absence of duress, the advisement of the client's right to decline medications, and the consequences of that in real life.

Bassman (2005) summarizes the arguments of clients' families, the mental health system, and society regarding involuntary interventions, including medication. From the client's perspective, involuntary treatment may alleviate suffering, pain, and embarrassment; and enhance recovery. However, it may also cause a loss of self-determination, liberty, and an abridgment of civil rights. It often means living with uncomfortable side effects. From the family's perspective, forced medication may mean improved perceptions of family members' own personal safety, but it can also cause considerable dissension among them. From the perspective of the system and society, forced medication may seemingly allow them to "do the right thing" but is clearly a form of social control.

INTERVENTIONS TO ASSIST IN MEDICATION ADHERENCE

This section focuses on specific strategies and techniques social workers can use to deal constructively with ambivalence or refusal and help clients increase appropriate adherence to their medication regimens. Assuming mutual engagement in a working relationship, intervention begins with ascertaining the pattern of adherence and the client's individual reasons for any non-adherence. Our approaches suggest assessment of the client's "health beliefs" and expectations about medication, including any ethnic or cultural influences on those processes. It suggests ascertaining the real desired outcomes for clients and their ability to make connections between taking medications and achieving those outcomes. Social workers can also assess whether the medication is accessible, affordable, and sufficiently simple to take and if family and friends support its use or merely tolerate it. Finally, social workers can take stock of their own attitudes and behaviors, and the attitudes of those around them, to consider their influence on a client's adherence. Our suggested interventions in cases when medication is declined rest on the principles of partnership and self-determination. In those rare cases when it is used, involuntary treatment should be "strictly time-limited, gentle, respectful and as non-intrusive as possible" (Parrish, 1993, p. 20).

An obvious strategy for intervention is *reflective discussion* with the client and perhaps their families to clarify assumptions and build knowledge to help in other interventions. In Chapter 8, we discuss many appropriate strategies, such as monitoring, coping with side effects, problem solving, decision-making, negotiation, and advocacy. Medication education also serves as a major intervention for medication non-adherence (see Chapter 7). In this chapter, we present a number of techniques associated with increased adherence. Although the distinction between an "educational" strategy and a "cognitive" or "behavioral" one may not be clear, the latter two usually focus on precise behaviors that present either barriers or cues to adherence, as opposed to the former's more global effort to increase knowledge and change attitudes.

Motivational Interviewing

Motivational interviewing (MI) is a client-centered, directive method for enhancing the motivation to change by exploring and resolving the client's ambivalence about a concern (Miller & Rollnick, 2002). It has become quite popular in the past 30 years as a means of engaging clients who are not explicitly motivated to address problems that are considered serious by significant others, if not by the clients themselves. Initially developed for the treatment of substance abuse, MI is now applied to other types of problems, including medication adherence. Typically a brief intervention, MI is characterized by collaboration rather than confrontation. Indeed, within this model, confrontation is perceived as a tactic that escalates client resistance. MI emphasizes listening reflectively to the client's concerns about taking medication and selectively emphasizing "change talk." The initial intervention goal is to build a client's motivation when they are ambivalent about medication, rather than focusing on actual behavior change. A client's perception of the (alleged) problem is thus the focus of the early part of the social worker's contacts.

A major influence on motivational interviewing is the Transtheoretical Stages of Change (TSOC) Model, developed to recognize the universality of ambivalence as people contemplate changing their behaviors (Connors, Donovan, & DiClemente, 2001; Prochaska & Norcross, 1994). In this model, the following six stages of change have been formulated:

- Pre-contemplation—the person does not believe he or she has a problem
- Contemplation—the person is contemplating change but unsure about the need
- Preparation—the person is poised to change and works on a strategy to do so
- Action—the person begins to take action
- Maintenance—sustained change has occurred for 6 months
- Relapse—in the event that the person slips back into old behaviors, the steps are revisited

Within the TSOC model, MI is designed to work with those who are either in *pre-contemplation or contemplation.*

The clinical perspective in motivational interviewing can be summarized as follows:

- Motivation to change is elicited from the client, not imposed from the outside.
- A client's motivation for enacting change relative to some medication issue is often impeded by ambivalence.
- It is the client's task to articulate and resolve his or her ambivalence.
- Readiness to change is a product of interpersonal interaction.
- Direct persuasion is not an effective method for resolving ambivalence.
- Practitioner comments and questions are useful in examining ambivalence.

Motivational interviewing works with the ambivalence of the client; the advantages and disadvantages of the situation with medication, and of changing, are openly considered. The social worker selectively reflects and affirms change talk and asks the client to elaborate on statements about change. The social worker seeks to create dissonance between a person's values and goals (in terms of health, future well-being, and family relationships) and the current status of his or her medication, so that the desire to change is bolstered. Another major focus of MI involves a client's *confidence* that he or she can succeed at change efforts (Miller & Rollnick, 2002).

Motivation is not a stable, internal quality of an individual but is affected by the interaction between the practitioner and client, and thus the nature of the helping relationship is emphasized (Killick & Allen, 1997). The social worker seeks to understand the client's perspective on the medication issue with reflective listening. He or she affirms the validity of that perspective and the client's freedom of choice in addressing the situation. Given this emphasis, client *resistance* is an invalid concept. A more appropriate term is client *reactance,* which is intended to describe a client's normal reactions to uncertainties about the purposes of the client–worker interaction. Reactance is thus a problem of the social worker rather than the client, signifying that the practitioner needs to adjust his or her interactions to match the client's position toward change. The responsibility for *how* behavior change occurs relative to a medication concern, or *if* it should change, is left to the client.

The four intervention principles of motivational interviewing are to:

Express empathy, because the feeling of being understood and accepted facilitates change

Develop discrepancy between how things are and should be

Roll with resistance; that is, avoid arguing

Support self-efficacy; the client's belief in the possibility of change

Four categories of change talk include pointing out the disadvantages of the status quo (the client's current experience of symptoms), pointing out the possible advantages of change, conveying optimism about change, and evaluating and encouraging a client's "intention" to change when it happens. The following guidelines help the practitioner to enact the above principles (Miller & Rollnick, 2002):

Begin where the client is. Do not assume that the client is ready to engage in change.

Explore the client's problem behaviors and reflect the client's perceptions. Listen with empathy to clients' concerns to accurately assess the person's relationship to the process of change.

Reinforce client statements about wanting to change. Attend to client expressions about change. Seek to create a discrepancy between the client's values and goals, such as long-term health, and how the medication-related problem may stand in the way.

Affirm clients' statements about their ability to change. In this way, confidence is built, and the individual feels empowered to take the first steps toward change.

Specific techniques of motivational interviewing include eliciting self-motivational statements, strategies to handle resistance, the decisional balance, and building self-efficacy.

Thus far there is limited evidence that MI enhances adherence to psychotropic medication. A systematic literature review by Drymalski and Campbell (2009) located five empirical studies of motivational interviewing used with clients who take antipsychotic medications. Two studies documented an increase in medication adherence among participants, while the other three found no differences between MI and the comparison intervention. A more general meta-analysis of 63 studies found that motivational interviewing produced significantly higher treatment-adherence outcomes in persons with a variety of chronic health issues (Bisonó, Manuel, & Forcehimes, 2006).

We now turn to another approach for addressing medication adherence that provides the social worker with intervention options when the client is non-adherent.

Dynamic Adherence

Dynamic adherence is a six-phase model that incorporates the role of the worker–client relationship and other factors that influence clients' decisions about medication adherence (Gearing, Townsend, MacKenzie, & Charlach, 2011). It reminds the social worker that adherence patterns may change for clients based on a variety of factors including the external information they receive, their subjective experiences of medication, financial factors, and their relationships with providers. This model is based on the premise that adherence is a function of rational decisions made by clients and that provider interventions can affect those decisions. The social worker should assume that medication adherence can be divided into a series of decision points that determine the client's degree of engagement with a medication intervention. Described below are each of the six stages of adherence with recommendations about the social worker's actions:

Treatment initiation. The client is prescribed medication but does not take it. In response, the social worker should use a clear approach to informed consent to improve the client's level of comfort involving the treatment recommendation, set realistic goals with the client about the desired and expected effects of medication, and elicit client preferences in analyzing costs and benefits related to specific medication choices.

Treatment trial. The client intially tries the medication but soon discontinues it. The social worker should then review the initial treatment decision and subsequent concerns with the client and address any worries not rooted in clinical evidence. The social worker may recalibrate the client's expectations to be more realistic about how the medications actually work and explore any disadvantages that might be modified.

Partial treatment acceptance. The client accepts the medication but does not agree to the prescribed dosage and schedule. The social worker can work with the client along with the physician to adjust the treatment plan, depending on the client's response to the medications, thus reinforcing the client's confidence that the plan can be renegotiated over time.

Intermittent treatment adoption. The client oscillates between periods of full medication adherence and partial or non-adherence. The social worker should focus on developing or maintaining a trusting relationship with the client in order to obtain honest information and understand potential obstacles or risks to medication use. The social worker helps the client feel comfortable enough to voice concerns around insurance and funding, symptom cycling, merging risks, and any decisions he or she has made regarding treatment.

Premature discontinuation following treatment adoption. The client is fully engaged with the treatment recommendation but stops taking the medication prematurely. In this scenario the social worker regularly monitors the client's mental status and prepares a rapid response to serious symptoms if they occur.

Adherence. The client is fully engaged with treatment recommendations and continues treatment maintenance. The social worker should maintain the relationship and monitor the client for any emerging obstacles or risks.

The dynamic adherence model takes into account that each client may have different degrees of engagement with medication intervention, and with the providers, over time. The following approach, developed in part by several consumer groups in the United States (Hall, 2007), provides further guidance in the social worker's dealings with clients who may refuse medication.

The Harm-Reduction Model

A harm-reduction approach means not being pro- or anti-medication, but supporting people to make their own decisions after carefully balancing the risks and benefits involved (Aldridge, 2012). The concept of harm reduction incorporates the following principles (Lenton & Single, 1998):

Pragmatism. The social worker accepts that non-adherence is common and takes the position that reduction of non-adherence-related harms may be a more feasible option than efforts to eliminate non-adherence entirely.

Prioritization of goals. Goals are hierarchical, with the social worker's immediate focus being on engaging clients in the intervention process by providing accessible and user-friendly services as a first step toward any decisions about adherence or non-adherence.

Humanist values. The social worker makes no moral judgments about a client's medication adherence or non-adherence.

Focus on risks and harms. The social worker provides interventions and responses that reduce risk, even if this involves the non-adherence of the client.

Maximize the range of available intervention options. The social worker balances, along with the client, the costs and benefits of using any services, including medications.

With these principles, a non-adherence, harm-reduction approach will unfold in four general steps. The social worker will share information and resources with the client related to continuing or coming off psychotropic medications, encourage a gradual rather than a sudden discontinuation of medications when indicated, support and monitor the client's mental and physical status during the withdrawal process, and always offering a range of alternative evidence-based psychosocial interventions.

The next approach to enhancing medication compliance includes a more structured approach to the challenge.

Compliance Therapy

A semi-structured three-phase intervention that rests on cognitive theory and motivational interviewing techniques has recently been described in the literature as "compliance therapy" (O'Donnell, et al., 2003; Hayward, Kemp, & David, 2000). Here each client individually participates in four to six sessions lasting 20 to 60 minutes each over the course of 2 to 3 weeks (approximately 5 hours total). Phase 1 involves a review of the person's illness, conceptualization of the illness, and stance toward treatment. Negative experiences are acknowledged, as are the consequences of non-adherence. Phase 2 explores the client's ambivalence toward treatment and the meaning of illness and medication use, including around issues of identity. In phase 3 the clinician introduces analogies of mental illness and treatment with that of physical illness, describes famous sufferers of mental illness, and tries to reframe medication use as an "insurance policy." Data suggests that adherence is improved, as are attitudes toward medications and the level of insight into illness. This model is particularly impressive because of its apparent focus on the client's lived experience.

Now we describe a range of more specific cognitive and behavioral approaches to medication adherence.

Cognitive and Behavioral Interventions

Behavioral strategies involve the systematic application of the principles of social learning and operant or respondent conditioning to problems with medication compliance. Positive reinforcement suggests that if taking medication is rewarded, adherence will likely increase in the future. To help clients and their families design such interventions, social workers can draw on many potential reinforcers, including consumables (food, drink), leisure activities (sports, gardening, hobbies), possessions (perfume, combs, books), activities (movies, special events, shopping), and other rewards (money, tokens). Social reinforcement (that is, providing shows of affection and verbal praise) is thought to be the most powerful action taken to increase adherence. With the permission of the client, families, peers, coworkers, roommates, or other people significant to clients can be educated to provide reinforcement for medication use.

Providing reminders, prompts, or cues is another useful and well-substantiated way to increase adherence if clients forget to take their medications. These prompts might include a note on the refrigerator door or on the bathroom mirror or a phone call from a family member or friend. Tailoring the medication means finding a way to fit the administration of the drug, or for that matter the prompt itself, to some idiosyncrasy or ritual of the client. Bentley, Rosenson, & Zito (1990) give the example of Harry, who learns to take his medication at 7:30 right before his favorite television show, "Wheel of Fortune." A Post-it® reminder stuck to the remote control summarizes the main reasons he takes his medication (helps him to stay calm and to sleep). Engineers are now designing prototypes of medication containers that may revolutionize medication administration, and the monitoring of adherence, in the future (e.g., Patel, et al., 2010).

Contracting is a more formal and often written agreement that specifies the contingencies for both adherence and non–adherence. Although familiar to most social workers, contracting often occurs implicitly rather than explicitly in everyday practice. With specific "if–then" statements, delineation of participants' roles, and planned reinforcements, contracting is also common to those who rely on behavioral techniques in other professions or areas of interventions. Bentley, et al. (1990) presents Tammy, whose social worker helps to create a sophisticated contract in partnership with the family. Tammy takes her medication for a number of points each day (the points decrease the more she has to be reminded) that she can later exchange for backup reinforcers, such as talking to a friend on the phone or renting a video. At the same time, her parents are learning about giving simple, matter-of-fact prompts (as opposed to nagging or unhelpful ones), such as "If you take your medication now, you will get 8 points."

Cognitive strategies are commonly used to increase medication adherence with people who have medical problems (Beck, 2001). Problem-solving, self-instruction, guided imagery, relaxation, reframing, and thought-stopping are helpful in a number of circumstances. For example, a social worker could lead a former drug abuser on antidepressants to imagine resisting offers of cocaine and reframing their thoughts of rejection and loneliness into stories of survival and hope. Clients could then learn how to recreate the imagery and practice the reframing at home.

Social workers can also review their own service delivery and organizational structures for ways to create a climate conducive to accepting diversity in client choices and supporting adherence to a well-planned and supported treatment regimen. For instance, making appropriate training available to staff or revising policies and procedures can help create this climate. While social workers must sometimes accept that all of those efforts do not work, this is not permission to give up but a call for persistence.

SUMMARY

This chapter has presented adherence as a major issue for clients, families, and mental health providers. Models of adherence give us insight into known risk and protective factors, and familiarity with legal and ethical issues provides even more insight into the complexity of addressing issues related to adherence.

Perhaps most important to remember is this: Health psychology research shows that when providers and family members support and reinforce choice and self-control, acknowledge the feelings of patients, and minimize external controls on behavior, then individuals develop self-regulation values and behaviors and improve their adherence to treatment (Williams, et al., 1998). Thus, especially because non-adherence is determined by multiple factors, achieving adherence and dealing productively with refusal over the long term calls for using a number of combined strategies such as self-monitoring, reinforcement, education, and cognitive, behavioral, and other psychosocial strategies in the context of a caring relationship.

TOPICS FOR DISCUSSION
AND LEARNING ACTIVITIES

1. Identify and discuss the personal values that seem to influence your thinking about the pros and cons of psychotropic medication use in particular situations in your practice setting. How do your values correspond with the National Association of Social Workers code of ethics?

2. Describe a real or hypothetical scenario from a field placement or practice experience in which you would feel justified in supporting the involuntary medication of a client (or might try to "convince" the client to accept medication). Next, describe a challenging scenario in which you would *not* support a coercive medication strategy. Defend your position in each case with your classmates.

3. Clients and their family members (parents, spouses, partners, and children) often disagree about whether the client should take medication for mental illness. Construct several scenarios in which this is the case. Engage in role playing in which a social worker must try to mediate this disagreement within the ethical bounds of his or her role. Discuss the actions of the social worker and any alternative actions the social worker might take.

4. Consider the following scenario for class discussion or role playing: A divorced, working African American female with two adult children and few friends is being treated for a generalized anxiety disorder. She has taken the prescription Valium for 4 years. The new physician (her previous physician has moved away) has just told the client that she must taper off the Valium and substitute a new medication that is not potentially addicting (buspirone). The client is fearful that her symptoms will worsen without her traditional medication regimen. She has been unable to hold jobs in the past, in part because of her anxiety, and she fears that she will lose her current job as a high school secretary. The social worker must reassure the client and then develop a plan with her for the transition between doctors and medications. How might the social worker proceed?

PART IV

✳

Future Directions

Chapter 10

Future Directions in Psychopharmacology: Implications
for Social Workers

10

Future Directions in Psychopharmacology: Implications for Social Workers

A number of scientific, social, and political issues have become prominent in psychopharmacology that will likely affect the roles of social workers and the future of the profession at large. These include the rapid appearance of new drug treatments; creative new delivery routes or treatment philosophies; the ongoing popularity of herbs and vitamins to address mental health concerns; and the debate about expanding prescription privileges among non-physician mental health care providers, such as nurses, psychologists, pharmacists, and social workers. We are also undoubtedly in the midst of a knowledge explosion that demands that social workers be both intentional and assertive about professional development with respect to psychopharmacology and the experience of clients who take psychiatric medications. We will discuss the implications of each of these developments for the profession. We begin with an overview of the drug development process (drawn from Laughren, 2010; Moncrieff, Hopker, & Thomas, 2005) and criticisms of that process that account for some controversies around psychotropic medication.

THE DRUG DEVELOPMENT PROCESS

The Food and Drug Administration (FDA) is the federal agency charged with overseeing drug testing and development, approving new drugs, and monitoring approved drugs. The FDA's Center for Drug Evaluation and Research (CDER) has responsibility for both prescription and over-the-counter drugs. The CDER does not test drugs itself but oversees the activities of the pharmaceutical companies as they work to get a drug into circulation. Getting FDA approval for a new drug is an expensive undertaking; on average it takes 10 to 15 years to get a new medicine from the laboratory to consumers at a total cost of up to $1 billion or more.

The starting point in drug research is the identification of a potential biological target presumably involved in a health or mental health condition. Once a relevant target (usually a neurotransmitter in the case of psychotropic drugs) has been identified and validated in biological studies, compounds are tested to find one or more that may have a therapeutic effect on the target. Hundreds of compounds may be evaluated for their activity in this process. "Me too" drugs, or those developed by one company to approximate the already-determined efficacy of another company's marketed drug, do not involve the testing of new chemical entities. A compound that *appears* to exhibit the desired activity is considered by the researcher to be a "hit." In the preclinical evaluation stage a team of scientists at the pharmaceutical company will evaluate a "hit" to ensure that it has appropriate properties to advance into further drug developments. This involves testing the compound in cell and tissue cultures and, later, in animals. In addition, the company establishes the properties of the chemical, that is, its makeup, stability, and solubility, and its suitability to be made into consumable formulations.

Drug developers must assess the major toxicities of the compound prior to use in humans, including its effects on the heart, lungs, brain, kidney, liver, and digestive systems. While many of these tests can be made using "in vitro" methods with isolated cells, others can only be made by using experimental animals, since only in an intact organism can the complex interplay of metabolism and toxicity be examined. Information gathered from this preclinical testing is submitted to the FDA as an Investigational New Drug (IND) application. The FDA has 30 days to decide if clinical trials will be allowed, and, if approved, the company can begin testing the drug in people.

After IND approval, three phases of clinical research and, later, post-marketing monitoring must be undertaken. In Phase 1, which is said to take about 2 years, researchers recruit 50 to 100 volunteers to evaluate the impact of the drug on a healthy person. In Phase 2, lasting approximately another 2 years, clinical trials are longer and involve participants who may actually benefit from the drug (100 to 300 volunteers). In Phase 3, larger numbers of participants (1000 to 3000) are used, and the drug's equivalence to standard therapies is assessed and compared to a placebo. Prescribers monitor these persons to assess efficacy and identify adverse events. The FDA requires that at least two major studies show statistically significant positive results for the drug. This phase takes about 18 months to complete. The process of drug development does not stop once human clinical trials are underway. Long-term or chronic toxicities are evaluated, as well as the drug's effects on other bodily systems not previously monitored (fertility, reproduction, immune system, etc.).

After the three phases of clinical trials are completed, the company can file a New Drug Application (NDA), which consists of a compilation of its research data and is often thousands of pages long. The FDA has 24 months to render a decision. During this time a team of CDER physicians, statisticians, chemists, pharmacologists, and other scientists reviews the sponsor's NDA and proposed labeling. If the drug is approved, the FDA creates a label for marketing the drug, which appears in the package insert and the *Physician's Desk Reference*. The label lists all possible side effects and what the drug's on-label use is. "On-label" use means the drug has specific FDA approval for marketing the drug to treat some disorder, while "off-label" use refers to other uses that prescribers may later find for the drug based on clinical experience and case reports. The company manufactures, markets, and distributes the new medicine. The FDA continuously monitors the drug after it is on the market for any newly discovered problems.

Many researchers, academics, and health care professionals are critical of the drug development process as described above, and their concerns include the following (Breggin, 1987; Cohen, 2011, 2009; Reinhart, 2007):

- The FDA does not engage in drug testing on its own; it relies on research generated and paid for by the pharmaceutical companies.

- The FDA does not regulate medications carefully enough and may be unduly influenced by the big business of the pharmaceutical industry.

- The FDA does not require that the pharmaceutical company make *all* of its data available for review in its NDA.

- Companies may conduct studies that show no significant results, but as long as two of them show positive results, the process can move forward.

- The FDA does not require testing to determine if cognitive impairment or brain dysfunction is associated with the treatments.

- The FDA does not require pharmaceutical companies to show that any consumers actually recover from their symptoms as a result of the drug.

There is significant public wariness about the drug companies, as we have presented in Chapter 1, due in part to widespread dissemination of their large profits and media stories about their role in suppressing information about negative effects of medications. As one example, a psychiatric survivor group called MindFreedom.org and drug maker Eli Lilly have fought in the courts about the availability of early data on the side effects of the drug olanzapine, which according to the advocacy group contains damning information. A related concern that has garnered much attention is the use of direct-to-consumer advertising by makers of psychiatric (and other) medication. Research shows that advertisements do not really adhere to the "fair balance" requirement or publicize sufficiently detailed information about a medication (Kaphingst, Rudd, DeJong, & Daltroy, 2004). We noted in Chapter 1, for example, social worker Jeff Lacasse's (2005) research that demonstrated that advertisements frequently present information about antidepressants that is inconsistent with scientific evidence, exaggerating the level of causal knowledge we have about the mechanism of action. Importantly for social workers, Lacasse contends that this bias in advertising also serves to undermine the use of psychosocial approaches to intervention. Because of the public's distrust of pharmaceutical companies, more attention is being paid to the relationships between those companies and the academic and governmental researchers doing clinical trials. Many medical journals now demand disclosure of these associations in peer-reviewed publications.

We should note that currently the majority of clinical trials focus on the therapeutic effect of specific drugs in the first 6 weeks of treatment. Clearly more research is needed about effectiveness that extends beyond the acute phase of a disorder or symptoms. In addition, most clinical trials are conducted comparing one drug to a placebo or, at most, one standard first-line medication. More research needs to be conducted comparing medications with each other and in conjunction with psychosocial treatments. Scholars are beginning to debate the ethics of allowing medication-free research, or the use of placebos on one hand, and the need to use standardized psychosocial interventions in conjunction with drug trials (Addington, Williams, Lapierre, & el-Geubaly, 1997; Carpenter, 1997; Carroll, 1997). Social workers need to be aware of all these issues in order to provide the best care possible to their clients who consume, and want to understand the risks and benefits of, these products.

NEW PHARMACEUTICAL TREATMENTS

Advances in molecular biology, particularly continuing research into neurotransmission and central receptor subtypes, are hoped to lead to greater pharmacological specificity in the coming years. The field has made progress toward discovering and refining drugs that affect aspects of neurotransmission precisely where it is needed but not where it is not, ideally leading to drugs that produce desired therapeutic effects with minimal side effects. Interestingly, innovation in psychotropic drug development has slowed in the past 20 years, due in part to the expense of the process but also the tendency of pharmaceutical companies to focus their efforts on producing medications similar to those already marketed by other companies (the "me too" phenomenon). According to Moncrieff and Cohen (2005), the dominant "disease-centered" model of how drugs work that is behind this philosophy is proving to be limited for the following reasons:

- Major hypotheses about the causes of mental illness are tentative, having been derived from selectively observed actions of drugs.
- Comparisons between drugs believed to have specific effects on certain conditions and drugs thought to have nonspecific effects fail to support the disease model.
- Outcome measures for various disorders include items that are responsive to nonspecific drug effects.
- Studies with healthy volunteers describe drug-induced states independent of the existence of a psychiatric condition.
- Animal tests show effects with drugs not usually thought of as specific treatments for the condition modeled by those tests.

A panel of academic, industry, and government representatives concluded several years ago that the development of new treatments for the symptoms of mental illness has been impeded by an incomplete understanding of the nature of mental illness and its effects on the brain (Nauert, 2006). Contrary to the prevailing "single disease model," combinations of several symptom groups may need to be addressed separately in developing new drugs. The most promising new direction of drug development appears to be focused on compounds that act on more than one target. In schizophrenia, for example, attention is being paid to a broader range of symptoms than before; those that may have a greater impact on a person's long-term functioning, such as cognitive impairment and depression. A related development is the increasing prevalence and acceptance of polypharmacy, the use of numerous medications at the same time. As one group of authors put it, "polypharmacy is a clinical way of life" (Preskorn, Harvey & Stanga, 1998). Studies show that between 30 and 80% of people taking antidepressants are also taking two other kinds of medication. Prescribers are trying to increase their client's therapeutic responses while decreasing adverse side effects by applying a more sophisticated understanding of pharmacodynamic and pharmacokinetic interactions among medications and foods.

Expanding on these ideas, Wiedemann (2011) notes that in the field of neurology there has been an upsurge of interest in searching for *biomarkers*; objectively measurable characteristics that may serve as indicators of the causes of illnesses, their course, and their modification by drug, psychosocial, and biological interventions. Possible biomarkers may include those determined by laboratory study (genes, neurotransmitters, hormones, cytokines, neuropeptides, and enzymes), electrophysiological markers (electroencephalography, magnetic encephalography, electrocardiograms, facial electromyography, and skin conductance), brain imaging techniques (cranial computed tomography, magnetic resonance imaging, magnetic resonance spectography, positron emission tomography, and single photon emission computed tomography), and behavioral approaches.

In terms of routes of administration, a number of controversial innovations are underway in both drug and somatic therapies. Some drugs may be made available that can be placed under the tongue, much like nitroglycerine in the treatment of angina, which may be a breakthrough for people who suffer from panic (Kim, Dyskin, & Goldsmith, 1992). In the treatment of depression, repetitive transcranial magnetic stimulation (RTMS) is being investigated, a process by which an electromagnetic coil is applied to the scalp to create a pulsating magnetic field that can produce neuron activation in localized areas of the brain (Montovani, Aly, Dagan, Allert, & Lisanby, 2012). The procedure is administered for a few weeks in an outpatient setting to a fully awake client in sessions lasting 15 to 30 minutes several times per week. Another new treatment for depression is vagus nerve stimulation (VNS), a procedure in which a pacemaker is implanted under the skin in the chest wall and attached with an electrode to the vagus nerve in the chest area (which extends into the brain) (Martin & Martin-Sanchez, 2012). The pacemaker is receptive to external programming from a computer that controls the intensity and frequency of the stimulations. In deep brain stimulation (DBS) electrodes are surgically implanted into brain areas thought to be associated with neurons involved in the targeted condition (Mathews, 2011). This treatment is said to have potential for helping persons with refractory depression and obsessive-compulsive disorder. Finally, single-enantiomer medication compounds are being developed that target neuron receptors that face in only one direction, as directionality has been found relevant to the actions of some neurotransmitters (Khan, Preskorn, & Wilamasena, 2006). One example of such a drug already on the market is the antidepressant escitalopram.

The coming years will likely usher in newer and more creative ways to incorporate health care reminders into the everyday lives of clients, as they have for persons receiving primary health care services. For example, in diabetes care, testing has shown that a voice messaging system is a useful adjunct for patients in monitoring their glucose levels, foot care, diet, and medication. These can improve both treatment adherence and client satisfaction with care (Piette & Mah, 1997).

HERBAL AND VITAMIN TREATMENTS

Herbs are low-growing plants with soft, succulent tissues, most commonly used for food seasoning and fragrances as well as medicinal purposes. *Vitamins* are organic substances that are essential in minute amounts for normal growth and health, because they help to convert foods into energy and tissues. There are 13 known vitamins, and, although the human body produces three of these, all 13 must be obtained from plant and animal foods to ensure healthy development.

Since the 1990s there has been a growing interest in this country among both the general public and health professionals in herbs and vitamins as primary or supplemental treatments for the symptoms of emotional distress. At present between 8 and 57% of psychiatric clients, most commonly those with depression and anxiety, use complementary medicines (Sarris, Panossian, Schweitzer, Stough, & Scholey, 2011). Our society has been skeptical of medicines that emerge from sources other than academic science, because of highly controlled procedures for drug manufacture and testing and the power of universities and medical professions to shape cultural attitudes. Of course, people around the world have used herbs and vitamins for centuries. Still, the evidence base for the use of these medicines is limited, and more randomized controlled trials of promising agents are needed. Further, the active ingredients in some herbal formulations have not been identified, which leads to problems with standardization of extracts and dose recommendations. "Alternative," a term coined by health professionals, emphasizes the secondary status of herbal or nutritional interventions. Others use the label "complementary" to more positively highlight their potential as additive therapeutic agents when used with standard medicines. In this section we provide a brief overview of the status of herbs and vitamins as alternative treatments.

A major trigger of the increased interest in herbal remedies for treating the symptoms of mental disorders was the 1996 publication in the *British Journal of Psychiatry* by Linde et al. (1996) of a meta-analysis of 23 European studies conducted between 1979 and 1995, indicating significant improvement in persons who took St.-John's-wort (hypericum) for mild to moderate depression. Results indicated that the herb, a plant that blooms in early summer in Europe, West Asia, and North Africa was as effective as several standard drugs including imipramine and amitriptyline. The authors concluded that subjects using the herb for 5 weeks to 2 months were three times as likely to experience significant mood improvement as subjects taking a placebo, with fewer side effects than standard drug therapies. It seemed to help about half of its users, an effectiveness rate comparable to many antidepressant drugs. It is speculated that hypericum has an inhibitory effect of serotonin and norepinephrine; another theory suggests MAO inhibition and inhibition of dopamine as well. The reaction to these claims by the medical profession in this country was one of skepticism (Schardt, 1998). Jacques Bradwejn, chief of psychiatry at the Royal Ottawa Hospital in Canada, expressed a typical view: the studies were reasonably well done but not comparable in quality to the kinds of studies necessary to have an antidepressant drug approved by the FDA.

Still, St.-John's-wort was the leading treatment for depression in Germany by the mid-1990s. Advocates pointed out that it does not interact with alcohol, is nonaddictive, includes no withdrawal symptoms, does not require a lengthy build-up period, enhances sleep and dreaming, and does not produce sedation. Its adverse effects, described as generally minor, include gastrointestinal discomfort, skin allergic reactions, itching, sensitivity to sunlight, and anxiety. Important in terms of accessibility, the herb represents a substantial cost savings to many consumers—an average monthly supply of hypericum costs only 10% as much as a standard SSRI drug.

Systematic reviews of published trials since that time continue to suggest that St.-John's-wort is more effective than a placebo, although comparative efficacy to standard antidepressants is less clearly established. Whiskey, Wernecke, and Taylor (2001) updated and expanded previous meta-analyses of St.-John's-wort (22 randomized controlled trials) and concluded that it was significantly more effective than a placebo but not different in efficacy from antidepressant medications. Adverse effects occurred more frequently with standard antidepressants than with St.-John's-wort. Another group of researchers more recently updated evidence from randomized trials regarding the effectiveness of hypericum (Linde, Berner, Egger, & Multrow, 2005). They performed a systematic review and meta-analysis of 37 double-blind, randomized, controlled trials that compared clinical effects of hypericum with either a placebo or a standard antidepressant in adults with depression. The larger placebo-controlled trials restricted to patients with major depression showed only minor effects over placebos, while the older and smaller trials not restricted to patients with major depression showed marked positive effects compared to standard drugs. The authors concluded that hypericum improved symptoms more than placebos and similarly to standard antidepressants in adults with mild to moderate depression. However, persons with major depression showed only minimal benefits compared with a placebo.

Evidence has been accumulating for the therapeutic effects of other herbs as well. Along with St.-John's-wort, kava is the most commonly used herbal medicine in the treatment of anxiety and depressive symptoms. One group of researchers conducted a systematic review for evidence of its efficacy in generalized anxiety disorders, social phobia, panic disorders, obsessive-compulsive disorders, and post-traumatic stress disorders and concluded that there is evidence supporting its use only in the treatment of generalized anxiety (Sarris & Kavanagh, 2009). More recently, Sarris et al. (2011) reviewed clinical trials of various herbs used in the treatment of mood and anxiety disorders. They located 66 controlled studies involving 11 herbal medicines, two of which (St.-John's-wort for depression and kava for anxiety disorders) demonstrated a high level of evidence. Preliminary positive evidence of antidepressant effects was for the herbs Echium amoenum, Crocus sativus, and Rhodiola rosea; and anti-anxiety effects for Matricaria recutita, Ginkgo biloba, Passiflora incarnata, Echium amoenum, and Scutellaria lateriflora.

Herbs and vitamins may also be used as adjunctive treatments for symptoms of mental disorders along with standard medications. Sarris, Kavanagh, and Byrne (2010) evaluated current evidence for the adjunctive use of nutritional and herbal medicines with antidepressants, mood stabilizers, and benzodiazepines. They concluded that encouraging evidence exists for the use of omega-3 fatty acids (found in marine and plant oils), SAM (a dietary supplement), folate (vitamin B9), and L-tryptophan (an amino acid) with antidepressants to enhance efficacy. Another systematic review of this type (Wernicke, Turner, & Priebe, 2001) identified potentially useful substances as ginkgo (a Chinese herb) and hydergine as cognitive enhancers, passion flower and valerian (herbs) as sedatives, SAM as an antidepressant, and selenium (a micro-nutrient) and folate to complement antidepressant drugs. Regarding cognitive enhancers, four researchers reviewed the clinical evidence for or against ginseng as a treatment for Alzheimer's disease (AD) (Lee et al., 2009). They reviewed the effectiveness of ginseng as an adjunct to drug therapy on cognitive function compared with conventional drug therapy. Their results suggested significant effects in favor of ginseng, although only two methodologically sound studies were available for review.

Traditional Chinese medicine has been used to treat schizophrenia-like symptoms for centuries (Rathbone et al., 2012). As in the United States, anti-psychotic drugs are the mainstay of treatment in China but some reports have suggested that Chinese herbal medicine is effective for psychosis and that combination treatments (drugs plus herbs) are useful to enhance antipsychotic efficacy or reduce adverse effects. In six of the seven studies reviewed by these authors, treatment was allocated according to a diagnosis of schizophrenia. The one study that incorporated traditional Chinese medical theory showed significant improvement in global state but was methodologically limited. Two studies used different herbal medicines and different antipsychotic medications. The herbal medicine group receiving either *dang gui cheng qi tang* or *xiao yao san* plus antipsychotics were significantly less likely to have an outcome of "no change or worse" compared with participants receiving only antipsychotic drugs. These results are broadly encouraging and suggest that combining herbal medicines with antipsychotics might be beneficial. In the context of these studies, the addition of herbal medicine did not worsen treatment compliance, and there is the suggestion that the addition of the herbal medicine made it easier for participants to accept the possible utility of standard antipsychotics.

Consumers frequently try herbal medicines with the assumption that they are safe, so the aim of another systematic review was to provide a summary of recent data on the adverse effects of herbal remedies (Ernst, 2003). Numerous case reports present a diverse array of possible adverse events including cerebral arteritis, cerebral edema, delirium, coma, confusion, encephalopathy, hallucinations, intracerebral hemorrhage, other types of cerebrovascular accidents, movement disorders, mood disturbances, muscle weakness, paresthesia (the feeling of "pins and needles" on the skin), and seizures. The authors concluded that herbal medicines can cause serious psychiatric and neurological adverse effects. Ten other human clinical trials met inclusion criteria for a systematic review of the possible adverse effects of kava. One study found that kava significantly improved visual attention and working memory (attributed to the ability of kava to inhibit reuptake of noradrenaline in the prefrontal cortex), while others found that kava could increase body sway and significantly impair visual attention during periods of high-cognitive demand (due to GABA pathway modulation).

Nutritional deficiency models regarding the cause of mental illness have been in existence for decades (Abou & Coppen, 1986). They do not receive much attention at present because they have been largely discounted. However, some researchers are producing evidence that vitamin deficiencies may be correlated with mental illness and that vitamins may play some role in treatment. The most commonly identified disorders and the vitamin deficiencies associated with them include alcoholism (thiamin), schizophrenia (niacin), depression (B6), and epilepsy (folate). Cobalamin deficiency has been associated with psychosis (Hutto, 1997).

Organic psychoses are occasionally observed in persons with B12 deficiency. It is widely accepted that a subset of cognitive disorders in old age may result from vitamin deficiency and thus be treatable with vitamin replacement therapy (Lachner, Steinle, & Regenold, 2012). But this is an unusual phenomenon. While some vitamin deficiencies initially present with psychiatric symptoms, it is erroneous to assume that they are generally the primary causes of reversible conditions. As noted earlier there is evidence that the vitamin supplement folate may be significant in reducing depression. In several studies low folate concentrations in the bloodstream have been noted in 15 to 38% of clients with depression. Low folate levels have also been associated with a poor response to antidepressant treatment in two studies (Fava et al., 1997; Wesson, Levitt, & Joffe, 1994). Folate has also shown in some studies to be associated with a positive response to lithium among persons with bipolar disorder. There is no cause-and-effect pathway suggested in these findings, but a deficiency of this substance is thought to be a contributing cause for mood disorders, since it is believed to be active in the process by which the body produces certain neurotransmitters. A folate deficiency may impede the processes of methylation and hydroxylation, which are important in the metabolism of neurotransmitters.

Regarding other disorders, some evidence exists for the utility of vitamin C, B6, and magnesium in supplementing the treatment of autistic children (Rossignol, 2009). Children with attention-deficit hyperactivity disorder are sometimes treated with a variety of vitamins and minerals, and some positive symptom outcomes have been reported from the experience (Curtis & Patel, 2008). Several studies also indicate that persons with tardive dyskinesia have low vitamin-E levels compared to controls, although efforts to treat the condition with vitamin E supplements have shown limited effectiveness (Howland, 2011).

What can social workers conclude from the emerging research on treating mental illnesses with herbs and vitamins? First of all, it makes common sense that if we recognize functioning as a biopsychosocial-spiritual phenomenon, improving physical and nutritional health is likely to contribute to improving mental health. Still, while the symptoms of some mental disorders may be positively impacted by good physical health, other symptoms and disorders may not. Second, the evidence does seem to support the positive effects of hypericum in treating milder depressions and kava for anxiety, and a folate deficiency may well contribute to depression and act as an inhibitor of antidepressant medication. Because so much of drug research has emerged from serendipitous findings over the years, it is also reasonable to speculate that alternative or complementary treatments will be effective for some persons. The best recourse for the social worker, it seems, is to be current with the literature in these areas and to encourage clients to talk to their prescribers about the range of remedies they might consider to maintain good physical health. These tasks clearly involve attention to the roles of consultant, counselor, advocate, educator, and researcher.

EXPANDING PRESCRIPTION-WRITING PRIVILEGES

Several health professions other than psychiatry and medicine, including nursing, pharmacy, psychology, and social work have either advocated for, or considered, expanding their roles in medication prescription. Their arguments are often based on concerns related to the shortage of prescribers in many parts of the country, especially rural areas, and on their perceived scope of actual or potential expertise. Nurse practitioners (advanced practice registered nurses, or APNs) have been able to prescribe medications in the United States for a half-century. They are credentialed to treat physical and mental conditions through assessment, physical exams, diagnostic tests, and treatments that include prescribing medications. APNs must hold national board certification in their area of specialty and be licensed through their state nursing boards. Because the profession is state-regulated, some APNs work independently of physicians while others are required to collaborate with them. The majority of states require that APNs hold a master's degree, a post-master's certificate, or a doctoral degree. Proposals are in place, however, that might require a Doctor of Nursing degree in order to work as an APN.

Doctoral training programs emerged in the pharmacy profession approximately 50 years ago to prepare those persons for work as medication specialists (Maine, 2008). The Board of Pharmaceutical Specialties now recognizes five specialties, one of which is psychopharmacy. The profession has long debated the extent of knowledge and skill required of students to serve as medication specialists, and since 2004 schools only recognize the Doctor of Pharmacy degree level of education. Over 25 years ago in the state of Washington, pharmacist advocates secured the first legislative recognition of their "collaborative practice authority" that permitted them to initiate and modify drug therapy under protocols with a prescriber. Models of patient care by which pharmacists assume responsibility for the selection, dosing, monitoring, and adjusting of medications can be found across the country and have led to such programs as pharmacy-based immunization and chronic-disease patient management. Forty-four states now recognize some level of collaborative practice authority for pharmacists although laws vary from state to state. Two states (New Mexico and North Carolina) have granted pharmacists independent authority to prescribe medications, but the number of pharmacists utilizing such authority in those states is small. The roles of medication-use specialists will likely expand in this era of health system reformation, and partnerships between pharmacists and clinical psychologists may even develop in the quest of both professions to expand the range of their services.

The profession of psychology has advocated for medication prescription privileges for reasons similar to those of social workers, including practicality and cost-effectiveness, specifically with the under-availability of psychiatrists and the lack of psychopharmacological training of regular physicians, who write the majority of psychotropic drug prescriptions in the United States. Hayes and Chang (2002) describe the evolution of psychology's efforts to obtain prescription privileges. These authors assert that such a development would be ultimately good for clients, as psychologists could apply their specialized skills in outcome evaluation to determine the best evidence-based courses of action for clients, whether it be medication, psychosocial therapy, or a combination of the two. Psychologists are already permitted to write prescriptions for the Indian Health Services, Department of Defense, Department of Veteran Affairs and in two states (New Mexico and Louisiana).

Some educators advocate for a new specialty in the profession, perhaps a doctorate in mental health or health psychology, and have written about two "paths" that psychologists might take, including the (traditional) primary care psychologist and the prescribing psychologist (McGrath & Sammons, 2011). The APA has developed a proposal for postdoctoral training programs in psychopharmacology, requiring approximately 300 contact hours (Campbell & Fox, 2010). It is estimated that approximately 1500 psychologists have already completed postdoctoral coursework in preparation for prescribing (Ax, Fagan, & Resnick, 2009) and approximately 60 psychologists were prescribing in New Mexico and Louisiana in the fall of 2008 (LeVine & Wiggins, 2010). The American Psychological Association (2006) has published a set of practice guidelines for its professionals involved in pharmacology and has developed a competency exam called the Psychopharmacology Examination for Psychologists (McGrath, 2010). Psychology professionals argue that psychologists with prescriptive authority would represent the only mental health profession with extensive training in *all* modalities that are appropriate to the amelioration of mental conditions. It is hoped that familiarity with both psychosocial and biological interventions, combined with training in the critical evaluation of research, will help psychologists resist excessive reliance on medications. The prescribing psychologist would be more effective than the general practitioner at determining when psychosocial versus biological interventions are warranted and more effective when informing the patient about the potential benefits of psychosocial intervention.

Of course, some psychologists are skeptical of the profession's move toward seeking prescription privileges, being concerned that they will lose what already makes them distinctive and risk becoming a conduit for pharmaceutical panaceas (Healy, 2003). Psychologists will spend hundreds of hours studying medical topics and, as a result, their clients will be more likely to receive medications as a primary or secondary component of treatment. It is argued that drug companies are entrepreneurs, not seekers of evidence-based practice, and that psychology would lose some of its dedication to empirical truth under their influence (as physicians allegedly do now). It is pointed out, for example, that there is as much evidence-based psychosocial interventions as for medications, but that psychologists might lose this perspective if they get into the business of prescribing. Further, research on effective combined treatments is not yet extensive enough to help providers make clearly informed decisions about using them. Finally, gaining prescription privileges might not enhance the status of the psychology profession, because it will likely open the floodgates for members of other professions, including social work, to advocate for the same privileges.

The early literature on social work and psychopharmacology (e.g., Brodsky, Fisher, & Weinstein, 1964; Hankoff & Galvin, 1968) rarely put forth the idea that social workers should seek training toward writing prescriptions. These articles mainly advanced the perspective that psychotropic medications represent a positive aspect of treatment for many people and that social workers need to develop their ability to participate actively as physicians' helpers. In the sole exception to this general position, Abroms and Greenfield (1973) suggested that social workers begin to work toward acquiring prescription privileges. They argued that this was a logical next step, given social work's person-in-environment perspective, the new emphasis on medication in the field of mental health, and the increasing complexity of cases faced by social workers. Elliot and Kintzer (1973) responded by arguing against this recommendation with two still-relevant concerns: (1) adding content on pharmacology to the social work curriculum would broaden an already overly general educational experience, and (2) it actually might work against the maintenance of a psychosocial intervention framework. Dziegielewski (1997) and Bentley (1997) argued both sides of the issue again with Dziegielewski posing the question "Why *not* us?" Then, noting the expansion of privileges beyond just the M.D., Dziegielewski advocates for the creation of relevant post-MSW training that would prepare them for taking on the task, if they so desired. Bentley on the other hand advocated for professional humility and a greater appreciation of other disciplines' contributions to the care of clients. In the 15 years since that debate, little else has appeared in the social work literature on the question. DeLeon and Pies (1994) also argued each side of this debate as it relates to nonphysician providers in general. DeLeon argued that adding prescription writing to any list of potential nonphysician activities among the helping professions would fill a desperate need for more holistic care, especially for those who have limited access to physicians. With improved curriculum and ongoing training and credentialing, this is a realistic goal. Pies disagreed, however, claiming that performance of a sound differential diagnosis with implications for treatment with psychotropic medication is a complex issue that goes well beyond the mere addition of course work in pharmacology.

Although we have made the case that expanding their knowledge base in psychopharmacology will help social workers respond well to their clients, we still do not embrace prescription writing as either feasible or desirable. The 2-year MSW curriculum is simply too packed as it is, with subjects including basic practice theory and skills, advanced human behavior, cultural diversity, social policy and services, and single-case research. In addition, clients seem best served by productive interdisciplinary relationships that stand the best chance of emerging when all parties respect and legitimize each other's expertise and acknowledge their own professional boundaries. Even though social work has recognized biological issues as a crucial aspect of the biopsychosocial perspective, prescription writing would probably only serve to confuse and blur the providers' roles and responsibilities. The absence of any swell of support for prescription privileges among social workers seems to support this view. "We do note that several Universities have and are developing a new DSW "advanced practice doctorate" in social work, some with considerable content on psychopharmacology. We await further developments around the degree in our field as we consider its implications, if any, of this on the potential for social workers to prescribe."

It is clear that all professions, including social work, that consider expanding their professional domain need to consider accountability issues and liability concerns. Even though we do not currently advocate seeking prescription privileges, we do support expanded knowledge and roles in medication management for social workers or, at the very least, significantly expanded application of existing skills to clients' concerns about psychotropic medication. But are social workers thus setting themselves up for increased liability risks? Will they be held liable for a failure to properly educate a client about missed doses, for example, or a failure to adequately monitor the side effects of medication, or coercing ambivalent clients into taking powerful medications with serious side effects? After all, even with the social worker's and the client's input, the prescriber is the one who makes the final decision about medications. In most cases, a nurse or pharmacist still distributes the medication. Interestingly, 20 years ago Littrell and Ashford (1995) asked "Is it proper for psychologists to discuss medication issues with clients?" The authors (both social workers) reviewed the ethics of nonmedical providers giving information about medications, including reviewing court cases that have emerged in pharmacy and nursing related to psychopharmacotherapy. Their conclusion is reassuring in terms of the thesis of this book. They say that prudent care not only finds these conversations permissible but also may be required as a part of the obligation to provide coordinated care.

KEEPING UP WITH DRUG DEVELOPMENTS
AND CLIENT EXPERIENCES

We have stressed our role as counselors, educators, consultants, and collaborators with clients and other providers and have emphasized our role in helping clients gain new knowledge and skills and make informed decisions. Clearly, to most effectively fulfill their roles, social workers also need to stay abreast of these developments through reading, in-service training, conferences, and collaborative discussions with colleagues and clients. Professional social work organizations can and do help by sponsoring training and increasing the coverage of such topics in their workshops, journals, newsletters, and brochures. Schools of social work may have a special obligation and opportunity to respond to the need for more psychopharmacological content in their explicit curriclum and through their continuing education offerings. In ever more settings, social workers should expand their roles as researchers by participating in the design and implementation of outcome studies or other inquiries that would inform responsive and compassionate care in the face of medication-related dilemmas. Indeed, social workers have a tremendous unfulfilled potential to increase knowledge through research, including how combined medication and psychosocial treatments affect client functioning.

The Internet offers perhaps one of the most accessible avenues for an individual social worker's professional development around psychiatric medication. Dziegielewski (2010), noting the World Wide Web as a major resource for clients as well, speaks of the Internet's empowering qualities and warns against information overload. Recognizing the bias and lack of objectivity of many sites, she encourages users to critically ask, among other things:

- Who owns and/or maintains the site?
- Is there a recognized professional body that reviews the contents? Are references made to professional literature?
- Are there links that support or supplement content? Is credit given to information sources? Are referral sources reputable and well-established?
- How often is the site updated?

Dubovsky and Dubovsky (2007) call for maintaining "healthy skepticism" about data from just about anywhere, but certainly from the Internet, drug representatives, or even hearsay around the office. They also note, however, that skepticism is not the same as cynicism. In that spirit, social workers are encouraged to exploit the resources of profit and not-for-profit sites as PsychCentral (http://psychcentral.com), WebMD (http://webmd.com), and National Alliance on Mental Illness (http://www.nami.org). Those three sites fared well in a recently published quality review of online resources for severe mental illness (see Guada & Venable, 2011). A list of potentially useful websites is offered in Table 10.1.

In addition to visiting websites, subscribing to online versions of such newsletters as *Psychiatric Times* or *Medscape Psychiatry & Mental Health* are additional options. Those savvy enough to subscribe to RSS ("rich site summary" or "really simple syndication") feeds can have links to targeted articles, videos, blogs, sent directly to their own files in a cataloged manner. Within social work more specifically, NASW now has a specialty section for "behavioral health" that maintains an up-to-date website of resources in general, and articles related to psychiatric medication can sometimes be found there.

Table 10.1 Websites with Information on Psychiatric Medications

http://www.samhsa.gov/
Substance Abuse and Mental Health Services
Site run by the federal government's Center for Mental Health Services, which provides free information via the Internet, phone, and publications to the public.

http://www.nimh.nih.gov
National Institute of Mental Health (NIMH)
Public information on specific disorders, diagnosis, and treatment with a section on NIMH research activities.

http://www.nami.org
National Alliance on Mental Illness (NAMI)
NAMI is a national advocacy group with a strong consumer and family member perspective, focusing on serious mental illnesses. This page leads to a number of NAMI articles focusing on disorders, medications, and research.

http://www.nmha.org/index.cfm
Mental Health America
This site gives access to fact sheets, pamphlets, merchandise, and position statements on a wide variety of mental health topics including disorders, medications, and suicide.

http://www.mentalhealth.com/p30-note.html
Internet Mental Health
Designed by Dr. Phillip Long, a Canadian psychiatrist, this is an encyclopedic-type site linking to medication information, drug research information, and other mental health links.

http://www.mentalhelp.net
MentalHelp.net
A comprehensive site linking to information on disorders and treatments, professional resources and journals. The site is sponsored by CMHC systems, a private, for-profit developer of information technology for human services.

http://www.psych.org
American Psychiatric Association
APA publishes the *Diagnostic and Statistical Manual* and sponsors a comprehensive website.

http://www.dr-bob.org/tips/
Dr. Bob's Psychopharmacology Tips
A unique site that allows you to search for tips (edited by Dr. Robert Hsiung) on psychopharmaceutical use from physician postings on the Interpsych discussion list. While not scientific, this site allows you to see direct opinions from prescribers on their experiences with psychopharmaceuticals.

http://www.medicinenet.com/medications/article.htm
MedicineNet.com
Site run by a "network of doctors" who want to provide up-to-date comprehensive health information to the public. This page gets you to the alphabetical medications index.

http://www.anxieties.com
Anxieties.com
A free self-help source directed at people with anxiety disorders. This page lists common medications, provides guidelines for their use, and offers detailed profiles of specific medications.

(Continued)

Table 10.1 *Continued*

http://www.schizophrenia.com
   Schizophrenia.com
A not-for-profit site (focusing on schizophrenia but has useful related information) provided by Brian Chiko in memory of his brother. This site has a useful section for students,
as well as sections for consumers, families, and professionals.

http://www.icspp.org/
   International Counselors, Social Workers, Psychiatrists, Psychologists, & Educators
This is Peter Breggin's site, author of numerous books critical of psychiatry and
medications. Find information on the dangers of drugs, book lists, reports, excerpts.

A key argument of this text is that social workers are in a unique place to respond with empathy and compassion to the medication-related decisions and dilemmas of clients and appreciate the meaning that medication has for their lives. Toward this end, it would be remiss to leave out another key way that social workers can "keep up"—by continuing to read newly published (and classic) first-person accounts of mental illness, trauma, emotional disorders, and behavioral challenges, especially those that focus on psychiatric medication use as a defining experience in their lives. Reading this important and growing genre of books can help keep social workers centered in the lived experience of clients and families and help them maintain their focus on the importance of compassion and empathy in all that they do. Powerful classics include Patty Duke's *A brilliant madness* (Duke & Hochman, 1992), Kay Jamison's *An unquiet mind: A memoir of moods and madness* (1995), Susan Kaysen's *Girl, interrupted* (1993), Kate Millet's *The looney bin trip* (1990), Lori Schiller's *The quiet room* (Shiller & Bennet, 1994), and Susan Sheehan's *Is there no place on earth for me?* (1982). A more recent book that focuses specifically on consumers' subjective experience with antidepressant medication in particular is David Karp's *Is it me or my meds?* (2006).

SUMMARY AND FINAL WORDS

In this chapter, we have made social workers aware of the drug development process; summarized how social workers might respond to new treatments and expanded prescription privileges among related professions; emphasized the increased use of herbal medicines for mental and emotional health concerns; and examined concerns about liability. We offered encouragement and resources for helping social workers "keep up" with relevant developments in the use of, and experience with, psychiatric medications.

In spite of many unanswered questions, we still envision social workers that hold fast to the principles of partnership, balance, and integration. We still see social workers who strive to fulfill their unique mission while working side by side with clients, families, prescribers, and other providers. We still see social workers who care deeply about their clients but whose concern is not contingent on the client doing what the social worker or agency thinks he or she should do or not do. They love their clients by abandoning the "I told you so's" and being there over the long haul. Clients, in return, offer us the gift of daily work that has meaning and purpose. Social workers who succeed in achieving the partnership we describe and embrace the roles we put forth are working not only to help improve the quality of their clients' lives but are also modeling the great promise of social work, a profession that is not afraid to pose difficult ethical questions, wrestle with complex cases, and confront its own future with vigor and pride.

TOPICS FOR DISCUSSION
AND LEARNING ACTIVITIES

1. Search the Internet and professional literature to learn about one medication that is in the "trial" stage. Determine how this drug is said to represent an improvement over other drugs in that general category. Find out how much research on human subjects has been done and what the preliminary results are. Be sure to note whether the report is sponsored by a drug company or a less-biased source.

2. Select three herbs or vitamins that are sometimes used to treat mental illnesses. Research the literature for articles on those substances and evaluate the current evidence for and against the effectiveness of that substance.

3. Some researchers are investigating invasive procedures that involve, for example, placing medication "pumps" into the brains of people with depression. Does such a possibility raise any ethical issues for human service professionals in addition to those already discussed in this book?

4. Organize a classroom debate about one or both of the following issues: Should clinical social workers seek psychotropic medication prescription-writing privileges? Should the field develop a post-MSW certificate in psychopharmacology?

5. Locate and rate the quality of several "anti-psychiatry" sites (such as http://www.mindfreedom.org) offering a critical perspective on the information found there? What might family members ask you about it and how would you respond?

Glossary

Absorption The process by which the bloodstream takes in a drug, most commonly through diffusion into the bowel wall. Absorption efficiency is affected by the chemical nature of the drug, its method of delivery, and the time of day, as well as the client's gender and physiology. Intravenous injection provides the most rapid form of drug absorption, followed by intramuscular injection and oral administration.

Acetylcholine (ah-SEAT-till-CO-leen) A type of neurotransmitter released by all neurons; controls the activity of the skeletal muscles, the heartbeat, some glandular functions, mood, sleep, and memory. It is essential to the transmission of brain/spinal-cord messages.

Acute stress disorder A diagnosis based on a person's development of incapacitating symptoms of anxiety within one month of experiencing a traumatic event. The disorder remits within four weeks; if symptoms persist, the person is diagnosed with a different anxiety disorder.

Adherence The degree to which the client follows a prescribed course of medication administration. It is used as an alternative term to "compliance," which has overtones of client passivity and "noncompliance," which has overtones of deviance.

Adjustment disorder According to the DSM-IV, an excessive and maladaptive response, lasting 6 months or less, to an identifiable external stressor. Psychosocial functioning of the individual is impaired beyond what would be expected given the known stressors. The disorder may include symptoms of depression and/or anxiety.

Adverse effects The physical, psychological, or social effects of a medication that are unintentional, unrelated to its therapeutic effect, and unpleasant or potentially harmful to the consumer. These are also referred to as side effects.

Advocacy role The role in which the social worker uses knowledge of law, mental illness, and advocacy strategies to help represent the wishes of the client to some decision-making authority, in hopes of achieving changes in practice and/or policy related to access to care or services.

Affect Feeling, emotion, or mood.

Aftercare Outdated term commonly used in the 1960s and 1970s that refers to all mental health services provided to people with mental illness after they have been discharged from a psychiatric hospital or other inpatient facility. Services are focused on coping, personal growth, skill building, and community adaptation. Terms more commonly used at present include psychosocial rehabilitation, case management, and community care.

Agitation   A state of tension in which a person's anxiety is manifested in increased psycho-motor activity, usually indicating perturbation.

Agoraphobia (ah-GORE-ah-FOE-bee-ah)   According to the DSM-IV, a type of panic disorder that arises when an individual becomes anxious about being alone outside the home to the extent of experiencing an incapacitating fear. The individual suffering from agoraphobia also fears having an unexpected panic attack in a public setting in which withdrawal is difficult or embarrassing.

Agranulocytosis (ay-GRAN-you-low-sigh-TOE-sis)   A dramatic decrease in the num-ber of infection-fighting white blood cells. This is a rare side effect of antipsychotic drugs, most notably of clozapine. Even in the case of clozapine, this disease is said to afflict only 1 to 2% of users, and its ill effects can be reversed if identified early and the drug is discontinued.

Akathisia (ack-ah-THEE-zsha)   The experience of extreme internal restlessness, accom-panied by muscle discomfort. Akathisia is an extrapyramidal side effect of antipsychotic drugs.

Amines (AM-meens)   Organic substances that are the building blocks for amino acids. GABA and glutamate are amino acids.

Amphetamine (am-FET-uh-MEEN)   A chemical substance that is the prototype of the current psychostimulant drugs. It is structurally similar to epinephrine, a natural substance that stimulates the peripheral nervous system.

Anorexia (an-or-EX-ee-ah)   An eating disorder (also known as anorexia nervosa) charac-terized by a self-imposed and deliberate restriction of food intake, regardless of appetite or nutritional needs, and leading to pronounced and physically harmful weight loss, possibly requiring hospitalization.

Anti-anxiety medications   All prescription medications specifically developed, or having demonstrated effectiveness, for alleviating the symptoms of anxiety disorders and other disorders in which anxiety is a prominent symptom. They include the benzodiazepines and buspirone, among other drugs.

Anticholinergic effects (ACEs) (AN-tie-koh-lin-UR-jick)   Adverse effects that result from the suppressive action of certain antipsychotic and antidepressant medications on the action of acetylcholine in the brain and peripheral nervous system. These effects include dry mouth, blurred vision, constipation, and urinary hesitancy.

Anticonvulsant drugs   Those medications, initially developed to treat persons with seizure disorders, that are also effective in the treatment of bipolar disorder. Carbamazepine and valproate are the best known.

Antidepressant drugs   All prescription medications specifically developed, or having dem-onstrated effectiveness, for alleviating the symptoms of depressive disorders. The medications include the monoamine oxidase inhibitors, cyclic antidepressants, and the selective serotonin reuptake inhibitors.

Antihistamines   A class of drugs that can impede the effects of naturally occurring chemical compounds in the body called histamines; these drugs can dilate capillaries, produce head-aches, and decrease blood pressure. They may be employed for their sedative and hypnotic properties and to treat extrapyramidal symptoms.

Antipsychotic drugs   All prescription medications specifically developed, or having dem-onstrated effectiveness, for alleviating the symptoms of psychosis and agitation in disorders such as schizophrenia, schizoaffective disorder, the manic phase of bipolar disorder, and other disorders in which such symptoms may be prominent.

Anxiety   The presence of high levels of physiological and psychological distress unconnected to any immediate threats in the environment. It is distinguished from fear by the fact that the threat is not known and by its serious and negative impact on psychosocial functioning. Anxiety is manifested in feelings of helplessness, self-doubt, self-absorption, and excessive preoccupation with perceived threats in the environment. The disorder may also be expressed as a variety of somatic complaints and symptoms, such as headaches and false "heart attacks," for which no organic cause can be found.

Aplastic anemia (ay-PLAS-tick)   A condition in which the body cannot produce a normal amount of red blood cells or cannot correct a deficiency in hemoglobin. It ordinarily occurs when a drug, toxic agent, radiation, or disease acts to inhibit the red blood cell production.

Arrhythmia (ah-RITH-me-ah)   Variation in the normal rhythm of the heartbeat, which normally ranges between 60 and 90 beats per minute in adults. The term for the high end (above 100 beats per minute) is tachycardia; the term for the low end (below 60 beats per minute) is bradycardia. Tachycardia or bradycardia may indicate heart disease or a drug adverse effect.

Attention-deficit/hyperactivity disorder (ADHD)   A mental disorder characterized by a persistent pattern (6 months or more) of inattention and/or hyperactivity and impulsivity in behavior that is more frequent and severe than typically observed in others at a comparable developmental level. ADHD is most often treated medically with psychostimulant drugs.

Autonomic nervous system (ought-oh-NAW-mick)   Regulates the involuntary processes of the internal organs and blood vessels. Many of the functions controlled by the autonomic nervous system are self-regulating or autonomous. It is comprised of two primary subsystems: the sympathetic and parasympathetic, which sometimes work in cooperation but at other times are antagonistic in their contrasting roles of "arousal" and "rest."

Autoreceptors   Receptors on presynaptic neurons that regulate the release of neurotransmitters.

Axon   A fiber projection from the neuron that serves to transmit signals to adjacent neurons. Contained within an axon are neurotransmitter substances. The axon terminal (or end) is also the site of the neurotransmitter release.

Balanced perspective   Maintaining a balance between competing and sometimes conflicting needs, rights, and aspirations of the individual, family, and society with regard to human behavior. Although the client's perspective should be preeminent, the effective collaboration needed for positive outcomes depends on balancing the perspectives of all stakeholders and participants.

Barbiturates (bar-BIT-sure-its)   A class of medications used as sedatives and hypnotics; popular from the late 19th through the mid-20th centuries. These medications are still available but have largely been replaced by the benzodiazepines.

Basal ganglia (BAY-zill GANG-lee-ah)   Structures located on both sides of the limbic system, involved in the regulation and initiation of movement and in a variety of neuropsychiatric symptoms, including dementia, major depression, and psychosis. These structures may be inadvertently affected by certain psychotropic drugs, resulting in adverse side effects.

Behavior disturbances   Marked changes, typical of psychotic disorders, in a person's behavior patterns. The disturbances may feature withdrawal, apathy, and bizarre actions.

Benzodiazepines (BENS-oh-dye-AZ-uh-peens)   A class of drugs used both as anti-anxiety drugs and as sedatives.

Beta-blockers (BAY-ta)   A class of drugs that reduces the physiological analogs of anxiety by blocking beta receptors in the autonomic nervous system. These drugs block receptors that stimulate the heartbeat and those that dilate blood vessels and air channels in the lungs. Although the drugs are not addicting, they are short-acting and do not remain long in the client's system.

Big Pharma   The pejorative term referring to pharmaceutical companies.

Bioavailability   The amount of a drug that reaches the bloodstream without being metabolized or chemically changed.

Biogenic amines (BYE-oh-JEN-ick AH-meens)   Neurotransmitters synthesized in the nerve terminals (as opposed to the cell body); the neurotransmitters affect nerve functioning through the synapses.

Bipolar disorder (BYE-pole-ur)   A disorder of mood in which, over time, a person experiences one or more manic episodes, usually accompanied by one or more major depressive episodes. There are two types of bipolar disorder. Bipolar I disorder is characterized by one or more manic episodes, usually accompanied by a major depressive episode. Bipolar II disorder is characterized by one or more major depressive episodes accompanied by at least one *hypomanic episode (see also)*.

Blood-brain barrier   A semipermeable barrier between the blood vessels and the brain. The medications and other compounds must be fat-soluble to pass through the parts of the barrier where the capillaries are tightly constricted. In areas where capillaries are not so tightly constricted, water-soluble substances may pass through.

Blood level   The measure of a drug's presence in the blood plasma at a given time.

Blood plasma level (peak)   The point at which the maximum amount of a dose of medication is present in the client's bloodstream.

Borderline personality disorder   Personality disorder characterized by emotional instability, narcissism, controlling behavior, identity diffusion, feelings of loneliness and abandonment, and troubled interpersonal relationships.

Bromides (BROH-mides)   Sedative medications introduced into mental health treatments in the second half of the 19th century and used until the mid-20th century. The chief result of such medications seems to have been the quieting of psychiatric wards rather than improvement of the clients' mental and emotional conditions.

Bulimia (boo-LEE-me-uh)   An eating disorder that is characterized by periods of uncontrollable binge eating followed by purging of ingested food or by other compensatory behaviors so as to prevent weight gain.

Buspirone (BUS-pih-rohn)   An anti-anxiety drug, classified as an azapirone, that, unlike the benzodiazepine drugs, does not carry the risk of physical addiction.

Calcium channel blockers   Primarily used in the treatment of cardiovascular disorders, this class of medications is under investigation as antimanic drugs. If effective, their relatively mild side-effect profiles, including safety during pregnancy, will make them attractive treatment alternatives.

Case management   An approach to social service delivery that attempts to ensure that clients with multiple, complex problems and disabilities receive the services they need in a timely, appropriate fashion.

Catecholamines (kat-ah-KOH-la-meens)   A group of biogenic amines, belonging to the catechol group, that play an important role in nervous system functioning, particularly regarding sleep, mood states, sexual behavior, and aggression.

Cell body   The central area of the neuron in which cell metabolism takes place.

Cell membrane   A barrier that separates the contents of the cell from the fluid enveloping it.

Cementing   A term that refers to any strategy or activity that leads to a better seal or connection between a client and a person or service to whom they are referred.

Central nervous system   The system of nerves comprising the brain and spinal cord that serves as the body's major nerve control system. It directs and regulates all parts of the body in receiving stimuli from external and internal environments, interpreting those stimuli, and organizing the body to react.

Cerebellum   Located in the hindbrain, the cerebellum controls bodily functions that operate below the level of consciousness, including posture, balance, and movement through space. It receives information directly from sense organs, muscles, and joints.

Cerebral cortex   The folded, outermost region of the cerebrum, responsible for primary sensory functioning, visual processing, long-term memory, motor and perceptual coordination and integration, language, thinking, and problem-solving. These functions are managed by the four lobes, each with a distinct function: the frontal lobe, the temporal lobe, the parietal lobe, and the occipital lobe.

Cerebrum   The largest and most imposing structure of the brain. Along with the cerebral cortex, it is the locus of higher mental functions, such as memory, reasoning, language, judgment, and abstract thought.

Chloral hydrate (KLO-roll HIDE-rate)   A generic sedative popular among hospital psychiatrists during the late 19th century for its expediency, despite grave side effects, in producing more manageable behaviors from clients.

Clearance   The measure of the amount of a drug excreted through pores and bodily secretions (such as saliva) in a given amount of time.

Community care   The range of treatments and support services available to clients outside of institutions; the level of care is usually less intensive or restricted. Medication management is often an important part of community care, inasmuch as it helps the client function more independently in the community.

Consultant role   The role in which the social worker helps to evaluate the client's need for medication, makes physician referrals, and consults with the psychiatrist/physician on treatment issues as needed. In this role, the worker avoids taking either adversarial or advocacy stances with respect to client medication adherence.

Continuity of care   The continuous provision of needed services for clients moving from one setting, or care provider, to another, including client and care provider collaboration in relocation, discharge contacts, and planning and follow-up.

Counselor role   The role in which the social worker helps the client problem-solve and make decisions about practical matters related to actual or possible medication use rather than about issues related to mental illness. It is a process of providing clients with information and advice, social skills, problem-solving skills, and assistance with goal-setting.

Cyclic antidepressant drugs (SIGH-click)   A group of antidepressant drugs, mostly developed between the late 1950s and mid-1980s, named for the varying number of chemical rings that determine the drugs' structure. These include heterocyclic, tricyclic, dicyclic, and monocyclic drugs.

Cyclothymia (SIGH-kloh-THIGH-mee-ah)   According to the DSM-IV, a mood disorder characterized by the manifestation of several hypomanic episodes and periods of depressed mood that do not meet the full criteria for mania or major depression. Psychotic symptoms are absent in cyclothymia.

Decision aid   Any type of resource or tool that is explicitly designed to help a person make a decision. Especially being developed and used around patient decisions in health care.

Decision-making (shared)   A collaborative process of decision-making between a client or patient and a practitioner or health care provider, who mutually work to exchange information, share experiences, and clarify preferences to arrive at decisions around care and treatment.

Deinstitutionalization   The mass release of institutionalized persons to the community over the course of three decades (from the 1950s to the 1980s). Specifically, the term refers to the reduced census at state hospitals.

Delusion   A false belief that is maintained even when contradicted by social reality. Delusions may include persecutory (people or forces are attempting to bring one harm), erotomanic (another person is in love with the individual), somatic (pertaining to body functioning), and grandiose beliefs (an exaggerated sense of one's power, knowledge, or identity); thought broadcasting (one's thoughts are overheard by others), thought insertion or withdrawal (others are putting thoughts into or taking thoughts out of one's head), delusions of being controlled (thoughts, feelings, or actions are imposed by an external force), and delusions of reference (neutral events have special significance for the person).

Delusional disorder A cognitive orientation to the external world characterized by *delusions (see above)* that persist for at least one month.

Dendrite (DEN-dright) The short extension of the neuron that is its "receiving end" for signals sent from other cells. The dendrite is located close to the axons of other cells but is separated by a short distance from the synaptic cleft.

Depression A disturbance in mood, characterized by a sadness that is out of the range of normal emotion. It may be primary (autonomous) or secondary to other physical and emotional conditions. "Clinical" depression is characterized by an intensity of mood that seems to permeate all aspects of the person's life.

Distribution The process by which a drug travels from the bloodstream to its target site by one of two routes: dissolving in blood plasma, which is relatively efficient in getting drugs to the target brain site, or attaching to proteins in the blood plasma, which is problematic because of individual differences in protein-binding rates. Only the unbound portion of the drug can cross into the brain. Most psychotropic drugs have a fairly high protein-binding rate.

Dopamine (DOPE-ah-meen) A type of neurotransmitter thought to be involved in disorders of cognition (such as schizophrenia), motor control systems, and limbic activity (emotional behavior).

Dose response The measure of therapeutic effect as a function of dosage.

Drug agonist (AG-un-ist) A drug that acts to facilitate or enhance the effect of another drug.

Drug antagonist A drug that acts against or hinders the effect of another drug.

Drug half-life The time it takes for the concentration of a drug within the body to fall to 50% of its previous (peak) level.

Dysthymic disorder (diss-THIGH-mick) A mood disorder that represents a generally depressed personality style, featuring symptoms that are similar to but less intense than those of major depression. The diagnosis requires two years of a continuously depressed mood (more bad days than good days). It often has an early age of onset (childhood through early adulthood) and produces impairments in school, vocational, and social functioning.

Dystonias (diss-TONE-ee-ahz) Uncoordinated, involuntary twisting movements of the jaw, tongue, or the entire body, produced by sustained muscle spasms.

Educator role The social worker's role of helping clients and their families understand the reasons for medication and other treatments, the benefits and risks of such treatments, and the various treatment options available to them.

Efferent (EHF-ur-rent) Nerve impulse conduction from the central nervous system outward to the periphery (muscles and glands).

Elimination All bodily processes that lower the concentration of a drug in the body. Metabolism, excretion (e.g., bodily wastes), and secretion (e.g., tears) are processes involved in elimination.

Enzymes (EN-zimes) Proteins in the body that facilitate chemical changes but are not affected by those changes. Enzymes are important catalysts for bodily functions, such as metabolism, which in turn can affect drug potency and rates of drug absorption.

Ethnopharmacotherapy (ETH-no-Farm-uh-co-Ther-uh-pee) The process of making decisions about psychotropic drug prescriptions based on an understanding of differences in the ways racial and ethnic groups respond to medication, based on genetic, environmental, and dietary factors.

Euthymic mood state (you-THIGH-mick) A generally positive mood state, or state of emotional wellness, marked by the absence of symptoms of mood disorders.

Excitatory (ex-SITE-uh-tore-ee) Activity or substance that stimulates nerve cell activity.

Excretion (ex-KREE-shun) The process following metabolism, in which the body eliminates a drug, generally through the bile, feces, urine, sweat, saliva, tears, or milk.

Extrapyramidal pathways (EX-truh-pee-RA-mid-ill) Long nerve pathways stretching from the cerebral cortex to the spinal cord and used by motor nerves. This diffuse set of neural structures influences movement, coordination, and posture.

Extrapyramidal symptoms (EPS) Side effects, including akathisia, dystonias, and parkinsonian effects, of antipsychotic drugs and the cyclic antidepressants.

Fat-soluble drugs Drugs that only dissolve in body tissues that absorb fat *(see also water soluble drugs)*. The concentration of fat-soluble drugs varies in proportion to the ratio of fat-to-water in the body. Individuals with proportionately more fat tissues than water tissues will have lower concentrations of fat-soluble drugs than those persons with proportionately more water tissues than fat tissues. Increased age is associated with higher fat-to-water ratios, and women tend to have greater fat-to-water ratios than men. Virtually all antipsychotic drugs are fat-soluble.

Fine motor movements Relating to coordinated small-muscle movements, such as those in the hands.

First-pass metabolism The initial, rather extensive, breakdown of a drug within the liver before the drug reaches the circulatory system. This substantially reduces the amount of drug available for the target site.

Forebrain The last of the three parts of the brain to evolve in embryonic development. The forebrain is highly specialized; it contains the limbic system, which is responsible for emotions and homeostasis of bodily functions and is a target of many psychotropic medications. In the forebrain is the location of the cerebrum and the cerebral cortex, centers of higher functioning processes, such as reasoning, decision-making, and abstract thought.

Frontal lobe One of four major hemispheres in the cerebrum of the human brain. It is located behind the forehead and controls the functions of speech, thought, and consciousness.

Gamma aminobutyric acid (GABA) (GAM-uh am-MEEN-oh-byu-TIE-rick ASS-id) An amino acid and neurotransmitter found throughout the central nervous system; GABA has a vital dampening effect on the excitability of nerve cells.

Generalized anxiety According to the DSM-IV, excessive and pervasive worrying that is difficult to control and that leads to restlessness, lack of focus, tachycardia, irritability, motor tension, heightened apprehension, and vigilance.

Glial cells (GLEE-ahl) A class of cells in the nervous system; these cells support neuron functioning and play an important role in neuronal activity by contributing to blood-brain barrier permeability of compounds entering and leaving the brain and central nervous system.

Glutamate (GLUE-tuh-mate) An excitatory neurotransmitter in the brain and a chemical precursor of GABA; obtained from food and metabolic processes. Glutamate is stored in and released from nerve terminals; its four types of receptors are found on the surfaces of virtually all neurons. Glutamate activity has a major influence on cognitive functions via the cortex and hippocampus, motor functions in the pyramidal and extrapyramidal systems, and on many cerebellar and sensory functions. This neurotransmitter may influence the development of a variety of mental disorders, including schizophrenia and Alzheimer's disease.

Gross motor movements Relating to large-muscle movements, such as those in the thigh.

Hallucinations Sense perceptions of external objects that are not present. These perceptions may be auditory, visual, gustatory (the perception of taste), tactile (feeling an object), somatic (an unreal experience within the body), and olfactory (a false sense of smell).

Health belief model Postulates that individuals will choose a course of action based on their motivational investment in the goal of that action and the perceived relevance of that goal to a recommended behavior. Medication education or any other change-based intervention will be effective insofar as they tap into a personal goal that the learner is motivated to achieve. For instance, a client may be motivated to take medications enabling him or her to work a steady job, which in turn makes it possible to sustain independent living.

Herbs   Low-growing plants with soft, succulent tissues; often used for medicinal purposes.

Hindbrain   The first part of the brain to evolve in embryonic development, the hindbrain consists of the brain stem, reticular formation, and the cerebellum, all of which regulate vital bodily functions (such as breathing rate and heartbeat), posture, balance, kinesthetic motion, and rudimentary memory functions, among others.

Hippocampus (hip-po-CAM-pus)   A brain structure that is part of the limbic system and thus concerned with emotion and motivation. The hippocampus appears to be important in learning and long-term memory; the structure also extends efferent neuron pathways (conduits for nerve impulses) to the hypothalamus.

Hypericum (high-PEAR-uh-some)   The active chemical agent in St.-John's-wort and other herbs that are used to treat mild depression.

Hypertension   High, life-threatening blood pressure, possibly due to hereditary predisposition and/or lifestyle (stress levels), health habits (smoking, overeating, food choices), and emotional habits (expressed and repressed hostility).

Hyperthymia (HIGH-per-THIGH-mee-ah)   An affective state characterized by heightened activity and emotional responses that exceed the norm but fall short of manic proportions.

Hypnotic drugs   Drugs that induce calmness when administered in low doses. Properly administered, hypnotic drugs do not induce sleep.

Hypomanic episode, hypomania (HIGH-po-MANE-ee-uh)   A mild form of mania that may be pleasurable for the person and may result in high social and occupational productivity. Its related behaviors are often socially acceptable and, consequently, the hypomanic person may receive positive reinforcement from friends and employers. The person has high self-esteem, a decreased need for sleep, a high energy level, an increase in overall productivity, and more intensive involvement in pleasurable activities. Hypomania, however, often leads to a full manic episode.

Hypothalamus (HIGH-poh-THAL-ah-muss)   A peanut-sized structure at the base of the brain; involved in the regulation of temperature, balance, appetite, fundamental emotional states, and sexual arousal.

Iatrogenic effects (eye-AT-tro-JEN-ik)   Harmful effects presumed to be inadvertently caused by the treatment itself.

Individual dignity   A fundamental value of the social work profession, arising from the notion that all people are intrinsically equal, regardless of status, income, religion, creed, color, language/dialect, ethnic group, ability, sexual orientation, etc.

Insight   In this context, the awareness of having a mental illness requiring intervention. Insight also means that the client understands that changes or exacerbations in symptoms are indicators that he or she is under stress and is reacting to it. The client is aware that he or she needs to take certain steps to reverse these changes.

Kindling process   Much as the burning of kindling wood and other flammables enables a beginning fire to take hold, this term describes the electrophysiological process of kindling that generates an action potential (electrochemical "fire") in a neuron, following repeated stimulation below the threshold level. Kindling is considered to be a causal process in the onset of a manic episode.

Lag time   The amount of time required for a drug to have its desired effect, depending on factors such as the body's tolerance of the drug; the drug's absorption, protein binding, and metabolizing rate; and individual differences in clients' physiologies.

Loose associations   The result of a disturbance in one's ability to control the innumerable threads that guide conscious thinking. The person's thinking consequently becomes illogical, confused, and incoherent.

Major depression   A mood disorder of at least 2 weeks duration in which a person experiences a depressed mood or loss of interest in nearly all common life activities. Symptoms may include depressed mood, diminished interest or pleasure in most activities, significant and unintentional weight loss or gain, insomnia or hypersomnia, feelings of physical agitation or retardation, loss of energy, feelings of worthlessness or excessive guilt, a diminished ability to think or concentrate, and persistent thoughts of death or suicide.

Mania, manic episode   A physiological and emotional state that persists for at least 2 weeks and in which a person's predominant mood is elevated, expansive, or irritable to a degree that seriously impairs social functioning. This state may be characterized by unrealistically inflated self-esteem, a decreased need for sleep, pressured speech, racing thoughts, distractibility, an increase in unrealistic goal-directed activities, and involvement in activities that have a potential for painful consequences.

Median effective dose   The dose of a drug that is known to produce a therapeutic effect in 50% of consumers. It is sometimes signified as ED50.

Medication (meaning of)   What taking medication symbolizes or conveys to oneself or others, including its emotional and psychological impact of sense of self and identity.

Medication education programs   Mental health service programs that provide clients and their families with information on drug dosages and uses, as well as potential physical, psychological, and social side effects associated with the use of psychotropic medication (*see also Psychoeducational programs*).

Mental hygiene movement   One of several social reform movements in the early 20th century concerned with public education, research, and prevention services. It was begun with the efforts of Clifford Beers, a Yale-educated psychiatric client, who helped found the National Committee on Mental Hygiene in 1909.

Metabolism (met–TAB–oh–liz–um)   The process by which the body breaks down a drug into its chemical derivatives that can then be eliminated from the body. The metabolic process is usually carried out by enzymes in the liver.

Metabolites (meh–TAB–oh–lights)   The chemical by-products of drug metabolism, substances that can still maintain a therapeutic effect on cognition or affect because they can be psychopharmacologically active, despite having been altered.

Midbrain   The second portion of the brain to evolve in embryonic development, the midbrain integrates and monitors many sensory functions and is the center for visual and auditory stimulation. Certain cells in the midbrain serve as relays for information passing from the sense organs to more sophisticated levels of the brain.

Monitor role   The role in which the social worker continues to help determine the outcomes, both positive and negative, of medication on social, psychological, and physical functioning through ongoing client system contact.

Monoamine oxidase (MAO) inhibitors (MAHN–oh–AM–meen OX–id–aze)   A class of drugs that were developed in the 1950s as the first antidepressants. These drugs are not widely used today because of the strict dietary regimes required to preclude adverse physical effects. They have been shown, however, to relieve some depressions that are not responsive to other antidepressants. There are two types of MAO inhibitors: type A, which breaks down norepinephrine and serotonin, and type B, which breaks down dopamine. Medications that selectively impact type A, still in development, may not produce the side effect of tyramine deamination.

Monoamines (MAHN–oh–AM–meens)   Neurotransmitters with a single amine (organic compound). This group includes dopamine, norepinephrine, epinephrine, acetylcholine, and serotonin.

Mood disorders   While most mental disorders negatively impact both the cognitive and emotional aspects of a person's life, these disorders most dramatically impact one's moods. Examples include major depression and generalized anxiety disorder.

Mood stabilizers   All prescription medications that have been specifically developed, or have demonstrated effectiveness, for stabilizing the moods of persons with bipolar disorder. Lithium, carbamazepine, and valproate are the most common mood stabilizers.

Moral treatment (of mental illness)   The predominant mental illness treatment model in America for the first half of the 19th century, based upon the notion that active rehabilitation and a structured life would help to steady uncontrolled thoughts and "problematic" emotions. Structured activities commonly included occupational therapy, religious exercises, sports, amusements, and reading. The typical time frame for such treatment was 6 weeks to 3 months.

Muscles (smooth)   Those muscles in the body that function involuntarily.

Narcissism (NAHR-siss-is-um)   Egocentrism, or self-centeredness, and self-preoccupation of excessive proportions.

Narcissistic injury (NAHR-siss-SISS-tick)   Occurs when an individual interprets a situation or event as a personal attack or a condemnation that wounds his or her core being. An individual with a mental illness who interprets the prescription of antipsychotic drugs as proof that "I must be sicker than I thought I was" has suffered a narcissistic injury.

Negative symptoms (of schizophrenia)   Those symptoms that represent a diminution of what would be considered normal affective behavior, including flat or blunted affect (the absence of expression), social withdrawal, non-communication, anhedonia (blandness) or passivity, and ambivalence in decision making. (*see also Positive symptoms*)

Neonatal withdrawal syndrome (NEE-oh-NATE-al)   Drug withdrawal symptoms experienced by a newborn child because of drug exposure and addiction in utero. Symptoms include insomnia, increased respiratory efforts and heart rate, and spontaneous body tremors. Behaviors that mark neonatal drug withdrawal symptoms can be recorded using the Neonatal Abstinence Score Tool.

Nervous system   The body's information-processing unit consisting of 100 billion nerve cells and the "action site" for psychotropic medications. It is comprised of the entire system of neurons and their supporting material. The nervous system is commonly divided into three branches: the central nervous system (brain and spinal cord), the peripheral nervous system (cranial, spinal nerves, and peripheral ganglia), and the autonomic nervous system (internal organs). The autonomic nervous system includes the sympathetic and the parasympathetic subsystems.

Neuroeconomics   The interdisciplinary study of the biological aspects of decision-making, specifically integrating neuroscience and behavioral economics.

Neurohormones (NEW-row-HOAR-moans)   Chemical messengers that are released into the bloodstream. They can be chemically indistinguishable from neurotransmitters.

Neuroleptic malignant syndrome (new-row-LEHP-tick)   A potentially fatal but rare toxic complication of antipsychotic drug treatment; usually occurs within 2 weeks of drug initiation. Symptoms include high fever, muscle rigidity, instability of the autonomic nervous system (e.g., rapid heartbeat), and alternating levels of consciousness (from confusion to coma).

Neuron (NEW-rahn)   A nerve cell, consisting of a cell body (nucleus and cytoplasm), a single axon, and several branched dendrites.

Neurotransmitter (NEW-row-TRANS-mit-er)   A chemical found in nerve cells; acts as a messenger by carrying electrical impulses between cells and along cell pathways. Some principle neurotransmitters in the nervous system include GABA, dopamine, serotonin, norepinephrine, acetylcholine, and glutamate.

Norepinephrine (NOR-epp-in-EH-frin)   A type of neurotransmitter secreted by the adrenal glands in response to arousal-provoking events such as stress. It influences affective behavior, alertness, anxiety, and tension.

Obsessive-compulsive disorder   An anxiety disorder characterized by uncontrollable recurrent thoughts or compulsive behaviors that are time-consuming and cause significant distress or social impairment.

Occipital lobes (ox-SIP-it-all)   An area of the cerebral cortex; serves as the foremost processing center for visual signals.

Organic mental disorders   Mental disorders that result from the temporary or permanent dysfunction of brain tissue; attributable to specific organic factors, such as aging, drug use, stroke, and metabolic disorders.

Orthostatic hypotension (OAR-thow-STAT-ick HI-poe-TEN-shun)   An abrupt lowering of blood pressure; can cause fainting, dizziness upon standing, or falling, particularly if the client is elderly. It is most commonly a side effect of some low-potency antipsychotic drugs, usually occurring during the early phase of treatment, before the body has had time to develop a tolerance.

Panic disorder   A condition in which panic attacks are experienced, followed by at least one month of persistent concerns about having another attack, concerns about the implications of the attack, or significant behavioral changes related to the attack. A panic attack is characterized by a period of intense fear or physiological discomfort with sudden onset and rapid buildup to a peak (usually within 10 minutes). The attack is often accompanied by a sense of imminent danger or impending doom and an urge to escape the situation.

Paranoia, paranoid ideation   A cognitive state that features systematized delusions and includes emotional experiences and behavior congruent with those delusions. The ideas and beliefs do not include hallucinations, and the person's intelligence is unaffected. The condition may be related to a mental disorder, such as a delusional disorder or schizophrenia or to a personality disorder.

Parasympathetic nervous system (PAIR-ah-SIMP-ah-THEH-tick)   That part of the autonomic nervous system that functions to support "at-rest" bodily processes, such as digestion. It is prominent in the body's conservation of energy reserves.

Parietal lobe (purr-EYE-it-ahl)   An area of the cerebral cortex responsible for the intellectual processing of sensory information (visual, tactile, auditory) and also for verbal and visual-spatial processing.

Parkinsonian effects (PARK-in-SO-nee-an)   Adverse effects resulting from some antipsychotic medications that mirror Parkinson's disease symptoms, such as reduction in motor abilities and coordination, shuffling gait, drooling, muscle rigidity, and tremors. The effect usually occurs within 5 to 90 days of drug initiation.

Partnership model of practice   A model of clinical practice with clients and families in which the social worker forges a nonthreatening alliance with the client/family that validates and respects their perspectives, concerns, strengths, and aspirations and that features a mutual, collaborative, and action-oriented helping process. This model is client-centered in its focus and in its goals, advocating for and representing the client system's needs, wants, and aspirations.

Peptides   Strings of amino acids.

Peripheral nervous system (purr-IF-ur-all)   The system of neurons branching from the central nervous system into the body from the lower brain and spinal cord. These nerves influence such sensations and actions as sight, smell, chewing and swallowing, and muscle movement.

Personality disorder   According to the DSM-IV, a personality is disordered when traits are inflexible, maladaptive, and cause significant distress or functional impairment. The idea of a personality as disordered is controversial among some human service professionals.

Pharmacodynamics (FARM-ah-co-dye-NAM-icks)   The study of the effects of a drug on the body. Factors affecting the effects of the drug include client age, gender, physical characteristics, and any organic pathologies.

Pharmacogenomics (Farm-uh-COE-jen-OH-mix)   A branch of pharmacology that considers the influence of genetic variation in drug response.

Pharmacokinetics (FARM-ah-co-kin-ET-icks)   All issues regarding how the human body handles a drug; in particular, the blood plasma concentration of a drug. Pharmacokinetics refers to the absorption, distribution, metabolism, and excretion of the medication.

Phenothiazine (FEE-no-THIGH-ah-zeen)   A type of antipsychotic drug used in the treatment of schizophrenia and other psychotic disorders.

Phobia (FOE-be-uh)   An irrational fear, manifesting a high level of anxiety that results in a person's conscious avoidance of the feared object, activity, or situation. Phobias may be specific (of birds, for example) or general (open spaces).

Physician's assistant role   A traditional role that social workers may still play but that was played most often through the 1970s when collaborating with physicians or psychiatrists. The social worker prepares the client for referral to the physician and enforces the directives of the physician with the client.

Placebo (pluh-SEE-bowe)   Any medication or inert substance that, by design or seren-dipity, relieves a consumer's symptoms not by pharmacologic action but by reinforcing the consumer's favorable expectancies about the intervention.

Polymorphisms (paul-ee-MORE-fizz-ums)   Naturally occurring variants in the structures of genes that may influence one's response to a psychotropic medication.

Polypharmacy (PAH-lee-FARM-ah-see)   The use of more than one drug for treatment of the same ailment.

Positive symptoms (of psychosis)   Those symptoms that represent bizarre exaggerations of normal behavior, including hallucinations, delusions, disorganized thought processes, and tendencies toward agitation.

Postpartum psychosis   A psychotic episode of the mother following childbirth, sometimes called puerperal psychosis. This disorder afflicts mothers within one month of delivery. Its causes are thought to include personality factors, life stressors, and endocrinological factors.

Postsynaptic membrane (post-sin-AP-tick)   The wall of the dendrite cell body, located at the opposite side of the synaptic cleft from the axon, on which receptor sites are located to receive neurotransmitter input and to pass an impulse through the rest of the cell.

Posttraumatic stress disorder (PTSD)   An emotional disorder in which, following exposure to a traumatic event, a person persistently reexperiences the event through memo-ries, dreams, or intense psychological distress. The person subsequently tends to avoid any stimuli associated with the trauma.

Potency   A drug's relative strength in standard units of measure (e.g., milligrams). Low-potency drugs, such as chlorpromazine, are given in high milligram amounts, while high-potency drugs, such as haloperidol, are given in low milligram doses.

Presynaptic terminal (pree-sin-AP-tick)   An axon ending that extends to the synapse and contains neurotransmitters to be released into the synaptic cleft during neuron activation.

Problem-solving   A systematic approach to helping clients become more effective prob-lem solvers. It includes six steps: (a) defining the problem, (b) generating possible solutions, (c) evaluating the pros and cons of each solution, (d) choosing the "best" solution, (e) planning how to carry out the solution, and (f) reviewing implementation.

Prodromal (pro-DRO-mull)   The phase during which a deteriorating state of health is recognized that later culminates in full-blown illness. During this phase there are subtle warning signs of the impending illness, indicators such as withdrawal, bizarre thoughts, or other behaviors recognized as precursors of a psychotic episode.

Progressivism   An early 20th-century middle-class movement of social reforms aimed at promoting harmony among social classes and races. Progressivism was a response to social change that threatened the upheaval of middle-class values, such as rationality, efficiency, and incremental upward mobility. Social work is, in part, an outgrowth of progressivism, given the profession's roots in "friendly visitors" to the urban poor to promote self-improvement and social harmony.

Prophylaxis (PRO-fill-AX-is)   Prevention of the recurrence of symptoms of a mental disorder with the ongoing supervised use of medications following the stabilization of symptoms. Dosages are generally lower during prophylaxis than during the active phase of an illness.

Protein binding   One of the routes of drug transport in the bloodstream, involving the attachment of the drug to plasma proteins in the blood. Drugs bound to the plasma are essentially lost, because only the unbound portion of the drug can pass into the brain. The protein-binding rate of drugs differs and has a corresponding effect on the amount of drug available for action.

Psychiatric social work   A term to describe a specialized area of social work practice, first developed in the early 20th century, that focuses on people who have mental illnesses or severe emotional distress.

Psychoeducational programs   Time-limited, open or closed groups conducted by mental health professionals for the purposes of educating and providing support to clients, family members, or significant other persons regarding issues related to mental illness, psychotropic medication, and other professional interventions.

Psychological side effects   The negative impact of taking medication on a client's self-image as a competent, self-directed individual.

Psychopharmacology   The study of drugs that affect thinking, emotion, and behavior.

Psychosocial rehabilitation   A global term that refers to all mental health services provided toward the goal of restoring the client to a level of functioning that will permit him or her to resume life in the community. This process operates on the premise that the best way to help clients progress toward greater self-sufficiency is to help them develop skills and competencies on individual, interpersonal, and social levels. Clients participate in structured activities aimed at improving emotional and cognitive resources, often including vocational training and counseling.

Psychostimulant drugs   All prescription medications that have been specifically developed, or have demonstrated effectiveness, for controlling the symptoms of attention-deficit/hyperactivity disorder and narcolepsy.

Psychotic disorders   A major group of mental disorders characterized in part by delusions, catatonic or grossly disorganized behavior, and hallucinations. Psychotic disorders are identi-fied in the DSM-IV as falling into two broad categories of schizophrenia and other psychotic disorders. The category of other psychotic disorders includes schizoaffective disorder, schizo-phreniform disorder, delusional disorder, brief psychotic disorder, shared psychotic disorder, psychotic disorder due to a general medical condition, and substance-induced psychotic disorder.

Psychotropic drugs (SIKE-oh-TROPE-ick)   Drugs that alter psychological functioning, mood, and thoughts.

Pyramidal nerve pathways (purr-RA-mid-ahl)   Long nerve pathways stretching from the cerebral cortex to the spinal cord. These are one of two pathways taken by motor nerves (the other being extrapyramidal). Pyramidal pathways carry messages to and from the central nervous system to control groups of muscles that contract simultaneously, such as those involved in gripping a pen.

Rapid cycling   A characteristic of approximately 10% of persons with bipolar disorder, in which over a 12-month period they experience four or more manic or depressive cycles.

Receptors   Special receiving areas in the dendrite, composed of nerve cell membranes that are partially exposed to the extracellular fluid and that recognize neuromessengers.

Remission   A state of cognitive, emotional, and behavioral functioning in which the symptoms of a mental illness have subsided to a significant degree. This state may be temporary or permanent.

Researcher role   The role of the social worker in documenting how medications affect the lives of clients and their families and in expanding the existing knowledge base of psycho-pharmacology. This role also encompasses collaborations with researchers in other disciplines.

Responder, response (partial)   The experience of a reduction in some symptoms of a mental disorder with the use of psychotropic medication, but the degree of symptom reduction is less than what was desired or what is typical for other users of the medication who have the same symptom profile.

Reticular formation (reh-TICK-you-lar)   A diffuse network of neurons that traces the midline of the brain stem, sending impulses up the brain stem to the cerebral cortex. This structure can activate the cortex into a state of wakefulness and transmits information about the environment. Some psychiatric motivational and arousal disorders can be attributed to problems in this area.

Reuptake   The process by which a neuron reabsorbs a neurotransmitter after it has been released into the synapse.

Schizoaffective disorder (SKIZ-oh-aff-FECK-tiv)   Defined by the DSM-IV as a continuous period of illness during which there are some symptoms of schizophrenia, such as delusions, hallucinations, grossly disorganized behavior; these symptoms occur concurrently with either a major depressive episode, a manic episode, or a mixed episode.

Schizophrenia (SKIZ-oh-FREN-ee-ah)   A disorder of the brain characterized by abnormal patterns of thought and perception as inferred from language and behavior. Schizophrenia is characterized by at least 6 months of continuous symptoms, including two or more positive symptoms (delusions, hallucinations, disorganized speech, and disorganized or catatonic behavior) for at least 1 month. There are five subtypes of schizophrenia: paranoid, disorganized, catatonic, undifferentiated, and residual.

Schizophreniform disorder (SKIZ-oh-FREN-ih-form)   A mental disorder that shares the symptomatology of schizophrenia but not the duration, lasting from 2 weeks to 6 months.

Sedation   A common effect of some psychotropic drugs; the milder form leads to reduced excitability and anxiety and the stronger form produces hypnotic (sleep-inducing) effects.

Sedative (SAID-uh-tiv)   Any medication that produces a state of decreased responsiveness to stimuli. The state may or may not be experienced as drowsiness.

Self-determination   A fundamental value of the social work profession arising from the belief that each individual is best equipped and, except for rare instances, most competent to judge what is best for himself or herself.

Self-monitoring (drug treatment)   The role of the client in noting and systematically recording the effects of drug treatment. The client's monitoring enables the client and the professional to assess the impact of taking a psychotropic drug. Self-monitoring includes observations of symptoms, medication-taking times, dosage, frequency, and adverse effects.

Serotonin (sair-ah-TONE-in)   A type of neurotransmitter that impacts sensory processes, muscular activity, and cognition. It is a factor in states of consciousness, basic bodily functions, complex sensory and motor activities, and mood. Serotonin is thought to be implicated in mood disorders, aggression, and schizophrenia.

Serotonin-reuptake inhibitors, serotonin-specific drugs   The newest group of antidepressant medications that functions by suppressing the reuptake or reabsorption of serotonin by the nerve cell. Sometimes called "atypical" because of their chemical distinctiveness from other antidepressants, these drugs cause less pronounced anticholinergic effects. As a result, they are more popular with many physicians and clients than many other antidepressants.

Sexual dysfunction   Changes in sexual desire in men and women, in addition to impotence in men and orgasmic dysfunction in women, that may result from the use of some psychotropic medications.

Side effects   *See Adverse effects.*

Skills training   A systematic approach to helping a client develop greater life skills, including these six steps: (a) discussing the rationale for the skill, (b) identifying the components of the skill, (c) modeling the skill, (d) role playing each skill component with the client, (e) evaluating the role play, and (f) applying the skill in real life.

Social psychiatry   A perspective on the practice of psychiatry developed by Adolf Meyer in the early 20th century. In Meyer's opinion, psychiatry needed to attend to prevention, teaching, and research in the service of comprehensive community treatment. He is said to have perceived a critical role for social workers in helping to bring about a suitable aftercare environment for clients.

Social side effects   The interpersonal, community, and organizational barriers that clients encounter when they take psychotropic drugs and are thus labeled as having mental illness.

Spinal cord   A long column of neural tissue that runs from the brain stem to the base of the spine. This structure is part of the central nervous system.

Stabilization   A stage in the process of recovery from an episode of mental illness in which the client's more extreme symptoms subside. Social functioning returns to normal within the limits of a protective, supportive environment, but the client requires ongoing intervention because he or she may still be at risk for relapse.

Steady state   The point at which a consistent level of medication is present in the bloodstream, such that the amount ingested is equal to the amount eliminated.

Stress–diathesis model (dye-ATH-uh-sis)   A model for understanding mental illness that takes into account the interplay between biological and environmental influences. The model asserts that while the causes of mental illness seem to be associated with genetic factors as well as abnormalities in brain chemistry and structure, the course of these disorders is in part related to environmental factors, such as skills in coping, social competence, and social support.

Sympathetic system   The part of the autonomic nervous system that functions during the expenditure of energy. The sympathetic system has an arousal function for the internal organs.

Sympathomimetic drugs (sim-PATH-oh-mi-MET-ick)   See *Psychostimulant drugs.*

Synapse (SIN-aps)   The bridge between one nerve cell and the next. Neurotransmitters flow across this space. The synapse is not a physical structure, but rather a point of juncture marked by the synaptic cleft (or gap).

Synaptic cleft   The gap between the axon of a sending neuron and the dendrite of a receiving neuron.

Synaptic vesicles   Small areas located on axon terminals; contain the molecules of a neurotransmitter produced in the cell body.

Tachycardia (tack-ah-CARD-ee-ah)   A form of heart arrhythmia; unusually rapid heartbeat (greater than 100 beats per minute) that may result from the side effects of antidepressant drugs acting on the autonomic nervous system.

Tardive dyskinesia (TAR-dive diss-kin-EASE-yah)   A serious and generally irreversible adverse effect of antipsychotic drugs. The symptoms of coordinated but involuntary rhythmic movements are commonly seen in facial movements, such as grimacing and lip tremors and in finger, hand, and trunk movements. Controversy exists regarding its prevalence. The longer a client takes antipsychotic drugs, the greater the likelihood that he or she may develop tardive dyskinesia.

Temporal lobe (TEM-pore-all)   One of four major hemispheres in the cerebrum of the human brain; located beneath the frontal lobe; it regulates memory, smell functions, and some aspects of speech.

Teratogenic drugs (tare-AT-uh-JEN-ick)   Any drug that carries a potential to cause damage to the fetus in a pregnant woman.

Thalamus (THOW-luh-muss)   A sensory relay station (for all but the olfactory senses) and an important integration and processing center for information passing from the lower body to the brain. The structure is essential to the perception of pain and helps to initiate consciousness and organize sensory signals.

Therapeutic index   A measure of the range of blood levels within which a drug's effects on the consumer are relatively safe. Drugs with a low therapeutic index, such as lithium, must be very closely monitored to avoid toxicity.

Thought disorders   While most mental disorders negatively impact both the cognitive and emotional aspects of a person's life, these disorders most dramatically impact one's cognitive functioning. Examples include schizophrenia and delusional disorders.

Three-party treatment relationships   The network of relationships in the treatment context including the client, medication prescriber (physician), and the social worker.

Tolerance   A person's reduced responsiveness to a drug as a function of the reduced sensitivity of significant nerve receptors over time.

Toxicity   A physical state in which the amount of an active drug in the body exceeds the amount required for therapeutic effect and which puts the consumer at risk for serious adverse effects.

Two-track model of treatment   The treatment of mental illness proceeding along two parallel tracks, including a medical track (biological) and a psychological or psychosocial track.

Vitamins   Organic substances (there are 13 in total) that are essential in minute amounts for the body's normal growth and activity; they help to convert foods into energy and tissues.

Water-soluble drugs   Drugs that dissolve in the water content of the body (other drugs dissolve in the body's fatty tissue). The concentration of water-soluble drugs varies in proportion to the ratio of water to fat in the body. Individuals with proportionately more fat than water will have lower concentrations of water-soluble drugs relative to those individuals with proportionately more fat. Increased age is associated with higher fat-to-water ratios, and women tend to have greater fat-to-water ratios than men. Lithium is the best example of a water-soluble psychotropic drug.

References

Abou, S. M. T., & Coppen, A. (1986). The biology of folate in depression: Implications for nutritional hypothesis of the psychoses. *Journal of Psychiatric Research, 20*(2), 91–101.

Abramson, J. S., & Mizrahi, T. (2003). Understanding collaboration between social workers and physicians: Application of a typology. *Social Work in Health Care, 37*(2), 71–100.

Abroms, G., & Greenfield, N. (1973). Drug-prescribing and the nonmedical therapist. *Clinical Social Work Journal, 1,* 132–134.

Adams, J. R., & Drake, R. E. (2006). Shared decision-making and evidence-based practice. *Community Mental Health Journal, 42*(1), 87–105.

Adams, S. G., & Howe, J. T. (1993). Predicting medication compliance in a psychotic population. *Journal of Nervous and Mental Disease, 181,* 558–560.

Addington, D., Williams, R., Lapierre, Y., & el-Guebaly, N. (1997). Placebos in clinical trials of psychotropic medication. *Canadian Journal of Psychiatry, 42*(3), 16–22.

Adelman, S. A. (1985). Pills as transitional objects: A dynamic understanding of the use of medication in psychotherapy. *Psychiatry, 48,* 246–253.

Administration for Children and Families (2010). *Child maltreatment 2009.* Washington, DC: Department of Health and Human Services

Agarwal, M. R., Sharma, V. K., Kishore-Kumar, K. V., & Lowe, D. (1998). Non-compliance with treatment in patients suffering from schizophrenia: A study to evaluate possible contributing factors. *International Journal of Social Psychiatry, 44*(2), 92–106.

Ahn, M. S., Yakutis, L., & Frazier, J. A. (2012). Use of antidepressants in children and adolescents. In A. J. Rothschild (Ed.), *The evidence-based guide to antidepressant medications* (pp. 189–225). Arlington, VA: American Psychiatric Publishing, Inc.

Aldebot, S., de Mamani, A. G., & Weisman, R. (2009). Denial and acceptance coping styles and medication adherence in schizophrenia. *Journal of Nervous and Mental Disease, 197*(8), 580–584.

Aldridge, M. A. (2012). Addressing non-adherence to antipsychotic medication: A harm-reduction approach. *Journal of Psychiatric and Mental Health Nursing, 19,* 85–96.

Altman, S., Haeri, S., Cohen, L. J., Ten, A., Barron, E., Galynker, I. I., et al. (2006). Predictors of relapse in bipolar disorder: A review. *Journal of Psychiatric Practice, 12*(5), 269–282.

American Psychiatric Association (APA). (2000). *Diagnostic and statistical manual of mental disorders* (4th ed., revised). Washington, DC: Author.

American Psychological Association (2006). *Report of the working group on psychotropic medications for children and adolescents.* Washington, DC: Author.

Anderson, H. (2008). Collaborative therapy. In K. Jordan (Ed.), *The quick theory reference guide: A resource for expert and novice mental health professionals* (pp. 417–426). Hauppauge, New York: Nova Science Publishers.

Andreasen, N. C. (1982). Negative symptoms of schizophrenia: Definition and reliability. *Archives of General Psychiatry, 39*, 784–788.

Andreasen, N. C., & Olsen, S. (1982). Negative vs. positive schizophrenia: Definition and validation. *Archives of General Psychiatry, 39*, 789–794.

Angell, M. (2004). *The truth about drug companies: How they deceive us and what to do about it.* New York: Random House.

Anuradha, K. (2004). Empowering families with mentally ill members: A strengths perspective. *International Journal for the Advancement of Counselling, 26*(4), 383–391.

Applegate, J. S., & Shapiro, J. R. (2005). *Neurobiology for clinical social work: Theory and practice.* New York: W.W. Norton.

Armstrong, L. (1993). *And they call it help: The psychiatric policing of America's children.* New York: Addison-Wesley.

Ascher-Svanum, H., Lafuze, J. E., Barrickman, P. J., Van Dusen, C., & Fompa-Loy, J. (1997). Educational needs of families of mentally ill adults. *Psychiatric Services, 48*, 1072–1074.

Asnaani, A., Richey, J. A., Dimaite, R., Hinton, D. E., Hofmann, S. G. (2010). A cross-ethnic comparison of lifetime prevalence rates of anxiety disorders. *Journal of Nervous and Mental Disease, 198*(8), 551–555.

Auge, M., & Herzlech, C. (Eds.). (1998). *The meaning of illness: Anthropology, history, and sociology.* New York: Harwood.

Awad, A. G., Voruganti, L. N., Heslegrave, R. J., & Hogan, T. P. (1996). Assessment of patient's subjective experience in acute neuroleptic treatment: Implications for compliance and outcome. *International Clinical Psychopharmacology, 11* (Suppl. 2), 55–59.

Ax, R. K., Fagan, T. J., & Resnick, R. J. (2009). Predoctoral prescriptive authority training: The rationale and a combined model. *Psychological Services, 6*(1), 85–95.

Bachur, J. A. (1986). A social work perspective. *The Gerontologist, 26*, 614–617.

Bainbridge, J. L., Page, R. L., & Ruscin, J. M. (2008). Elucidating the mechanism of action and potential interactions of MAO-B inhibitors. *Neurologic Clinics, 26*(3, Suppl. 1), S85–S96.

Baird, C. (2011). Prescription drug abuse: Just the facts.. *Journal of Addictions Nursing, 22*(1–2), 72–74.

Baker, F. M. (1994). Psychiatric treatment of older African Americans. *Hospital & Community Psychiatry, 45*, 32–37.

Baldessarini, R. J., Tondo, L., Davis, P., Pompili, M., Goodwin, F. K., & Henne, J. (2006). Decreased risk of suicides and attempts during long-term lithium treatment: A meta-analytic review. *Bipolar Disorders, 2006, 8*[5, pt 2], 625–639.

Balon, R. (2001). Positive and negative aspects of split treatment. *Psychiatric Annals, 31*(10), 598–603.

Barker, R. L. (1998). *The social work dictionary* (7th ed.) (p. 35). Silver Spring, MD: National Association of Social Workers.

Barkley, R. A., Conners, C. K., Barclay, A., Gadow, K., Gittleman, R., Sprague, R., & Swanson, J. (1991). *Task force report: The appropriate role of clinical child psychologists in the prescribing of psychoactive medication for children.* Washington, DC: American Psychological Association.

Barnes, T. R. E. (1989). A rating scale for drug-induced akathisia. *British Journal of Psychiatry, 154*, 672–676.

Barnett, K. B. (2012). *Dosed: The medication generation grows up.* Boston: Beacon Press.

Barondes, S. H. (1994). Thinking about Prozac. *Science, 263*(5150), 1102–1103.

Barsky, A. E. (2010). *Ethics and values in social work: An integrated approach for a comprehensive curriculum.* New York: Oxford University Press.

Bassman, R. (2005). Mental illness and the freedom to refuse treatment: Privilege or right. *Professional Psychology: Research and Practice, 36*(5), 488–497.

Baumesiter, A. A., & Francis, J. L. (2002). Historical development of the dopamine hypothesis of schizophrenia. *Journal of the History of the Neurosciences, 11*(3), 265–277.

Beck, E. M., Cavelati, M., Kvrgic, S., Kleim, B., & Vauth, R. (2011). Are we addressing the 'right stuff' to enhance adherence in schizophrenia? Understanding the role of insight and attitudes towards medication. *Schizophrenia Research, 132*(1), 42–49.

Beck, J. S. (2001). A cognitive therapy approach to medication compliance. In J. Kay (Ed.), *Review of Psychiatry, 20*(2), (pp. 113–141). Washington, DC: American Psychiatric Association.

Beitman, B. D., Blinder, B. J., Thase, M. E., Riba, M., & Safer, D. L. (2003). *Integrating psychotherapy and pharmacotherapy: Dissolving the mind–brain barrier.* New York: Norton.

Beitman, B. D., & Klerman, G. L. (Eds.). (1991). *Integrating pharmacotherapy and psychotherapy.* Washington, DC: American Psychiatric Press.

Bell, A. C., & D'Zurilla, T. J. (2009). Problem-solving therapy for depression: A meta-analysis. *Clinical Psychology Review, 29*(4), 348–353.

Ben Armor, L. (2012). Antipsychotics in pediatric and adolescent patients: A review of comparative safety data. *Journal of Affective Disorders, 138*(Suppl.), S22–S30.

Benítez, C. I. P., Smith, K., Vasile, R. G., Rende, R., Edelen, M. O., & Keller, M. B. (2008). Use of benzodiazepines and selective serotonin reuptake inhibitors in middle-aged and older adults with anxiety disorders: A longitudinal and prospective study. *American Journal of Geriatric Psychiatry, 16*(1), 5–13.

Bentley, K. J. (2010). The meaning of psychiatric medication in a residential program for adults with serious mental illness. *Qualitative Social Work, 9*(4), 479–499.

Bentley, K. J. (1997). Should clinical social workers seek psychotropic medication privileges? No! In B. Thyer (Ed.), *Controversial issues in social work practice* (pp. 159–164). Boston: Allyn/Bacon.

Bentley, K. J. (1991). Voluntary recruitment of psychiatric patients for clinical research. *International Journal of Mental Health, 20,* 94–107.

Bentley, K. J., & Collins, K. (2013). Psychopharmacological treatment for child and adolescent mental disorders. In C. Franklin, M. B. Harris, & P. A. Meares (Eds.), *The school services sourcebook: A guide for school-based professionals* (2nd ed.) (pp. 53–72). New York: Oxford University Press.

Bentley, K. J., & Reeves, J. (1992). Integrating psychopharmacology into social work curriculum: Suggested content and resources. *Journal of Teaching in Social Work, 6,* 41–48.

Bentley, K. J., Rosenson, M., & Zito, J. (1990). Promoting medication compliance: Strategies for working with families of mentally ill people. *Social Work, 35,* 274–277.

Bentley, K. J., & Walsh, J. (1998). Advances in psychopharmacology and psychosocial aspects of medication management: A review for social workers. In J. B. W. Williams & K. Ell (Eds.), *Recent advances in mental health research: Implications for social workers* (pp. 309–342). Silver Spring, MD: National Association of Social Workers.

Bentley, K. J., Walsh, J., & Farmer, R. (2005a). Roles and activities of social workers with psychiatric medication: Results of a national survey. *Social Work, 50,* 295-303.

Bentley, K. J., Walsh, J. & Farmer, R. (2005b). Referring clients for psychiatric medication: Best practices for social workers. *Best Practices in Mental Health, 1,* 59-71.

Berger, F. M. (1970). Anxiety and the discovery of the tranquilizers. In F. J. Ayd & R. Blackwell (Eds.), *Discoveries in biological psychiatry* (pp. 115–129). Philadelphia: J. B. Lippincott.

Bernstein, G. A., Crosby, R. D., Perwien, A. R., & Borchardt, C. M. (1996). Anxiety rating for children-revised: Reliability and validity. *Journal of Anxiety Disorders, 10*(2), 97–114.

Beyer, B. (1990). What philosophy offers to the teaching of thinking. *Educational Leadership, 47*(5), 55–60.

Bhattacharjee J., & El-sayeh, H. G. (2010). Aripiprazole versus typical antipsychotic

drugs for schizophrenia. *Cochrane Collaboration,* DOI: 10.1002/14651858
.CD006617.pub3.

Bigelow, L. B., & Berthot, B. D. (1989). The psychiatric symptom assessment scale (PSAS). *Psychopharmacology Bulletin, 25*(2), 168–179.

Bisonó, A. M., Manuel, J. K., & Forcehimes, A. A. (2006). In W. T. O'Donohue & E. R. Levensky (Eds.), *Promoting treatment adherence: A practical handbook for health care providers* (pp. 71–84). Thousand Oaks, CA: Sage Publications.

Blanco, C., Patel, S. R., Liu, L., Jiang, H., Lewis-Fernandez, R., Schmidt, A. B., et al. (2007). National trends in ethnic disparities in health care. *Medical Care, 45*(11), 1012–1019.

Blech, J. (2006). *Inventing disease and pushing pills: Pharmaceutical companies and the medicalization of normal life.* London: Routledge.

Bond, A. L., & Lader, M. H. (1996). *Understanding drug treatment in mental health care.* West Sussex, England: John Wiley & Sons.

Botsford, A. L., & Rule, D. (2004). Evaluation of a group intervention to assist aging patients with permanency planning for an adult offspring with special needs. *Social Work, 49*(3), 423–431.

Brabbins, C., Butleer, J., & Bentall, R. (1996). Consent to neuroleptic medication for schizophrenia: Clinical, ethical and legal issues. *British Journal of Psychiatry, 168,* 540–544.

Bradley, S. (2003). The psychology of the psychotherapist-psychopharmacology triangle: The client, the clinicians and the medication. *Social Work in Mental Health, 1*(4), 29–50.

Bradley, S. (1990). Non-physician psychotherapist—physician pharmacotherapist: A new model for concurrent treatment. *Psychiatric Clinics of North America, 13*(2), 307–322.

Breggin, P., & Cohen, D. (2007). *Your drug may be your problem: How and why to stop taking psychiatric medication* (2nd ed.). New York: DaCapo Press.

Breggin, P. R. (2008). *Medication madness: A psychiatrist exposes the dangers of mood-altering medications.* New York: St. Martin's Press.

Breggin, P. R. (1987). *Psychiatric drugs: Hazards to the brain.* New York: Springer.

Brennan, J. W. (1995). A short-term psychoeducational multiple-family group for bipolar patients and their families. *Social Work, 40*(6), 737–743.

Breslau, J., Aguilar-Gaxiola, S., Kendler, K. S., Su, M., Williams, D., Kessler, R. C. (2006). Specifying race-ethnic differences in risk for psychiatric disorder in a USA national sample. *Psychological Medicine, 36*(1), 57–68.

Brodsky, C., Fisher, A., & Weinstein, M. (1964). Modern treatment of psychosis: New tasks for social therapies. *Social Work, 9,* 71–78.

Brody, H. (1988). The symbolic power of the modern personal physician: The placebo response under challenge. *Journal of Drug Issues, 18*(2), 149–161.

Brody, H., & Miller, F. G. (2011). Lessons from recent research about the placebo effect: From art to science. JAMA: *Journal of the American Medical Association, 306*(23), 2612–2613.

Bronstein, L. R. (2003). A model for interdisciplinary collaboration. *Social Work, 48*(3), 297–306.

Brown, P. (1985). *The transfer of care: Psychiatric deinstitutionalization and its aftermath.* Boston: Routledge & Kegan Paul.

Browne, T. A. (2006). Social work roles and health-care settings. In S. Gehlert & T. A. Browne (Eds.), *Handbook of social work* (pp. 23–2). New York: John Wiley & Sons.

Buckalew, L., & Sallis, R. (1986). Patient compliance and medication perception. *Journal of Clinical Psychology, 42,* 49–53.

Budd, R. J., Hughes, I. C. T., & Smith, J. A. (1996). Health beliefs and compliance with antipsychotic medication. *British Journal of Clinical Psychology, 35*(3), 393–397.

Buelow, G., Hebert, S., & Buelow, S. (2002). *Psychotherapist's resource on psychiatric medications: Issue of treatment and referral.* Belmont, CA: Brooks/Cole Thomson Learning.

Bulmash, E., Harkness, K. L., Stewart, J. G., & Bagby, R. M. (2009). Personality, stressful life events, and treatment response in major depression. *Journal of Consulting and Clinical Psychology, 77*(6), 1067–1077.

Bureau of Labor Statistics, U.S. Department of Labor (2011). Social Workers. *Occupation Outlook Handbook, 2008–2009 ed.,* http://www.bls.gov/oco/.

Burgess, S., Geddes, J., Hawton, K., Taylor, M. J., Townsend, E., Lamison, K., & Godwin, G. (2009). Lithium for maintenance treatment of mood disorders. *Cochrane Collaboration,* DOI: 10.1002/14651858.CD003013.

Burns, C., Smith, A., Hyer, K., Jacobsen, H., Lowry, L., Reed, C., et al. (2000). Training the interdisciplinary team in primary care. *National Academies of Practice Forum, 2*(2), 95–100.

Burroughs, V. J., Maxey, R. W., & Levy, R. A. (2002) Racial and ethnic differences in response to medicines: Towards individualized pharmaceutical treatment. *Journal of the National Medical Association, 94* (10, Suppl.), 1–26.

Bursztajn, H., & Barksy, A. J. (1985). Facilitating patient acceptance of a psychiatric referral. *Archives of Internal Medicine, 145,* 73–75.

Burti, L., & Mosher, L. R. (Eds.). (2003). Attitudes, values and beliefs of mental health workers. *Epidemiologia e Psichiatria Sociale, 12*(4), 227–231.

Busch, F. N., & Gould, E. (1993). Treatment by a psychotherapist and a psychopharmacologist: Transference and countertransference issues. *Hospital & Community Psychiatry, 44,* 772–774.

Byrne, M. K., Deane, F. P., Lambert, G., & Coombs, T. (2004). Enhancing medication adherence: Clinician outcomes from the Medication Alliance training program. *Australian and New Zealand Journal of Psychiatry, 38*(4), 246–253.

Caley, C. F. (2011). Interpreting and applying CYP450 genomic test results to psychotropic medication. *Journal of Pharmacy Practice, 24*(5), 439–446.

Cameron, J. K., & Mauksch, L. B. (2002). Collaborative family healthcare in an uninsured primary care population: Stages of integration. *Family, Systems & Health, 20,* 343–363.

Campbell, L. F., & Fox, R. (2010). The evolution of training guidelines in pharmacotherapy for psychologists. In R. E. Moore & B. A. Moore (Eds.), *Pharmacotherapy for psychologists: Prescribing and collaborative roles* (pp. 29–47). Washington, DC: American Psychological Association.

Caplan, P. J. (1995). *They say you're crazy: How the world's most powerful psychiatrists decide who's normal.* Reading, MA: Addison-Wesley.

Carpenter, W. T. (1997). The risk of medication-free research. *Schizophrenia Bulletin, 23,* 11–18.

Carrick, R., Mitchell, A., Powell, R., & Lloyd, K. (2004). The quest for well-being: A qualitative study of the experience of taking antipsychotic medication. *Psychology and Psychotherapy, 77,* 19–33.

Carroll, K. M. (1997). Manual-guided psychosocial treatment: A new virtual requirement for pharmacotherapy trials. *Archives of General Psychiatry, 54,* 923–928.

Carter, C., Swift, R. M., & Turnbull, J. M. (1996). When are long-term anxiolytics warranted? *Patient Care, 30*(5), 165–176.

Carter, R. (1999). *Helping someone with mental illness: A compassionate guide for family, friends and caregivers.* New York: Three Rivers Press.

Casper, R. C., Belanoff, J., & Offer, D. (1996). Gender differences, but no racial differences, in self-reported psychiatric symptoms in adolescents. *Journal of the Academy of Child and Adolescent Psychiatry, 35*(4), 500–508.

Cassidy, C. M., Rabinovitch, M., Schmitz, N., Joober, R., & Malla, A. (2010). A comparison study of multiple measures of adherence to antipsychotic medication in first-episode psychosis. *Journal of Clinical Psychopharmacology, 30*(1), 64–67.

Caudill, T. S., Lurie, N., & Rich, E. (1992). The influence of pharmaceutical industry advertising on physician prescribing. *Journal of Drug Issues, 22*(2), 331–338.

Chessick, C. A., Allen, M. H., Thase, M. E., da Chuna, A., Kapczinski, F., de Lima, M., et al. (2009). Azapirones for generalized anxiety disorder. *Cochrane Collaboration*, DOI: 10.1002 /14651858.CD006115.

Chewing, B., Bylund, C. L., Shah, B., Arora, N. K., Gueguen, J. A., & Makoul, G. (2012). Patient preferences for shared decisions: A systematic review. *Patient Education and Counseling*, 86(1), 9–18.

Chewning, B., & Sleath, B. (1996). Medication decision-making and management. *Social Science & Medicine*, 42, 389–398.

Choy, Y. (2007). Managing side effects of anxiolytics. *Primary Psychiatry*, 14(7), 68–76.

Chubinsky, P., & Rappaport, N. (2006). Medication and the fragile alliance: The complex meanings of psychotropic medication to children, adolescents and families. *Journal of Infant, Child and Adolescent Psychotherapy*, 5(1), 111–123.

Clark, R. E., Xie, H., & Brunette, M. F. (2004). Benzodiazepine prescription practices and substance abuse in persons with severe mental illness. *Journal of Clinical Psychiatry*, 65(2), 151–155.

Clary, C., Dever, A., & Schweizer, E. (1992). Psychiatric inpatients' knowledge of medication at hospital discharge. *Hospital & Community Psychiatry*, 43, 140–143.

Clayton, A. H. (2005). Gender differences in clinical psychopharmacology. *Journal of Clinical Psychiatry*, 66(9), 1191.

Clayton, A. H., & Balon, R. (2009). The impact of mental illness and psychotropic medications on sexual functioning: The evidence and management. *Journal of Sexual Medicine*, 6(5), 1200–1211.

Clemens, S. E. (2004). Recognizing vicarious traumatization: A single session group model for trauma workers. *Social Work With Groups*, 27(2–3), 55–74.

Cohen, D. (2011). Psychopharmacology and clinical social work practice. In J. R. Brandell (Ed.), *Theory and practice of clinical social work* (pp. 763–810). Newbury Park, CA: Sage.

Cohen, D. (2009). Needed: Critical thinking about psychiatric medication. *Social Work in Mental Health*, 7(1–3), 42–61.

Cohen, D. (2002). Research on the drug treatment of schizophrenia: A critical appraisal and implications for social work education. *Journal of Social Work Education*, 38(2), 217–139.

Cohen, D. (1988). Social work and psychotropic drug treatments. *Social Service Review*, 62, 576–599.

Cohen, D., & McCubbin, M. (1990). The political economy of tardive dyskinesia: Asymmetries in power and responsibility. *Journal of Mind and Behavior*, 11, 465–488.

Cohen, I. M. (1970). The benzodiazepines. In F. J. Ayd & R. Blackwell (Eds.), *Discoveries in biological psychiatry* (pp. 130–141). Philadelphia: J. B. Lippincott.

Cohen, L. S. (2007). Treatment of bipolar disorder during pregnancy. *Journal of Clinical Psychiatry*, 68(Suppl. 9), 4–9.

Cohen, N. L. (1993). Stigmatization and the "noncompliant" recidivist. *Hospital & Community Psychiatry*, 44, 1029.

Colom, F., Vieta, E., Reinares, M., Martinez-Aran, A., Torrent, C., Goikolea, J. M. et al. (2003). Psychoeducation efficacy in bipolar disorders: Beyond compliance enhancement. *Journal of Clinical Psychiatry*, 64, 1101–1105.

Colom, F., & Vieta, E. (2004). A perspective on the use of psychoeducation, cognitive-behavioral therapy and interpersonal therapy for bipolar patients. *Bipolar Disorders*, 6(6), 480–486.

Connaway, R. S. (1975). Teamwork and social worker advocacy: Conflicts and possibilities. *Community Mental Health Journal*, 11, 381–388.

Connors, G., Donovan, D., & DiClemente, C. (2001). *Substance abuse treatment and stages of change: Selecting and planning interventions.* New York: Guilford.

Conrad, P. (1985). The meaning of medications: Another look at compliance. *Social Science and Medicine*, 20, 29–37.

Consedine, N. S., Sabag-Cohen, S., & Krivoshekova, Y. S. (2007). Ethnic, gender, and socioeconomic differences in young adults' self-disclosure: Who discloses what and to whom? *Cultural Diversity and Ethnic Minority Psychology*, 13(3), 254–263.

Cook, J. A., Copeland, M. E., Corey, L., Buffington, E., Jonikas, J. A., Curtis, L. C., et al. (2010). Developing the evidence base for peer-led services: Changes among participants following Wellness Recovery Action Planning (WRAP) education in two statewide initiatives. *Psychiatric Rehabilitation Journal, 34*(2), 113–120.

Cooper, W. O., Hickson, G. B., & Ray, W. A. (2004). Prescriptions for contraindicated category X drugs in pregnancy among women enrolled in TennCare. *Pediatric and Perinatal Epidemiology, 18*, 106–111.

Copeland Center for Wellness and Recovery (2010). Retrieved on February 8, 2012, from http://copelandcenter.com/.

Copeland, M. E. (2008). *The WRAP story: First person accounts of personal and system recovery and transformation.* West Dummerton, VT: Peach Press.

Corrigan, P. W., Lawson, J. E., & Kuwabara, S. A. (2010). Social psychology of the stigma of mental illness: Public and self-stigma models. In J. E. Maddux & J. P.Tanney (Eds.), *Social psychological foundations of clinical psychology* (pp. 51–68). New York: Guilford.

Corsini, R. J., & Wedding, D. (2004). *Current psychotherapies* (7th ed.). Itasca, Ill: F. E. Peacock.

Corty, E., Lehman, A. F., & Myers, C. P. (1993). Influence of psychoactive substance use on reliability of psychiatric diagnosis. *Journal of Counseling and Clinical Psychology, 61*, 165–170.

Coryell, W. (2009). Maintenance treatment in bipolar disorder: A reassessment of lithium as the first choice. *Bipolar Disorders, 11*(Suppl. 2), 77–83.

Cowles, L. A., & Lefcowitz, M. (1992). Interdisciplinary expectations of the medical social worker in the hospital setting. *Health & Social Work, 17*(1), 57–65.

Cramer, J. A., & Rosenheck, R. (1999). Enhancing medication compliance for people with serious mental illness. *Journal of Nervous and Mental Disease, 187*, 53–55.

Crawford, V., Crome, I. B., & Clancy, C. (2003). Co-existing problems of mental health and substance misuse (dual diagnosis): A literature review. *Drugs: Education, Prevention & Policy, 10*(Suppl.), S1–S74.

Crowe, M., Wilson, L., & Inder, M. (2011). Patients' reports of the factors influencing medication adherence in bipolar disorder: An integrated review of the literature. *International Journal of Nursing Studies, 48*(7), 894–903.

Cubine, T., Bentley, K. J., Poe, J., & McCafferty, P. (1999). The MESA model of family-professional education: Virginia's experience in enhancing collaboration. *Arete, 25*, 46–57.

Cummings, C. M., & Fristad, M. A. (2007). Medications prescribed for children with mood disorders: Effects of a family-based psychoeducational program. *Experimental and Clinical Psychopharmacology, 15*(6), 555–562.

Curtis, L. T., & Patel, K. (2008). Nutritional and environmental approaches to preventing and treating autism and attention deficit hyperactivity disorder (ADHD): A review. *Journal of Alternative and Complementary Medicine, 14*(1), 79–85.

Curtis, S. M. (2004). The perception of stress and anxiety among mentally ill substance abusers. *Dissertation Abstracts International, 64*(7-B), 3517.

Dane, B. O., & Simon, B. L. (1991). Resident guests: Social workers in host settings. *Social Work, 36*, 208–213.

Dang, A., Garg, A., & Rataboli, P. V. (2011). Role of zolpidem in the management of insomnia. *CNS Neuroscience & Therapeutics, 17*(5), 387–397.

Dassa, D., Boyer, L., Benoit, M., Bourcet, A., Raymondet, P., & Bottai, R. (2010). Factors associated with medication non-adherence in patients suffering from schizophrenia: A cross-sectional study in a universal coverage health care system. *Australian and New Zealand Journal of Psychiatry, 44*(10), 921–928.

Dassori, A. M., Miller, A. L., Velligan, D., Slanda, D., Diamond, P., & Mahurin, R. (1998). Ethnicity and negative symptoms in patients with schizophrenia. *Cultural Diversity and Mental Health, 4*(1), 65–69.

Davidson, M., & Jamison, P. (1983). The clinical social worker and current psychiatric drugs: Some introductory principles. *Clinical Social Work Journal, 11,* 139–150.

Davis, T. S., Gavazzi, S. M., Scheer, S. D., KwonKwon, A., Lammers, A., Fristad, M. A., & Uppal, R. (2011). Measuring family caregiver perceptions of support in caring for children and youth with mental health concerns. *Journal of Social Service Research, 37*(5), 500–515.

Dean, A. J., Wragg, J., Draper, J., & MecDermott, B. M. (2011). Predictors of medication adherence in children receiving psychotropic medication. *Journal of Paediatrics and Child Health, 47*(6), 350–355.

Deegan, P. E. (2000). Spirit breaking: When the helping professions hurt. *The Humanistic Psychologist, 28*(1–3), 194–209.

Deegan, P. E. (2007). The lived experience of using psychiatric medication in the recovery process and a shared decision-making program to support it. *Psychiatric Rehabilitation Journal, 31*(1), 62–69.

Deegan, P. E., & Drake, R. E. (2006). Shared decision making and medication management in the recovery process. *Psychiatric Services, 57*(11), 1636–1639.

DeGeest, S., Abraham, I., Gemoets, H., & Evers, G. (1994). Development of the long-term medication behavior self-efficacy scale: Qualitative study for item development. *Journal of Advanced Nursing, 19*(2), 233–238.

DeLeon, P. H., & Pies, R. W. (1994). Should non-physician mental health professionals be allowed to prescribe medicine? In S. A. Kirk & S. D. Einbinder (Eds.), *Controversial issues in mental health* (pp. 177–188). Boston: Allyn & Bacon.

DeNavas-Walt, C., Proctor, B. D., & Smith, J. (2008). *Income, poverty, and health insurance coverage in the United States: 2006.* Washington, DC: U.S. Census Bureau.

Dennis, C. L. (2010). Postpartum depression peer support: Maternal perceptions from a randomized controlled trial. *International Journal of Nursing Studies, 47*(5), 560–568.

Dere-Meyer, C., Bender, B., Metzl, E., Diaz, K. (2011). Psychotropic medication and

art therapy: Overview of literature and clinical considerations. *Arts in Psychotherapy, 38*(1), 29–35.

Devane, C. L. (1990). *Fundamentals of monitoring psychoactive drug therapy.* Baltimore: Williams & Wilkins.

Dewan, M. J. (1999). Are psychiatrists cost-effective? An analysis of integrated versus split treatment. *American Journal of Psychiatry, 156,* 324–326.

Diamond, R. J., & Scheifler, P. L. (2007). *Treatment collaboration: Improving the therapist, prescriber, client relationship.* New York: W. W. Norton.

Diflorio, A., & Jones, I. (2010). Is sex important? Gender differences in bipolar disorder. *International Review of Psychiatry, 22*(5), 437–452.

Dixon, L., Lyles, A., Scott, J., Lehman, A., Postrado, L., Goldman, H., & McGlynn, E. (1999). Services to families of adults with schizophrenia: From treatment recommendations to dissemination. *Psychiatric Services, 50,* 233–238.

Dixon, L., McNary, S., & Lehman, A. F. (1998). Remission of substance use disorder among psychiatric inpatients with mental illness. *American Journal of Psychiatry, 155*(2), 239–243.

Dixon, L., Weiden, P., Torres, M., & Lehman, A. (1997). Assertive community treatment and medication compliance in the homeless mentally ill. *American Journal of Psychiatry, 154*(9), 1302–1304.

Dixon, L. B., Lucksted, A., Medoff, D. R., Burland, J., Stewart, B., Lehman, A. F., Fang, L. J., Sturm, V., Brown, C., & Murry-Swank, A. (2010). Outcomes of a randomized study of a peer-taught family-to-family education program for mental illness. *Psychiatric Services, 62*(6), 591–597.

Docherty, J. P. (1986). Psychopharmacology evaluation: Psychosocial issues. In D. C. Jimerson & J. P. Docherty (Eds.), *Psychopharmacology consultation* (pp. 118–129). Washington, DC: American Psychiatric Press.

Dolder, C. R., & Jeste, D. V. (2003). High risk patients. *Biological Psychiatry, 53*(12), 1142–1145.

Doran, C. D. (2008). *Prescribing mental health medication: The practitioner's guide.* New York: Routledge.

Dore, M. N., Nelson-Zlupko, L., & Kaufmann, E. (1999). "Friends in need": Designing and implementing a psychoeducational group for school children from drug-involved families. *Social Work, 44*(2), 179–190.

Dow, M. G., Verdi, M. B., & Sacco, W. P. (1991). Training psychiatric patients to discuss medication issues: Effects on patient communication and knowledge of medications. *Behavior Modification, 15*(1), 3–21.

Draine, J., & Solomon, P. (1994). Explaining attitudes toward medication compliance among a seriously mentally ill population. *Journal of Nervous and Mental Disease, 182,* 50–54.

Drake, R. E., & Deegan, P. E. (2009). Shared decision making is an ethical imperative. *Psychiatric Services, 60,* 1007.

Drake, R. E., O'Neal, E. L., & Wallach, M. A. (2008). A systematic review of psychosocial research on psychosocial interventions for people with co-occurring severe mental and substance use disorders. *Journal of Substance Abuse Treatment, 34*(1), 123–138.

Drymalski, W. M., & Campbell, T. C. (2009). A review of motivational interviewing to enhance adherence to antipsychotic medication in patients with schizophrenia: Evidence and recommendations. *Journal of Mental Health, 18*(1), 6–15.

Dubovsky, S. L., & Dubovsky, A. N. (2007). *Psychotropic drug prescriber's survival guide: Ethical mental health treatment in the age of Big Pharma.* New York: W.W. Norton & Company.

Duke, P., & Hochman, G. (1992). A brilliant madness: Living with manic-depressive illness. New York: Bantam.

Duncan, J. C., & Rogers, R. (1998). Medication compliance in patients with chronic schizophrenia: Implications for the community management of mentally disordered offenders. *Journal of Forensic Sciences, 43,* 1133–1137.

DuPaul, G. J., Power, T. J., Anastopoulos, A. D., & Reid, R. (1998). *ADHD Rating Scale-IV: Checklists, norms, and clinical interpretations.* New York: Guilford Press.

Dziegielewski, S. F. (1997). Should clinical social workers seek psychotropic medication privileges. Yes! In B. Thyer (Ed.), *Controversial issues in social work practice* (pp. 152–158, 164–165). Boston: Allyn/Bacon.

Dziegielewski, S. F. (2010). *Social work practice and psychopharmacology: A person-in-environment approach* (2nd ed.). New York: Springer Publishing Co.

D'Zurilla, T. J. (1986). *Problem-solving therapy: A social competence approach to clinical intervention.* New York: Springer.

D'Zurilla, T. J., & Nezu, A. M. (2010). Problem-solving therapy. In K. S. Dobson (Ed.), *Handbook of cognitive-behavioral therapies* (3rd ed.) (pp. 197–225). New York: Guilford Press.

Eckman, T. A., & Liberman, R. P. (1990). A large-scale field test of a medication management skills training program for people with schizophrenia. *Psychosocial Rehabilitation Journal, 13,* 31–35.

Eckman, T. A., Liberman, R. P., Phipps, C. C., & Blair, K. E. (1990). Teaching medication management skills to schizophrenic patients. *Journal of Clinical Psychopharmacology, 10*(1), 33–38.

Eckman, T. A., Wirshing, W. C., Marder, S. R., Liberman, R. P., Johnston-Cronk, K., Zimmerman, K., & Mintz, J. (1992). Technique for training schizophrenic patients in illness self-management: A controlled trial. *American Journal of Psychiatry, 149,* 1549–1555.

Egger, J. F., & Hebert, C. (2011). Buspirone: Anxiolytic, antidepressant, or neither? *Psychiatric Annals, 41*(3), 166–175.

El-Gabalawy, R., Mackenzie, C. S., Shooshtari, S., & Sareen, J. (2011). Comorbid physical health conditions and anxiety disorders: A population-based exploration of prevalence and health outcome among older adults. *General Hospital Psychiatry, 33*(6), 556–564.

Elliot, C., & Kintzer, C. (1973). No prescription pads for social workers. *Clinical Social Work Journal, 1,* 134–136.

Elwyn, G., Edwards, A., Kinnersley, P. & Grol, R. (2000). Shared decision making and the concept of equipoise: The competences of invoving patients in healthcare choices. *British Journal of General Practice, 50,* 892–897.

Ennis, R. H. (1989). Critical thinking and subject specificity: Clarification and needed research. *Educational Researcher, 18*(3), 4–10.

Ergaz, Z., & Ornoy, A. (2010). Psychotropic drugs and lactations: To nurse or not to nurse. In S. Tyano, M. Keren, H. Herman, & J. Cox (Ed.), *Parenthood and mental health: A bridge between infant and adult psychiatry* (pp. 385–399). New York: Wiley-Blackwell.

Ernst, E. (2003). Serious psychiatric and neurological adverse effects of herbal medicines: A systematic review. *Acta Psychiatrica Scandinavica, 108*(2), 83–91.

Even, C., Richard, H., & Thuile, J. (2007). Characteristics of voluntary participants versus nonparticipants in a psychoeducation program for euthymic patients with bipolar disorder. *Journal of Nervous and Mental Disease, 195*(3), 262–265.

Falloon, I., Boyd, J., & McGill, C. (1984). *Family care of schizophrenia: A problem-solving approach to the treatment of mental illness.* New York: Guilford Press.

Fancher, T. L., Lee, D., Cheng, J. K. Y., Yang, M. S., & Yang, L. (2012). Interventions to improve adherence to psychotropic medication in clients of Asian descent: A systematic review. *Asian American Journal of Psychology,* Online First Publication, April 30, 2012. DOI:10.1037/a0027803

Fang, L., & Schinke, S. P. (2007). Complementary alternative medicine use among Chinese Americans: Findings from a community mental health service population. *Psychiatric Services, 58*(3), 402–404.

Faravelli, C., Rosi, S., Scarpato, M. A., Lampronti, L., Amedei, S. G., & Rana, N. (2006). Threshold and subthreshold bipolar disorders in the Sesto Fiorentino Study. *Journal of Affective Disorders, 94*(1–3), 111–119.

Farmer, R. (2003). Gender and psychotropics: Toward a third wave framework. *British Journal of Social Work, 33*(5), 611–623.

Farmer, R. (2009). *Neuroscience and social work practice: The missing link.* Thousand Oaks, CA: Sage Publications.

Farrel, D., Fischer, J., McCabe, P. C. (2010). Tardive dyskinesia with typical and atypical antipsychotic medications in children and adolescents. In P. C. McCabe and S. R. Shaw (Eds.), *Psychiatric disorders: Current topics and interventions for educators* (pp. 60–70). Thousand Oaks, CA: Corwin Press.

Fava, M., Borus, J. S., Alpert, J. E., & Nierenberg, A. A. (1997). Folate, vitamin B-sub-1-sub-2, and homocysteine in major depressive disorder. *American Journal of Psychiatry, 154*(3), 426–428.

Fawzi, W., Abdel Mohsen, M. Y., Hashem, A. H., Moussa, S., Coker, E., & Wilson, K. C. M. (2012). Beliefs about medications predict adherence to antidepressants in older adults. *International Psychogeriatrics, 24*(1), 159–169.

Fenton, W. S., Blyler, C. R., & Heinssen, R. K. (1997). Determinants of medication compliance in schizophrenia: Empirical and clinical findings. *Schizophrenia Bulletin, 23,* 637–651.

Fincke, B. G., Miller, D. R., & Spiro, A. (1998). The interaction of patient perception of overmedication with drug compliance and side effects. *Journal of General Internal Medicine, 13*(3), 182–185.

Finnell, D., & Ditz, K. A. (2007). Health diaries for self-monitoring and self-regulation: Applications to individuals with serious mental illness. *Issues in mental health nursing, 28*(12), 1293–1307.

Flockhart, D. A., & Oesterheld, J. R. (2000). Cytochrome P450-mediated drug interactions. *Child & Adolescent Psychiatric Clinics of North America, 9*(1), 43–76.

Floersch, J. (2003). The subjective experience of youth psychotropic treatment. *Social Work in Mental Health, 1*(4), 51–69.

Floersch, J., Townsend, L., Longhofer, J., Munson, M. Winbush, V., Kranke, D., Faber, R., Thomas, J., Jenkins, J. H., & Findling, R. L. (2009). Adolescent experience of psychotropic treatment. *Transcultural Psychiatry, 46*(1), 157–179.

Flynn, L. M. (1994). The impact of managed care. *Advocate* (newsletter of the National

Alliance for the Mentally Ill), *16*(2), 1, 16, 23.

Fong, R., & Furuto, S. (Eds.). (2001). *Culturally competent practice: Skills interventions, and evaluations.* Boston: Allyn & Bacon.

Forte, J. A. (2004). Symbolic interactionism and social work: A forgotten legacy, Part 2. *Families in Society, 85*(2), 521–530.

Foxx, R. M., & Bittle, R. G. (1989). *Thinking it through: Teaching a problem-solving strategy for community living: Curriculum for individuals with chronic mental illness.* Champaign, IL: Research Press.

France, C. M., Lysaker, P. H., & Robinson, R. P. (2007). The "chemical imbalance" explanation for depression: Origins, lay endorsement, and clinical implications. *Professional Psychology, 38*(4), 411–420, DOI:10.1037/0735-7028.38.4.441.

Franchini, L., Bongiorno, F., Spagnolo, C., Florita, M., Santoro, A., Dotoli, D., Barbini, B., & Smeraldi, E. (2006). Psychoeducational group intervention in addition to antidepressant therapy as relapse prevention strategy in unipolar patients, *Clinical Neurology: Journal of Treatment Evaluation, 3*(4), 282–285.

Frank, E., Perel, J. M., Mallinger, A. G., Thase, M. E., & Kupfer, D. J. (1992). Relationship of pharmacologic compliance to long-term prophylaxis in recurrent depression. *Psychopharmacology Bulletin, 28*, 231–235.

Frank, J. D., & Frank, J. B. (1993). *Persuasion and healing: A comparative study of psychotherapy* (3rd ed.). Baltimore: Johns Hopkins University Press.

Franson, K. L., & Smith, S. L. (1998). Compliance: Problems and opportunities. *Clinics in Geriatric Medicine, 14*(1), 7–16.

Fraser, M., Richman, J., & Galinsky, M. (1999). Risk, protection, and resilience: Toward a conceptual framework of social work practice. *Social Work Research, 23*, 131–143.

Fristad, M. A., Goldberg-Arnold, J. S., & Gavazzi, S. M. (2002). Family psychoeducation: An adjunctive intervention for children with bipolar disorder. *Biological Psychiatry, 53*(11), 1000–1008.

Fukui, S., Starnino, V. R., Susana, M., Davidson, L. J., Cook, K., Rapp, C. A., & Gowdy, E. A. (2011). Effect of Wellness Recovery Action Plan (WRAP) participation on psychiatric symptoms, sense of hope, and recovery. *Psychiatric Rehabilitation Journal, 34*(3), 214–222.

Gardner, A., & Boles, R. G., (2011). Beyond the serotonin hypothesis: Mitochondria, inflammation and neurodegeneration in major depression and affective spectrum disorders. *Progress in Neuro-Psychopharmacology & Biological Psychiatry, 35*(3), 730–743.

Gearing, R. E., Townsend, L., MacKenzie, M., & Charlach, A. (2011). Reconceptualizing medication adherence: Six phases of dynamic adherence. *Harvard Review of Psychiatry,* 177–188.

Geddes, J. R., Burgess, S., Hawton, K., Jamison, K., & Goodwin, G. M. (2004). Long-term lithium therapy for bipolar disorder: Systematic review and meta-analysis of randomized controlled trials. *American Journal of Psychiatry, 161*(2), 217–222.

Gellad, W. F., Grenard, J. L., & Marcum, Z. A. (2011). A systematic review of barriers to medication adherence in the elderly: Looking beyond cost and regimen complexity. *American Journal of Geriatric Pharmacotherapy (AJGP), 9*(1), 11–23.

Geller, R. E., & Goldberg, J. F. (2007). A review or evidence-based psychotherapies for bipolar disorder. *Primary Psychiatry, 14*(3), 59–69.

Geller, B., Tillman, R., Bolhofner, K., & Zimerman, B. (2008). Child bipolar I disorder: Prospective continuity with adult bipolar I disorder; characteristics of second and third episodes; predictors of 8-year outcome. *Archives of General Psychiatry, 65*(10), 1125–1133.

Gerhart, U., & Brooks, A. (1983). The social work practitioner and anti-psychotic medication. *Social Work, 28*, 454–459.

Gerhart, U. C. (1990). *Caring for the chronic mentally ill.* Itasca, IL: F. E. Peacock.

Ghaemi, S. N. (Ed.) (2002). *Polypharmacy in psychiatry. New York: Marcel Dekker, Inc.*

Ghormley, C., Basso, M., Candlis, P., & Combs, D. (2011). Neuropsychological impairment corresponds with poor understanding of informed consent disclosures in persons diagnosed with major depression. *Psychiatry Research, 187*(1–2), 106–112.

Gibbons, R. D., Brown, C. H., Hur, K., Marcus, S. M., Bhaumik, D. K., Erkens, J. A., Herings, R. M. C., & Mann, J. J. (2007). Early evidence on the effects of regulators' sucidally warnings on SSRI prescriptions and suicide in children and adolescents. *American Journal of Psychiatry, 164*(9), 1356–1363.

Gibbs, L. (1991). *Scientific reasoning for social workers.* New York: Macmillan.

Gibelman, M. (1993). School social workers, counselors, and psychologists in collaboration: A shared agenda. *Social Work in Education, 15*(1), 45–51.

Gilmour, J., Harrison, C., Asadi, L., Cohen, M. H., & Vohra, S. (2011). Referrals and shared or collaborative care: Managing relationships with complementary and alternative medication practitioners. *Pediatrics, 128* (Suppl. A), S181–S186, DOI:10.1542/peds.2010-2720G.

Ginsberg, L., Nackerud, L., & Larrison, C.R. (2004). *Human biology for social workers: Development, ecology, genetics and health.* Boston: Pearson Education.

Ginsberg, L. D. (2006). Carbamazepine extended-release capsules: A retrospective review of its use in children and adolescents. *Annals of Clinical Psychiatry, 18*(Suppl. 1), 9–14.

Glynn, S. M., Marder, S. R., Liberman, R. P., Blair, K., Wirshing, W. C., Wirshing, D. A., Ross, D., & Mintz, J. (2002). Supplementing clinic-based skills-training with manual-based community support sessions: Effect on social adjustment of patients with schizophrenia. *American Journal of Psychiatry, 159*(5), 829–837.

Goldbeck, R., Tomlinson, S., & Bouch, J. (1999). Patients' knowledge and views of their depot neuroleptic medication. *Psychiatric Bulletin, 23*(8), 467–470.

Goldberg, A. I., Cohen, G., & Rubin, A. H. E. (1998). Physician assessments of patient compliance with medical treatment. *Social Science & Medicine, 47,* 1873–1876.

Goldberg, R. S., Riba, M., & Tasman, A. (1991). Psychiatrists' attitudes toward prescribing medication for patients treated by nonmedical psychotherapists. *Hospital & Community Psychiatry, 42,* 276–280.

Goldsmith, D. R., Wagstaff, A. J., Ibbotson, T., & Perry, C. M. (2004). Spotlight on lamotrigine in bipolar disorder. *CNS Drugs, 18*(1), 63–67.

Gomory, T., Wong, S., Cohen, D., & Lacasse, J. (2011). Clinical social work and the biomedical industrial complex. *Sociology and Social Welfare, 38*(4), 135–165.

Gonzalez, E. A., Mustelier, M. M., & Rey, J. A. (2005). Geriatric psychopharmacology. In S. S. Bush & T. A. Martin (Eds.), *Geriatric neuropsychology: Practice essentials.* (pp. 401–428). Philadelphia, PA: Taylor & Francis.

Gonzalez-Pinto, A., Reed, C., Novick, D., Bertsch, J., & Haro, J. M. (2010). Assessment of medication adherence in a cohort of patients with bipolar disorder. *Pharmacopsychiatry, 43*(7), 263–270.

Goodwin, G. M., Bowden, C. L., Calabrese, J. R., Grunze, H., Kasper, S., White, R., Greene, P., & Leadbetter, R. (2004). A pooled analysis of 2 placebo-controlled 18-month trials of lamotrigine and lithium maintenance in bipolar I disorder. *Journal of Clinical Psychiatry, 65*(3), 432–441.

Goozner, M. (2004). *The $800 million pill: The truth behind the cost of drugs.* Berkeley: University of California Press.

Gould, N. (2010). *Mental health social work in context.* London: Routledge.

Gray, C. (1998, October 3). *The joys and struggles of the collegial relationship in the best interests of the client.* Presentation at Psychopharmacology for Clinical Social Workers and Other Mental Health Professionals, sponsored by The Greater Washington Society for Clinical Social Work and the National Catholic School of Social Service, Washington, DC.

Green, K. (1998). *Home care survival guide.* Philadelphia: Lippincott.

Greene, R. R. (2009). Power factors in social work practice. In R. R. Greene &

N. Kropft (Eds.), *Human behavior theory: A diversity framework* (2nd rev. ed.). (pp. 251–274). New Brunswick, NJ: Aldine Transaction.

Greider, K. (2003). *The big fix: How pharmaceutical industry rips off American consumers.* New York: PublicAffairs.

Grenard, J. L., Munjas, B. A., Adamns, J. L., Suttorp, M., Maglione, M., McGlynn, E. A., & Gelad, W. F. (2011). Depression and medication adherence on the treatment of chronic diseases in the United States: A meta-analysis. *Journal of General Internal Medicine, 26*(10), 1175–1182.

Griffiths, C. A. (2006). The theories, mechanisms, benefits, and practical delivery of psychosocial educational interventions for people with mental health disorders. *International Journal of Psychosocial Rehabilitation, 11*(1), 21–28.

Grof, P., & Muller-Oerlinghausen, B. (2009). A critical appraisal of lithium's efficacy and effectiveness: The last 60 years. *Bipolar Disorders, 11*(Suppl. 2), 10–19.

Guada, J., & Venable, V. (2011). A comprehensive analysis of the quality of online health-related information regarding schizophrenia. *Health & Social Work, 36*(1), 45–53.

Gutheil, T. G. (1977). Improving patient compliance: Psychodynamics in drug prescribing. *Drug Therapy, 7,* 82–83, 87, 89–91, 95.

Haas, G. L., Garratt, L. S., & Sweeney, J. A. (1998). Delay to first antipsychotic medication in schizophrenia: Impact on symptomatology and clinical course of illness. *Journal of Psychiatric Research, 32* (3–4), 151–159.

Hall, W. (2007) *Harm reduction guide to coming off psychiatric drugs.* Icarus Project and Freedom Center:,San Francisco.

Hallowell, E. M., & Ratey, J. J. (1994). *Driven to distraction: Recognizing and coping with attention deficit disorder from childhood through adulthood.* New York: Pantheon.

Hamann, J., Leuct, S., & Kissling, W. (2003). Shared decision-making in psychiatry. *Acta Psychiatrica Scandinavia, 107,* 403–409.

Hamann, J., Mendel, R., Cohen, R., Heres, S., Ziegler, M., Bühner, M., & Kissling, W. (2009). Psychiatrists' use of shared decision making in the treatment of schizophrenia: Patient characteristics and decision topics. *Psychiatric Services, 60*(8), 1107–1112.

Hamilton, M. (1959). The assessment of anxiety states by rating. *British Journal of Medical Psychology, 32,* 50–55.

Hamrin, V., McCarthy, E. M., & Tyson, V. (2010). Pediatric psychotropic medication initiation and adherence: A literature review based on social exchange theory. *Journal of Child and Adolescent Psychiatric Nursing, 23*(3), 151–172.

Hamrin, V., & Pachler, M. (2007). Pediatric bipolar disorder: Evidence-based psychopharmalogical treatments. *Journal of Child and Adolescent Psychiatric Nursing, 20*(1), 40–58.

Hancock, L. (1996). Mother's little helper. *Newsweek, 127*(12), 51–56.

Hankoff, L., & Galvin, J. (1968). Psychopharmacological treatment and its implications for social work. *Social Work, 13,* 40–47.

Hanwella, R., Senanayake, M., & de Silva, V. (2011). Comparative efficacy and acceptability of methylphenidate and atomoxetine in treatment of attention deficit hyperactivity disorder in children and adolescents: A meta-analysis. *BMC Psychiatry, 11,* .

Harrison, J. N., Cluxton-Keller, F., & Gross, D. (2011). Antipsychotic medication prescribing trends in children and adolescents. *Journal of Pediatric Health Care, 26*(2), 139–145.

Harrison, W. D., Drolen, C. S., & Atherton, C. R. (1989). Role discrepancies in state hospital social work. *Social Casework, 70,* 622–626.

Hasson-Ohayon, I., Kravetz, S., Meir, T., & Rozencwaig, S. (2009). Insight into severe mental illness, hope, and quality of life of persons with schizophrenia and schizoaffective disorders. *Psychiatry Research, 167*(3), 231–238.

Hausner, R. (1985–1986). Medication and transitional phenomena. *International Journal of Psychoanalytic Psychotherapy, 11,* 375–407.

Hayes, S. C., & Chang, G. (2002). Invasion of the body snatchers: Prescription privileges, professional schools, and the drive to create a new behavioral *Clinical Psychology: Science and Practice, 9,* 264–269.

Haynes, R. B., McDonald, H. P., & Garg, A. X. (2002). Helping patients follow prescribed treatment: Clinical applications. *Journal of the American Medical Association, 288*(22), 2880–2883.

Haynes, R. B., Yao, X., Degani, A., Kripalani, S., Garg, A., & McDonald HP (2005) Interventions for enhancing medication adherence (Review). *Cochrane Database of Systematic Reviews.* CD000011, DOI:000010.001002/14651858.CD14000011.pub14651852.

Hayward, P., Kemp, R., & David, A. (2000). Compliance therapy: A collaborative approach to psychiatric medication. In B. Martindale, A. Bateman, & F. Margison (Eds.), *Psychosis: Psychological approaches and their effectiveness,* (pp. 50–67). London: Gaskell/Royal College of Psychiatrists.

Healy, D. (2003). Psychopharmacology 102 (... What they neglected to mention in psychopharmacology 101). *Clinical Psychologist, 56*(2), 10–17.

Healy, D. (2004). *Let them eat Prozac: The unhealthy relationship between the pharmaceutical industry and depression.* New York: New York University Press.

Healy, D., & Thase, M. E. (2003). Is academic psychiatry for sale? *British Journal of Psychiatry, 182I,* 388–390.

Heller, N. R., & Gitterman, A. (2011). Introduction to social problems and mental health/illness. In N. R. Heller & A. Gitterman (Eds.) *Mental health and social problems: A social work perspective* (pp. 1–17). New York: Routledge.

Helman, C. G. (1981). "Tonic," "fuel," and "food": Social and symbolic aspects of the long-term use of psychotropic drugs. *Social Science & Medicine, 15B,* 521–533.

Henkin, A. B., & Dee, J. R. (1998). Collaboration in human services: Skills assessment for effective interpersonal communication. *Professional Development: International Journal of Continuing Social Work, 1*(1), 22–30.

Henry, D. B., Pavuluri, M. N., Youngstrom, E., & Birmaher, B. (2008). Accuracy of brief and full forms of the Child Mania Rating Scale. *Journal of Clinical Psychology, 64*(4), 368–381.

Henry, J. D., Rendell, P. G., Scicluna, A., Jackson, M., & Phillips, L. H. (2009). Emotion experience, expression, and regulation in Alzheimer's disease. *Psychology and Aging, 24*(1), 252-257.

Hepworth, D., Rooney, R., Rooney, G. D., & Gottfried-Strom, K. (2012). *Direct social work practice: Theory and skills* (8th ed.). Belmont, CA: Brooks/Cole.

Hewitt, J., & Coffey, M. (2005). Therapeutic working relationships wit people with schizophrenia. *Journal of Advanced Nursing, 52*(5), 561–570.

Heyduk, L. J. (1991). Medication education: Increasing patient compliance. *Journal of Psychosocial Nursing and Mental Health Services, 29*(12), 32–35.

Heyscue, B. E., Levin, G. M., & Merrick, J. P. (1998). Compliance with depot antipsychotic medication by patients attending outpatient clinics. *Psychiatric Services, 49*(9), 1232–1234.

Higgins, P. B. (1995). Clozapine and the treatment of schizophrenia: Implications for social work practice. *Health & Social Work, 20,* 124–132.

Hindmarch, I., Patat, A., Stanley, N., Paty, I., & Rigney, U. (2001). Residual effects of zalepon and zolpidem following middle of the night administration five hours to one hour before awakening. *Human Psychopharmacology: Clinical and Experimental, 16*(2), 159–167.

Hirschowitz, J., Kolevzon, A., & Garakani, A. (2010) The pharmacological treatment of bipolar disorder: The question of modern advances. *Harvard Review of Psychiatry, 18*(5), 266–278.

Hochman, M. E. (2006). Children of depressed parents are more vulnerable. *Health Science,* June 5, p. C3.

Hoffman, J. S. (1990). Integrating biologic and psychologic treatment: The need for a unitary model. *Psychiatric Clinics of North America, 13*(2), 369–372.

Hong, J., Reed, C., Novick, D., Haro, J. M., & Aguado, J. (2011). Clinical and economic consequences of medication nonadherence in the treatment of patients with a manic/mixed episode of bipolar disorder: Results from the European Mania in Bipolar Longitudinal Evaluation of Medication (EMBLEM) study. *Psychiatry Research, 190*(1), 110–114.

Hosch, H. M., Barrientos, G. A., Fierro, C., & Ramirez, J. I. (1996). Predicting adherence to medications by Hispanics with schizophrenia. *Hispanic Journal of Behavioral Sciences, 17*(3), 320–333.

Howland, R. H. (2011). Drug therapies for tardive dyskinesia: Part 2. *Journal of Psychosocial Nursing and Mental Health Services, 49*(7), 17–20.

Huang, X., Lei, Z., & El-Mallach, R. S. (2007). Lithium normalizes elevated intracellular sodium. *Bipolar Disorder, 9*(3), 298–300.

Hughes, S., & Cohen, D. (2010). Understanding the assessment of psychotropic drug harms in clinical trials to improve social workers' role in medication monitoring. *Social Work, 55*(2), 105–115.

Hunter, R., Kennedy, E., Song, F., Gadon, L., & Irving, C. B. (2010). Risperidone versus typical antipsychotic medication for schizophrenia. *Cochrance Collaboration,* DOI: 10.1002/14651858. CD000440.

Hutto, B. R. (1997). Folate and cobalamin in psychiatric illness. *Comprehensive Psychiatry, 38*(6), 305–314.

Ingersoll, R. E., & Rak, C. F. (2006). *Psychopharmacology for helping professionals: An integral exploration.* Belmont, CA: Brooks/Cole Centage.

Insel, K. C., Reminger, S. L., & Hsiao, C. P. (2006). The negative association of independent personality and medication adherence. *Journal of Aging and Health, 18*(3), 407–418.

Ivanoff, A., & Stern, S. B. (1992). Self-management in health and mental health settings: Evidence of maintenance and generalization. *Social Work Research & Abstracts, 28*(4), 32–38.

Ivey, A. E., & Ivey, M. B. (1999). *Intentional interviewing and counseling: Facilitating client development in a multicultural society* (4th ed.). Pacific Grove, CA: Brooks/Cole.

Jacobvitz, D. (1990). Treatment of attentional and hyperactivity problems in children with sympathomimetic drugs: A comprehensive review. *Journal of the American Academy of Child and Adolescent Psychiatry, 29,* 677–688.

Jamison, K. R., & Akiskal, H. S. (1983). Medication compliance in patients with bipolar disorder. *Psychiatric Clinic of North America, 6,* 175–192.

Janicak, P. G., Marder, S. R., & Pavuluri, M. N. (2011). *Principles and practice of psychopharmacology* (5th ed.). Philadelphia, PA: Wolters Kluwer Health/Lippincott Williams & Wilkins.

Jenkins, J., Strauss, M. E., Carpenter, E. A., Miller, D., Floersch, J., & Sajatovic, M. (2005). Subjective experience of recovery from schizophrenia-related disorders and atypical antipsychotics. *International Journal of Social Psychiatry, 51*(3), 211–227.

Jensfold, M. F. (1996). Nonpregnant reproductive-age women, Part 1: The menstrual cycle and psychopharmacology. In M. F. Jensfold, U. Halbreich, & J. A. Hamilton (Eds.), *Psychopharmacology and women* (pp. 139–161). Washington, DC: American Psychiatric Press.

Jeste, D. V., & Caligiuri, M. P. (1993). Tardive dyskinesia. *Schizophrenia Bulletin, 19,* 303–312.

Johnson, F. N. (1984). *The history of lithium therapy.* London: Macmillan.

Johnson, H. C. (1989). Resisting the evil empire: Comments on "Social work and psychotropic drug treatments." *Social Service Review, 63,* 657–660.

Johnston H. F., & Frehling, J. J. (2008). Psychopharmalogical approaches with children and adolescents. In R. J. Morris & T. R. Kratochwill (Eds.), *The practice of child therapy* (4th ed.). (pp. 455–494). Mahwah, NJ: Lawrence Erlbaum Associates.

Joyal, C. C., Côté, G., Meloche, J., & Hodgins, S. (2011). Severe mental illness and aggressive behavior: On the importance of considering subgroups. *International Journal of Forensic Mental Health, 10*(2), 107–117.

Julien, R. M. (2011). *A primer of drug action: A comprehensive guide to the actions, uses, and side-effects of psychoactive drugs* (12th ed.). New York: Worth Publishers.

Julius, R. J., Novitsky, M. A., & Dubin, W. R. (2009). Medication adherence: A review of the literature and implications for clinical practice. *Journal of Psychiatric Practice, 15*(1), 34–44.

Kabat-Zinn, J., Massion, A. O., Kristeller, J., Peterson, L. G., Fletcher, K. E., Phert, L., Lenderking, W. R., & Santorelli, S. F. (1992). Effectiveness of a meditation-based stress reduction program in the treatment of anxiety disorders. *American Journal of Psychiatry, 149*, 936–943.

Kabat-Zinn, J. (2003) Mindfulness-based stress reduction (MBSR). *Constructivism in the Human Services,* 8(2), 73–107.

Kail, B. L. (1989). Drugs, gender, and ethnicity: Is the older minority woman at risk? *Journal of Drug Issues, 19*(2), 171–189.

Kane, J., Honigfeld, G., Singer, J., & Meltzer, H. (1988). Clozapine for the treatment-resistant schizophrenic: A double-blind comparison with chlorpromazine. *Archives of General Psychiatry, 45*, 789–796.

Kanter, J. (1989). Clinical case management: Definition, principles, components. *Hospital & Community Psychiatry, 40*, 361–368.

Kaphingst, K. A., Rudd, R. E., DeJong, W., & Daltroy, L. H. (2004). Literacy demands of product information intended to supplement television direct-to-consumer prescription drug advertisements. *Patient Education and Counseling, 55*(2), 291–300.

Karp, D. (2006). *Is it me or my meds?* Boston: Harvard University Press.

Karp, D. A. (2001). *The burden of sympathy: How families cope with mental illness.* New York: Oxford University Press.

Kasper, J., Hoge, S., Feucht-Haviar, T., Cortina, J., & Cohen, B. (1997). Prospective study of patients' refusal of antipsychotic medication under a physician discretion review procedure. *Archives of General Psychiatry, 154*, 483–489.

Keast, J. (2011). *A study of mental health provider enacted stigma: A conceptual model derived from client and family experience.* Manuscript under review.

Kellner, R. (1986). The brief depression rating scale. In N. Sartorius and T. A. Bans (Eds.), *Assessment of depression* (pp. 179–183). New York: Springer-Verlag.

Kelly, K. V. (1992). Parallel treatment: Therapy with one clinician and medication with another. *Hospital & Community Psychiatry, 43*, 778–780.

Kendler, K. S., & Schaffner, K. F. (2011). The dopamine hypothesis of schizophrenia: An historical and philosophical analysis. *Philosophy, Psychiatry, & Psychology, 18*(1), 41–63.

Keshavan, M. S., & Kennedy, J. S. (1992). *Drug-induced dysfunction in psychiatry.* New York: Hemisphere Publishing.

Kessler, R. C., Demiger, O., Frank, R. G., Olfson, M., Pincus, H. A., Walters, E. E., Wang, P., Wells, K. B., & Zaslavsky, A. M. (2005). Prevalence and treatment of mental disorders, 1990 to 2003. *New England Journal of Medicine, 352*(24), 2515–2523.

Khan, A. Y., Preskorn, S. H., & Wilamasena, K. (2006). Seingle enantiomer drugs: Should they be developed? *Essential Psychopharmacology, 7*(1), 15–23.

Killick, S., & Allen, C. (1997). 'Shifting the balance': Motivational interviewing to help behaviour change in people with bulimia nervosa. *European Eating Disorders Review* 5(1), 35–41.

Kim, H., & Salyers, M. P. (2008). Attitudes and perceived barriers to working with families of persons with severe mental illness: Mental health professionals' perspectives. *Community Mental Health Journal, 44*(5), 337–345.

Kim, S. W., Dysken, M. W., & Goldsmith, S. R. (1992). Target symptom oriented treatment of panic attacks with sublingual alprazolam: A case report. *Annals of Clinical Psychiatry, 4*(2), 147–149.

King, N., & Ross, A. (2003). Professional identities and interprofessional relations: Evaluation of collaborative community schemes. *Social Work in Health Care, 38*(2), 51–72.

Kirkcaldy, B. D., Furnham, A. F., & Siefen, R. G. (2011). Culture, psychopharmacology, and well being. In B. D. Kircaldy (Ed.), *The art and science of health care: Psychology and human factors for practitioners* (pp. 51–77). Cambridge, MA: Hogrefe Publishing.

Kleinman, D. L., & Cohen, L. J. (1991). The decontextualization of mental illness: The portrayal of work in psychiatric drug advertisements. *Social Science & Medicine, 32*(8), 867–874.

Klerman, G. L. (1990). The psychiatric patient's right to effective treatment: Implications of *Osheroff v. Chestnut Lodge. American Journal of Psychiatry, 147,* 409–418.

Kline, N. S. (1970). Monoamine oxidase inhibitors: An unfinished picaresque tale. In F. J. Ayd & R. Blackwell (Eds.), *Discoveries in biological psychiatry* (pp. 194–204). Philadelphia: J. B. Lippincott.

Koelch, M., Schnoor, K., & Fegert, J. M. (2008). Ethical issues in psychopharmacology of children and adolescents. *Current Opinion in Psychiatry, 21*(6), 598–605.

Kolb, D. A. (1984). *Experiential learning: Experience as the source of learning and development.* New Jersey: Prentice Hall.

Komossa, K., Rummel-Kluge, C., Hunger, H., Schwarz, S., Bhoopathi, P. S, Kissling, W., & Leucht, S. (2010). Ziprasidone versus other atypical antipsychotics for schizophrenia. *Cochrane Collaboration,* DOI: 10.1002/14651858. CD006624.pub2.

Komossa, K., Rummel-Kluge, C., Schmid, F., Hunger, H., Schwarz, S., Srisurpanont, M., Kissling, W., & Leucht, S. (2010). Quetiapine versus other atypical antipsychotics for schizophrenia. *Cochrane Collaboration,* DOI: 10.1002/14651858. CD006569.pub3.

Komossa, K., Rummel-Kluge, C., Schwarz, S., Schmid, F., Hunger, H., Kissling, W., & Leucht, S. (2011). Risperidone versus other atypical antipsychotics for schizophrenia. *Cochrane Collaboration,* DOI: 10.1002/14651858.CD006626.pub2.

Kopp, J. (1988). Self-monitoring: A literature review of research and practice. *Social Work Research & Abstracts, 4*(4), 8–20.

Kramer, P. D. (1993). *Listening to Prozac: A psychiatrist explores antidepressant drugs and the remaking of self.* New York: Viking.

Kranke, D., Guada, J., Kranke, B., & Floersch, J. (2012). What do African American youth with a mental illness think about help-seeking and psychiatric medication? Origins of stigmatizing attitudes. *Social Work in Mental Health, 10*(1), 53–71.

Kranke, D. A., Floersch, J., Kranke, B. O., & Munson, M. R. (2011). A qualitative investigation of self-stigma among adolescents taking psychiatric medication. *Psychiatric Services, 62*(8), 893–899.

Kuhn, R. (1970). The imipramine story. In F. J. Ayd & R. Blackwell (Eds.), *Discoveries in biological psychiatry* (pp. 205–217). Philadelphia: J. B. Lippincott.

Lacasse, J. R. (2005). Consumer advertising of psychiatric medications biases the public against nonpharmacological treatment. *Ethical Human Psychology and Psychiatry, 7*(3), 175–179.

Lacasse, J. R., & Leo, J. (2011). Knowledge of ghost-writing and financial conflicts-of-interest reduces the perceived credibility of biomedical research. *BMC Research Notes, 4,* 27.

MLacasse, J. R., & Leo, J. (2010). Ghost-writing at elite academic medical centers in the United Sates, *PLoS Medicine, 7*(2), e1000230, DOI:10.1371/journal. pmed.1000230.

Lacasse, J. R., & Leo, J. (2005). Serotonin and depression: A disconnect between the advertisements and the scientific literature. *PLoS Medicine, 2*(12), e392, 1211–1216.

Lachner, C., Steinle, N. I., Regenold, W. T. (2012). The neuropsychiatry of vitamin B_{12} deficiency in elderly patients. *Journal of Neuropsychiatry and Clinical Neurosciences, 24*(1), 5–15.

Landsverk, S. S., & Kane, C. F. (1998). Antonovsky's sense of coherence: Theoretical basis of psychoeductaion in schizophrenia. *Issues in Mental Health Nursing, 19,* 419–431.

Lang, A., Berghofer, G., Kager, A., Steiner, E., Schmitz, M., Schidl, F., & Rudas, S. (2003). Predictors of insight into mental illness among psychotic and non-psychotic patients. *European Journal of Psychiatry, 17*(4), 213–222.

Laughren, T. P. (2010). What's next after 50 years of psychiatric drug development: An FDA perspective. *Journal of Clinical Psychiatry, 71*(9), 1196–1204.

Law, J. (2006). *Big pharma: How the world's biggest drug companies control illness*. London: Constable & Robinson.

Lawless, L. L., & Wright, G. J. (2000). *How to get referrals: A mental health professionals guide to strategic marketing*. New York: Wiley.

Lawrence, J. D., Lawrence, D. B., & Carson, D. S. (1997). Optimizing ADHD therapy with sustained-release methylphenidate. *American Family Physician, 55*(5), 1705–1712.

Lawson, W. B. (2000). Issues in pharmacotherapy for African Americans. In P. Ruiz (Ed.), *Ethnicity and psychopharmacology* (pp. 37–47). Washington, DC: American Psychiatric Press.

Leake, C. D. (1970). The long road for a drug from idea to use: The amphetamines. In F. J. Ayd & R. Blackwell (Eds.), *Discoveries in biological psychiatry* (pp. 69–84). Philadelphia: J. B. Lippincott.

Leckband, S. G., Bishop, J. R., & Ellingrod, V. L. (2007). Pharmacogenomics in psychiatry. *Journal of Pharmacy Practice, 20*(3), 252–264.

Lee, H., Kane, I., Sereika, S. M., Cho, R. Y., & Jolley, C. J. (2011). Medication-taking behaviors in young adults with schizophrenia: A pilot study. *Journal of Psychiatric and Mental Health Nursing, 18*(5), 418–424.

Lee, J. A. B. (2003). *The empowerment approach to social work practice* (2nd ed.). New York: Columbia University Press.

Lee, M. S., Yang, E. J., Kim, J. I., & Ernst, E. (2009). Ginseng for cognitive function in Alzheimer's disease: A systematic review. *Journal of Alzheimer's Disease, 18*(2), 339–344.

Lefley, H. P. (1993). Involuntary treatment: Concerns of consumers, families and society. *Innovations and Research, 2*, 7–9.

Lens, V. (2004). Principled negotiation: A new tool for case advocacy. *Social Work, 49*(3), 506–513.

Lenton, S., & Single, E. (1998) The definition of harm reduction. *Drug & Alcohol Review, 17*, 213–220.

Leo, J., & Lacasee, J. R. (2008). The media and the chemical imbalance theory of depression. *Sociology, 45*, 35–45, DOI 10.1007/s12115-007-9047-3.

Le Quach, P., Mors, O., Christensen, T. O., Krarup, G., Jorgensen, P., Bertelsen, M., Jeppesen, P., Petersen, L., Thorup, A., & Nordentoft, M. (2009). Predictors of poor adherence to medication among patients with first-episode schizophreni-spectrum disorder. *Early Intervention in Psychiatry, 3*(1), 66–74.

Leventhal, H., Diefenbach, M., & Leventhal, E. A. (1992). Illness cognition: Using common sense to understand treatment adherence and affect cognition interactions. *Cognitive Therapy and Research, 16*, 143–163.

LeVine, E. S., & Wiggins, J. (2010). In the private practice setting: A survey of the experiences of prescribing psychologists. In R. E. Moore & B. A. Moore (Eds.), *Pharmacotherapy for psychologists: Prescribing and collaborative roles,* (pp. 153–171). Washington, DC: American Psychological Association.

Levy, S. T. (1977). Countertransference aspects of pharmacotherapy in the treatment of schizophrenia. *International Journal of Psychoanalytic Psychotherapy, 6*(1), 15–30.

Lewinsohn, P. M., Clarke, G. N., & Hoberman, H. M. (1989). The Coping With Depression Course: Review and future directions. *Canadian Journal of Behavioral Sciences, 21*(14), 470–493.

Liberman, R., Kane, J., Vaccaro, J., & Wirshing, W. (1987, October). *Negotiating medication issues with schizophrenic patients*. Workshop conducted at the Institute on Hospital & Community Psychiatry, Boston, MA.

Liberman, R. P. (1988). Coping with chronic mental disorders: A framework for hope. In R. P. Liberman (Ed.), *Psychiatric rehabilitation of chronic mental patients* (pp. 1–28). Washington, DC: American Psychiatric Press.

Licht, R. W., Nielsen, J. N., Gram, L. S., Vertergaard, P., & Bedz, H. (2010). Lamotrigine versus lithium as maintenance treatment in bipolar I disorder: An open, randomized effectiveness study mimicking clinical practice. The 6th trial of the Danish University antidepressant group. *Bipolar Disorders, 12*(5), 483–493.

Lin, K., & Shen, W. W. (1991). Pharmacology for southeast Asian psychiatric patients. *Journal of Nervous and Mental Disease, 179*(6), 346–350.

Linde, K., Berner, M., Egger, M., & Mulrow, C. (2005). St. John's wort for depression: Meta-analysis of randomised controlled trials. *British Journal of Psychiatry, 186*, 99–107.

Linde, K., Ramirez, G., Mulrow, C. D., Pauls, A., Weidenhamer, W., & Melchart, D. (1996). St. John's Wort for depression: An overview and meta-analysis of randomized clinical trials. *British Medical Journal, 313*(7052), .

Liptak, A. (2008). U.S. imprisons 1 in 100 adults, report finds. *New York Times*, Feb 29, New York Times Company.

Liraud, F., Droulout, T., Parrot, M., & Verdoux, H. (2004). Agreement between self-rated and clinically assessed symptoms in subjects with psychosis. *Journal of Nervous and Mental Disease* 192(5), 352–356.

Littrell, J., & Ashford, J. B. (1994). The duty of social workers to refer for medications: A study of field instructors. *Social Work Research, 18*(2), 123–128.

Littrell, J., & Ashford, J. B. (1995). Is it proper for psychologists to discuss medications with clients? *Professional Psychology, 26*, 238–244.

Liu, H. Y., Potter, M. P., Woodworth, K. Y., Yorks, D. M., Petty, C. R., Wozniak, J. R., Faraone, S. V., & Biederman, J. (2011). Pharmacologic treatments for pediatric bipolar disorder: A review and meta-analysis. *Journal of the American Academy of Child & Adolescent Psychiatry, 50*(8), 749–762.

Lloyd, A., Horan, W., Borgaro, S. R., Stokes, J. M., & Harvey, P. D. (1998). Predictors of medication compliance after hospital discharge in adolescent psychiatric patients. *Journal of Child & Adolescent Psychopharmacology*, 8(2), 133–141.

Lobos, C. A., Komossa, K., Rummel-Kluge, C., Hunger, H., Schmid, F., Schwarz, S., & Leucht, S. (2010). Clozapine versus other atypical antipsychotics for schizophrenia. *Cochrane Collaboration,* DOI: 10.1002/14651858.CD006633.pub2.

Loffler, W., Kilian, R., Toumi, M., & Angermeyer, M. C. (2003) Schizophrenic patients' subjective reasons for compliance and noncompliance with neuroleptic treatment. *Pharmacopsychiatry 36*, 105–112.

Lukens, E. P., & McFarlane, W. R. (2006). Psychoeducation as evidence-based practice: Considerations for practice, research, and policy. In A. R. Roberts & K. R. Yeager (Eds.), *Foundations of evidence-based social work practice* (pp. 291–313). New York: Oxford.

MacPherson, R., Double, D. B., Rowlands, R. P., & Harrison, D. M. (1993). Long-term psychiatric patients' understanding of neuroleptic medication. *Hospital & Community Psychiatry, 44*, 71–73.

Mailick, D., & Ashley, A. (1981). Politics of interprofessional collaboration: Challenge to advocacy. *Social Casework, 65*, 131–137.

Mailick, M. D., & Jordan, D. (1977). A multimodel approach to collaborative practice in health care settings. *Social Work in Health Care, 2*, 445–457.

Maine, L. L. (2008). Collaborative practice in pharmacy: Substance or semantics? *Psychological Services, 5*(2), 198–199.

Malhotra, A. K., Lencz, T., Correll, C. U., & Kane, J. M. (2007). Genomics and the future of pharmacotherapy in psychiatry. *International Review of Psychiatry, 19*(5), 523–530.

Mantovani, A., Aly, M., Dagan, Y., Allart, A., & Lisanby, S. H. (2012). Randomized sham controlled trial of repetitive transcranial magnetic stimulation to the dorsolateral prefrontal cortex for the treatment of panic disorder with comorbid major depression. *Journal of Affective Disorders, 139*(12), 111–118.

Maples, N. J., & Velligan, D. I. (2008). Cognitive Adaptation Training: Establishing environmental supports to bypass cognitive deficits and improve functional outcomes. *American Journal of Psychiatric Rehabilitation, 11*, 164–180.

Marder, S. R. (2003). Overview of partial compliance. *Journal of Clinical Psychiatry, 64*(Suppl. 16), 3–9.

Marks, I. M. (1987). *Fears, phobias, and rituals: Panic, anxiety, and their disorders.* New York: Oxford University Press.

Martin J. L. R., & Martin-Sanchez, E. (2012). Systematic review and meta-analysis of vagus nerve stimulation in the treatment of depression: Variable results based on study designs. *European Psychiatry, 27*(3), 147–155.

Mason, S. E., & Pollack, D. (1998). Prozac, families and the law: Implications for social work practice. *Clinical Social Work Journal, 26,* 317–332.

Masud, M. I., Sobhan, T., & Ryals, T. (2002). Effects of commonly used benzodiazepines on the fetus, the neonate, and the nursing infant. *Pscyhiatric Services, 53*(1), 39–49.

Mathews, D. J. H. (2011). Deep brain stimulation, personal identity, and policy. *International Review of Psychiatry, 23*(5), 486–492.

Mattessich, P.W. (1992). *Collaboration— What makes it work: A review of research literature on factors influencing successful collaboration.* St. Paul, MN: Amherst H. Wilder Foundation.

Mazure, C. M. (Ed.) (1995). *Does stress cause psychiatric illness?* Washington, DC: American Psychiatric Press.

McCabe, S. E., Cranford, J. A., &, West, B. T. (2008). Trends in prescription drug use and dependence, co-occurrence with other substance use disorders, and treatment utilization: Results from two national surveys. *Addictive Behaviors, 33* (10), 1297–1305.

McCandless-Glimcher, L., McKnight, S., Hamera, E., Smith, B. L., Peterson, K. A., & Plumlee, M. N. (1986). Use of symptoms by schizophrenics to monitor and regulate their illness. *Hospital & Community Psychiatry, 37,* 929–933.

McCann, T. V., Clark, E., & Lu, S. (2008). The self-efficacy model of medication adherence in chronic mental illness. *Journal of Nursing and Healthcare of Chronic Illness, 17,* 329–340.

McCollum, A., Margolin, C., & Lieb, J. (1978). Consultation on psychoactive medication. *Health & Social Work, 3*(4), 72–98.

McFarlane, W. R., (2002). *Multifamily groups in the treatment of severe psychiatric disorders.* New York: Guilford.

McGrath, R. E. (2010). Prescriptive authority for psychologists. *Annual Review of Clinical Psychology, 6,* 21–47.

McGrath, R. E., & Sammons, M. (2011). Prescribing and primary care psychology: Complementary paths for professional psychology. *Professional Psychology: Research and Practice, 42*(2), 113–120.

McIntosh, D. E., & Trotter, J. S. (2006). Early onset bipolar spectrum disorder: Psychopharmacological, psychological, and educational management. *Psychology in the Schools, 43*(4), 451–460.

McMiller, T. P., & Weisz, J. R. (1996). Help-seeking preceding mental health clinic intake among African-American, Latino, and Caucasian youths. *Journal of the Academy of Child and Adolescent Psychiatry, 35*(8), 1086–1094.

McPhillips, M., & Sensky, T. (1998). Coercion, adherence or collaboration? Influences on compliance with medication. In T. Wykes, N. Tarrier, & S. Lewis (Eds.). *Outcome and innovation in psychological treatment of schizophrenia* (pp. 161–177). Chichester, England: Wiley.

Meder, J., Morawiec, M., Sawicka, M. (1998). Evaluation of the Medication Management Module in Poland. *International Review of Psychiatry, 10*(1), 62–66.

Meeks, T. W., & Jeste, D. V. (2008). Older individuals. In K. T. Mueser & D. V. Jeste (Eds)., *Clinical handbook of schizophrenia* (pp. 390–397). New York: Guilford.

Meltzer-Brody, S. E. (2001). St. John's wort: Clinical status in psychiatry. *CNS Spectrum, 6*(10), 835–840.

Melvin, C. L., Carey, T. S., Goodman, F., Oldham, J. M., Williams, J. W., & Ranney, L. H. (2008). Effectiveness of antiepileptic drugs for the treatment of bipolar disorder: Findings from a systematic review. *Journal of Psychiatric Practice*, *14*(1), 9–14.

Mendoza, R., & Smith, M. W. (2000). The Hispanic response to psychotropic medication. In P. Ruiz (Ed.), *Ethnicity and psychopharmacology*, (pp. 55–82). Washington, DC: American Psychiatric Press.

Michalak, E. E., Yatham, L. N., & Lam, R. W. (2005). Perceived quality of life in patients with bipolar disorder: Does group psychoeducation have an impact? *Canadian Journal of Psychiatry*, *50*(2), 95–100.

Miklowitz, D. J. (2011). *The bipolar disorder survival guide: What you and your family need to know* (2nd ed.). New York: Guilford Press.

Miklowitz, D. J., George, E. L., Axelson, D. A., Kim, E. Y., Birmhauer, B., Schenk C., Beresford, C., Craighead, W. E., & Brent, D. A. (2004). Family focused treatment for adolescents with bipolar disorder. *Journal of Affective Disorders*, *82* (Suppl. 1), s113–s128.

Miklowitz, D. J., & Goldstein, M. J. (1997). *Bipolar disorder: A family-focused treatment approach.* New York: Guilford.

Miklowitz, D. J., Simoneau, T. L., George, E. L., Richards, J. A., Kalbag, A., Sachs-Ericsson, N., & Suddath, R. (2000). Family-focused treatment of bipolar disorder: 1-year effects of a psychoeducational program in conjunction with pharmacotherapy. *Biological Psychiatry*, *48*(6), 582–592.

Miller, J. G. (1995). Criminal justice: Social work roles. *Encyclopedia of Social Work*, (19th ed). Washington, DC: National Association of Social Workers.

Miller, L., Bishop, J. R., Fischer, J. H., Geller, S. E., & Macmillan, C. (2008). Balancing risks: Dosing strategies for antidepressants near the end of pregnancy. *Journal of Clinical Psychiatry*, *69*(2), 323–324.

Miller, W., & Rollnick, S. (2002). *Motivational interviewing: Preparing people to change addictive behavior* (2nd ed.). New York: Guilford.

Millet, K. (1990). *The looney bin trip.* New York: Simon & Schuster.

Minkoff, K. (2001). "Substance use and medication treatment": Reply. *Psychiatric Services*, *52*(9), 1255–1256.

Misdrahi, D., Petit, M., Blanc, O., Bayle, F. & Llorca, P. M. (2012). The influence of therapeutic alliance and insight on medication adherence in schizophrenia. *Nordic Journal of Psychiatry*, *66*(1), 49–54.

Mistler, L. A., & Drake, R. E. (2008). Shared decision making in antipsychotic management. *Journal of Psychiatric Practice*, *14*(6), 333–344.

Mizrahi, T., & Abramson, J. (1985). Sources of strain between physicians and social workers. Implications for social workers in health care settings. *Social Work in Health Care*, *10*(3), 33–51.

Mizrahi, T., & Abramson, J. (2000). Collaboration between social workers and physicians: Perspectives on a shared case. *Social Work in Health Care*, *31*(3), 1–24.

Moncrieff, J., & Cohen, D. (2005). Rethinking models of psychotropic drug action. *Psychotherapy and Psychosomatics*, *74*(3), 145–153.

Moncrieff, J., Hopker, S., Thomas, P. (2005). Psychiatry and the pharmaceutical industry: Who pays the piper? *Psychiatric Bulletin*, *29*(3), 84–85.

Montejano, L., Sasané, R., Hodgkins, P., Russo, L., & Huse, D. (2011). Adult ADHD: Prevalence of diagnosis in a US population with employer health insurance. *Current Medical Research and Opinion*, *27*(Suppl. 2), 5–11.

Montgomery, S. A. (2006). Guidelines in major depressive disorder, and their limitations. *International Journal of Psychiatry in Clinical Practice*, *10*(Suppl. 3), 3–9.

Morgan, R. D., Kroner, D. G., Varghese, F., Flora, D. B., Mills, J. F., & Steffan, J. S. (2012). Treating offenders with mental illness: A research synthesis. *Law and Human Behavior*, *36*(1), 37–50.

Morris, L. S., & Schulz, R. M. (1993). Medication compliance: The patient's perspective. *Clinical Therapeutics*, *15*(3), 593–606.

Morrison, P., Gaskill, D., Meehan, T., Lunney, P., Lawrence, G., & Collings, P. (2000). The use of the Liverpool University Neuroleptic Side-Effect Rating Scale (LUNSERS) in clinical practice. *Australian & New Zealand*

Journal of Mental Health Nursing, 9(4), 166–176.

Morse, E. V., Simon, P. M., & Balson, P. M. (1993). Using experiential training to enhance health care professionals' awareness of patient compliance issues. *Academic Medicine, 68*(9), 693–697.

Mueser, K. T., Corrigan, P. W., Hilton, D. W., Tanzman, B., Schaub, A., Ginger-ich, S., Essock, S. M., Tarrier, N., Morey, B., Vogel-Scibilia, S., & Herz, M. I. (2002). Illness management and recovery: A review of research. *Psychiatric Services, 53,* 1272–1284.

Mueser, K. T., & Gingerich, S. (1994). *Coping with schizophrenia: A guide for families.* Oakland, CA: New Harbinger Publications.

Nash, M. (2011). Improving mental health service users' physical health through medication monitoring: A literature review. *Journal of Nursing Management, 19*(3), 360–65.

National Alliance on Mental Illness (NAMI) (2012). *About NAMI.* http://www.nami.org/template.cfm?section=About_NAMI.

National Association of Social Workers (NASW) (2008). *Code of ethics.* Washington, DC: Author.

National Association of Social Workers (NASW) (2011). *Mental health issue fact sheet.* Washington, DC: Author.

National Institute of Health (NIH) (2003). *Older adults: Depression and suicide facts.* NIH Publication No. 03-4593. Washington, DC: Author.

Nauert, R. (2006). New model for psycho-tropic drugs. *PsychCentral News,* http://psychcentral.com/news/2006/12/04/new-model-for-psychotropic-drugs/452.html.

Neighbors, H. W., Trierweiler, S. J., Ford, B. C., & Murdoff, J. R. (2003). Racial differences in DSM diagnosis using a semi-structured instrument: The importance of clinical judgment in the diagnosis of African-Americans. *Journal of Health and Social Behavior, 44*(3), 237–256.

Neill, J. R. (1989). A social history of psy-chotropic drug advertisements. *Social Science and Medicine, 28*(4), 333–338.

Nevins, D .B. (1990). Psychoanalytic per-spectives on the use of medication for mental illness. *Bulletin of the Menninger Clinic, 54*(3), 323–329.

Nightengale, B. S., Crumley, J. M., Liao, J., Lawrence, B. J., & Jacobs, E. W. (1998). Economic outcomes of antipsychotic agents in a Medicaid population: Tradi-tional agents vs. risperidone. *Psychophar-macology Bulletin, 34,* 373–382.

O'Donnell, C., Donohoe, G., Sharkey, L., Owens, N., Migone, M., Harries, R., Kinsella, A., Larkin, C., & O'Callaghan, E. (2003). Compliance therapy: A ran-domised controlled trial in schizophrenia. *British Medical Journal, 327*(7419), 834.

Olfson, M., & Pincus, H. A. (1994). Use of benzodiazepines in the community. *Archives of Internal Medicine, 154*(11), 1235–1241.

Ortega, A. N., Rosenheck, R., Alegria, M. & Desai, R. A. (2000). Acculturation and the lifetime risk of psychiatric and sub-stance use disorders among Hispanics. *Journal of Nervous and Mental Disease, 188*(11), 728–735.

O'Shea, M., Bicknell, L., & Whatley, D. (1991). Brief multifamily psychoeducation programs for schizophrenia: Strategies for implementation and management. *Ameri-can Journal of Family Therapy, 19*(1), 33–44.

Pacheco, J., Beevers, C. G., McGeary, J. E., & Schnyer, D. M. (2012). Memory monitoring performance and pfc activity are associated with 5-httlpr genotype in older adults. *Neuropsychologia, 50*(9), 2257-2270.

Pare, D. A., & Larner, G. (2004). *Collabora-tive practice in psychology and therapy.* New York: Haworth.

Parrish, J. (1993). Involuntary use of inter-ventions: Pros & cons. *Innovations and Research, 2,* 15–22.

Patel, U. B., Ni, Q., Clayton, C., Lam, P., & Parks, J. (2010). An attempt to improve antipsychotic medication adherence by feedback of medication possession ratio scores to prescribers. *Population Health Management, 13*(5), 269–274.

Patorno, E., Bohn, R. L., Wahl, P. M., Avorn, J., Patrick, A. R., Liu, J., & Schneeweiss, S. (2010). Anticonvulsant medications and the risk of suicide, attempted suicide, or violent death. *JAMA: Journal of the American Medical Association, 303*(14), 1401–1409.

Patterson, J., Albala, A. A., McChahill, M. E., & Edwards, T. M. (2009). *The therapist's guide to psychopharmacology*. New York: Guilford Press.

Paul, R., & Elder, L. (2009). *Critical thinking: Concepts and tools*. Tomales, CA: Foundation for Critical Thinking Press.

Paulose-Ram, R., Safran, M. A., Gu, Q., & Orwig, D. (2007). *Trends in psychotropic medication use among U.S. adults*. New York: John Wiley & Sons.

Paykina, N., & Greenhill, L. L. (2007). Pharmacological treatments for attention-deficit/hyperactivity disorder. In P. E. Nathan & J. M. Gorman (Eds.), *A guide to treatments that work* (3rd ed.), (pp. 29–70). New York: Oxford University Press.

Pellegrino, E. D. (1976). Prescribing and drug ingestion symbols and substances. *Drug Intelligence and Clinical Pharmacy, 10*, 624–630.

Pekkala, E., & Merinder, L. (2007). Psychoeducation for schizophrenia. *Cochrane Database of Systematic Reviews,* 1. New York: John Wiley and Sons.

Pena, S. D. J. The fallacy of racial pharmacogenomics (2011). *Brazilian Journal of Medical and Biological Research, 44*(4), 268–275.

Perlis, R. H., Welge, J. A., Vornik, M. S., Herschfeld, R. M. A., & Keck, P. E. (2006). Atypical antipsychotics in the treatment of mania: A meta-analysis of randomized, placebo-controlled trials. *Journal of Clinical Psychiatry, 67*(4), 509–516.

Pert, C. B. (1999). *Molecules of emotion: The science behind mind-body medicine*. New York: Touchstone.

Pescosolido, B. A., Perry, B. L., Martin, J. K., McLeod, J. D., & Jensen, P. S. (2007). Stigmatizing attitudes and beliefs about treatment and psychiatric medications for children with mental illness. *Psychiatric Services, 58*(5), 613–618.

Peselow, E. D., Fieve, R. R., Difiglia, C., & Sanfilipo, M. P. (1994). Lithium prophylaxis of bipolar illness: The value of combination treatment. *British Journal of Psychiatry, 164*(2), 208–214.

Petersen, M. (2008). *Our daily meds: How the pharmaceutical companies transformed themselves into slick marketing machines and hooked the nation on prescription drugs*. New York: Sarah Crichton Books.

Petr, C. G. (1998). *Social work with children and their families*. New York: Oxford.

Peuskens, J. (1995). Risperidone in the treatment of patients with chronic schizophrenia: A multi-national, multi-centre, double-blind, parallel group study versus haloperidol. *British Journal of Psychiatry, 166*, 712–726.

Pharoah, F. M., Rathbone, J., Mari, J. J., & Streiner, D. (2003). Family intervention for schizophrenia. The Cochrane Database of Systematic Reviews, Issue 3, Art. No. CD000088. DOI: 10.1012/14651858.

Piat, M., Sabetti, J., Couture, A., Sylvestre, J., Provencher, H., Botschner, J., & Stayner, D. (2009). What does recovery mean for me? Perspectives of Canadian mental health consumers. *Psychiatric Rehabilitation Journal, 32*(3), 199–207.

Piette, J. D., & Mah, C. A. (1997). The feasibility of automated voice messaging as an adjunct to diabetes outpatient care. *Diabetes Care, 20*, 15–21.

Pilette, W. L. (1988). The rise of three-party treatment relationships. *Psychotherapy, 25*, 420–423.

Pilling, S., Bebbington, P., Kuipers, E., Garety, P., Geddes, J., Orbach, G., & Morgan, C. (2002). Psychological treatments in schizophrenia: I. Meta-analysis of family intervention and cognitive behavior therapy. *Psychological Medicine, 32*(5), 763–782.

Pollio, D. E., North, C. S., & Foster, D. A. (1998). Content and curriculum in psychoeducation groups for families of persons with severe mental illness. *Psychiatric Services, 49*, 816–822.

Pollio, D. E., North, C. S., & Reid, D. L. (2006). Living with severe mental illness—What families and friends must know: Evaluation of a one-day psychoeducational workshop. *Social Work, 51*(1), 31–38.

Pollack, S. (2005). Taming the shrew: Regulating prisoners through women-centered mental health programming. *Critical Criminology, 13*(1), 612–616.

Popper, C. W. (1995). Balancing knowledge and judgment. *Child and Adolescent Psychiatry Clinics of North America, 4*, 483–513.

Posternak, M. A., & Zimmerman, M. (2007). Therapeutic effect of follow-up assessment on antidepressant and placebo response rates in antidepressant effect trials: Meta-analysis. *British Journal of Psychiatry, 190*(4), 287–292.

Potocky, M. (1993). An art therapy group for clients with chronic schizophrenia. *Social Work with Groups, 16*(3), 73–82.

Potter, G. G., Plassman, B. L., Burke, J. R., Kabeto, M. U., Langa, K. M., Llewellyn, D. J., Rogers, M. A. M., & Steffens, D. C. (2009). Impairment and dementia in African Americans and Whites. *Alzheimer's & Dementia, 5*(6), 445–453.

Powell, A. D. (2001). The medication life. *Journal of Psychotherapy Practice and Research, 10*(4), 217–222.

Pray, J. E. (1991). Responding to psychosocial needs: Physician perceptions of their referral practices for hospitalized patients. *Health & Social Work, 16*(3), 184–192.

Preskorn, S. H., Harvey, A. T., & Stanga, C. (1998). Drug interactions and their role in patient care. In A. J. Rush (Ed.), *Mood and anxiety disorders* (pp. 145–164). Philadelphia: Current Science.

Price, S. K., & Bentley, K. J. (under review). Psychopharmacological decision-making among pregnant and postpartum women and health providers: Informing compassionate women's health care.

Prochaska, J., & Norcross, J. (1994). *Systems of psychotherapy: A transtheoretical analysis* (3rd ed.). Pacific Grove, CA: Brooks/Cole.

Qato, D., Alexander, G. C., Conti, R. M., Johnson, M., Schumm, P., & Lindau, T. (2008). Use of prescription and over-the-counter medications and dietary supplements among older adults in the United States. *Journal of the American Medical Association, 300*(24), 2867–2878.

Quilty, L. C., De Fruyt, F., Rolland, J. P., Kennedy, S. H., Rouillon, P. F., & Bagby, R. M. (2008). Dimensional personality traits and treatment outcome in patients with major depressive disorder. *Journal of Affective Disorders, 108*(3), 241–250.

Raboch, J., Kališová, L., Nawka, A., Kitzlerová, E., Onchev, G., Karastergiou, A., Magliano, L., Dembinskas, A., Kiejna, A., Torres-Gonzales, F., Kjellin, L., Priebe, S., & Kallert, T. W. (2010). Use of coercive measures during involuntary hospitalization: Findings from ten European countries. *Psychiatric Services, 61*(10), 1012–1017.

Ramirez, L. F. (1996). Ethnicity and psychopharmacology in Latin America. *Mount Sinai Journal of Medicine, 63*(5–6), 330–331.

Ransom, S., Azzarello, L. M., & McMillan, S. C. (2006). Methodological issues in the recruitment of cancer pain patients and their caregivers. *Research in Nursing & Health, 29*(3), 190–198.

Rapp, R. C. (2007). The strengths perspective: Proving "my strengths" and "it works." *Social Work, 52*(2), 185–186.

Rappaport, N., & Chubinsky, P. (2000). The meaning of psychotropic medications for children, adolescents, and their families. *Journal of the American Academy of Child & Adolescent Psychiatry, 39*(9), 1198–1200.

Rassool, G. H. (2006). Understanding dual diagnosis: A review. In H. G. Rassool (Ed.), *Dual diagnosis nursing.* (pp. 3–15). Malden, MA: Blackwell Publishing.

Rathbone, J., Zhang, L., Zhang, M., Xia, J., Liu, X., Yang, Y., & Adams, C. E. (2012). Chinese herbal medicine for schizophrenia. *Cochrane Library,* DOI: 10.1002/14651858.CD003444.pub2.

Rea, M. M., Tompson, M. C., Miklowitz, D. J., Goldstein, M. J., Hwang, S., & Mintz, J. (2003). Family-focused treatment versus individual treatment for bipolar disorder: Results of a randomized clinical trial. *Journal of Consulting and Clinical Psychology, 71*(3), 482–492.

Reid, W. H., Pham, V. A., & Rago, W. (1993). Clozapine use by state programs: Public mental health systems respond to a new medication. *Hospital & Community Psychiatry, 44*, 739–743.

Reinhart, U. E. (2007). The pharmaceutical sector in health care. In F. A. Sloan & C. R. Hsieh (Eds.), *Pharmaceutical innovation: Incentives, competition, and cost-benefit analysis in international perspective* (pp. 25–53). New York: Cambridge University Press.

Reist, D., & VandeCreek, L. (2004). The pharmaceutical industry's use of gifts and educational events to influence prescription practices: Ethical dilemmas for psychologists. *Professional Psychology: Research and Practice, 35*(4), 329–335.

Relman, A. S., & Angell, M. (2002). America's other drug problem: How the drug industry distorts medicine and politics. *Time Magazine,* p. 27–29, 32–41.

Remler, M., & Cohen, D. (1992). Should the right of mental patients to refuse treatment with psychotropic drugs be severely curtailed? In E. Gambrill & R. Pruger (Eds.), *Controversial issues in social work* (pp. 301–315). Boston: Allyn & Bacon.

Renner, J. A., Baxter, J., Suzuki, J., & Ciraulo, D. A. (2011). Substance abuse and depression. In D. A. Ciraulo & R. I. Shader (Eds.), *Pharmacotherapy of depression* (2nd ed.), (pp. 239–274). New York: Springer Science.

Reynolds, N. R., Martin, F., Nanyonga, R. C., & Alonzo, A. A. (2012). Self-regulation: The common-sense model of illness representation. In V. H. Rice (Ed.), *Handbook of stress, coping, and health: Implications for nursing research, theory, and practice* (2nd ed.), (pp. 465–483). Thousand Oaks, CA: Sage Publications.

Rhodes, L. A. (1984). "This will clear your mind": The use of metaphors for medications in psychiatric settings. *Culture, Medicine and Psychiatry, 8,* 49–70.

Rice, A. H. (2000). Interdisciplinary collaboration in health care: Education, practice and research. *National Academies of Practice Forum, 2*(1), 59–73.

Riolo, S. A., Nguyen, T. A., Greden, J. F., & King, C. A. (2005). Prevalence of depression by race/ethnicity: Findings from the National Health and Nutritional Examination Survey III. *American Journal of Public Health, 95*(6), 998–100.

Robb, A. S., & Joshi, P. T. (2008). Newer drugs. In B. Geller & M. P. DelBello (Eds.), *Treatment of bipolar disorder in children and adolescents* (pp. 126–152). New York: Guilford Press.

Roe, D., Goldblatt, H., Baloush-Klienman, V., Swarbrick, M., & Davidson, L. (2009). Why and how people decide to stop taking psychiatric medication: Exploring the subjective process of choice. *Psychiatric Rehabilitation Journal, 33*(1), 38–46.

Rosenfeld, P. J. (2007). Poison or cure: Meanings of medication in schizophrenia. *Journal of the American Academy of Psychoanalysis and Dynamic Psychiatry, 35*(2), 189–201.

Rosenson, M., & Kasten, A. M. (1991). Another view of autonomy: Arranging for consent in advance. *Hospital & Community Psychiatry, 17,* 1–7.

Ross, C., & Pam, A. (1995). *Pseudoscience in biological psychiatry: Blaming the body.* New York: John Wiley and Sons.

Rossignol, D. (2009). Novel and emerging treatments for autism spectrum disorders: A systematic review. *Annals of Clinical Psychiatry, 21*(4), 213–236.

Rothbaum, B. O., & Astin, M. C. (2000). Integration of pharmacotherapy and psychotherapy for bipolar disorder. *Journal of Clinical Psychiatry, 61*(Suppl. 9), 68–75.

Rothman, J. (1989). Client self-determination: Untangling the knot. *Social Service Review, 63*(4), 598–612.

Rouget, B. W., & Aubry, J. M. (2007). Efficacy of psychoeducational approaches on bipolar disorders: A review of the literature. *Journal of Affective Disorders, 98*(1–2), 11–27.

Rubinow, D. R., & Schmidt, P. J. (2003). Menstrual cycle-related and perimenopause-related affective disorders. In O. Wolkowitz & A. J. Anthony (Eds.), *Psychoneuroendocrinology: The scientific basis of clinical practice* (pp. 245–279). Washington, DC: American Psychiatric Publishing.

Ruffolo, M. C., Kuhn, M. T., & Evans, M. E. (2006). Developing a parent-professional team leadership model in group work: Work with families with children experiencing behavioral and emotional problems. *Social Work, 51*(1), 39–47.

Rungruangsiripan, M., Sitthimongkol, Y., Maneesriwongul, W., Talley, S., & Vorapongsathorn, T. (2011). Mediating role of illness representation among social support, therapeutic alliance, experience of medication side effects, and medication adherence in persons with schizophrenia. *Archives of Psychiatric Nursing, 25*(4), 269–283.

Ryan, R. M., & Deci, E. L. (2008). A self-determination theory approach to psychotherapy: The motivational basis for effective change. *Canadian Psychology, 49*(3), 186–193.

Rynn, M., Puliafico, A., Heleniak, C., Rikhi, P., Ghalib, K., & Vidair, H. (2011). Advances in pharmacotherapy for pediatric anxiety disorders. *Depression and Anxiety, 28*(1), 76–87.

Sadock, B. J., & Sadock, V. A. (2009). *Kaplan & Sadock's comprehensive textbook of psychiatry* (9th ed.). Philadelphia, PA: Wolters Kluwer Health/Lippincott Williams & Wilkins.

Saija, S., & Mortimer, A. M. (2011). *Practice questions in psychopharmacology.* London: Springer Healthcare.

Saleeby, D. (2011). Some basic ideas about the strengths perspective. In F. J. Turner (Ed.), *Social work treatment: Interlocking theoretical approaches* (5th ed.), (pp. 477–485). New York: Oxford University Press.

Saleeby, D. (1985). In clinical social work is the body politic? *Social Service Review, 59,* 578–592.

Saleeby, D. (1992). Introduction: Beginnings of a strength approach to practice. In D. Saleeby (Ed.), *The strengths perspective in social work practice* (pp. 41–44). New York: Longman.

Sammons, M. T., & Schmidt, N. B. (Eds.). (2001). *Combined treatment for mental disorders: A guide to psychological and pharmacological interventions.* Washington, DC: American Psychological Association.

Sands, R. G. (1989). The social worker joins the team: A look at the socialization process. *Social Work in Health Care, 14*(2), 1–14.

Sarris, J., & Kavanagh, D. J. (2009). Kava and St. John's wort: Current evidence for use in mood and anxiety disorders. *Journal of Alternative and Complementary Medicine, 15*(8), 827–836.

Sarris, J., Kavanagh, D. J., & Byrne, G. (2010). Adjuvant use of nutritional and herbal medicines with antidepressants, mood stabilizers and benzodiazepines. *Journal of Psychiatric Research, 44*(1), 32–41.

Sarris, J., Panossian, A., Schweitzer, I., Stough, C., & Scholey, A. (2011). Herbal medicine for depression, anxiety and insomnia: A review of psychopharmacology and clinical evidence. *European Neuropsychopharmacology, 21* (12), 841–860.

Sarwer-Foner, G. J. (1975). Psychiatric symptomatology: Its meaning and function in relation to the psychodynamic action of drugs. In H. C. B. Denbar (Ed.), *Psychopharmacological treatment: Theory and practice* (pp. 201–224). New York: Marcel Dekker.

Scahill, L., Solanto, M., & McGuire, J. (2008). The science and ethics of placebo in pediatric psychopharmacology. *Ethics & Behavior, 182,* 266–285.

Schardt, D. (1998). Herbs for nerves. *Nutrition Action Newsletter, 25*(8), 8–12.

Schatzberg, A. F., & Nemeroff, C. B. (2009). *The American psychiatric publishing textbook of psychopharmacology* (4th ed.). Washington, DC: American Psychiatric Publishing.

Scheid, T. L. (2003). Managed care and the rationalization of mental health services. *Journal of Health and Social Behavior, 44*(2), 142–161.

Schiller, L., & Bennett, A. (1994). *The quiet room.* New York: Warner.

Schmit, J. (2004, August 17). Drugmaker admitted fraud, but sales flourish. *USA Today,* p. A, 2A.

Schneider, B., Scissons, H., Arney, L., Benson, G., Derry, J., Lucas, K., Misurelli, M., Nickerson, D., & Sunderland, M. (2004). Communication between people with schizophrenia and their medical professionals: A participatory research project. *Qualitative Health Research, 14*(4), 562–577.

Schulte, S. J., Meier, P. S., Stirling, J., Berry, M. (2010). Understanding dual diagnosis: A risk factor for dropout of addiction treatment. *Mental Health and Substance Use: Dual Diagnosis, 3*(2), 94–109.

Seale, C., Chaplin, R., Lelliott, P., & Quirk, A. (2006). Sharing decisions in consultations involving anti-psychotic medication: A qualitative study of psychiatrists' experiences. *Social Science and Medicine, 62*, 2861–2873.

Segal, E. A., Gerdes, K. E., & Steiner, S. (2013). *An introduction to the profession of social work: Becoming a change agent* (4th ed.). Belmont, CA: Brooks/Cole.

Shah, B. K., & Chewing, B. (2011). Concordance between observer reports and patient survey reports of pharmacists' communication behaviors. *Research in Social & Administrative Policy, 7*(3), 272–280.

Sharfstein, S. S. (2005). Big pharma and American Psychiatry: The good, the bad and the ugly. *Psychiatric News, 40*(16), 3.

Sharfstein, S. S. (2008). Big pharma and American psychiatry (Editorial). *Journal of Nervous and Mental Disease, 196*(4), 265–266.

Sheehan, S. (1982). *Is there no place on earth for me?* New York: Random House.

Sheikh, J. I., Cassidy, E. L., Doraiswamy, P. M., Salomon, R. M., Hornig, M., Holland, P. J., Mandel, F. S., Clary, C. M., & Burt, T. (2004). Efficacy, safety, and tolerability of sertraline in patients with late-life depression and comorbid medical illness. *Journal of the American Geriatrics Society, 52*(1), 86–92.

Shelton, D., Ehret, M. J., Wakai, S., Kapetanovic, T., & Moran, M. (2010). Psychotropic medication adherence in correctional facilities: A review of the literature. *Journal of Psychiatric and Mental Health Nursing, 17*, 603–613.

Shim, R. S., Compton, M. T., Rust, G., Druss, B. G., & Kaslow, N. J. (2009). Race-ethnicity as a predictor of attitudes toward mental health treatment seeking. *Psychiatric Services, 60*(10), 1336–1341.

Shoemaker, S. J., & de Oliveira, D. R. (2008). Understanding the meaning of medications for patients: The medication experience. *Pharmacy World Science, 30*, 86–91.

Simpson, G. M., & Angus, J. W. S. (1970). A rating scale for extrapyramidal side effects. *Acta Psychiatrica Scandinavia, 212*, 11–19.

Singh, I. (2007). Clinical implications of ethical concepts: Moral self-understandings in children taking methylphenidate for ADHD. *Clinical Child Psychology and Psychiatry, 12*(2), 167–182.

Skolnick, P. (Ed.). (1997). *Antidepressants: New pharmacological strategies.* Totowa, NJ: Humana Press.

Smith, S. (2010). Gender differences in antipsychotic prescribing. *International Review of Psychiatry, 22*(5), 472–484.

Soloff, P. H., Price, J. C., Mason, N. S., Becker, C., & Meltzer, C. C. (2009). *Gender, personality, and serotonin-2A receptor binding in healthy subjects.* http://dx.doi.org/10.1016/j.pscychresns.2009.08.007.

Soyer, D. (1963). The right to fail. *Social Work, 8*(3), 72–78.

Spaniol, L., Zipple, A., & FitzGerald, S. (1984). How professionals can share power with families: Practical approaches to working with families of the mentally ill. *Psychosocial Rehabilitation Journal, 8*(2), 77–84.

Spaulding, W., & Nolting, J. (2006). Psychotherapy for schizophrenia in the year 2030: Prognosis and prognostication. *Schizophrenia Bulletin, 32*(Suppl. 1), S94–S105.

Spencer, T. J., Biederman, J., & Wilkins, T. (1998). Pharmacotherapy of ADHD with antidepressants. In R. A. Barkley (Ed.), *Attention-deficit hyperactivity disorder: A handbook for diagnosis and treatment* (2nd ed.), (pp. 552–563). New York: Guilford Press.

Srisurapanont, M., Maneeton, B., Maneeton, N., Lankappa, S., & Gandhi, R. (2010). Quetiapine for schizophrenia. *Cochrane Collaboration,* DOI: 10.1002/14651858.CD000967.pub2.

Stacey, D. Légaré, F., Pouliot, S., Kryworuchko, J.. & Dunn, S. (2010). Shared decision-making models to inform an interprofessional perspective on decision making: A theory analysis.

Patient Education and Counseling, 80(2), 164–172.

Stahl, S. M. (2008). *Stahl's essential psychopharmacology: Neuroscientific basis and practical applications* (3rd ed.). New York: Cambridge University Press.

Steele, M., Jensen, P. S., & Quinn, D. M. P. (2006). Remission versus response as the goal of therapy in ADHD: A new standard for the field? *Clinical Therapeutics: International Peer-Reviewed Journal of Drug Therapy, 28*(11), 1892–1908.

Stein, D. J. (2012). Psychopharmalogical enhancement: A conceptual framework. *Philosophy, Ethics, and Humanities in Medicine, 7*(5), DOI: 10.1186/1747-5341-7-5.

Stone, A. A. (1990). Law, science, and psychiatric malpractice: A response to Klerman's indictment of psychoanalytic psychiatry. *American Journal of Psychiatry, 147*, 419–427.

Storosum, J. G., Elferick, A. J. A., van Zweiten, B. J., van der Brink, W., Gersons, B. P. R., van Strick, R., & Broekmans, A. W. (2001). "Short-term efficacy of tricyclic antidepressants revisited: A meta-analytic study": Erratum. *European Neuropsychopharmacology, 11*(4), 325.

Stowe, Z. N. (2007). The use of mood stabilizers during breastfeeding. *Journal of Clinical Psychiatry, 68*(Suppl. 9), 22–28.

Stromm-Gottfried, K. (2009). Enacting the educator role: Principles for practice. In A. R. Roberts and G. J. Greeene (Eds.) *Social workers' desk reference* (pp. 437–441), New York: Oxford Press.

Sturm, R., & Klap, R. (1999). Use of psychiatrists, psychologists and Masters-level therapists in managed behavioral health care carve-out plans. *Psychiatric Services, 50*, 504–508.

Sussman, M., Friedman, M., Korn, J. R., Hassan, M., Kim, J., & Menzin, J. (2012). The relationship between use of antidepressants and resource utilization among patients with manic or mixed bipolar disorder episodes: Findings from a managed care setting. *Journal of Affective Disorders, 138*(3), 425–432.

Swann, A. C., & Ginsberg, D. L. (2004). Special needs of women with bipolar disorder. *CNS Spectrums, 9*(8), 1–11.

Swartz, M. S., Swanson, J. W., Hiday, V. A., Borum, R., Wagner, R., & Burns, B. J. (1998). Taking the wrong drugs: The role of substance abuse and medication noncompliance in violence among severely mentally ill individuals. *Social Psychiatry and Psychiatric Epidemiology, 33* (Suppl. 1), S75–S80.

Swazey, J. P. (1974). *Chlorpromazine in psychiatry: A study of therapeutic innovation.* Cambridge, MA: MIT Press.

Szasz, T. (1994). *Cruel compassion: Psychiatric control of society's unwanted.* New York: John Wiley.

Talen, M. R., Fraser, J. S., & Cauley, K. (2002). From soup to nuts: Integrating clinical psychology training into primary healthcare settings. *Family, Systems & Health, 20*, 419–429.

Taurines, R., Gerlach, M., Warnke, A., Thome, J., & Wewetzer, C. (2011). Pharmacotherapy in depressed children and adolescents. *World Journal of Biological Psychiatry, 12*(Suppl. 1), 11–15.

Teter, C. J., Falone, A. E., Bakaian, A. M., Tu, C., Ongur, D., & Weiss, R. D. (2011). Medication adherence and attitudes in patients with bipolar disorder and current versus past substance use disorder. *Psychiatry Research, 190*(2–3), 253–258.

Thompson, R., & Weisberg, S. (1990). Families as educational consumers: What do they want? What do they receive? *Health & Social Work, 15*, 221–227.

Tobias, M. (1990). Validator: A key role in empowering the chronically mentally ill. *Social Work, 35*, 357–359.

Todman, M., Gordon-Leeds, D., & Taylor, S. (1997). Attitude toward medication and perceived competence among chronically psychotic patients. *Psychological Reports, 80*(pt. 1, 3), 809–810.

Torniainen, M., Suvisaari, J., Partonen, T., Castaneda, A. E., Kuha, A., Perälä, J., Saarni, S., Lönnqvist, J., & Tuulio-Henriksson, A. (2011). Sex differences in cognition among persons with schizophrenia and healthy first-degree relatives. *Psychiatry Research, 188*(1), 7–12.

Toprac, M. G., Dennehy, E. B., Carmody, T. J., Crismon, M. L., Miller, A. L., Trivedi, M. H., Suppes, T., & Rush, A. J. (2006). Implementation of the Texas Medication Algorithm Project Patient and Family Education Program. *Journal of Clinical Psychiatry, 67*(9), 1362–1372.

Toprac, M. G., Rush, A. J., Conner, T. M., Crismon, M. L., Dees, M., Hopkins, C., Rowe, V., & Shon, S. P. (2000). The Texas Medication Algorithm Project Patient and Family Education Program: A consumer-guided initiative. *Journal of Clinical Psychiatry, 61*(7), 477–484.

Torres, I. J., DeFreitas, C. M., DeFreitas, V. G., Bond, D. J., Kunz, M., Honer, W. G., Lam, R. W., & Yatham, L. N. (2011). Relationshp between cognitive functioning and 6-month clinical and functional outcomes in patients with first manic episode bipolar I disorder. *Psychological Medicine, 41*(5), 971–982.

Toseland, R., Zaneles-Palmer, J., & Chapman, D. (1986). Teamwork in psychiatric settings. *Social Work, 31*, 46–52.

Tracy, A. B. (1994). *Prozac: Panacea or Pandora.* West Jordan, VT: Cassia Publications.

Tung, W. C. (2011). Cultural barriers to mental health services among Asian Americans. *Home Health Care Management & Practice, 23*(4), 303–305.

Turner, S. E., & Cooley-Quille, M. R. (1996). Socioecological and socio-cultural variables in psychopharmacology research: Methodological considerations. *Psychopharmacology Bulletin, 32*(2), 183–192.

Udechuku, A., Nguyen, T., Hill, B., & Szego, K. (2010). Antidepressants in pregnancy: A systematic review. *Australian and New Zealand Journal of Psychiatry, 44*(11), 978–996.

Ulus, F. (2001). Substance use and medication treatment. *Psychiatric Services, 52*(9), 1255.

United States Census Bureau (2012). http://www.census.gov/#.

Urrutia, G. (1994). Medication refusal: Clinical picture and outcome after use of administrative review. *Bulletin of the American Academy of Psychiatry and the Law, 22*, 595–603.

Usher, K. (2001). Taking neuroleptic medications as the treatment for schizophrenia: A phenomenological study. *Australian and New Zealand Journal of Mental Health Nursing, 10*, 145–155.

Valenstein, E. T. (1998). *Blaming the brain: The truth about drugs and mental health.* New York: Free Press.

Valenstein, M., Barry, K. L., Blow, F. C., Copeland, L., & Ullman, E. (1998). Agreement between seriously mentally ill veterans and their clinicians about medication compliance. *Psychiatric Services, 49*, 1043–1048.

Van Dorn, R., Volavka, J., Johnson, N. (2012). Mental disorder and violence: Is there a relationship beyond substance use? *Social Psychiatry and Psychiatric Epidemiology, 47*(3), 487–503.

Vasudev, A., Macritchie, K., Vasudev, K., Watson, S., Geddes, J., & Young, A. H. (2011). Oxcarbazepine for acute affective episodes in bipolar disorder. *Cochrane Collaboration,* DOI: 10.1002/14651858.CD004857.pub2.

Vasudev, K., Macritchie, K., Geddes, J., Watson, S., & Young, A. H. (2009). Topiramate for acute affective episodes in bipolar disorder. *Cochrance Collaboration,* DOI: 10.1002/14651858.CD003384.pub2.

Velligan, D. I., Weiden, P. J., Sajatovic, M., Scott, J., Carpenter, D., Ross, R., & Docherty, J. P. (2009). Strategies for addressing adherence problems in patients with serious and persistent mental illness: Recommendations from the Expert Consensus Guidelines. *Journal of Psychiatric Practice, 16*(5), 306–323.

Vieta, E. (2005). Improving treatment adherence in bipolar disorder through psychoeducation. *Journal of Clinical Psychiatry, 66*(Suppl. 1), 24–29.

Vieta, E., & Suppes, T. (2008) Bipolar II disorder: Arguments for and against a distinct diagnostic entity. *Bipolar Disorders, 10*(Suppl. 1p2), 163–178.

Vourlekis, B., & Ell, K. (2007). Best practice case management for improved medical adherence. *Social Work in Health Care, 44*(3), 161–177.

Walker, S. (1996). *A dose of sanity*. New York: Wiley & Sons.

Walkup, J. T., Albano, A. M., Piacentini, J., Birmaher, B., Compton, S. N., Sherrill, J. T., Ginsburg, G. S., Rynn, M. A., McCracken, J., Waslick, B., Iyengar, S., March, J. S., & Kendall, P. C. (2008). Cognitive behavioral therapy, sertraline, or a combination in childhood anxiety. *New England Journal of Medicine, 359*(26), 2753–2766.

Walsh, C. B. (1993). This prescription may be hazardous to your health: Who is accountable to the patient? *Journal of Clinical Psychopharmacology, 13*(1), 68–70.

Walsh, J. (1995) Social work practice and mental illness: Symbolic interactionish as a framework for intervention. *Journal of Applied Social Science, 23*, 71–85.

Walsh, J. (2000). *Clinical case management with persons having mental illness: A relationship-based perspective*. Pacific Grove, CA: Brooks/Cole.

Walsh, J. (2010). *Psychoeducation in mental health*. Chicago: Lyceum.

Walsh, J. (2013). *The recovery philosophy and direct social work practice*. Chicago: Lyceum.

Walsh, J., Farmer, R., Taylor, M. F., & Bentley, K. J. (2003). Ethical dilemmas of practicing social workers around psychiatric medication: Results of a national study. *Social Work in Mental Health, 1*(4), 91–105.

Ware, N. C., Tugenberg, T., & Dickey, B. (2004). Practitioner relationships and quality of care for low-income persons with serious mental illness. *Psychiatric Services, 55*(5), 555–559.

Warren, P. A. (Ed.) (2011). *Behavioral health disability: Innovations in prevention and management*. New York: Springer.

Watnabi, A. (2006). Theoretical review of assertiveness inventories: Issues in the measurement of four theoretical dimensions. *Japanese Journal of Educational Psychology, 54*(3), 420–433.

Weick, A., Rapp, C., Sullivan, W. P., & Kisthardt, W. (1989). A strengths perspective for social work practice. *Social Work, 34*, 350–354.

Weiden, P., Rapkin, B., Mott, T., Zygmut, A., Goldman, D., Horvitz-Lennon, M., & Frances, A. (1994). Rating of medication influences (ROMS) scale in schizophrenia. *Schizophrenia Bulletin, 20*, 297–307.

Weiden, P. J., Mackell, J. A., & McDonnell, D. D. (2004). Obesity as a risk factor for antipsychotic noncompliance. *Schizophrenia Research, 66*(1), 51–57.

Weil, M. (1982). Research on issues in collaboration between social workers and lawyers. *Social Service Review, 56*, 393–405.

Weinberger, A. H., & George, T. P. (2009). Nicotine and tobacco use in patients with schizophrenia. In J. M. Meyer & H. A. Nasrallah, (Ed.). *Medical illness and schizophrenia* (2nd ed.), (pp. 223–243). Arlington, VA: American Psychiatric Publishing.

Wernicke, U., Turner, T., & Priebe, S. (2001). Complimentary medicines in psychiatry: Review of effectiveness and safety. *British Journal of Psychiatry, 188*, 109–121.

Wesson, V. A., Levitt, A. J., & Joffe, R. T. (1994). Change in folate status with antidepressant medication. *Psychiatry Research, 53*(3), 313–322.

Wettstein, R. M. (1992). Legal aspects of prescribing. In M. S. Keshavan & J. S. Kennedy (Eds.). *Drug-induced dysfunction in psychiatry* (pp. 9–19). New York: Hemisphere Publishing.

Whiskey, E., Wernike, U., & Taylor, D. (2001). A systematic review and meta-analysis of Hypercom perforatum in depression: A comprehensive clinical review. *International Clinical Psychopharmacology, 16*(5), 239–252.

Wiedemann, K. (2011). Biomarkers in development of psychotropic drugs. *Dialogues in Clinical Neuroscience, 13*(2), 225–234.

Wilder, C. M., Elbogen, E. B., Moser, L. L., Swanson, J. W., & Swartz, M. S. (2010). Medication preferences and adherence among individuals with severe mental illness and psychiatric advance directives. *Psychiatric Services, 61*(4), 380–385.

Wilk, R. J. (1994). Are the rights of people with mental illness still important? *Social Work, 39*, 167–177.

Willetts, R. (1980). Advocacy and the mentally ill. *Social Work, 25,* 372–377.

Williams, G. C., Rodin, G. C., Ryan, R. M., Grolnick, W. S., & Deci, E. L. (1998). Autonomous regulation and long-term medication adherence in adult outpatients. *Health Psychology, 17,* 269–276.

Wilson, S. R. (1993). Patient and physician behavior models related to asthma care. *Medical Care, 31*(Suppl.), MS49–MS60.

Wilson, W. H., & Claussen, A. M. (1993). New antipsychotic medications: Hope for the future. *Innovations & Research, 2,* 3–11.

Wing, Y. K., Chan, E., Chan, K., Lee, S., & Shek, C. C. (1997). Lithium pharmacokinetics in Chinese manic-depressive patients. *Journal of Clinical Psychopharmacology, 17*(3), 179–184.

Winkler, D., Willeit, M., Wolf, R., Stamenkovic, M., Tuchsler, J., Pirek, E., Konstantinidis, A., Schindler, S., Barnas, C., & Kasper, S. (2003). Clonazepam in the long-term treatment of patients with unipolar depression, bipolar and schizoaffective disorder. *European Neuropsychopharmacology, 13*(2), 129–134.

Winslade, W. (1981). Ethical issues. In E. A. Serafetinides (Ed.). *Psychiatric research in practice: Biobehavioral terms* (pp. 227–240). New York: Grune & Stratton.

Wolraich, M. L. (2003). Annotation: The use of psychotropic medications in children: An American view. *Journal of Child Psychology and Psychiatry, 44*(2), 159–168.

Woodward, A. T. (2011). Discrimination and help-seeking: Use of professional services and informal support among African Americans, Black Carribeans, and non-Hispanic Whites with a mental disorder. *Race and Social Problems, 3*(3), 146–159.

Xu, Y., Okuda, M., Hser, Y., Hasin, D., Liu, S., Grant, B. F., Blanco, C. (2011). Twelve-month prevalence of psychiatric disorders and treatment-seeking among Asian American/Pacific Islanders in the United States: Results from the national epidemiological survey on alcohol and related conditions. *Journal of Psychiatric Research, 45*(7), 910–918.

Yen, C., Cheng, C., Huang, C., Yen, J., Ko, C., & Chen, C. (2008). Quality of life and its association with insight, adverse effects of medication and use of atypical antipsychotics in patients with bipolar disorder and schizophrenia in remission. *Bipolar Disorders, 10*(5), 617–624.

Yeung, K. S. S., Ho, A. P. Y., Lo, M. C. H., & Chan, E. A. (2010). Social work ethical decision making in an interdisciplinary context. *British Journal of Social Work, 40*(5), 1573–1590.

Young, R. C. (2005). Evidence-based pharmacological treatment of geriatric bipolar disorder. *Psychiatric Clinics of North America, 28,* 837–869.

Young, R. C., Biggs, J. T., Ziegler, V. E., & Meyer, D. A. (1978). A rating scale for mania: Reliability, validity, sensitivity. *British Journal of Psychiatry, 133,* 429–435.

Youssef, F. (1984). Adherence to therapy in psychiatric patients: An empirical investigation of the impact of patient education. *International Journal of Nursing Studies, 21,* 51–57.

Zaretsky, A. E., Rizvi, S., & Parikh, S. V. (2007). How well do psychosocial interventions work in bipolar disorder? *The Canadian Journal of Psychiatry, 52*(1), 14–21.

Zarit, S. H., & Zarit, J. M. (2007). *Mental disorders in older adults: Fundamentals of assessment and treatment* (2nd ed.). New York: Guilford Press.

Ziedonis, D., Williams, J., Corrigan, P., & Smelson, D. (2000). Management of substance abuse in schizophrenia. *Psychiatric Annals, 30*(1), 67–75.

Zipple, A. M., Langle, S., Spaniol, L., & Fisher, H. (1990). Client confidentiality and the family's need to know: Strategies for resolving the conflict. *Community Mental Health Journal, 26,* 533–545.

Name Index

A

Abdel Mohsen, M. Y., 203
Abou, S. M. T., 271
Abramson, J. S., 20, 21
Abroms, G., 274
Adams, C. E., 270
Adams, J. R., 193
Adams, S. G., 244
Addington, D., 266
Adelman, S. A., 182
Administration for
    Children and
    Families, 27
Agarwal, M. R., 249
Aguado, J., 242
Aguilar-Gaxiola, S., 162
Ahn, M. S., 158
Akiskal, H. S., 173
Albala, A. A., 152, 154, 156
Albano, A. M., 28
Aldebot, S., 249
Aldridge, M. A., 257
Alegria, M., 163
Alexander, G. C., 30
Allart, A., 267
Allen, C., 255
Allen, M. H., 130
Alonzo, A. A., 245
Alpert, J. E., 271
Altman, S., 114
Aly, M., 267
Amedei, S. G., 120
American Psychiatric
    Association
    (APA), 19, 86, 87,
    110, 111, 225
American Psychological
    Association
    (APA), 156, 172,
    273

Anastopoulos, A. D., 225
Anderson, H., 36
Andreasen, N. C., 223
Angell, M., 15
Angermeyer, M. C., 246
Angus, J. W. S., 223
Anuradha, K., 38
Applegate, J. S., 13
Armstrong, L., 17
Arora, N. K., 232
Asadi, L., 176
Ascher-Svanum, H., 201
Ashford, J. B., 175, 275
Ashley, A., 22, 236
Asnaani, A., 164
Astin, M. C., 198
Atherton, C. R., 20
Aubry, J. M., 198
Auge, M., 83
Avorn, J., 120
Awad, A. G., 182
Ax, R. K., 273
Axelson, D. A., 211
Azzarello, L. M., 203

B

Bachur, J. A., 42
Bagby, R. M., 228
Bainbridge, J. L., 102
Baird, C., 165
Baldessarini, R. J., 114
Balon, R., 151, 174
Baloush-Klienman, V., 193
Balson, P. M., 247
Barker, R. L., 40
Barkley R. A., 49
Barksy, A. J., 178
Barnas, C., 121
Barnes, T. R. E., 223
Barnett, K. B., 83, 159

Barondes, S. H., 16
Barrickman, P. J., 201
Barron, E., 114
Barsky, A. E., 251
Bassman, R., 251, 252
Basso, M., 200
Baumesiter, A. A., 73
Baxter, J., 164
Bayle, F., 243, 247
Bebbington, P., 198
Beck, E. M., 244
Beck, J. S., 259
Becker, C., 147
Bedz, H., 119
Beevers, C. G., 153
Beitman, B. D., 14, 172
Belanoff, J., 146
Bell, A. C., 228–229
Ben Armor, L., 157
Bender, B., 227
Benítez, C. I. P., 155
Bennett, A., 278
Benoit, M., 244, 247
Bentall, R., 252
Bentley, K. J., 11, 12, 17,
    43, 44, 48, 152,
    171, 175, 177,
    179, 180, 181,
    182, 183, 184,
    188, 196, 200,
    216, 217, 237,
    259, 274
Beresford, C., 211
Berger, F. M., 125
Berghofer, G., 216
Berner, M., 269
Bernstein, G. A., 224
Berry, M., 164
Bertelsen, M., 248
Bertsch, J., 248
Beyer, B., 7
Bhattacharjee J., 96

Bhaumik, D. K., 159
Bicknell, L., 203
Biederman, J., 139, 159
Biggs, J. T., 224
Birmaher, B., 28, 224
Birmhauer, B., 211
Bishop, J. R., 149, 161
Bisonó, A. M., 256
Bittle, R. G., 231
Blair, K., 205, 206, 235
Blanc, O., 243, 247
Blanco, C., 163
Blech, J., 15
Blinder, B. J., 14
Blyler, C. R., 242
Bohn, R. L., 120
Boles, R. G., 76
Bolhofner, K., 111
Bond, A. L., 175
Bond, D. J., 199
Borchardt, C. M., 224
Borus, J. S., 271
Botschner, J., 35
Botsford, A. L., 199
Bottai, R., 244, 247
Bouch, J., 196
Bourcet, A., 244, 247
Bowden, C. L., 118
Boyd, J., 204
Boyer, L., 244, 247
Brabbins, C., 252
Bradley, S., 173, 174
Breggin, 1999
Breggin, P., 248, 265
Brennan, J. W., 199
Brent, D. A., 211
Breslau, J., 162
Brodsky, C., 274
Brody, H., 72, 182
Broekmans, A. W., 105
Bronstein, L. R., 22
Brooks, A., 6, 41, 236

Brown, C., 209
Brown, C. H., 159
Brown, P., 14, 252
Browne, T. A., 37
Brunette, M. F., 165
Buckalew, L., 246
Budd, R. J., 249
Buelow, J. R., 177, 180
Buelow, S., 177, 180
Buffington, E., 221
Bühner, M., 192
Bulmash, E., 228
Bureau of Labor Statistics, 25
Burgess, S., 114
Burke, J. R., 162
Burland, J., 209
Burns, C., 22
Burroughs, V. J., 162
Bursztajn, H., 178
Burt, T., 30
Burti, L., 36
Busch, F. N., 175
Butleer, J., 252
Bylund, C. L., 232
Byrne, G., 270
Byrne, M. K., 247

C

Calabrese, J. R., 118
Caley, C. F., 162
Caligiuri, M. P., 154
Cameron, J. K., 22
Campbell, L. F., 273
Campbell, T. C., 256
Candlis, P., 200
Caplan, P. J., 15
Carey, T. S., 117
Carmody, T. J., 201, 206
Carpenter, D., 245
Carpenter, E. A., 182
Carpenter, W. T., 266
Carrick, R., 182
Carroll, K. M., 266
Carson, D. S., 137
Carter, C., 128
Carter, R., 226
Casper, R. C., 146
Cassidy, C. M., 243
Cassidy, E. L., 30
Castaneda, A. E., 148
Caudill, T. S., 19
Cauley, K., 22
Cavelati, M., 244
Chan, E., 36, 164
Chan, K., 164
Chang, G., 273
Chaplin, R., 192
Chapman, D., 21
Charlach, A., 244, 256
Chen, C., 225
Cheng, C., 225
Cheng, J. K. Y., 164
Chessick, C. A., 130
Chewing, B., 232
Chewning, B., 232, 239
Cho, R. Y., 222
Choy, Y., 151

Christensen, T. O., 248
Chubinsky, P., 182
Ciraulo, D. A., 164
Clancy, C., 165
Clark, E., 244
Clark, R. E., 165
Clarke, G. N., 198
Clary, C., 30, 196
Clayton, A. H., 147, 151
Clayton, C., 259
Clemens, S. E., 199
Cluxton-Keller, F., 157
Coffey, M., 40
Cohen, 1999
Cohen, B., 250
Cohen, D., 6, 11, 14, 42, 43, 48, 195, 217, 248, 251, 265, 266
Cohen, G., 243
Cohen, I. M., 125
Cohen, L. J., 19, 114
Cohen, L. S., 151
Cohen, M. H., 176
Cohen, N. L., 243
Cohen, R., 192
Coker, E., 203
Collings, P., 223
Collins, K., 17
Colom, F., 198
Colom, F., 210
Combs, D., 200
Compton, M. T., 160
Compton, S. N., 28
Connaway, R. S., 236
Connors, G., 254
Conrad, P., 245
Consedine, N. S., 162
Conti, R. M., 30
Cook, J. A., 221
Cook, K., 221
Cooley-Quille, M. R., 160, 163
Coombs, T., 247
Cooper, W. O., 150
Copeland, M. E., 220, 221
Coppen, A., 271
Corey, L., 221
Correll, C. U., 80
Corrigan, P., 165
Corrigan, P. W., 83, 198, 228
Corsini, R. J., 40
Cortina, J., 250
Corty, E., 165
Côté, G., 251
Couture, A., 35
Cowles, L. A., 21
Coryell, W., 114
Craighead, W. E., 211
Cramer, J. A., 242
Cranford, J. A., 165
Crawford, V., 165
Crismon, M. L., 201, 206
Crome, I. B., 165
Crosby, R. D., 224
Crowe, M., 244, 248
Crumley, J. M., 18

Cubine, T., 200
Cummings, C. M., 211
Curtis, L. C., 221
Curtis, L. T., 272
Curtis, S. M., 165

D

da Chuna, A., 130
Dagan, Y., 267
Daltroy, L. H., 265
Dane, B. O., 20, 21
Dang, A., 131
Dassa, D., 244, 247
Dassori, A. M., 163
David, A., 258
Davidson, L., 193, 221
Davidson, M., 6, 12, 43
Davis, P., 114
Davis, T. S., 38
Dean, A. J., 248
Deane, F. P., 247
Deci, E. L., 35, 260
Dee, J. R., 22
Deegan, P. E., 34, 36, 192, 193
DeFreitas, C. M., 199
DeFreitas, V. G., 199
De Fruyt, F., 228
Degani, A., 246
DeGeest, S., 244
DeJong, W., 265
DeLeon, P. H., 274
de Lima, M., 130
deMamani, A. G., 249
Dembinskas, A., 250
Demiger, O., 25
DeNavas-Walt, C., 27
Dennehy, E. B., 201, 206
Dennis, C. L., 149
de Oliveira, D. R., 182
Dere-Meyer, C., 227
Desai, R. A., 163
de Silva, V., 139
Dever, A., 196
Dewan, M. J., 180
Diamond, P., 163
Diamond, R. J., 39, 218
Diaz, K., 227
Dickey, B., 34
DiClemente, C., 254
Diefenbach, M., 244
Difiglia, C., 114
Diflorio, A., 148
Dimaite, R., 164
Ditz, K. A., 222
Dixon, L., 196, 249
Dixon, L. B., 209
Docherty, J. P., 216, 245
Dolder, C. R., 154
Donohoe, G., 258
Donovan, D., 254
Doraiswamy, P. M., 30
Doran, C. D., 86, 92, 146, 153, 155, 164, 167
Dore, M. N., 199
Double, D. B., 196
Dow, M. G., 232

Draine, J., 245
Drake, R. E., 36, 166, 192, 193
Draper, J., 248
Drolen, C. S., 20
Droulout, T., 220
Drug Enforcement Agency (DEA), 136
Druss, B. G., 160
Drymalski, W. M., 256
Dubin, W. R., 196, 242, 247
Dubovsky, A. N., 16, 276
Dubovsky, S. L., 16, 276
Duke, P., 278
Duncan, J. C., 249
Dunn, S., 193
DuPaul, G. J., 225
Dysken, M. W., 267
Dziegielewski, S. F., 274, 276
D'Zurilla, T. J., 228–229, 231

E

Eckman, T. A., 201, 205, 206, 233
Edelen, M.O., 155
Edwards, A., 193
Edwards, T. M., 152, 154, 156
Egger, J. F., 130
Egger, M., 269
Ehret, M. J., 33
Elbogen, E. B., 252
Elder, L., 7
Elferick, A. J. A., 105
El-Gabalawy, R., 155
El-Guebaly, N., 266
Ell, K., 37
Ellingrod, V. L., 161
Elliot, C., 274
El-Mallach, R. S., 114
El-sayeh, H. G., 96
Elwyn, G., 193
Ennis, R. H., 7
Ergaz, Z., 149
Erkens, J. A., 159
Ernst, E., 270, 271
Essock, S. M., 198, 228
Evans, M. E., 199
Even, C., 198

F

Faber, R., 157, 182
Fagan, T. J., 273
Falloon, I., 204
Fancher, T. L., 164
Fang, L., 164
Fang, L. J., 209
Faraone, S. V., 159
Faravelli, C., 120
Farmer, R., 13, 44, 146, 171, 175, 177, 180, 196, 216, 217, 237

Farrel, D., 157
Fava, M., 271
Fawzi, W., 203
Fegert, J. M., 134
Fenton, W. S., 242
Feucht-Haviar, T., 250
Fieve, R. R., 114
Fincke, B. G., 246
Findling, R. L., 157, 182
Finnell, D., 222
Fischer, J., 157
Fischer, J. H., 149
Fisher, A., 274
Fisher, H., 11
Flockhart, D. A., 161
Floersch, J., 83, 157, 162,
    182, 186
Flora, D. B., 33
Flynn, L. M., 19
Fompa-Loy, J., 201
Fong, R., 160
Food and Drug Admin-
    istration (FDA),
    88, 112, 146, 263
Forcehimes, A. A., 256
Ford, B. C., 162
Forte, J. A., 181
Foster, D. A., 196
Fox, R., 273
Foxx, R. M., 231
France, C. M., 14
Frances, A., 242, 244
Franchini, L., 198
Francis, J. L., 73
Frank, E., 245
Frank, J. B., 228
Frank, J. D., 228
Frank, R. G., 25
Franson, K. L., 242, 247
Fraser, J. S., 22
Fraser, M., 14
Frazier, J. A., 158
Frehling, J. J., 156
Friedman, M., 109
Fristad, M. A., 38, 211
Fukui, S., 221
Furnham, A. F., 160
Furuto, S., 160

G

Gadon, L., 95, 96
Galinsky, M., 14
Galvin, J., 274
Galynker, I. I., 114
Garakani, A., 118
Gardner, A., 76
Garety, P., 198
Garg, A., 131, 246
Garratt, L. S., 177
Gaskill, D., 223
Gavazzi, S. M., 38, 211
Gearing, R. E., 244, 246,
    256
Geddes, J., 114, 119, 120,
    198
Geddes, J. R., 114
Gellad, W. F., 243, 245,
    247

Geller, R. E., 198
Geller, B., 111
Geller, S. E., 149
George, E. L., 211
George, T. P., 165
Gerdes, K. E., 27, 30
Gerhart, U., 6, 41, 236
Gerhart, U. C., 39, 236,
    237
Gerlach, M., 158
Gersons, B. P. R., 105
Ghaemi, S. N., 146
Ghalib, K., 159
Ghormley, C., 200
Gibbons, R. D., 159
Gibbs, L., 8
Gibelman, M., 20
Gilmour, J., 176
Gingerich, S., 198, 228,
    229
Ginsberg, D. L., 120
Ginsberg, L., 13, 120
Ginsburg, G. S., 28
Gitterman, A., 19
Glynn, S. M., 235
Godwin, G., 114
Goikolea, J. M., 210
Goldbeck, R., 196
Goldberg, A. I., 243
Goldberg, R. S., 174, 180
Goldberg-Arnold, J. S.,
    211
Goldblatt, H., 193
Goldburg, J. F., 198
Goldman, D., 242, 244
Goldman, H., 196
Goldsmith, D. R., 118
Goldsmith, S. R., 267
Goldstein, M. J., 198, 210
Gomory, T., 6
Gonzalez, E. A., 155
Gonzalez-Pinto, A., 248
Goodman, F., 117
Goodwin, F. K., 114
Goodwin, G. M., 114,
    118
Goozner, M., 15
Gordon-Leeds, D., 243
Gottfried-Strom, K., 40,
    228, 229, 230,
    233, 235, 238
Gould, E., 175
Gould, N., 12
Gowdy, E. A., 221
Gram, L. S., 119
Grant, B. F., 163
Gray, C., 174
Greden, J. F., 162
Green, K., 199, 200, 203
Greene, P., 118
Greene, R. R., 37
Greenfield, N., 274
Greenhill, L. L., 140
Greider, K., 15
Grenard, J. L., 242
Grenard, J. L., 243, 245,
    247
Griffiths, C. A., 197
Grof, P., 114

Grol, R., 193
Grolnick, W. S., 260
Gross, D., 157
Grunze, H., 118
Gu, Q., 146
Guada, J., 83, 162, 276
Gueguen, J. A., 232
Gutheil, T. G., 182

H

Haas, G. L., 177
Haeri, S., 114
Hall, W., 257
Hallowell, E. M., 133
Hamann, J., 192, 193
Hamera, E., 216
Hamilton, M., 224
Hamrin, V., 113, 248
Hankoff, L., 274
Hanwella, R., 139
Harkness, K. L., 228
Haro, J. M., 242, 248
Harries, R., 258
Harrison, C., 176
Harrison, D. M., 196
Harrison, J. N., 157
Harrison, W. D., 20
Harvey, A. T., 267
Hashem, A. H., 203
Hasin, D., 163
Hassan, M., 109
Hasson-Ohayon, I., 216
Hausner, R., 182
Hawton, K., 114
Hayes, S. C., 273
Haynes, R. B., 246
Hayward, P., 258
Healy, D., 16, 274
Hebert, C., 130
Hebert, S., 177, 180
Heinssen, R. K., 242
Heleniak, C., 159
Heller, N. R., 19
Helman, C. G., 181
Henkin, A. B., 22
Henne, J., 114
Henry, D. B., 224
Henry, J. D., 110
Hepworth, D., 40, 228,
    229, 230, 233,
    235, 238
Heres, S., 192
Herings, R. M. C., 159
Herschfeld, R. M. A.,
    120
Herz, M. I., 198, 228
Herzlech, C., 83
Heslegrave, R. J., 182
Hewitt, J., 40
Heyduk, L. J., 200
Heyscue, B. E., 249
Hickson, G. B., 150
Higgins, P. B., 41
Hill, B., 150
Hilton, D. W., 198, 228
Hindmarch, I., 131
Hinton, D. E., 164
Hirschowitz, J., 118

Ho, A. P. Y., 36
Hoberman, H. M., 198
Hochman, G., 278
Hochman, M. E., 27
Hodgins, S., 251
Hodgkins, P., 133
Hoffman, J. S., 173
Hofmann, S. G., 164
Hogan, T. P., 182
Hoge, S., 250
Holland, P. J., 30
Honer, W. G., 199
Hong, J., 242
Honigfeld, G., 95
Hopker, S., 263
Hornig, M., 30
Horvitz-Lennon, M.,
    242, 244
Hosch, H. M., 163
Howe, J. T., 244
Howland, R. H., 90, 154,
    226, 272
Hser, Y., 163
Hsiao, C. P., 228
Huang, C., 225
Huang, X., 114
Hughes, I. C. T., 249
Hughes, S., 42
Hunger, H., 95, 96
Hunter, R., 95, 96
Hur, K., 159
Huse, D., 133
Hutto, B. R., 271
Hwang, S., 210
Hyer, K., 22

I

Ibbotson, T., 118
Inder, M., 244, 248
Ingersoll, R. E., 54, 86,
    146
Insel, K. C., 228
Irving, C. B., 95, 96
Ivanoff, A., 220
Ivey, A. E., 40
Ivey, M. B., 40
Iyengar, S., 28

J

Jackson, M., 110
Jacobs, E. W., 18
Jacobsen, H., 22
Jacobvitz, D., 138
Jamison, K., 114, 173,
    278
Jamison, P., 6, 12, 43
Janicak, P. G., 54, 86,
    146, 149
Jenkins, J., 157, 182
Jensen, P. S., 137, 203
Jensfold, M. F., 149
Jeste, D. V., 154
Jiang, H., 163
Joffe, R. T., 271
Johnson, H. C., 11
Johnson, M., 30
Johnson, N., 251

Johnston H. F., 156
Jolley, C. J., 222
Jones, I., 148
Jonikas, J. A., 221
Joober, R., 243
Jordan, D., 20
Jorgensen, P., 248
Joshi, P. T., 121
Joyal, C. C., 251
Julien, R. M., 54, 86, 146
Julius, R. J., 196, 242, 247

K

Kabat-Zinn, 2003, 218
Kabeto, M. U., 162
Kager, A., 216
Kail, B. L., 163
Kalbag, A., 211
Kališová, L., 250
Kallert, T. W., 250
Kane, C. F., 197
Kane, I., 222
Kane, J., 80, 95, 233, 235
Kanter, J., 173
Kapczinski, F., 130
Kapetanovic, T., 33
Kaphingst, K. A., 265
Karastergiou, A., 250
Karp, D., 12, 226, 278
Kaslow, N. J., 160
Kasper, J., 250
Kasper, S., 118, 121
Kasten, A. M., 252
Kaufmann, E., 199
Kavanagh, D. J., 270
Kaysen, S., 278
Keast, J., 11
Keck, P. E., 120
Keller, M. B., 155
Kellner, R., 223
Kelly, K. V., 174, 175
Kemp, R., 258
Kendall, P. C., 28
Kendler, K. S., 73, 162
Kennedy, E., 95, 96
Kennedy, J. S., 16
Kennedy, S. H., 228
Keshavan, M. S., 16
Kessler, R. C., 25, 162
Khan, A. Y., 268
Kiejna, A., 250
Kilian, R., 246
Killick, S., 255
Kim, E. Y., 211
Kim, H., 38
Kim, J., 109, 270
Kim, S. W., 267
King, C. A., 162
King, N., 22
Kinnersley, P., 193
Kinsella, A., 258
Kintzer, C., 274
Kirkcaldy, B. D., 160
Kishore-Kumar, K. V., 249
Kissling, W., 95, 96, 192, 193
Kisthardt, W., 34

Kitzlerová, E., 250
Klap, R., 180
Kleim, B., 244
Kleinman, D. L., 19
Klerman, G. L., 17, 172
Kline, N. S., 100
Ko, C., 225
Koelch, M., 134
Kolb, D. A., 201
Kolevzon, A., 118
Komossa, K., 95, 96
Konstantinidis, A., 121
Kopp, J., 218
Korn, J. R., 109
Kramer, P. D., 16
Kranke, B., 83, 162
Kranke, D., 83, 157, 162, 182
Krarup, G., 248
Kravetz, S., 216
Kripalani, S., 246
Krivoshekova, Y. S., 162
Kroner, D. G., 33
Kryworuchko, J., 193
Kuha, A., 148
Kuhn, M. T., 199
Kuhn, R., 101
Kuipers, E., 198
Kunz, M., 199
Kupfer, D. J., 245
Kuwabara, S. A., 83
Kvrgic, S., 244
KwonKwon, A., 38

L

Lacasse, J. R., 6, 13, 14, 15, 16, 19, 265
Lachner, C., 271
Lader, M. H., 175
Lafuze, J. E., 201
Lam, P., 259
Lam, R. W., 199, 209
Lambert, G., 247
Lamison, K., 114
Lammers, A., 38
Lampronti, L., 120
Landsverk, S. S., 197
Lang, A., 216
Langa, K. M., 162
Langle, S., 11
Lapierre, Y., 266
Larkin, C., 258
Larner, G., 36
Larrison, C. R., 13
Laughren, T. P., 263
Law, J., 15
Lawless, L. L., 176
Lawrence, B. J., 18
Lawrence, D. B., 137
Lawrence, G., 223
Lawrence, J. D., 137
Lawson, J. E., 83
Lawson, W. B., 163
Leadbetter, R., 118
Leake, C. D., 135
Leckband, S. G., 161
Lee, D., 164
Lee, H., 222

Lee, J. A. B., 34
Lee, M. S., 270
Lee, S., 164
Lefcowitz, M., 21
Lefley, H. P., 250
Légaré, F., 193
Lehman, A., 165, 196, 209, 249
Lei, Z., 114
Lelliott, P., 192
Lencz, T., 80
Lens, V., 237
Lenton, S., 257
Leo, J., 13, 14, 15, 16
Le Quach, P., 248
Leucht, S., 95, 96
Leucht, S., 192, 193
Leventhal, E. A., 244
Leventhal, H., 244
Levin, G. M., 249
LeVine, E. S., 273
Levitt, A. J., 271
Levy, R. A., 162
Levy, S. T., 182
Lewinsohn, P. M., 198
Lewis-Fernandez, R., 163
Liao, J., 18
Liberman, R., 233, 235
Liberman, R. P., 14, 201, 205, 206, 233, 235
Licht, R. W., 119
Lieb, J., 6, 39
Lin, K., 164
Lindau, T., 30
Linde, K., 268, 269
Liptak, A., 32
Liraud, F., 220
Lisanby, S. H., 267
Littrell, J., 175, 275
Liu, H. Y., 159
Liu, J., 120
Liu, L., 163
Liu, S., 163
Llewellyn, D. J., 162
Llorca, P. M., 243, 247
Lloyd, A., 243
Lloyd, K., 182
Lo, M. C. H., 36
Lobos, C. A., 96
Loffler, W., 246
Longhofer, J., 157, 182
Lönnqvist, J., 148
Lowe, D., 249
Lowry, L., 22
Lu, S., 244
Lucksted, A., 209
Lukens, E. P., 197
Lunney, P., 223
Lurie, N., 19
Lyles, A., 196
Lysaker, P. H., 14

M

Mackell, J. A., 246
Mackenzie, C. S., 155
MacKenzie, M., 244, 256
Macmillan, C., 149

MacPherson, R., 196
Macritchie, K., 119, 120
Magliano, L., 250
Mah, C. A., 268
Mahurin, R., 163
Mailick, D., 22, 236
Mailick, M. D., 20
Makoul, G., 232
Malhotra, A. K., 80
Malla, A., 243
Mallinger, A. G., 245
Mandel, F. S., 30
Maneesriwongul, W., 247
Mann, J. J., 159
Mantovani, A., 267
Manuel, J. K., 256
Maples, N. J., 222
March, J. S., 28
Marcum, Z. A., 243, 245, 247
Marcus, S. M., 159
Marder, S. R., 54, 86, 146, 149, 235, 249
Margolin, C., 6, 39
Mari, J. J., 198
Marks, I. M., 124
Martin, F., 245
Martin, J. K., 203
Martinez-Aran, A., 210
Martin J. L. R., 267
Martin-Sanchez, E., 267
Mason, N. S., 147
Mason, S. E., 17
Masud, M. I., 151
Mathews, D. J. H., 267
Mattessich, P. W., 22
Mauksch, L. B., 22
Maxey, R. W., 162
Mazure, C. M., 14
McCabe, P. C., 157
McCabe, S. E., 165
McCafferty, P., 200
McCandless-Glimcher, L., 216
McCann, T. V., 244
McCarthy, E. M., 248
McChahill, M. E., 152, 154, 156
McCollum, A., 6, 39
McCracken, J., 28
McCubbin, M., 14
McDonald H. P., 246
McDonnell, D. D., 246
McFarlane, W. R., 197, 207
McGeary, J. E., 153
McGill, C., 204
McGlynn, E., 196
McGrath, R. E., 273
McGuire, J., 158
McIntosh, D. E., 120
McKnight, S., 216
McLeod, J. D., 203
McMillan, S. C., 203
McMiller, T. P., 163
McPhillips, M., 244
MecDermott, B. M., 248
Meder, J., 233

Medoff, D. R., 209
Meehan, T., 223
Meeks, T. W., 154
Meier, P. S., 164
Meir, T., 216
Melchart, D., 268
Meloche, J., 251
Meltzer, C. C., 147
Meltzer, H., 95
Melvin, C. L., 117
Mendel, R., 192
Mendoza, R., 163
Menzin, J., 109
Merinder, L., 197
Merrick, J. P., 249
Metzl, E., 227
Meyer, D. A., 224
Michalak, E. E., 209
Migone, M., 258
Miklowitz, D. J., 198, 210, 211, 226
Miller, A. L., 163, 201, 206
Miller, D., 182, 246
Miller, F. G., 72
Miller, J. G., 32
Miller, L., 149
Miller, W., 254, 255
Millet, K., 278
Mills, J. F., 33
Minkoff, K., 167
Mintz, J., 210, 235
Misdrahi, D., 243, 247
Mistler, L. A., 192
Mitchell, A., 182
Mizrahi, T., 20, 21
Moncrieff, J., 263, 266
Montejano, L., 133
Montgomery, S. A., 101
Moran, N., 33
Morawiec, M., 233
Morey, B., 198, 228
Morgan, C., 198
Morgan, R. D., 33
Morris, L. S., 242, 246
Morrison, P., 223
Mors, O., 248
Morse, E. V., 247
Mortimer, A. M., 54, 86, 146
Moser, L., 252
Mosher, L. R., 36
Mott, T., 242, 244
Moussa, S., 203
Mueser, K. T., 198, 228, 229
Muller-Oerlinghausen, B., 114
Mulrow, C., 268, 269
Munson, M., 157, 182
Murdoff, J. R., 162
Murry-Swank, A., 209
Mustelier, M. M., 155
Myers, C. P., 165

N

Nackerud, L., 13
Nanyonga, R. C., 245

Nash, M., 217
National Alliance for the Mentally Ill (NAMI), 9, 18, 201, 208, 277
National Alliance on Mental Illness, 276, 277
National Association of Social Workers (NASW), 11, 25, 44, 45
National Institute of Health, 30, 182
Nauert, R., 267
Nawka, A., 250
Neighbors, H. W., 162
Neill, J. R., 19
Nelson-Zlupko, L., 199
Nemeroff, C. B., 54, 86, 146, 167
Nevins, D .B., 182
Nezu, A. M., 228, 231
Nguyen, T., 150, 162
Ni, Q., 259
Nielsen, J. N., 119
Nierenberg, A. A., 271
Nightengale, B. S., 18
Nolting, J., 40
Norcross, J., 254
Nordentoft, M., 248
North, C. S., 196, 199, 208
Novick, D., 242, 248
Novitsky, M. A., 196, 242, 247

O

O'Callaghan, E., 258
O'Donnell, C., 258
Oesterheld, J. R., 161
Offer, D., 146
Okuda, M., 163
Oldham, J. M., 117
Olfson, M., 25, 126
Olsen, S., 223
Onchev, G., 250
O'Neal, E. L., 166
Orbach, G., 198
Ornoy, A., 149
Ortega, A. N., 163
Orwig, D., 146
O'Shea, M., 203
Owens, N., 258

P

Pacheco, J., 153
Pachler, M., 113
Page, R. L., 102
Pam, A., 14
Panossian, A., 268, 270
Pare, D. A., 36
Parikh, S. V., 198
Parks, J., 259
Parrish, J., 253
Parrot, M., 220
Partonen, T., 148

Patat, A., 131
Patel, K., 272
Patel, S. R., 163
Patel, U. B., 259
Patorno, E., 120
Patrick, A. R., 120
Patterson, J., 152, 154, 156
Patterson, J., 154
Paty, I., 131
Paul, R., 7
Paulose-Ram, R., 146
Pauls, A., 268
Pavuluri, M. N., 54, 86, 146, 149, 224
Paykina, N., 139
Pekkala, E., 197
Pellegrino, E. D., 181
Pena, S. D. J., 160
Perälä, J., 148
Perel, J. M., 245
Perlis, R. H., 120
Perry, B. L., 203
Perry, C. M., 118
Pert, C. B., 63
Perwien, A. R., 224
Pescosolido, B. A., 203
Peselow, E. D., 114
Petersen, M., 15
Peterson, K. A., 216
Petit, M., 243, 247
Petr, C. G., 134
Petty, C. R., 159
Pham, V. A., 18
Pharoah, F. M., 198
Phillips, L. H., 110
Phipps, C. C., 205, 206
Piacentini, J., 28
Piat, M., 35
Pies, R. W., 274
Piette, J. D., 268
Pilette, W. L., 173
Pilling, S., 198
Pincus, H. A., 25, 126
Pirek, E., 121
Plassman, B. L., 162
Plumlee, M. N., 216
Poe, J., 200
Pollack, D., 17
Pollack, S., 32
Pollio, D. E., 196, 199, 208
Pompili, M., 114
Popper, C. W., 158
Posternak, M. A., 72
Postrado, L., 196
Potocky, M., 227
Potter, G. G., 162
Potter, M. P., 159
Pouliot, S., 193
Powell, A. D., 191
Powell, R., 182
Power, T. J., 225
Pray, J. E., 20, 21
Preskorn, S. H., 267, 268
Price, J. C., 147
Price, S. K., 152
Priebe, S., 270
Prochaska, J., 254

Proctor, B. D., 27
Provencher, H., 35
Puliafico, A., 159

Q

Qato, D., 30
Quilty, L. C., 228
Quinn, D. M. P., 137
Quirk, A., 192

R

Rabinovitch, M., 243
Raboch, J., 250
Rago, W., 18
Rak, C. F., 54, 86, 146
Ramirez, G., 268
Ramirez, L. F., 164
Rana, N., 120
Ranney, L. H., 117
Ransom, S., 203
Rapkin, B., 242, 244
Rapp, C., 34, 221
Rapp, R. C., 36
Rappaport, N., 182
Rassool, G. H., 165
Rataboli, P. V., 131
Ratey, J., 133
Rathbone, J., 198, 270
Ray, W. A., 150
Raymondet, P., 244, 247
Rea, M. M., 210
Reed, C., 22, 242, 248
Reeves, J., 43
Regenold, W. T., 271
Reid, D. L., 199, 208
Reid, R., 225
Reid, W. H., 18
Reinares, M., 210
Reinhart, U. E., 265
Reist, D., 15
Relman, A. S., 15
Reminger, S. L., 228
Remler, M., 251
Rende, R., 155
Rendell, P. G., 110
Renner, J. A., 164
Resnick, R. J., 273
Rey, J. A., 155
Reynolds, N. R., 245
Rhodes, L. A., 181
Riba, M., 14, 174, 180
Rice, A. H., 21, 22
Rich, E., 19
Richard, H., 198
Richards, J. A., 211
Richey, J. A., 164
Richman, J., 14
Rigney, U., 131
Rikhi, P., 159
Riolo, S. A., 162
Rizvi, S., 198
Robb, A. S., 121
Robinson, R. P., 14
Rodin, G. C., 260
Roe, D., 193
Rogers, M. A. M., 162
Rogers, R., 249

Rolland, J. P., 228
Rollnick, S., 254, 255
Rooney, G. D., 40, 228, 229, 230, 233, 235, 238
Rooney, R., 40, 228, 229, 230, 233, 235, 238
Rosenfeld, P. J., 181
Rosenheck, R., 163, 242
Rosenson, M., 43, 252, 259
Rosi, S., 120
Ross, A., 22
Ross, C., 14
Ross, D., 235
Ross, R., 245
Rossignol, D., 271
Rothbaum, B. O., 198
Rothman, J., 35
Rouget, B. W., 198
Rouillon, P. F., 228
Rowlands, R. P., 196
Royal Ottawa Hospital (Canada), 269
Rozencwaig, S., 216
Rubin, A. H. E., 243
Rubinow, D. R., 147
Rudas, S., 216
Rudd, R. E., 265
Ruffolo, M. C., 199
Rule, D., 199
Rummel-Kluge, C., 95, 96
Rungruangsiripan, M., 247
Ruscin, J. M., 102
Rush, A. J., 201, 206
Russo, L., 133
Rust, G., 160
Ryals, T., 151
Ryan, R. M., 35, 260
Rynn, M., 28, 159

S

Saarni, S., 148
Sabag-Cohen, S., 162
Sabetti, J., 35
Sacco, W. P., 232
Sachs-Ericsson, N., 211
Sadock, B. J., 54, 86, 146
Sadock, V. A., 54, 86, 146
Safer, D. L., 14
Safran, M. A., 146
Saija, S., 54, 86, 146
Sajatovic, M., 182, 245
Saleebey, D., 36
Saleeby, D., 34, 173
Sallis, R., 246
Salomon, R. M., 30
Salyers, M. P., 38
Sammons, M., 172, 273
Sands, R. G., 21
Sanfilipo, M. P., 114
Sareen, J., 155
Sarris, J., 268, 270
Sarwer-Foner, G. J., 182

Sasané, R., 133
Sawicka, M., 233
Scahill, L., 158
Scarpato, M. A., 120
Schaffner, K. F., 73
Schardt, D., 269
Schatzberg, A. F., 54, 86, 146, 167
Schaub, A., 198, 228
Scheer, S. D., 38
Scheid, T. L., 19
Scheifler, P. L., 39, 218
Schenk, C., 211
Schidl, F., 216
Schiller, L., 278
Schindler, S., 121
Schinke, S. P., 164
Schmid, F., 95, 96
Schmidt, A. B., 163
Schmidt, N. B., 172
Schmidt, P. J., 147
Schmit, J., 17
Schmitz, M., 216
Schmitz, N., 243
Schneeweiss, S., 120
Schneider, B., 34
Schnoor, K., 134
Schnyer, D. M., 153
Scholey, A., 268, 270
Schulte, S. J., 164
Schulz, R. M., 242, 246
Schumm, P., 30
Schwarz, S., 95, 96
Schweitzer, I., 268, 270
Schweizer, E., 196
Scicluna, A., 110
Scott, J., 196, 245
Seale, C., 192
Segal, E. A., 27, 30
Senanayake, M., 139
Sensky, T., 244
Sereika, S. M., 222
Shah, B., 232
Shapiro, J. R., 13
Sharfstein, S. S., 16
Sharkey, L., 258
Sharma, V. K., 249
Sheehan, S., 278
Sheikh, J. I., 30
Shek, C. C., 164
Shelton, D., 33
Shen, W. W., 164
Sherrill, J. T., 28
Shim, R. S., 160
Shoemaker, S. J., 182
Shooshtari, S., 155
Siefen, R. G., 160
Simon, B. L., 20, 21
Simon, P. M., 247
Simoneau, T. L., 211
Simpson, G. M., 223
Singer, J., 95
Singh, I., 134
Single, E., 257
Sitthimongkol, Y., 247
Skolnick, P., 131
Slanda, D., 163
Sleath, B., 232, 239
Smelson, D., 165

Smith, A., 22
Smith, B. L., 216
Smith, J., 27, 249
Smith, K., 155
Smith, M. W., 163
Smith, S., 148, 242, 247
Sobhan, T., 151
Solanto, M., 158
Soloff, P. H., 147
Solomon, P., 245
Song, F., 95, 96
Soyer, D., 36
Spaniol, L., 11
Spaulding, W., 40
Spencer, T. J., 139
Spiro, A., 246
Srisurpanont, M., 96
Stacey, D., 193
Stahl, S. M., 54, 86, 146
Stamenkovic, M., 121
Stanga, C., 267
Stanley, N., 131
Starnino, V. R., 221
Stayner, D., 35
Steele, M., 137
Steffan, J. S., 33
Steffens, D. C., 162
Steiner, E., 216
Steiner, S., 27, 30
Steinle, N. I., 271
Stern, S. B., 220
Stewart, B., 209
Stewart, J. G., 228
Stirling, J. S., 162
Stone, A. A., 17
Storosum, J. G., 105
Stough, C., 268, 270
Stowe, Z. N., 149
Strauss, M. E., 182
Streiner, D., 198
Stromm-Gottfried, K., 199, 201
Sturm, R., 180
Sturm, V., 209
Su, M., 162
Suddath, R., 211
Sullivan, W. P., 34
Suppes, T., 121, 201, 206
Susana, M., 221
Sussman, M., 109, 121
Suvisaari, J., 148
Suzuki, J., 164
Swann, A. C., 120
Swanson, J. W., 252
Swarbrick, M., 193
Swartz, M. S., 249, 252
Swazey, J. P., 88
Sweeney, J. A., 177
Swift, R. M., 128
Sylvestre, J., 35
Szasz, T., 248
Szego, K., 150

T

Talen, M. R., 22
Talley, S., 247
Tanzman, B., 198, 228
Tarrier, N., 198, 228

Tasman, A., 174, 180
Taurines, R., 158
Taylor, D., 269
Taylor, M. F., 180, 216, 217, 237
Taylor, M. J., 114
Taylor, S., 243
Ten, A., 114
Thase, M. E., 14, 16, 130, 245
Thomas, J., 157, 182
Thomas, P., 263
Thome, J., 158
Thompson, R., 201
Thuile, J., 198
Tillman, R., 111
Tobias, M., 39
Todman, M., 243
Tomlinson, S., 196
Tompson, M. C., 210
Tondo, L., 114
Toprac, M. G., 201, 206
Torniainen, M., 148
Torrent, C., 210
Torres, I. J., 199
Torres, M., 249
Torres-Gonzales, F., 250
Toseland, R., 21
Toumi, M., 246
Townsend, E., 114
Townsend, L., 157, 182, 244, 256
Tracy, A. B., 16
Trierweiler, S. J., 162
Trivedi, M. H., 201, 206
Trotter, J. S., 120
Tuchsler, J., 121
Tugenberg, T., 34
Tung, W. C., 163
Turnbull, J. M., 128
Turner, S. E., 160, 163
Turner, T., 270
Tuulio-Henriksson, A., 148
Tyson, V., 248

U

Udechuku, A., 150
Ulus, F., 166
Uppal, R., 38
Urrutia, G., 250
Usher, K., 182

V

Vaccaro, J., 233, 235
Valenstein, E. T., 5, 15
Valenstein, M., 243
VandeCreek, L., 15
van der Brink, W., 105
Van Dorn, R., 251
Van Dusen, C., 201
van Strick, R., 105
van Zweiten, B. J., 105
Varghese, F., 33
Vasile, R. G., 155
Vasudev, A., 119
Vasudev, K., 119, 120

Vauth, R., 244
Velligan, D., 163, 222, 245
Venable, V., 276
Verdi, M. B., 232
Verdoux, H., 220
Vertergaard, P., 119
Vidair, H., 159
Videka, L., 178
Vieta, E., 121, 198, 210
Vogel-Scibilia, S., 198, 228
Vohra, S., 176
Volavka, J., 251
Vorapongsathorn, T., 247
Vornik, M. S., 120
Voruganti, L. N., 182
Vourlekis, B., 37

W

Wagstaff, A. J., 118
Wahl, P. M., 120
Wakai, S., 33
Walker, S., 15
Walkup, J. T., 28
Wallach, M. A., 166
Walsh, C. B., 18
Walsh, J., 26, 43, 44, 48, 171, 175, 177, 179, 180, 181, 196, 200, 216, 217, 227, 229, 237

Walters, E. E., 25
Wang, P., 25
Ware, N. C., 34
Warnke, A., 158
Warren, P. A., 43
Waslick, B., 28
Watnabi, A., 233
Watson, S., 119, 120
Wedding, D., 40
Weick, A., 34
Weiden, P., 242, 244, 245, 246, 249
Weidenhamer, W., 268
Weil, M., 20
Weinberger, A. H., 165
Weinstein, M., 274
Weisberg, S., 201
Weisman, R., 249
Weisz, J. R., 163
Welge, J. A., 120
Wells, K. B., 25
Wernicke, U., 270
Wernike, U., 269
Wesson, V. A., 271
West, B. T., 165
Wettstein, R. M., 18
Wewetzer, C., 158
Whatley, D., 203
Whiskey, E., 269
White, R., 118
Wiedemann, K., 267
Wiggins, J., 273

Wilamasena, K., 268
Wilder, C. M., 252
Wilk, R. J., 251
Wilkins, T., 139
Willeit, M., 121
Willetts, R., 237
Williams, D., 162
Williams, G. C., 260
Williams, J., 165
Williams, J. W., 117
Williams, R., 266
Wilson, K. C. M., 203
Wilson, L., 244, 248
Wilson, S. R., 217
Winbush, V., 157, 182
Wing, Y. K., 164
Winkler, D., 121
Winslade, W., 11
Wirshing, D. A., 235
Wirshing, W., 233, 235
Wolf, R., 121
Wolraich, M. L., 156
Wong, S., 6
Woodward, A. T., 163
Woodworth, K. Y., 159
Wozniak, J. R., 159
Wragg, J., 248
Wright, G. J., 176

X

Xie, H., 165
Xu, Y., 163

Y

Yakutis, L., 158
Yang, E. J., 270
Yang, L., 164
Yang, M. S., 164
Yao, X., 246
Yatham, L. N., 199, 209
Yen, C., 225
Yen, J., 225
Yeung, K. S. S., 36
Yorks, D. M., 159
Young, A. H., 119, 120
Young, R. C., 113, 224
Youngstrom, E., 224
Youssef, F., 244

Z

Zaneles-Palmer, J., 21
Zaretsky, A. E., 198
Zarit, J. M., 30
Zarit, S. H., 30
Zaslavsky, A. M., 25
Zhang, L., 270
Zhang, M., 270
Ziedonis, D., 165
Ziegler, M., 192
Ziegler, V. E., 224
Zimerman, B., 111
Zimmerman, M., 72
Zipple, A. M., 11
Zito, J., 43, 259
Zygmut, A., 242, 244

Subject Index

Page numbers in italics indicate materials in tables or figures

A

Abilify. *See* Aripiprazole
Absorption, 68, 147
ACE. *See* Anticholinergic effects
Acetophenazine, *90, 91*
Acetylcholine, 64–65
Activist learners, 201–202
Acute dystonias, *91,* 92, 226
Adapin. *See* Doxepin
Adderall, 138
   See also Amphetamines
ADHD. *See* Attention deficit
   hyperactivity disorder
   (ADHD)
ADHD Rating Scale-IV, 225
Adherence
   interventions to assist, 253–259
      behavioral interventions,
         258–259
      cognitive interventions,
         258–259
      compliance therapy, 258
      dynamic adherence, 256–257
      harm-reduction approach,
         257–258
      motivational interviewing,
         253–256
   legal and ethical issues of,
      250–253
   measuring, 243
   medication education for, 196
   models for understanding,
      243–250
      client characteristics and,
         244–245
      illness of symptoms, 248–250
      self-efficacy model, 243–244
      social environment, 247–248
      treatment, 246–247
   older adults and, 153–154
   See also Nonadherence

Adolescents
   adverse effects in, 157–159
   anti-anxiety medications for, 159
   antidepressant medications for,
      158
   antipsychotic medications for,
      157–158
   anxiety disorders in, 159
   depression in, 156, 158–159
   ethical issues in drug treatment of,
      134–135
   interventions involving,
      156–157, 159
   mood disorders in, 158
   mood-stabilizing medications
      for, 158
   SSRIs for, 158–159
   tardive dyskinesia (TD) in, 157
   See also Children
Adult learners, 199
Advanced practice registered nurses
   (APNs), 272
Adverse effects, 72, 80–83
   of anti-anxiety medications, 127,
      127, 128
   anticholinergic effects, 81
   of anticonvulsants, *119*
   of antipsychotic medications, 89,
      90–92, *91,* 93–94, *94*
   vs. benefits, 11–12
   of benzodiazepines, 127, *127*
   of buspirone, 130
   in children and adolescents,
      157–159
   of cyclic antidepressants, *106,*
      106–107
   lithium (lithium carbonate), *115,*
      115–116, *116*
   MAO inhibitors, *103*
   of mood-stabilizing medications,
      119

   nonadherence and, 246
   physical, 81–83
   during pregnancy, 149, 150–151
   psychological, 83
   sexual, 81, 151–152
   social, 83
   steps for coping with, 225–228
Advocacy, 236–238
Advocates, 41–42, 48
Affective disorders. *See* Mood
   disorders
African Americans
   medication response in, 162
   polypharmacy and, 162
   schizophrenia and, 162
   treatment-seeking behavior
      of, 162
Age factor, in adverse physical
   effects, 82
Aging, 30–32
Agonists, 64
Agranulocytosis, 95, 226
Akathisia, 81, *91,* 93, 226
Akineton. *See* Biperiden
Alcohol abuse
   anti-anxiety medications and, 167
   mental illness and, 167
Alprazolam, *94, 126*
Alternative treatments, 268–272
Alzheimer's disease (AD), 154, 270
Amantadine, *94*
Ambien. *See* Zolpidem
American Psychological Association
   (APA), 156, 172, 273
Amines, 64
Amitriptyline, 105
Amoxapine, *105*
Amphetamines, 135–136
Amygdala, *56*
Anafranil. *See* Clomipramine
Anger, 220, 227, 230

Antagonists, 64
Anti-anxiety medications, 26, 77–78, 124
  adverse effects of, 127, *127*, 128
  alcohol abuse and, 167
  antidepressants and, 131
  antihistamines, 131
  benzodiazepines, 77–78, 125–128
  buspirone, 128–130
  case examples, 131–133
  for children and adolescents, 159
  currently available, 125–130
  for older adults, 155–156
  origins of, 125
  during pregnancy, 151
  zolpidem, 131
  See also specific types
Anticholinergic effects (ACE), 81, 89, *91*, 105, 108, 154, 155
Anticonvulsants, 117–120
  adverse effects of, *119*
  carbamazepine, 118, *119,* 120
  lamotrigine, 118, 119, *119*
  valproate, 118, *119*
Antidepressant medications, 13, 14, 16, 26, 74–76, 99–100
  for ADHD, 139–140
  for anxiety disorders, 131
  for bipolar disorder, 120–121
  case examples, 109–110
  for children and adolescents, 158
  classes of (*See* Cyclic antidepressants; Monoamine oxidase (MAO) inhibitors; Selective serotonin reuptake inhibitors (SSRIs))
  currently available, 101–102
  introduction of, 15–16
  older adults and, 153, 155
  origins of, 100–101
  during pregnancy, 150
  risk of suicide, 17
  See also specific types
Antihistamines, 78, 131
Antimanic medications. *See* Carbamazepine; Lithium (Lithium carbonate); Valproate
Antipsychiatrists, 5
  awareness of, 5–7
Antipsychotic medications, 26, 73–74
  adjunctive medications with, 93–94, *94*
  adverse effects of, 89, 90–92, *91*, 93–94, *94*
  case examples, 97–99
  for children and adolescents, 157–158
  currently available, 89–92
  drug interactions with, 97
  first-generation drugs, 92–94
  gender differences and, 148
  high-potency, 158
  for older adults, 153, 154
  origins of, 88–89
  during pregnancy, 151
  second-generation drugs, 94–96
  See also specific types
Antipsychotics, 270

Antiseizure medications, 77
An unquiet mind: A memoir of moods and madness (Jamison), 278
Anxiety disorders
  antidepressants for, 131
  in children and adolescents, 159
  in older adults, 155
  symptoms of, 124
  treatment of (*See* Anti-anxiety medications)
Anxiety Rating for Children–Revised, 224
Aplastic anemia, 226
APNs. *See* Advanced practice registered nurses
Aripiprazole, 74, *90, 91,* 96
Artane. *See* Trihexyphenidyl
Art therapy, 227
Asendin. *See* Amoxapine
Asian Americans
  medication response in, 163–164
  mental health services, use of by, 163
  tardive dyskinesia (TD) and, 164
Atenolol, *129*
Ativan. *See* Lorazepam
Atomoxetine, 79, *136,* 139
Attention deficit hyperactivity disorder (ADHD), 78–79, 133–134
  alternative drugs for, 139–140
  antidepressants for, 139–140
  case examples, 140–143
  clonidine for, 139
  monitoring, 225
  psychostimulants for, 136–139
Atypical antidepressants, 108, *108*
Auditory hallucinations, 87
Autism, 159
Autonomic nervous system, 58
Autoreceptors, 63
Aventyl. *See* Nortriptyline
Axons, 59, *61*
Azapirone. *See* Buspirone

B
B12 deficiency, 271
Balanced perspective, 10–12
  costs *vs.* benefits of, 11–12
  individual, family, and society, rights of, 10–11
  ineffective collaboration, 10–12
Barcelona bipolar disorders group, 210
Barnes Akathisia Scale, 223
Basal ganglia, 57
BDRS. *See* Brief Depression Rating Scale
Behavioral family therapy project (Falloon), 204–205
Behavioral interventions, 258–259
Behavioral strategies, 258
Benadryl. *See* Diphenhydramine
Benzodiazepines, 77–78, 125–128, *126,* 147, 148, 151, 155–156, 161, 164, 165
  abuse of, 127, 128
  adverse effects of, 127, *127*
  drug interactions with, 128, *129*

  therapeutic effect, 126–127
  withdrawal symptoms, *128*
Benztropine, 93, *94*
Beta-blockers, 78, 93, 130
Big Pharma, 14–16
Binding activity, neurotransmitters, 63
Bioavailability, 69
Biological and ecological determinism, tension between, 13
Biology and psychology, integration of, 173
Biomarkers, 267
Biperiden, *94*
Bipolar disorder, 110–111, 147, 148, 159, 165, 167
  anticonvulsants for, 117–120
  antidepressants for, 120–121
  case examples, 121–124
  lithium for, 112, 113–117
  substance abuse and, 165
  types, 111
  See also Mood-stabilizing medications
Bipolar I disorder, 111, 148
Bipolar II disorder, 111, 148
Blood-brain barrier, 149
Blood level, 69
Blood-placenta barrier, 149
Brain, 54–59, *56*
Brain imaging techniques, 267
Brain stem, 55, *56,* 57
Breast-feeding, lithium and, 115
Brief Depression Rating Scale (BDRS), 223–224
A brilliant madness (Duke), 278
British Journal of Psychiatry, 268
Bupropion, 108, *108*
Bupropion (Wellbutrin, Zyban), 76
Bureaucratic paternalism, 11
Buspirone, 78, 128–130, *129*
  adverse effects of, 130
  therapeutic benefits, 130

C
Calcium channel blockers, 121
Carbamazepine, 77, 118, 120
  for children and adolescents, 156
  during pregnancy, 151
Care, parallel and integrated, 172–175
Case advocacy, 238
Case managers, 25–26
CAT. *See* Cognitive Adaptation Training
Catapres. *See* Clonidine
Catecholamines, 65
Cause advocacy, 238
CDER. *See* Center for Drug Evaluation and Research (CDER)
Celexa. *See* Citaprolam
Cellular-molecular theory, 75
Cementing, 179
Center for Drug Evaluation and Research (CDER), 263, 264
Central nervous system
  brain and, 54–59
  nerve cells and, 59–63

Centrax. *See* Prazepam
Cerebellum, *56, 57*
Cerebral cortex, *56,* 58
Cerebrum, *56,* 58
Child Mania Rating Scale-Parent (CMRS-P), 224
Child protective services (CPS), 27
Children
 ADHD in (*See* Attention deficit hyperactivity disorder (ADHD))
 adverse effects in, 157–159
 cognitive-behavioral therapy (CBT) and, 159
 dosages in, 157–159
 ethical issues in drug treatment of, 134–135
 medication education for, 203
 nonadherence and, 243
 psychopharmacological assessment of, 157
 special concerns for, with medications, 159
 See also Adolescents
Child welfare, 27–30
Chinese herbal medicine, 270
Chlordiazepoxide, *126,* 148
Chlorpromazine, 88–89, *90, 91,* 92, 95
Chlorprothixene, *90, 91*
Citaprolam, *107*
Clearance, 70
Client, medication-related dilemma, 11–12
Client advocacy, 236–238
Client-centered practice, 35–36
Client-clinician relationship, 36–37, 53–54
Clients
 characteristics of, and adherence, 244–245
 problem-solving training for, 228–232
 rights of, 10–11, 236–237, 250–253
 self-advocacy for, 237–238
 self-monitoring by, 217–223
 shared decision-making and, 191–193
 strengths and limits of, 34–35
 WRAP plan, 221
Clinical social workers, 26
Clomipramine, *105*
Clonazepam, *94,* 121, *126,* 155
Clonidine, *94, 136*
Clorazepate, *126*
Clozapine, 74, *90, 91,* 95
Clozaril. *See* Clozapine
CMRS-P. *See* Child Mania Rating Scale-Parent
Cobalamin deficiency, 271
Code of ethics, 44
Cogentin. *See* Benztropine
Cognitive Adaptation Training (CAT), 222
Cognitive interventions, 258–259
Cognitive strategies, 259
Collaboration, effective
 balanced perspective and, 10–12

interdisciplinary, 19–22
 partnership model of practice for, 33–38
 traditional collaboration, 21
Collaboration, in parallel and integrated care, 172–175
Communication skills, 232–235
Community care, 41
Compazine. *See* Prochlorperazine
Compliance therapy, 258
Consultants, 39–40, 48
Content, education programs, 212–213
 absorption and predicted response, 212
 addictiveness and withdrawal, 212
 adherence, 213
 benefits of medication, 212
 communication/negotiation, 213
 dosage and equivalents, 212
 emerging trends and research, 213
 forms of drugs, 212
 interactions, 212
 rationale for medication use, 212
 self-administration principles, 213
 side effects, 212
 types of drugs, 212
Contraceptives, oral, 148, 149
Contracting, 259
Copeland Center for Wellness and Recovery, 220
Coping strategies, for adverse effects, 225–228
Corgard. *See* Nadolol
Corrections and jails, 32–33
Cortex, 57–58
Counselors, 40, 48
Critical perspective, 5–10
 antipsychiatry, awareness of, 5–7
 critical thinking, application of, 7–10
Cyamemazine, *90*
Cyclic antidepressants, 75–76, 104, *105,* 105–107
 adverse effects of, *106,* 106–107
 dose levels, *105,* 105–106
 drug interactions with, *106*
 older adults and, 155
Cylert. *See* Pemoline
Cymbalta. *See* Duloxetine
Cytochrome (CYP) P450 enzyme, 148, 161

D
dang gui cheng qi tang, 270
DBS. *See* Deep brain stimulation
Decision-making, 191–193
 See also Shared decision-making
Decision science, 191
Deep brain stimulation (DBS), 267
Deinstitutionalization, 32–33
Delusions, 87
Dendrites, 59, *61*
Depakote. *See* Divalproex sodium; Valproate
Department of Defense, 273
Department of Veteran Affairs, 273
Depression, 99–100

alternative treatments for, 268–272
 in children and adolescents, 156, 158–159
 late-onset, 154
 symptoms of, 100
Desipramine, *105*
Desoxyn. *See* Methamphetamine
Desyrel. *See* Trazodone
Dexedrine. *See* Dextroamphetamine
Dexmethylphenidate, *136*
Dextroamphetamine, 79, *136,* 137, 138
Diagnosis factor, in adverse effects, 82
Diagnostic and Statistical Manual of Mental Disorders (DSM-IV-TR), 34
Diazepam, *94, 126,* 148, 155
Diphenhydramine, 93, *94, 151*
 during pregnancy, 151
Distribution, 68–69, 147–148
Disulfram, 167
Divalproex sodium, *113*
Dopamine, 64, 65–66, 73–74, 147, 148, 151, 165
Dopamine receptor antagonists, 148
Dose response, 71
Doxepin, *105*
Drug development process, 263–266
Drug-induced psychoses, 166
Drug metabolism, 148, 160–161, 163, 168
Duloxetine, *108*
Dynamic adherence, 256–257
 six stages of, 256–257
Dyskinesia, 81
 See also Tardive dyskinesia (TD)

E
Educators, 42–43, 48
Effective negotiation, 233
Effexor. *See* Venlafaxine
Elavil. *See* Amitriptyline
Eldepril. *See* Selegiline
Electrophysiological markers, 267
Elimination, 69
Empowerment practice, 34
Environmental factors, in mental illness, 24–25
Epinephrine, 65
Erectile dysfunction, 13
Erotomanic delusions, 87
Escitalopram, *107*
Eskalith. *See* Lithium (Lithium carbonate)
Estazolam, *126*
Estrogen, 147, 148
Ethical code, 44
Ethical concerns, in referrals, 180
Ethical issues
 relating to adherence, 250–253
 role of, in medication monitoring, 216–217
Ethnicity factor
 in adverse effects, 82–83
 in medication response, 160–164
Ethnopharmacotherapy, 160–164

Ethoprozapine, *94*
Excretion, 69–70
Extrapyramidal nerve pathways, 58
Extrapyramidal symptoms (EPSs),
     81, 82, 89, 98

F
Falloon program, 204–205
Family Focused Treatment (FFT),
     210–211
   for adolescents, 211
Family members
   appreciating perspective of, 38
   collaboration with, 33
   communication skills for, 232–235
   forced interventions by, 253
   influences of, on adherence, 248
   rights of, 10–11
   role of, in medication monitoring,
     216
Family survival workshop, 208
Family-to-Family program,
     208–209
Fanapt. *See* Iloperidone
FDA. *See* Food and Drug
     Administration
Fenfluramine, 159
Fluoxetine, 107, *107*
Fluphenazine, *90, 91,* 98
Flurazepam, *126*
Fluvoxamine, *107*
Folate, 270–272
Food and Drug Administration (FDA),
     146, 150, 157, 158, 263–265
Forebrain, *56,* 57
Frontal lobes, *56, 58*

G
GABA. *See* Gamma-aminobutyric
     acid
Gabapentin, *113*
GAF. *See* Global Assessment of
     Functioning scale
Gamma-aminobutyric acid
     (GABA), 64, 66 , 77, 118,
     119–120, 147
Gender differences
   in different effects of medications,
     82
   general considerations in, 146
Geodon. *See* Ziprasidone
Ghostwriting, 15
Ginkgo, 270
Girl, interrupted (Kaysen), 278
Glial cells, 54
Global Assessment of Functioning
     scale (GAF), 225
Glutamate (glutamic acid), 64,
     66–67
Grandiose delusions, 87
Group psychoeducation program,
     209–210
Guanfacine, *136*
Gustatory hallucinations, 87

H
Halazepam, *126*
Haldol. *See* Haloperidol
Half-life, 70

Hallucinations, 87
Hallucinogenic drugs, 165
Haloperidol, 71, *90, 91,* 98, 159
Hamilton Anxiety Rating Scale
     (HARS), 224
Harm-reduction model, 257–258
   principles, 257
HARS. *See* Hamilton Anxiety
     Rating Scale
Health, 30–32
Health belief model, 244
Health care professionals
   psychopharmacology practice
     and, 19
Health care provider, negotiating
     medication issues with,
     232–235
Herbal treatments, 268–272
Hindbrain, 55, *56,* 57
Hippocampus, *56,* 57
Hispanics
   enzyme differences in, 163
   medication response in, 162–163
Hispanics, medication response in,
     162–163
Holistic perspective, 21
Homeostasis, 57
Hormonal contraceptives, 147
Hormone replacement therapies,
     147
Hospitals, 30–32
Human behavior, brain functions
     and, 54–55
Hypericum, 268–269, 272
Hypothalamus, *56,* 57

I
Illness-related factors, affecting
     adherence, 249
Iloperidone, *90*
Imipramine, *105,* 148, 167
IND. *See* Investigational New Drug
Inderal. *See* Propranolol
Indian Health Services, 273
Individual rights, 10–11
Inpatient social workers, 7
Integrated care, 172–175
Interdisciplinary collaboration,
     19–22
   benefits of, 21
Internet, 276
Interventions
   to assist medication adherence,
     253–259
   behavioral, 253–259
   cognitive, 253–259
   historical context of, 24–25
   involving children and
     adolescents, 156–157, 159
   involving older adults, 154, 156
   multiple family, 207
   with patients exhibiting mental
     illness and substance abuse,
     165–167
   reflective discussion, 253
   self-management, 220–222
Invega. *See* Paliperidone
Investigational New Drug
     (IND), 264

Involuntary treatment, 250–253
Ions, 59
Is it me or my meds? (Karp), 278
Isocarboxazid, *102*
Is there no place on earth for me?
     (Sheehan), 278

K
Kava, 269–272
Kemadrin. *See* Procyclidine
Klonipin. *See* Clonazepam

L
Lag time, 71–72
Lamictal. *See* Lamotrigine
Lamotrigine, *113,* 118, 119
Late-onset depression, 154
Latuda. *See* Lurasidone
Learned intermediary, 18
Learners
   activist, 201–202
   pragmatist, 202
   reflector, 202
   theorist, 202
Learning readiness, 203
Legal concerns, in referrals, 180
Legal issues, relating to adherence,
     250–253
Lexapro, 131
   See also Escitalopram
Limbic system, *56,* 57–58
Lipid, 59
Lithane. *See* Lithium (Lithium
     carbonate)
Lithium (Lithium carbonate),
     76–77, 93, 94, 112,
     113–117, 120, 121
   adverse effects, *115,* 115–116, *116*
   for children and adolescents,
     157, 159
   for older adults, 155
   during pregnancy, 115, 151
   for relapse prevention, 114–115
   toxicity, 115–116, *116*
Lithobid. *See* Lithium (Lithium
     carbonate)
Lithonate. *See* Lithium (Lithium
     carbonate)
Lithotabs. *See* Lithium (Lithium
     carbonate)
Liverpool University Neuroleptic
     Side Effect Rating Scale
     (LUNSERS), 223
Lopressor. *See* Metoprolol
Lorazepam, *94,* 121, *126*
Loxapine, *90, 91*
Loxitane. *See* Loxapine
L-tryptophan, 270
Ludiomil. *See* Maprotilene
LUNSERS. *See* Liverpool Univer-
     sity Neuroleptic Side Effect
     Rating Scale
Lurasidone, *90*
Luvox. *See* Fluvoxamine

M
Malignant syndrome, *91*
Manerix. *See* Moclobemide
Mania

symptoms of, 111
See also Bipolar disorder
Mania Rating Scale (MRS), 224
Manic episodes, 111
Maprotilene, *105*
Marijuana, 165
Marplan. *See* Isocarboxazid
Meaning, of psychiatric medication, 180–191
  as basis of gratitude and source of victory over past struggles, 187
  for children and adolescents, 182
  metaphors and symbols, 181–182
  as necessary for relapse prevention and protection of humanness, 188
  as positive force across dimensions of functioning, 184–185
  as primarily an internal and individual experience, 186
  as prominent part of story and evolution of one's mental illness, 186–187
  as symbol of differentness and dependency, 188
  themes, 183–191
  as tolerated fact of life, 185
  typology of, *183*
Medication education, 195–214
  content recommendations for, 212–213
  demand for, 196
  impact on compliance, 198
  implementing and evaluating, 199–204
  abilities of learners, 199–200
  assessing one's performance, 202
  for children, 203
  creating environment for, 200
  knowledge of material, 200–201
  learners acquisition of educational outcomes, 202
  objectives for, 199
  for older adults, 203
  recruitment challenges, 203–204
  specific needs of learners, 199–200
  using appropriate teaching methods, 201–202
  programs, 204–211
  content of, 204–206
  education for adolescent clients, 211
  family focused treatment, 210–211
  family survival workshop for schizophrenia, 208
  family-to-family, 208–209
  group psychoeducation for bipolar disorder, 209–210
  multifamily group intervention for schizophrenia, 207–208
  multi-family psychoeducational group for depression, 211
  patient and family education program, 206–207

training, special, 201
Medication Event Monitoring System, 222
Medication management, 215–240
  advocacy in, 236–238
  ethical issues, 216–217
  negotiating with health care providers, 232–235
  partnership in, *239*
  problem solving in, 228–232
Medication Management Module (MMM), 201, 205–206
Medication monitoring, 215–240
  for adverse effects, 225–228
  ethical issues, 216–217
  using existing measures for, 223–225
Medication-monitoring protocols, 220–223
Medication response
  gender differences in, 146–149
  racial and ethnic differences in, 160–164
  substance abuse and, 164–167
Medications
  movement of, through body, 67–70
  serotonin-antagonist, 153
  sexual adverse effects of, 151–152
  See also Psychotropic medications
Medulla, *56*
Medulla oblongata, 55
Mellaril. *See* Thioridazine
Mental health, 25–27
Mental health settings, social workers in, 173–174
Mental illness
  alcohol abuse and, 167
  historical context for treatment of, 24–25
  risk and resistance model of, 14
  societal attitudes toward, 247–248
  stress-diathesis model of, 14, 197, 204, 212
  stress-vulnerability-coping-competence, 205
  substance abuse and, 164–167
Mentalism, 35
Mentally ill
  rights of, 10–11
  See also Clients
Mesoridazine, *90, 91*
Metabolism, 69, 148
  drug, 148, 160–161, 163, 168
  older adults and, 153
Metabolites, 69
Metaphors, in meaning of medication, 181–182
Methamphetamine, *136,* 138
Methylphenidate, *136,* 137, 138
Methylphenidate (Ritalin), 79
Metoprolol, *94, 129*
MFPG. *See* Multi-Family Psychoeducational Group
MI. *See* Motivational interviewing
Midazolam, *126*
Midbrain, *56,* 57
MindFreedom.org, 265
Mirtazepine, *108,* 152

MMJ. *See* Monthly Medication Journal
MMM. *See* Medication Management Module
Moban. *See* Molindone
Moclobemide, *102*
Molindone, *90, 91*
Monitoring role, 40–41, 48
Monoamine oxidase (MAO) inhibitors, 75, *102,* 102–104
  adverse effects, *103*
  food and drug interactions with, *103,* 103–104, *104*
  older adults and, 102, 155
  type A, 104
  type B, 104
Monthly Medication Journal (MMJ), 222
Mood, 99
Mood disorders
  in children and adolescents, 158
  in women, 148–149
  See also Antidepressant medications; Mood-stabilizing medications
Mood-stabilizing medications, 26, 76–77, 110–111
  adverse effects of, *119*
  anticonvulsants, 117–120
  case examples, 121–124
  for children and adolescents, 158
  currently available, 112–113, *113*
  drug interactions with, *117*
  lithium, 112, 113–117
  origins of, 112
  during pregnancy, 151
Motivational interviewing (MI), 253–256
  client's confidence, 255
  clinical perspective in, 254
  guidelines, 255
  intervention principles of, 255
  Transtheoretical Stages of Change (TSOC) model, 254
MRS. *See* Mania Rating Scale
Multifamily Group Intervention (MFI), 207
Multi-Family Psychoeducational Group (MFPG), 211

N
Nadolol, *129*
Naltrexone, 159, 167
NAMI. *See* National Alliance for the Mentally Ill
Nardil. *See* Phenylzine
National Alliance on Mental Illness (NAMI), 18, 208, 276
National Association of Social Workers, 44
Navane. *See* Thiothixene
NDA. *See* New Drug Application
Nefazodone, *108,* 152
Negotiating with Health Care Providers, 233
Nerve cells (neurons), 54, 59–63, *60–62*
  functions, 62–63

Nervous system
autonomic, 58
brain and, 54–59
peripheral, 58
See also Central nervous system
Neurohormones, 57
Neuroleptic malignant syndrome, 81, 89, 90, 226
Neurontin. See Gabapentin
Neurotin, illegal marketing of, 17
Neurotransmitters, 63–67, 147
New Drug Application (NDA), 264
New Hampshire Medicaid, 165
Nonadherence, 241–260
legal and ethical issues of, 250–253
protective factors for, 249
rates of, 242
risks for, 249
See also Adherence
Norepinephrine, 64, 65
Norflex. See Orphenadrine
Norpramin. See Desipramine
Nortriptyline, 105, 148
Nurses, 217
Nutritional deficiency models, 271

O
Obsessive-compulsive behaviors, 158
Occipital lobes, 56, 58
Off-label drugs, 265
Olanzapine, 90, 91, 95–96, 265
Older adults
anxiety and, 155
cardiovascular efficiency and, 153
medication education for, 153, 203
medication use and, 152–155
nonadherence, 243
phobic disorders, 155
physiological changes in, 152–153
Olfactory hallucinations, 87
Omega- 3 fatty acids, 270
On-label drugs, 265
Oral contraceptives, 148, 149
Orap. See Pimozide
Organic psychoses, 271
Orphenadrine, 94
Orthostatic hypotension, 81, 226
Outpatient social workers, 7
Oxazepam, 126
Oxcarbazepine, 113, 119

P
Paliperidone, 90
Parallel and integrated care, 172–175
Parasympathetic nervous system, 58
Parietal lobes, 56, 58
Parkinsonian effects, 81
Parkinsonism, 91
Parnate. See Tranylcypromine
Paroxetine, 107
Parsidol. See Ethoprozapine
Partnership model of social work practice, 25, 33–38
balancing rights and, 10–11
client-centered practice, 35–36

client-clinician relationship, 35–36
family member's perspective, 38
participants' strengths and limits, 34–35
principles of, 33–38
social worker as resource, 37–38
Pathology-based classification schemes, 34
Pathways, 55
Patient and family education program, 206–207
Paxil. See Paroxetine
Peak level, 69
Pemoline, 79, 136, 136, 138–139
Peripheral nervous system, 58
Perphenazine, 90, 91
Persecutory delusions, 87
Personality factor, in adverse effects, 82
PFEP. See Patient and Family Education Program
Pharmacists, 273
Pharmacodynamics, 69–72
Pharmacogenomics, 161
Pharmacokinetics, 67–70
"Pharmacological Calvinism," 146
Pharm-CAT, 222
Phenylzine, 102, 102, 131
Physicians
collaboration with, 20–21
negotiating medication issues with, 232–235
pharmaceutical industry, collaboration with, 18–19
Physician's assistant, 38–39, 48
Physician's Desk Reference, 264
Pimozide, 90
Placebo effect, 72
Polymorphisms, 161
tricyclic antidepressants and, 161
Polypharmacy, 153, 162, 167, 267
Pons, 55, 56
Postpartum psychosis, 150
Postsynaptic terminal, 59
Potency, 71
Power differentials, 217
Pragmatist learners, 202
Prazepam, 126
Pregnancy
adverse effects in, 149, 150–151
mood-stabilizing medications during, 151
psychotropic medications during, 149, 150
Prescription-writing privileges, 272–275
Presynaptic terminal, 59
Problem-solving skills, 198, 202, 207, 210
Problem-solving training, 228–232
Prochlorperazine, 90
Procyclidine, 94
Professional values, 40
Progesterone, 147
Prolixin. See Fluphenazine
Propranolol, 94, 129, 159
Protective factors, to moderate mental illness, 12–14

Protriptyline, 105, 105
Prozac, 16
See also Fluoxetine
PSAS. See Psychiatric Symptom Assessment Scale
PsychCentral, 276
Psychiatric medication
Psychiatric medications, websites on, 277–278
Psychiatric social work, rise of, 24–25, 38
Psychiatric Symptom Assessment Scale (PSAS), 223
Psychiatric Times or Medscape Psychiatry & Mental Health, 276
Psychiatry, association of social work with, 6
Psychoeducational program, 203
Psychologists, 273–274
Psychology and biology, integration of, 173
Psychopharmacology, 20, 79–80
alternative treatments for, 268–272
Big Pharma, 14–16
and biology, 12–13
collaborative practice authority, 273
drug development process, 263–266
early literature on, 274
future trends in, 263–279
nervous system and, 54–59
and neuroscience, 12–13
neurotransmitters and, 63–67
pharmacists, 273
psychodynamic approaches, 17
psychologists, 273–274
psychopharmacology Examination, 273
scientific and sociopolitical dimensions of, 12–22
vulnerability and stressors, 14
See also Psychotropic medications
Psychopharmacology Examination for Psychologists, 273
Psychopharmacy, 272
Psychosis, 87
symptoms of, 87
Psychosocial interventions, effects of, 24–25
Psychosocial rehabilitation, 19
Psychostimulants, 78–79, 133
adverse effects of, 137, 137
currently available, 136–139
origins of, 135–136
Psychotherapy, and depression, 14
Psychotic disorders
in children, 17
costs vs. benefits of, 11–12
in older adults, 154
social workers and psychiatric medication, 10–11
Psychotropic medications
administration of, 267–268
advances in, 266–268
adverse effects of (See Adverse effects)
anti-anxiety, 77–78
antidepressants, 74–76

antipsychotics, 73–74
in children, 17
for children and adolescents, 156
classes of, 73–79
clients, medication-related
dilemma, 11–12
drug advertisements, 19
effects of, 70–72
gender differences in, 146
improper medication, 18
mood-stabilizers, 76–77
movement of, through body,
67–70
older adults and, 153, 155
and pharmaceutical industry, 15
prescription-writing privileges
for, 272–275
psychopharmacology, 79–80
racial and ethnic differences in
responses to, 160–164
right to refuse, 250–253
self-regulation of, 245
social attitudes toward, 247–248
social workers' roles with, 25–26
substance abuse and, 166–167
See also specific types
Pyramidal nerve pathways, 58

Q
Quazepam, *126*
Quetiapene, *90*
Quetiapine, 96

R
Really simple syndication (RSS), 276
Receptors, 58
Referrals, 175–180
collaborative relationships with
prescribers, 176–177
excellence in, 176
following up results of, 179–180
managing legal and ethical
concerns in, 180
overview, 175–176
preparing clients and families for
evaluation, 178–179
timing of, 177–178
Reflector learners, 202
Relapses
prevention, 114–115
TSOC, 254
warning signs of, 204
Remenstrual dysphoric disorder,
149
Remeron. *See* Mirtazepine
Repetitive transcranial magnetic
stimulation (RTMS), 267
Researchers, 43, 48
Reticular formation, 55
Reuptake, 63
Rich site summary (RSS), 276
Risk and resistance model, of mental
illness, 14
Risperdal. *See* Risperidone
Risperidone, *90, 91,* 95, 98
Ritalin. *See* Methylphenidate
Ritalin, overuse of, 17
RTMS. *See* Repetitive transcranial
magnetic stimulation

S
SAM, 270
SANS. *See* Scale for the Assessment
of Negative Symptoms
SAPS. *See* Scale for the Assessment
of Positive Symptoms
Sarafem. *See* Escitalopram
Scale for the Assessment of Negative
Symptoms (SANS), 223
Scale for the Assessment of Positive
Symptoms (SAPS), 223
Schizophrenia, 147, 148, 162, 163,
165–166, 167
substance abuse and, 165–166,
167
School settings, social workers
in, 173
Sedation, 81
Selective serotonin reuptake inhibi-
tors (SSRIs), 76, 78, *107,*
107–109, 147, 149, 151, 167
adverse effects of, 108, *109*
for children and adolescents,
158–159
drug interactions with, *109*
effectiveness, 108
older adults and, 155
Selegiline, *102,* 104
Self-advocacy, 237–238
Self-care, 87
Self-determination, 35–36, 252–253
Self-efficacy model, 243–244
Self-monitoring, of medications,
217–223
Self-regulation model, 245
Serentil. *See* Mesoridazine
Seroquel. *See* Quetiapene
Serotonin, 64, 66
Serotonin and norepinephrine
reuptake inhibitors
(SNRIs), 76
Serotonin-enhancing drugs, 151
Serotonin-mediated activities, 147
Sertraline, 78, *107*
Serzone. *See* Nefazodone
Sex differences
in adverse effects, 82
different effects of medications in,
146–151
Sex steroids, 147
Sexual dysfunction, 81, 152
Shared decision-making
as collaborative process, 192
defined, 192
informed choice *vs.,* 192
in practice, 193
in psychiatry, 192–193
Simpson-Angus Neurological Rating Scale, 223
Skills-training process, 234–235
Social justice perspective, 4–5
Social work, rise of psychiatric,
25–26
Social workers, 20
case scenarios for, 26–27, 28–30,
31–32, 33
categories of, 38–43, 48–49
interdisciplinary collaboration by,
19–22

medication-related activities of,
44–48, *46–47*
mental health services, providers
of, 25–26
in parallel and integrated care
settings, 172–175
professional values of, 44
referrals and, 175–180
as resources, 37–38
roles and activities of, 25–33
in various settings, 172–175
women, 20
Social work perspective, 4–5
critical thinking, 7–10
and disiplinary context, 19–22
lens, 4
person-in-environment, 4
social justice, 4–5
strengths and empowerment, 5
Society, rights of, 10–11
Society for Medical Decision
Making, 191
Somatic hallucinations, 87
Sonata. *See* Zaleplon
Spinal cord, *56,* 58
SSRIs. *See* Selective serotonin
reuptake inhibitors
Steady state, 69
Stelazine. *See* Trifluoperazine
St.-John's-wort, 268–270
Strattera. *See* Atomoxetine
Strengths and empowerment
perspective, 5
Strengths perspective, 34–35
Stress-diathesis model, 14, 197,
204, 212
Substance abuse
adherence problems and,
242–243, 251, 254
mental illness and, 164–167
Suicidal behavior
atomoxetine and, 139
lithium and, 114
in older adults, 154
Surmontil. *See* Trimipramine
Symbolic interactionism, 181
Symbols, in meaning of medication,
181–182
Symmetrel. *See* Amantadine
Sympathetic nervous system, 58
Sympathomimetics. *See*
Psychostimulants
Symptom checklist, 218, *219*
Synapses, 59, *61*
Synaptic cleft, 59
Synaptic vesicles, 63

T
Tachycardia, 81
Tactile hallucinations, 87
Taractan. *See* Chlorprothixene
Tardive, defined, 81
Tardive dyskinesia (TD), 81, 90, *91,* 92
in children and adolescents, 157
coping with, 226
gender differences in, 148
in older adults, 154
substance abuse and, 165
vitamin E levels and, 272

Teaching methods, selecting, 201–202
Tegretol. *See* Carbamazepine
Temazepam, *126*
Temporal lobes, *56,* 58
Tenex. *See* Guanfacine
Tenormin. *See* Atenolol
Teratogenic, 149, 151
Tercian. *See* Cyamemazine
Texas Medication Algorithm (TMA), 206
Thalamus, *56,* 57–58
The looney bin trip (Millet), 278
Theorist learners, 202
The quiet room (Schiller), 278
Therapeutic index, 71
Therapist, 40
Thioridazine, *90, 91*
Thiothixene, *90, 91*
Thorazine. *See* Chlorpromazine
Thought broadcasting, 87
Thought insertion, 87
Thought withdrawal, 87
Tindal. *See* Acetophenazine
TMA. *See* Texas Medication Algorithm
Tofranil. *See* Imipramine
Tolerance, 72
Topamax. *See* Topiramate
Topiramate, *113,* 119–120
Tourette's syndrome, 156, 159
Toxicity, 70
Traditional collaboration, 21
Transformational collaboration, 21
Transtheoretical Stages of Change (TSOC), 254

action, 254
contemplation, 254
maintenance, 254
pre-contemplation, 254
preparation, 254
relapse, 254
Tranylcypromine, 101, 102, *102,* 131
Trazodone, *108*
Treatment monitoring, 202
Treatment-resistant schizophrenia, 18
Triazolam, *126*
Tricyclic antidepressants (TCAs), 147
Trifluoperazine, *90, 91*
Triflupromazine, *90, 91*
Trihexyphenidyl, 93, *94*
Trilafon. *See* Perphenazine
Trileptal. *See* Oxcarbazepine
Trimipramine, *105*
TSOC. *See* Transtheoretical Stages of Change
Tyramine, 103, 104
Tyrosine, 65

U
Unitary approach, 173
United States Census Bureau, 160
Updating drug developments, 275–278
Uric acid diathesis, 112

V
Vagus nerve stimulation (VNS), 267
Valium. *See* Diazepam
Valproate, 118

during pregnancy, 151
Valproic acid, 77, *117,* 119
Venlafaxine, *108,* 152
Vesprin. *See* Triflupromazine
Visual hallucinations, 87
Vitamin deficiencies, 271
Vitamin treatments, 268–272
Vivactil. *See* Protriptyline
VNS. *See* Vagus nerve stimulation

W
WebMD, 276
Websites, on psychiatric medications, 277–278
Weight gain, 82
Wellbutrin. *See* Bupropion
Wellness Recovery Action Plan (WRAP), 220–221
Women
    different effects of medications in, 146–151
    with mood disorder, 82, 148–149
WRAP. *See* Wellness Recovery Action Plan (WRAP)

X
Xanax. *See* Alprazolam
xiao yao san, 270

Z
Zaleplon, *129*
Ziprasidone, *90, 91,* 96
Zoloft. *See* Sertraline
Zolpidem, *129*
Zyban. *See* Bupropion
Zyprexa. *See* Olanzapine